W9-ABI-447

Gramley Library
Salem College
Winston-Salem, NC 27108

NOVEL BEGINNINGS

PATRICIA MEYER SPACKS

Novel Beginnings

EXPERIMENTS IN EIGHTEENTH-CENTURY

ENGLISH FICTION

Gramley Library
Salem College
Winston-Salem, NC 27108

YALE UNIVERSITY PRESS   NEW HAVEN & LONDON

Yale Guides to English Literature

Yale Guides to English Literature survey topics in English literature from *Beowulf* to the contemporary scene. Each volume of the series is intended for students and general readers.

Published with assistance from the Annie Burr Lewis Fund and the Mary Cady Tew Memorial Fund.

Copyright © 2006 by Patricia M. Spacks.
All rights reserved.
This book may not be reproduced, in whole or in part, including illustrations, in any form (beyond that copying permitted by Sections 107 and 108 of the U.S. Copyright Law and except by reviewers for the public press), without written permission from the publishers.

Printed in the United States of America.

Library of Congress Cataloging-in-Publication Data
Spacks, Patricia Ann Meyer.
Novel beginnings : experiments in eighteenth-century English fiction / Patricia Meyer Spacks.
p.   cm. — (Yale guides to English literature)
Includes bibliographical references and index.
ISBN-13: 978-0-300-11031-9 (alk. paper)
ISBN-10: 0-300-11031-6 (alk. paper)
1. English fiction—18th century—History and criticism. 2. Experimental fiction, English—History and criticism. 3. Literary form—History—18th century. I. Title. II. Series.
PR858.E982S66 2006
823'.509—dc22
2005024209

A catalogue record for this book is available from the British Library.

The paper in this book meets the guidelines for permanence and durability of the Committee on Production Guidelines for Book Longevity of the Council on Library Resources.

10   9   8   7   6   5   4   3   2   1

For Aubrey Williams

Blest with a *Taste* exact, yet unconfin'd;
A *Knowledge* both of *Books* and *Humankind;*
Gen'rous Converse; a *Soul* exempt from *Pride;*
And *Love to Praise,* with *Reason* on his Side.

CONTENTS

ACKNOWLEDGMENTS

MORE THAN ANYTHING ELSE I have written, this book is indebted to my students—particularly to the several generations of graduate students with whom I have discussed eighteenth-century fiction and by whom I have been stimulated and enlightened. I am also profoundly grateful to Myra Jehlen, who read and reread key chapters, always helping me to achieve greater clarity and precision and often provoking me to fresh thought. Like my other writing during the past fifteen years, this book has profited from my weekly lunches and literary discussions with Jerome McGann. Bruce Redford provided valuable suggestions at an early stage of my thinking; and Aubrey Williams, to whom the book is dedicated, helped me, as so often before, by innumerable enlivening conversations.

CHAPTER ONE

The Excitement of Beginnings

THE YEAR 1719 PRODUCED two fictional best sellers in England: Daniel Defoe's *Robinson Crusoe* and Eliza Haywood's *Love in Excess*. Literacy was rising, and an increasingly large and eager audience now devoured fiction in many forms. Just over twenty years later, Samuel Richardson would publish *Pamela*, which generated controversy as well as excitement, stimulating parodies, continuations, and other printed responses. These conspicuous instances suggest that the novel—which hardly yet knew itself to be "the novel"—already engaged wide and enlarging attention.

Robinson Crusoe, as even many children still know, narrates the vicissitudes of a mariner shipwrecked on a desert island. *Love in Excess* consists of a series of semi-erotic tales, linked by a group of participants acquainted with one another, and resolved by the happy marriage of a man who has previously enjoyed many amatory adventures. *Pamela* tells of a fifteen-year-old servant girl who resists her master's attempts at seduction or rape until he finally marries her. She then must withstand the violent disapproval of her husband's aristocratic sister. As these examples indicate, the early novel investigated a range of subjects. If its writers paid lip service to the classic ideal that literature must both please and instruct, they increasingly emphasized the first of these goals even while proclaiming allegiance to the second. They often stressed also their claims to factuality. Richardson announced himself as only the "editor" of Pamela's letters;

Defoe prefixed to several of his novels elaborate announcements of their literal truth.

To call the works of Defoe, Haywood, and Richardson examples of "the early novel," however, makes literary history neater than the facts justify. Both the starting point and the definition of the novel remain debatable. Certainly prose fiction has existed since classic times. Daphnis pursued Chloe through the pages of Longus in the second century. Even earlier, imagined by Apuleius, Lucian metamorphosed into an ass and enjoyed marvelous adventures. The ancient Greeks produced romances; so did the Middle Ages, throughout Europe and Asia. By the sixteenth and seventeenth centuries, elaborate French romances, translated, had won wide readership in England. These romances—considered by moralists, because of their stress on love, a threat to the moral well-being of young women—centered on beautiful maidens of high rank whose numerous wooers confronted daunting and interminable trials in the service of their beloved. Written in elaborate prose, narrated at a leisurely pace and with lavish detail, the romances told stories with little immediate connection to the lives of their readers. They belonged to the realm of fantasy and accordingly—like popular romances of our own time—satisfied imaginative needs.

Beginning a story of the novel with the beginning of the eighteenth century, then, is an arbitrary choice. Much that was written earlier both prepares for and anticipates what would emerge from presses between 1700 and 1800. Yet that arbitrary stretch of time saw an explosion of new energies, a sequence of fictional experiments, that justifies special attention. Early in the century one innovation emerged that would itself account for much subsequent change. Such writers as Daniel Defoe began to organize fictions around the careers of imagined working-class or middle-class characters—not Everyman or Everywoman or, like John Bunyan in *Pilgrim's Progress*, Christian Man; not, like Aphra Behn in *Oroonoko*, exotic "savages" with extraordinary capacities; but sea captains and maidservants assigned individualized natures and following individualized life courses. The repercussions of that development still continue to resound.

To speak of "ordinary people" as central figures in the new novel is not to say that eighteenth-century novels were necessarily "realistic." On the contrary: the story I want to tell focuses especially on deviations from realism. It is primarily because novels depict characters with physical needs and ordinary occupations in relatively familiar settings that they have so often been described as realistic. Moreover, as I will soon suggest more fully, novels of this period often reflect in recognizable ways the assumptions and disturbances of the society from which they emanate. The facts of the world we inhabit measure reality for most of us, and eighteenth-century fiction frequently draws on facts of experience. Yet to call it realistic for these reasons requires ignoring a great deal that it also does: for instance, the degree to which it relies on palpable artifice, trades in wish fulfillment, and depends on plotting that is too neat to correspond to the course of actual lives. In this chapter I propose, among other things, to initiate investigation of aspects of the early novel that the expectation of realism may obscure and to call attention to the complicated workings of fantasy in eighteenth-century fiction. I shall return to this subject from several angles.

During the period that concerns us, some novelists showed new interest in delineating detailed psychological experience. Others provided abundant details of the social world. Their work conformed, therefore, in a limited sense to customary standards of realism as offering a plausible illusion of actuality. But many relied heavily on techniques of exaggeration often associated with satire, though crucial also to sentimentalism; and almost all presented plots answering more to desire than probability. The novels' realistic aspects matter: their attention to and reflection of social problems, their interest in the implications of social class, and their effort to investigate psychological depths. Those aspects do not, however, comprise all that matters. To think of eighteenth-century fiction as dominated by realism makes it more difficult to see its complexity and range and to experience its variety of riches.

From one point of view, anything short of accounts of ogres and enchanters belongs to the territory of realism. Yet the generalizing designation obscures the formal variety of eighteenth-century narrative, the multiple technical possibilities it explores, the broad spectrum, from credible to barely credible, that marks the period's fiction. In 1957 Ian Watt declared "formal realism" to be the crucial characteristic of the eighteenth-century English novel, citing Defoe, Richardson, and Fielding as principal cases in point and ignoring a large number of less conspicuous novelists. Almost fifty years later, thanks partly to the generations of critics that followed Watt, we are in a position to see a more complicated, confusing, and compelling picture, taking into consideration a larger group of variously ambitious writers. Approaching these novels from a new angle, I hope to recapture the multiplicity of eighteenth-century fiction, partly by bracketing the issue of realism and making an effort to start anew.

I propose, in other words, to tell a fresh story about the eighteenth-century novel. That many stories yet remain to be told is an important polemic point. The eighteenth century, like every other period defined by literary histories, offers abundant variety. Like other narratives of literary history—like, indeed, *all* stories—my story will necessarily flatten some of actuality's diversity for the sake of coherence and economy, but it will attempt to convey the excitement and power of an era of radical literary experiment. The entire eighteenth century composed such an era. Energy is its hallmark, primary evidence of the impetus of the new—newness suggested by the very designation *novel*. By the century's end, the novel had become the dominant literary genre. Henry Fielding, as early as the 1740s, had half-jokingly tried to assimilate his new genre to the epic, claiming to be writing, in *Joseph Andrews,* a "comic Epic-Poem in Prose" (4). Although it would never claim the epic's high dignity, the novel indeed came to fulfill a traditional epic function by articulating the nation's values and its complicated sense of itself in a period of dramatic change.

Examining the century's novels primarily as literature, rather than as social documents or exemplars of a single movement, I shall call attention to the narrative dexterity exemplified in the work of almost forgotten writers as well as in that of their better-known contemporaries. My story of a century's fiction will also celebrate the act and process of reading, aspiring to bring to the attention of twenty-first-century readers the pleasures of encountering unfamiliar assumptions and unfamiliar ways of representing character and action.

This study concerns itself with literary causes and effects rather than social causes and with the experience of reading rather than theories of writing. Watt's brilliant *The Rise of the Novel,* arguing the importance to the novel of a new social class and of increasing stress on individualism, inaugurated a sequence of significant inquiries into social forces that bear on the novel's development. Along with subsequent investigations—the work, for example, of Michael McKeon, J. Paul Hunter, Nancy Armstrong, and Catherine Gallagher (see Suggestions for Further Reading)—it laid the groundwork for understanding the eighteenth-century interpenetration of the social and the literary. My own enterprise calls attention to another vital aspect of understanding: concentrating on the texts. My story depends on staying close to the novels themselves in order both to delineate their individuality and to suggest connections among them. For purposes of this inquiry, I treat male and female novelists as members of a single species. Much valuable recent work has concentrated on the special contributions of women writers considered as a group. Such criticism has helped to create a situation in which it becomes possible to think about the way that men and women simultaneously shaped the course of English fiction.

First, though, something about the cultural context these novels inhabited. The growing population of literate English men and women could find many kinds of prose besides that of romance narratives to fulfill their imaginative needs, even before the novel developed. Lines spoken on the stage and printed in published plays provided colloquial, witty, socially alert versions of speech in the service of often familiar but freshly imagined and elaborated plots. Drama flourished in the Restoration and the early eighteenth century, as it had flourished in the Renaissance, but its dominant mode had shifted. Now comedy triumphed in the theater—comedy that frequently skirted the obscene or pornographic. Love, in Restoration comedy, figured often as game or battle, or both. Audiences became accustomed to rapid action and to verbal repartee that both furthered the action and entertained its participants and its audience. The period's tragedies likewise emphasized the rhetorical, declaring and demonstrating the power of language. Type characters worked effectively in comedy and tragedy alike: the bold warrior, the naive country woman, the rake-hero. They would show up again in the novels that succeeded Restoration plays. The audiences that flocked to the theater in this period were unwittingly preparing themselves for the advent of increasingly complicated novelistic forms.

More than the various energies of published prose, however, contributed to the course of subsequent fiction. Social changes impinged upon, even helped to determine, the shape of the evolving novel. All eras, obviously, are marked by change, but especially dramatic shifts occurred in England during the eighteenth century. For most of the century the nation remained at peace. After the Peace of Utrecht in 1714, marking the end of the War of the Spanish Succession, no further armed conflict involved

England (politically united with Scotland in 1707) until the American colonists rebelled. Within this context of military quiescence, however, unrest continued.

An inexorable process of urbanization persisted, even heightened, throughout the century. Urbanization meant, in most instances, movement toward London, imagined by those existing in rural poverty as a place of infinite opportunity. The enclosure of common land in the country to enlarge the estates of big landholders intensified the neediness of the rural population, and on occasion deprived them of occupation. By 1800 Wordsworth could mention "the encreasing accumulation of men in cities" as a sign of national malaise (160). Men, and women, too, made their way to London, only to endure, often, misery and degradation. Entrepreneurial gifts and energy might find abundant reward, legal or illegal, but the city remained—as many novels would remind their readers—a place of physical and moral danger, threatening some residents by the depredations of criminals and others by the lure of criminality.

Criminality was rampant in eighteenth-century London, in an era of draconian punishment: a fictional Moll Flanders and her real-life counterparts risked hanging for stealing a length of cloth. Crimes against property carried heavy penalties, for property—not only land, the traditional measure of wealth, but money and objects—assumed ever-increasing importance. Money (along with love) provided a crucial subject for the novel, as well as one of the period's central preoccupations.

We take money for granted now—not its possession, but the fact of it in the world. Money had been a fact for a long time when the eighteenth century began, but the power it represented attracted special attention during this period. Accumulating new meanings in the culture, money became a new kind of fact. The literary situation reflected actualities of the society at large. In earlier times writers of verse and prose had profited from a system of patronage: wealthy men and women, usually aristocrats, bestowed gifts and sinecures on authors whom they favored, thus providing them with somewhat precarious means of support. Dependent on the favor of the great, writers might be tempted to flattery as a mode of livelihood. The lack of social status accorded to most writers bore some relation to this fact.

The old patronage system, slowly and at first partially, gave way to more direct methods of selling literature. "Subscription" provided one popular mode. Usually a stationer, or publisher (occasionally an author directly), would solicit advance purchases of a forthcoming book; the rich would sometimes agree to buy multiple copies. As subscribers accumulated, lists, frequently ordered by rank, were often published before the book itself, providing credibility to the literary venture. Writers would thus not only get advance payment; they would reap certain benefits of the old patronage system as well. Moreover, they would have some assurance of an audience.

Other systems also operated. A writer who could not win over a publisher on other terms might agree to pay the costs of printing, with profits beyond those costs to accrue mainly to the author. The stationers themselves might assume financial responsibility for printing, paying the author a fixed sum and profiting from any sales beyond their initial commitment. Although inexperienced authors usually accepted the payment offered, more seasoned writers might negotiate the amount. As the century progressed, these sums became increasingly large.

With general literacy spreading, the market for literature expanded. Hard evidence is difficult to come by; we lack dependable figures about the number of readers and writers in the seventeenth and eighteenth centuries. Historians agree, though, that the capacity to read and write expanded across social levels, creating a new audience, so that by the end of the eighteenth century the expectation that a child would become literate had been fully normalized. Publishing as well as writing became increasingly profitable, and it spread across the country. In the late seventeenth century, virtually all publishers worked in London. A hundred years later, hundreds of presses flourished in small towns across England.

It was now possible for more than a tiny minority to make a living by writing—particularly by writing fiction. This fact came to assume special importance for women, to whom few legitimate and profitable occupations were open. Writing as a trade was minimally respectable for women, vaguely associated with prostitution, but it did not disgrace a woman practitioner as definitively as, say, acting on the stage. Numerous women came to support themselves and, often, their families by producing appealing novels. Such an occupation engaged only a minute proportion of needy women, but it symbolized an opening of female opportunity as well as constituting a literal resource for many. A striking number of prefaces and dedications, as the century went on, alleged that the female writer had risked publication only in order to provide for her children, her husband, or an aged parent.

Despite the large number of women who wrote fiction, relatively few retained even name recognition into the twentieth century. Until recently, perhaps only Frances Burney would have represented women novelists before Jane Austen in the consciousness of most students. The relative invisibility of female eighteenth-century novelists may derive partly from the fact that few wrote the kind of richly populated, "realistic" works popularized by Defoe, Fielding, and Smollett. As we shall see, women were major experimenters, and they had a large contemporary audience. By late in the century, lending libraries had expanded this audience, charging a fee for the loan of books. Their regular patrons included many women, and women, as well as men, wrote for them.

To be sure, novels remained a dubiously respectable literary form, perhaps partly because women wrote and read so many of them. Moralists insisted on fiction's power to corrupt. Samuel Johnson, who dominated the literary scene through the middle years of the century, offered rigid prescriptions for novelistic propriety. If novels furthered morality, they might offer valuable insight into human behavior, but such insight had no value, according to Johnson, unless it suggested modes of aspiration. "Mixed" characters, combining virtue and vice (characters like Henry Fielding's Tom Jones), were necessarily dangerous to readers' moral capacities. Johnson himself participated actively in a club of literary men—men who wrote, for the most part, poetry or moral essays or art criticism, not fiction. He made a living from his writing (late in life he received a government pension), but most of that writing avoided the fanciful. The association of women with novel writing suggested, to some minds, the triviality of both. And women's often expressed need to profit from such writing also implicitly denigrated them as persons: declared financial motivation for literary production suggested something less than the high moral purpose traditionally assigned to literature. It is perhaps worth noting that the best-known male novelists of the century—Defoe, with many forms of employment; Fielding, a magistrate; Richardson, a printer; Smollett, a physician; Sterne, a clergyman—had gainful occupations apart from fiction writing.

Literature could be, and was, recognized as a commodity like others, substance for commerce, its transactions involving multiplying numbers of people. Such implication of literature in commerce accompanied a great expansion of commerce in other realms as well. England was becoming a commercial nation, and the fact had vast reverberations.

More than domestic buying and selling was involved. By treaty and by conquest, what had been a country was becoming an empire, with far-flung opportunities for trade. Early in the century Alexander Pope could celebrate in verse a vision of trees rushing into the ocean to become the ships bringing wealth and power to the nation. A taste for luxury (much decried by moralists) developed concomitantly. English women required Chinese tea and porcelain, Indian cashmere and spices, sugar from the Caribbean, coffee and jewels and silks from around the world. Extensive trade in slaves helped to support prosperity. England did not permit slavery within its borders, but its merchants engaged freely in the transportation and sale of human cargoes.

The women who entertained themselves with porcelain and jewels, women of the upper classes, were allowed little occupation beyond needle-work, shopping, visiting, and polite accomplishments. Their leisure status reflected positively on the wealth of their husbands. If they lacked hus-bands, they belonged to fathers. Few had money under their own control. In a sense, they did not even control their children: in case of divorce or sepa-ration, children of both sexes belonged to their fathers. With many social forces impinging on their opportunities, a few women yet made not only money but reputation: a place for themselves on the literary scene, writing novels, poetry, moral essays, and treatises on Shakespeare. Moreover, by the second half of the century at least a small group of intellectual women had devised equivalents for the French salons at which distinguished women held court. The so-called Bluestockings encouraged one another's writing and self-esteem and provided a new kind of female activity.

During the reign of George III (1760–1820), the population of Great Britain almost doubled, from seven and a half million to more than four-teen million. The probable reason for the increase was that more people were being kept alive. Medical advances paralleled industrial ones, as the rapid development of manufacturing that we now know as the Indus-trial Revolution began to take hold. Men discovered more ways to make fortunes, from plundering India to manufacturing pottery. The growing accumulation of money in private hands changed the traditional balance of power. Once Tory landholders had ruled the country; for much of the eighteenth century Whig oligarchs assumed control. Money could translate into political power, as well as power over physical conditions.

The importance of money registered not only with those who accumulated great fortunes but with the ever more numerous members of what would come to be called the middle class. An increasingly sharp separation between the occupations of women and men developed, as men claimed the responsibility of working in the world outside the home, without the aid of their spouses—"work" including both manufacture and trade, in stocks as well as commodities. Speculation involved increasing numbers of people. In 1720 the collapse of the South Sea Bubble brought widespread financial disaster. (The South Sea Company, which held a monopoly on British trade with islands of the South Seas and South America, had assumed responsibility for the national debt and attracted many eager purchasers for its stock. After achieving enormously inflated values, stock prices suddenly fell, and thousands lost their investment.) Subsequent legislation helped to forestall future such disasters, and financial markets flourished later in the century.

As more money became available to more people, the fact affected marital arrangements. Aristocrats had long arranged their children's marriages on the basis of property interests, planning matches in order to consolidate or enlarge estates. Now men in the process of aggrandizing their wealth might see the possibilities of using a daughter's marriage to elevate the family's social status, and those of high status but relatively limited financial resources could imagine that a daughter's match might indirectly improve their monetary positions. Even the young, of both sexes, might consider the possibility of marrying for money.

The issue of money's relation to marriage comes up almost obsessively in the century's novels, which frequently concern themselves with domestic matters. Even in works by such writers as Tobias Smollett, who interests himself more in adventure than in romance or marriage, a male protagonist's financially advantageous marriage provides a happy ending more satisfactory than would romantic love alone. Such protagonists, however, marry for love, not for the sake of money, which provides only an agreeable concomitant to romance. In many novels, desire for wealth with marriage marks the false values of the old: the young defy their elders' prudence to marry instead for romantic reasons. The generational conflict of prerogatives often plays itself out as a struggle over the right of the young to make their own marital choices. Yet almost never do two young people propose to marry *without* financial wherewithal. Such a course seems literally inconceivable.

Money also figures novelistically in ways quite remote from marriage. Whether an eighteenth-century fiction deals with prostitution or politics, confinement or adventure, untrammeled lawbreaking or trammeled domesticity—and the period's novels concern themselves with all these matters—it almost invariably makes money a large component of plot. In contrast with the dramas and romances of previous periods, the fiction of the eighteenth century declares its relation to actual experience partly by insisting on the role of money in fictional experience.

By late in the century, social questions about the distribution of money had become increasingly pressing. The rising tide of prosperity, abundance, and luxury by no means floated all boats. In the context of two wars, the need to consider issues of equality became increasingly apparent. The revolution of the American colonies not only defeated British military might; it also challenged assumptions about the "natural" community of feeling between the English and the Americans and about the "natural" dominance of the British. By extension, it raised questions about everything that had been automatically considered natural. Then, at the century's end, the French Revolution fomented radical ideas of human equality and radical possibilities of action. The prospect that events comparable to those in France could take place in England exhilarated some, terrified many others.

Well before the revolution in France, increasing awareness of misery around them troubled many affluent Britons. The hypocrisy of founding much national prosperity on the slave trade while forbidding slave ownership in England would hardly bear examination. The inhumanity of that trade became a subject of public agitation. The suffering and inequities in prisons also exercised reformers, who publicized for a previously unaware middle- and upper-class audience injustices of a long-accepted system. New consciousness of human rights helped to provoke concern about education: What was the best system for educating boys? How much education should girls have? Where should they get it? By the century's end, the "woman question" had reached popular consciousness, and the deliberately unconventional lives of women like Mary Wollstonecraft were arousing discussion.

The ferment surrounding such issues as those I have mentioned

Gramley Library
Salem College
Winston-Salem, NC 27108

figured openly in novels. Henry Fielding, in *Amelia,* took a conservative view on the subject of the learned woman; his sister Sarah, in *David Simple,* suggested an opposed position. The horrors of prisons emerge vividly in William Godwin's *Caleb Williams. The Old Manor House* (Charlotte Smith) offers a view of the American Revolution from the point of view of a British soldier fighting in it. Frances Burney, in several novels, discussed with subtlety and force the power of money. The early novel paid attention to the problems of the society that generated it.

My present interest in literary effects rather than social causes calls attention, however, to other problems. What did the new novel look like? It presented a startling variety of faces. The novel included the providential narratives of Henry Fielding, the psychological concentration of Samuel Richardson, the amatory fictions of Eliza Haywood, the political romans à clef of Delarivier Manley, the extravagant plottings of Jane Barker, the virtually psychotic social scenes of Frances Burney, the wild musings of Laurence Sterne, the sentimental parables of Sarah Fielding and Henry Mackenzie, the Gothic indulgence of Horace Walpole, Ann Radcliffe, and Matthew Lewis, the political allegories of Robert Bage. It is hard to imagine a summary characterization that would apply to all these works.

At this point, the novelists I have mentioned constitute only a list of names; they will assume fuller definition in the subsequent chapters, as will their multiplicity of narrative experiments. Despite their varied approaches, most of the novelists here to be considered shared new ideas about what makes a story worth attending to, ideas implicit in their turn toward "ordinary people" as characters. If the composers and compilers of epic assumed that readers valued heroic ideals of conduct, if writers of romance predicated their enterprise on the conviction that readers wished for imaginative encounters with a world unknown and impossible, the new novelists tacitly argued that readers might enjoy engaging situations and characters already more or less familiar.

The question of social rank in effect condenses this issue. Epic heroes virtually by definition held high social positions, positions of leadership. Heroes of romance, knights if not princes, inhabited a world remote in time and space in which they figured among the most distinguished inhabitants. Moll Flanders, in contrast, born in Newgate Prison, belongs initially to the lowest social class and rises to some version of the middle class. Tom Jones, a foundling, eventually inherits money and a position

among the landed gentry, but, neither prince nor aristocrat, he is of illegitimate birth. Jane Barker, as we shall see, describes a lady of "distinction,"
her precise status unspecified, engaged in washing dishes. Richardson's
first heroine is a servant. Smollett's protagonists often go to sea. These
characters occupy themselves as readers might and inhabit social spheres
that readers might inhabit.

Yet such imagined characters by no means always resolutely assert
their Englishness. The action of *Love in Excess* takes place in France and
Italy; Jane Barker's many little stories are frequently enacted on the Continent; Delarivier Manley claims to have translated a manuscript from
Italian—as, much later in the century, do Horace Walpole and, later still,
Ann Radcliffe. Such early fiction writers as Penelope Aubin often locate
their characters in France. By and large, writers who eschew British settings thereby declare their affinities with French seventeenth-century romances, which typically narrate fanciful events on the fancifully delineated
continent of Europe. Such writers also, however, convey a sense of literary
activity as transnational.

The figures who populate eighteenth-century novels need money,
which they may find, lose, inherit, earn, steal, beg, borrow, or be given.
Their counterparts in romance require neither money nor, apparently, food.
The novel's characters hire coaches, which may leak or overturn or collide
with obstacles. They concern themselves with love, but also with survival.
They make minor mistakes as well as catastrophic ones. More often than
they fight duels or battles, they stop at inns or attend balls. In short, they
do things that ordinary readers would recognize and understand.

Their fictional predecessors had on occasion also done ordinary
things, but in a far different context. The tradition of religious allegory,
of which John Bunyan's *Pilgrim's Progress* remains the most familiar exemplar, made room for the narration of commonplace events assigned
large meanings. Bunyan's allegory (1678–84) won enormous readership
(second only to the Bible), ostensibly because of its religious purpose but
certainly also for its imaginative power. It narrates the experience of an archetypal Christian man—assigned the name Christian—as he undertakes
a strenuous journey in an effort to save his soul. He bears on his back a
heavy burden of sin, of which he has no power to divest himself. Along
the way, he faces such obstacles as the dungeon of the giant Despair, the
treacherous Slough (swamp) of Despond, and the allurements of Vanity

Fair, which offers a full range of worldly enticements. Predictably, and rather quickly, he triumphs over each in turn (assisted in some instances by characters with names like Help), winning his way at last to the peace and fulfillment of heaven.

Although Protestant tradition effectively predetermines the trajectory and outcome of Christian's journey, the narrative generates local tension and cumulative excitement by the immediacy and cogency of its figures for familiar experience. When Christian, at the beginning of the "strait and narrow way" he must follow to salvation, comes to the house of Interpreter, its master shows him into a parlor full of dust. A man comes in to sweep it, raising choking clouds of dirt. Then Interpreter calls for a maidservant to sprinkle the floor with water, which enables her to sweep without discomfort to the room's inhabitants. The parlor, Interpreter subsequently explains, is the unsanctified heart of man; the male servant is the Law, the maidservant the Gospel. The episode shows how knowledge of the Gospel subdues sin, whereas the Law only stirs it up.

The event has minor importance in the allegory's total structure, but it exemplifies Bunyan's gift for discovering potential meaning in trivial details of ordinary life. Few men or women would fail to understand the account of a common household expedient for subduing dust. To assign significance to such a familiar experience reinforces the general message of allegory: that all of life has consequence. In more fully developed happenings, sequences in which Christian (who has been joined by his townsman Faithful) faces real obstacles and danger, the constant reference to the everyday both lends the allegory plausibility and furthers awareness that the story, alluding as it does to Everyman and Everywoman, holds direct relevance for the reader.

At Vanity Fair, for instance, the travelers find a variety of goods for sale: "At the fair are all such merchandise sold, as houses, lands, trades, places, honours, preferments, titles, countries, kingdoms, lusts, pleasures, and delights of all sorts, as whores, bawds, wives, husbands, children, masters, servants, lives, blood, bodies, souls, silver, gold, pearls, precious stones, and what not" (78). The list, calculated to keep the reader off balance, places ordinary concomitants of middle-class and working-class lives in conjunction with appurtenances of the rich. Preferments and lusts may be readily denounced as lures to vice—but what of houses and lands, husbands and wives, bodies and souls? As one thinks about the conjunctions and implications of the sequence, it becomes increasingly disturbing. A working man might endanger his soul simply by having children and valuing them more highly than he values his Christian responsibilities. Christian and Faithful, stand-ins for devout readers, suffer both pain and shame in this ostensible place of pleasure, reminding the reader that salvation does not come easily. They are mocked, whipped, and caged, blamed for all mishaps. Envy, Superstition, and Pickthank testify against them at their trial; the judge declares them deserving of immediate death. A corrupt jury condemns them to the most cruel death that can be devised, a fate that Faithful promptly suffers. Christian, however, escapes the prison, joined by a new companion, Hopeful.

This plot sequence exemplifies Bunyan's characteristic technique. He points the allegory by the names assigned to characters, by textual interpolations, and by references to Scripture. He uses repetition to reinforce doctrinal points. Thus Christian and Faithful tell their stories over and over, to various audiences, dwelling particularly on their mistakes. But Bunyan also supplies adventure, suspense, difficulties that seem hard to surmount—and surprises such as Faithful's death. (That good man, however, ascends immediately to heaven.)

Although the transparent narrative structure of *Pilgrim's Progress* appears hardly a product of the writer's devising, so much does it reflect and logically contain the story, that structure carries its own cumulative effect. The work's protagonist undertakes a journey; the work's structure simply follows that journey, one place and one problem after another. When Christian reaches the end of his progress, the book comes to an end. The structure, however, powerfully reinforces—indeed, powerfully creates—the allegory's meaning. The one-thing-after-another succession of events, with no obvious progression of complexity or impact, corresponds to the pattern of human lives, in which intricacy of connection may appear after the fact, but day-to-day experience consists precisely of one thing after another in no discernable logical sequence. The narrative's building suspense comes from the lack of predictability in the story's ordering. We expect the happy ending (as I said before, the conclusion is implicit from the beginning), but we don't know how Christian will get to the end of his journey. The effective identification between reader and character depends heavily on narrative arrangement.

Readers can respond to Bunyan's text on many levels. They may react to the ingenuity with which points of Protestant doctrine are embodied; they may merely read a simple, but exciting, story; they may give it credence because of the abundant commonplace references; they may see themselves in the characters. The devices Bunyan used for divine allegory would resurface in the eighteenth-century novel, where they won readers for less clearly defined purposes, and ostentatiously simple sequencing of events would create its effects in novels as well.

English adaptations of romance, although they rarely trafficked in the everyday, laid the ground in other ways for a kind of fiction more closely related to its readers' experience. Aphra Behn's *Oroonoko* (1688), like Bunyan's work greatly popular, employed a romance hero in the form of an African prince, experimenting with setting and character as well as suggesting fresh political and ethical insights. The eighteenth-century novel would follow Behn's lead in finding indirect ways to comment on existing social and political arrangements.

Oroonoko provides a female narrator, an exotic setting, and a new kind of exciting story. Neither its intentions nor its methods resemble Bunyan's. In many respects a fully developed novel, it tells a tale about an African prince sold into slavery in Surinam from the point of view of an English woman who claims to have witnessed the events she reports and emphasizes that she never deviates from literal truth. Oroonoko, in her account, is wonderfully handsome, wonderfully heroic, and wonderfully "civil," able to speak French and English, conversant with European as well as African political events. His sense of honor far exceeds that of most Englishmen he encounters; the narrative consistently emphasizes this fact. In all these respects—physical prowess and beauty, impeccable behavior, chivalric honor—he epitomizes the romance hero.

Because of his high rank, but also, finally, because of his high accomplishments, all the local slaves accept Oroonoko's leadership. Indeed, they virtually worship him. Finally he leads them to escape, in an effort to regain their freedom and return to their own country. Captured and betrayed, he meets his death by torture with the utmost heroism. The narrative concludes in these words: "Thus died this great man, worthy of a better fate, and a more sublime wit than mine to write his praise: Yet, I hope, the reputation of my pen is considerable enough to make his glorious name to survive to all ages, with that of the brave, the beautiful, and the constant *Imoinda* [Oroonoko's wife]" (224).

The sacrificial death of the heroic figure and his wife, after the hero has both fought bravely and inspired bravery in others, constitutes a version of the high exploits that mark the activities of male protagonists in romance. The French romances most familiar to English readers characteristically ended in marriage rather than death, but *Oroonoko*, like them, glorifies the "brave," "beautiful," "constant" woman and the power of true love. Its celebration of a black—*very* black: the point is emphasized—African hero is surprising. Yet more startling is the female narrator's consistent implication that Oroonoko's virtues exceed those of his English counterparts, to whom there is constant implicit reference. The explicit story here concerns the nobility and accomplishment of a "great man"; the subtext involves the situation of women (English women) and the importance of a female perspective. Behn's fiction, in other words, offers the kind of intricate suggestiveness more often associated with the later novel. It achieves its energy partly by a structure that places constant emphasis on the narrator's situation, reminding us (as many later novels would also do) that story depends on point of view, that what the narrator sees derives not only from where she is but from who she is. Responding to the imaginative needs of its readers, it also hints moral and social reflections. It foretells eighteenth-century developments.

Not only allegory and romance prepared for the novel. The line between "fact" and "fiction" remained wobbly in the late seventeenth and early eighteenth century, and the consequent blurring rarely seemed to trouble either literary critics or moralists. The widely circulated "confessions" of criminals, for instance, characteristically purporting to have been composed on the eve of their writers' execution, had usually been written by other hands than those of the alleged confessor and often rested on a scant foundation of fact. Criminal biographies similarly extrapolated freely on the basis of meager actual knowledge. Books of advice to the young included didactic stories, purportedly but not literally true, intended to entice readers toward moral improvement. Popular periodicals and pamphlets mingled reportage with fancy. Works claiming to record travel to faraway places provided an opportunity for relatively unchecked inventiveness. Such miscellaneous genres trained their readers to expect imaginative stimulation of a sort soon to become increasingly the province of acknowledged fiction.

The eighteenth-century novel, then, had many recognizable forebears,

but its ways of developing the hints they offered were by no means predictable. If, as I have claimed, the eighteenth century from beginning to end
was marked by fictional experiment, that fact registered the exhilarating
sense of possibility attending the absence of established rules. The novel in
its newness enjoyed few rules of composition. Its precedents might come
from fiction, journalism, drama, moral essay—a great range of generic
opportunity. It in effect made itself up as it went along, constantly inventive not only of new kinds of scene and character but, in consequence,
of new precedents for itself. The multiplied stories of the century's early
fiction, the Gothic extravagances of the final years—both declare the ex-
pansiveness of novelistic self-imagining.

It may prove useful to sketch at the outset some of the polarities between
which novelists might range. I'll start with novelistic pace. Even now,
no determinate ideal governs a novelist's choice of pace, and individual
works may adopt leisurely or rapid movement according to their aims.
The possible extremes, in this as in other matters, were possibly farther
apart in the eighteenth century. Only twenty years separate the publication of Jane Barker's *The Lining of the Patch Work Screen* (1726) from
Richardson's *Clarissa* (1747–48), a great novel paced so slowly that it risks
tedium: Samuel Johnson claimed that if you read it for the plot, you'd hang
yourself. Modern abridgements, which may expunge half to two-thirds of
the original text, retain the plot in a form less likely to encourage suicide
but eliminate much of what makes its development so prolonged; lovers
of Richardson's novel maintain that such abridgements destroy, or greatly
weaken, the work's impact. Abridgements, for example, typically excise
an interminable series of letters from the clergyman Brand—letters that
serve minimal plot function, that communicate a disagreeable personality,
and that interfere with the narrative of Clarissa's dying. Yet these dreary
communications crucially involve the reader in the frustration Clarissa
feels in her losing game with death, as she tries to reconcile with her
family, thwarted at every turn by Brand's steadily derogatory reports on
her—reports dictated not by conscious malice but by egotism and moral
blindness.

Few later writers (one might instance the Rousseau of *La nouvelle
Héloïse,* who deliberately modeled his work after Richardson's, and of
course Proust) have attempted comparable prolongation. Barker, in con-

trast, proceeds at a breakneck speed likewise rarely (if ever) matched. She offers a vague frame story, continued from one volume to the next of the trilogy to which her novel belongs, but the substance of the fiction comprises an extended series of interpolated tales, greatly compressed, rapidly told, virtually any of them implying the substance of an entire novel in itself. The sharp contrast between the speeds of the two narratives calls attention to strongly differentiated views of a novel's aims. By the century's end, one may discern a "normalized" pace for the novel, a kind of midpoint between Barker's tumultuous speed and Richardson's excruciating slowness. Novelists could and did vary from the norm, as they continue to do, but the swings between one novel and another rarely again proved so intense and so unpredictable.

Equally striking is the distance between a kind of fiction sparing of concrete detail and the dense circumstantiality of a book like *Robinson Crusoe,* in which objects and appearances become the impetus of plot. To stick with the two authors I have already cited: as the velocity of her narratives might lead one to expect, Barker supplies many stories that tell us nothing at all about how rooms look, what people wear, how tall they are, what objects surround them, what landscape or cityscape they walk through. Yet in isolated moments her rapid plots can slow down to make space for a few striking details: for instance, the gloves and lace worn by a female servant in *A Patch-Work Screen for the Ladies,* the middle volume of Barker's trilogy. Each detail of apparel bears a weight of significance, as does the velvet upholstery of the chair the servant sits in. *Clarissa* obviously has room for as much descriptive data as the novelist wishes to insert—a fact that makes more startling the total absence of specificity in many scenes. Richardson, too, though, far more elaborately than Barker, will pause to report, for instance, every sordid element of the room in a bailiff's house where Clarissa is confined for debt. The novelist concerns himself mainly with the insides of people's heads, but the insides of their houses may also receive his full attention.

As these instances will suggest, novelists were less likely to eschew detail altogether than to use it parsimoniously and purposefully. Even fictions as dense with people as *Tom Jones,* as dense with trivial event as *Tristram Shandy,* rarely poured out the kind of physical information that might give imaginative reality to the settings their characters inhabit. The fullest detail appears in the fiction of such novelists as Defoe, for whom a character's physical circumstances had powerful determinant force, and Frances Burney, in whose works the minutiae of social environment accounted for much psychological fact. What Moll Flanders wore, what she stole, what she saw in prison—such elements are crucial to Defoe's effects. They help explain why many readers find his novels realistic, despite, for instance, their reliance on more abundant unlikely coincidences than life customarily offers. The asserted teleology of the realistic novel has a powerful effect on readers: Defoe fulfills their expectations. But he satisfies more eclectic expectations as well.

The most crucial polarities of plot in the period are singleness versus multiplicity. In matters of pacing and detail, the century's development culminated in a middle-of-the-road norm. Plot development was different: it moved inexorably from multiplicity toward unity. By the 1790s, Elizabeth Inchbald could still publish, in *A Simple Story*, a novel with a double plot—but not without making manifest efforts to unify its two schemes of action. Up to, and even after, the century's midpoint, however, it was by no means a foregone conclusion that unity would prove preferable to diversity as a basis for plot structure. Even the works of such important novelists as Henry Fielding and Tobias Smollett made heavy use of so-called interpolated stories—tales by often minor characters that critics from later periods often see as interrupting the main sequence of action. If, though, one drops the assumption that fictional excellence demands plot unity, it becomes possible to see that the multiplication of apparently irrelevant stories speaks to the universal desire for narrative per se. Sentimental novels in particular continued until late in the century to employ structures depending on the introduction of one story after another, told by various unfortunate protagonists to a central figure who provides in his own person (such figures are usually male) the principal unifying element of the plot.

But the idea of unity, with its Aristotelian precedent, developed increasing power as the novel began to make greater claims for its own relevance and importance. In the 1790s, Godwin told the story of how he plotted *Caleb Williams*. He began with the end, he said, having a clear vision of the dénouement. Then he plotted backward, constructing his novel's events so that each one contributed to the outcome. Even the long, baggy Gothic novels of Ann Radcliffe attend carefully to causality and sequence. If a character tells a story in such novels, we can be sure that the story will bear directly on how a complicated sequence of events works itself out. Plot carries meaning in fictional structures, and unified plots could enforce their meanings in more lucid and direct fashion than the earlier multiplots—which is by no means to imply that multiplied plots don't create striking effects of their own, as we shall see.

The spectrum of possibility between complete realism and complete fantasy, of course, provides a crucial range of opportunity. The notion of realism suggests to most readers at least significant *possible* correspondence between fictional representations and actuality. The characters and actions of a novel are not taken to be literally real, but the way the characters act, what they do, bears some recognizable relation to our knowledge of what human beings are like and how they behave. In a "realistic" novel, as I have already pointed out, details of setting and social circumstance as well as character delineate a world that appears plausible. (Indeed, in our own time historians have not infrequently assumed that they could mine the texts of eighteenth-century novels for data about actual circumstances.) The sequence of cause and effect that forms the plot in realistic fiction also strikes the reader as believable—as a sequence of events that could conceivably take place. The problems that characters face in such fiction resonate with readers who know of or have experienced comparable problems; the resulting sense of recognition often obviates awareness of the strong element of fantasy also operative in plotting.

Disputes about the nature of realism or about the degree to which any given novel merits the label "realistic" frequently reflect not only different ways of looking at the literary work but disparate notions of what reality means. If, for instance, one believes that the unconscious mind contains a chaos of contradictory impulses and perceptions, it becomes possible to argue that a novel eschewing orderly development is more profoundly realistic than one pursuing a sequential plot. In common usage, however, realism is usually linked to density of detail and plausibility of action.

Whatever one's definition of realism, the assumption that eighteenth-century novels aspire to it can lead the reader into trouble by obscuring salient aspects of the fiction. We can readily agree that the density of social texture in *Tom Jones* gives the novel the kind of plausibility that we associate with realism. Large questions remain, nonetheless, about the usefulness of seeing this novel as primarily realistic. Its plot may remind us of Miss Prism's pronouncement in *The Importance of Being Earnest* that in fiction the good end happily and the bad unhappily. That, she explains, is what fiction means. Just so in *Tom Jones*. An innocent seduced maiden appears; the man who has wronged her is persuaded to marry her. A hardworking family exists in dreadful poverty; a savior shows up. Blifil gets his comeuppance; Tom gets his inheritance and his girl. Moreover, one knows from the beginning that everything will come out happily.

The pleasure *Tom Jones* provides arguably derives mainly from its artifice. The nineteenth-century poet Samuel Taylor Coleridge and the twentieth-century critic Ronald Crane agreed that Fielding's novel has a perfect plot. That is to say, its contrivances mesh flawlessly; its parts add up to a coherent whole; its events have consequences; no gun goes unfired. The narrator takes rather ostentatious pride in the neatness of his arrangements, frequently calling attention to it, and particularly to what he has deliberately concealed until revelation will have maximum effect. The elaborate authorial constructions show off the narrator's dexterity and call attention to his control of his readers—that control he flaunts, plays with, and appears to employ sometimes for its own sake alone.

I shall examine *Tom Jones* more fully in a forthcoming chapter. For the moment, it is enough to observe that the artifice playing a large part in creating the novel's effects must be acknowledged in order to understand the work's accomplishment. This observation may call attention to the difficulty of categorizing much of the period's fiction. The novel's appropriate function in depicting some version of reality competed (as it always competes) with the possibility of its rendering or relying on unrealistic fantasy in the service of readers' entertainment or enlightenment. Throughout the century, these two fundamental sources of plot and image vied with each other. Realism won, in the sense that nineteenth-century fiction often depended on characterization, detail, and sometimes even plot that attempted verisimilitude. Yet through the nineteenth century and into our own time, the competition has continued, with elements of fantasy quite remote from actuality making their way into fiction and sometimes almost completely controlling its structure and content.

The relative triumph, until quite recently, of realism, at least in "serious" fiction, meant that critics and historians looking back at the eighteenth century from the vantage point of the twentieth or twenty-first have tended to see most distinctly the line of development bearing the most obvious affinities to the major literary trends of later periods. In other words, they have read the nineteenth century back into the eighteenth. The other kinds of innovation that abounded in the eighteenth century have therefore been obscured. It will be the task of this book to look especially at the period's new directions that have never fully been followed up.

The story of a century's fiction that I propose to tell provides no consistent plot of development. Indeed, the growth of the novel enacts no teleology, despite retrospective impositions. In a situation that both allowed aspiring novelists to make use of conventions developed in many literary forms and authorized them to invent new conventions, one can speculate that writers might imagine or half-imagine competing directions that the evolving form might take. Their fictions sketch many potential lines of development. The conceivable alternatives do not end with something called realism, as opposed to something called fantasy. In the first place, neither of those categories ever emerges absolute and unmixed. We should think, rather, of possibilities along an axis extending between the imagined poles of realism and fantasy. Such possibilities include, toward the realistic pole, life stories that follow an imaginary protagonist from birth to death, or at least childhood to maturity. Stories of this sort can dwell mainly on external events or they can focus on the internal life—a fact that suggests another fictional direction, toward narratives of consciousness. Fictions containing multiple plots, as many early novels abundantly do, can also utilize multiple conventions, combining realism and fantasy, narration of external and internal events. Novels of sentiment, while making direct reference to social actualities, may indulge in fantasies of superhuman virtue as well as superhuman distress. The conventions of romance may dictate plots entirely controlled by love (an aspect of the novel that greatly concerned moralists), bypassing all the impediments that real experience puts in the way of total concentration on romantic relationships.

Of course a wide range of possibility for the novel, including lines of development unknown in the eighteenth century, remains in the twenty-first century, and publishers' lists give evidence of continued experimentation in many directions. Novelists now, however, work within or against a long tradition. Readers consequently can locate what they read in relation to what has gone before. Eighteenth-century readers, sometimes not even aware that they were reading fiction, could refer to fewer precedents beyond their own experience and that of their acquaintances. In the process of reading, novels would often have felt like something new. If they felt familiar, as *Robinson Crusoe* might have felt familiar by analogy with the factual narrations of literal seafarers, the familiarity could be misleading, by eliding the new form's fictionality.

We can only surmise, though, what it would have felt like to read novels when they were still in the process of defining their shape for the first time. Although some discussions of the putative immorality of *Tom Jones* and *Tristram Shandy* survive, although personal letters occasionally offer testimony about someone's immediate reaction to a new work of fiction, little evidence remains of detailed personal responses to the developing genre. Yet how these novels are read and are to be read matters as much as how they are written—matters perhaps even more as we think about them now. The situation of the twenty-first-century reader makes part of the story of the novel for our own time. Originally intended to entertain as well as to instruct, many of the works here considered attracted large audiences at the outset. Their power to yield pleasure and enlightenment remains even now, although the kind of illumination they provide probably differs from what the first readers discovered, and their entertainment may also have altered its nature. It is important to remember, though, that the claim these novels make on us is not only historical. The books remain readable. Indeed, they offer abundant rewards to the attentive reader, who will implicitly and explicitly, in imagined form, be invoked as part of the ensuing discussion.

Aspiring to coherence, literary history, like other kinds of history, seeks organizational principles. Social or literary theory has often supplied the principles to make sense out of the abundance of verbal production, offering a vantage point from which to approach multiple texts. The flavor of individual works disappears, though, as a generalizing thesis blurs their idiosyncrasies. Everything can start to sound alike, one work after another demonstrating the oppression of women or the hegemony of wealth. My own organization depends on the idea of multiplicity—and, more important, on the idea of reading. Only by procrustean stretching and lopping or by draconian exclusion can one fit the variety of eighteenth-century fiction under a single rubric. To read and respond individually to a range of novelistic patterns and effects more accurately conveys the appropriate impression of wonderfully productive multiplicity. Such an approach can neither achieve nor aspire to full "coverage," or, for that matter, exhaustive readings of specific texts. It can, however, call attention to issues engaged, techniques devised, and pleasure provided in the many works of fiction England produced in the eighteenth century.

The narrative that follows will tell of varied engagements with the problems of creating fiction. It focuses not on where the novel comes from but on what the novel in its varied early manifestations *is*, not on how the novel reflects or comments on social conditions but on how it shapes itself to engage interest and provide enlightenment. I propose to examine a number of novels in sufficient detail at least to adumbrate the special flavor, dominant structure, and peculiar delight offered by each. This procedure, I hope, will heighten both understanding and appreciation of the period's fiction in all its variety.

For organizational purposes I have grouped the novels under consideration—the well known and unfamiliar alike—into loose categories designed to facilitate comparison. These categories suggest both substantive and formal aspects of the works in question. Some classifications have been deliberately chosen to violate common assumptions about lines of kinship in eighteenth-century fiction. Manley, Haywood, and Behn are customarily grouped as female writers of erotic fiction. To locate Manley and Haywood in the company of Daniel Defoe and Charles Johnstone (author of that strange work *Chrysal: or, The Adventures of a Guinea*) illuminates new aspects of the two women as writers and rescues them from the female ghetto to which they are customarily consigned. Putting *A Sentimental Journey* and Sarah Fielding's unjustly neglected *The Cry* in conjunction with a group of epistolary novels sharpens perception of an important aspect of epistolary fiction and declares some unexpected connections.

Other classifications offer few obvious surprises in themselves. The chapters on sentimental novels and on the Gothic, for instance, present on the whole predictable texts for contemplation. Such less startling groupings provide opportunities for differentiation, allowing us to examine the diverse procedures and effects that can be obscured by generalizing labels. Sophia Lee's *The Recess* (another remarkable, little-known work) and M. G. Lewis's *The Monk* have little in common beyond their mutual use of cavernous spaces as the locale for unpredictable events, yet both plausibly belong to the category of Gothic.

To some extent, I must confess, my primary desire is to rescue such books as *The Recess, The Cry,* and *Memoirs of Miss Sidney Bidulph,* a powerful first-person narrative about a woman's suffering. To read them is in effect to rescue them: to pay attention to their individual qualities immediately makes clear how other readers might profit from attending to them too. I want also, though, to reveal the richness of books whose titles everyone knows—*Pamela, Tristram Shandy, Tom Jones.* And, as I have already indicated, I am eager to tell a story of eighteenth-century fictional productivity as a whole.

The subsequent chapters are largely organized under capacious labels (usually suggesting both content and form) that provide a basis for groupings. That form and content relate closely to one another is hardly a new idea. Their intimate synergy lies at the heart of the novel's capacity to transmute experience into art. The novel of development shapes itself in relation to the course of human life; the novel of adventure follows an episodic structure. In this respect it resembles the novel of sentiment—which, using the episodic structure to different ends, consequently makes of it quite a different thing. In the novel of adventure, individual episodes constitute complete mini-narratives, with climax and resolution. The novel of sentiment, making feeling its object, achieves emotional effect by fragmentary structure, often refusing resolution for its episodes. The unlikelihood of completion can determine both its subject and its shape. "Sentiment" and "adventure," like "development," then, designate structural arrangements as well as subject matter.

My organizing labels, however, are only temporary conveniences—not classifications intended to organize the period into rigid categories. Many of the century's fictions draw on more than a single subgenre. The categories by which I have classified them are rarely, if ever, exclusive; they are merely useful for the moment. *Tom Jones* is a novel of development, and I've treated it in the chapter on novels of this sort. But it is also a picaresque novel with certain characteristics of sentimental fiction as well. No formal taxonomy can comprehend the richness and variety of the period's fiction. *Formal* doesn't necessarily mean formal; categories are not definitive. The loose groupings here offered constitute ways of attending to novels in conjunction with one another, of beginning to look at what they are like. To do so—to think about the individual tone and substance of individual novels, and about how novels resemble one another—may help to recapture the vitality and daring of the early fictional enterprise and to suggest the rewards that eighteenth-century fiction offers its modern and postmodern readers. The story of the novel, like that of other literary genres, necessarily involves attention to developing conventions. The novel, as I have already suggested, drew some of its conventions from other genres and invented many of its own. Conventions as they first articulate themselves of course don't feel like conventions; they represent immediate responses to narrative problems. Inasmuch as they offer solutions to such problems, they provide a resource for subsequent novelists to draw on. The subgenres that I allude to consist of clusters of conventions, gradually developed or seized on from their first appearance. The convention that fictional letter writers have infinite time and opportunity to pursue their correspondences, for instance, is essential to the epistolary novel. Authors need not bother to elucidate why this is the case within their fictions, any more than the writers of earlier French romances needed to explain how their heroes nourished themselves when consigned to a wilderness for many years. Yet matters not explained can carry as much significance as the explicit substance of a text.

Most of the following chapters will focus on a cluster of novelists, usually rather closely linked in time. The loose chronological arrangement, however, on occasion yields to other local principles of organization. Thus the chapter that concentrates on *Tristram Shandy* also draws on other works from throughout the century to ponder how novelists can mingle disparate novelistic conventions—a matter that calls attention to the necessary arbitrariness of designating *Pamela*, say, an epistolary novel rather than a romance.

The story to be told contemplates subject matter from the sensational, as utilized by early novelists, to the political, a late-century preoccupation, and the forms associated with the varieties of subject. We begin with early narratives of adventure.

CHAPTER TWO

Novels of Adventure

NO MAN BUT AN IDIOT ever wrote except for money, Dr. Johnson told Boswell. No woman either, he might have added. Early novelists, men and women alike, impelled to make their livings from writing needed to engage paying audiences. Exploring new possibilities for prose fiction, many decided that adventure supplied an obvious hook. Sarah Fielding in the opening pages of her 1754 novel, *The Cry,* makes it clear that she expects her audience to want "a number of surprising incidents and adventures" (11). Although she does not propose to satisfy this desire, she acknowledges that adventure easily arouses the reader's interest. If a protagonist suffers many hardships, "the reader's fears will be alarm'd for her safety; his pleasure will arise on seeing her escape from the teeth of a lion, or the paws of a fierce tiger; if he has conceived any regard for the virtuous sufferer, he will be delighted when she avoids being taken captive" (12).

The imagined plot to which Fielding alludes presumably derives from her reading of seventeenth-century romances that provided prolonged stories of love in which male protagonists dared greatly for the sake of their frequently threatened beloved—fighting with numerous opponents, surviving years of wandering in the wilderness—but these romances followed fixed and predictable patterns. As the eighteenth century began, fiction writers' implicit definition of adventure enlarged, no longer de-

pending on knights, giants, lions, and tigers. Some explored erotic implications of the love plot; some allowed women to become protagonists;
some made politics an arena for excitement; some stranded a traveler on
a desert island or investigated a prostitute's struggle for survival; some
used the structure of adventure as a pretext for disjunction. A sampling of
publications from the century's early years illustrates the evolving forms
and expanding content of the period's fiction. The later period, as even a
single representative will suggest, found new uses for the idea of adventure, even while returning to techniques of earlier fiction.

The works grouped together do not often receive attention in conjunction with one another. Manley and Haywood are usually grouped as
writers of "amatory fiction"; Mary Davys and Penelope Aubin, acknowledged as precursors to the full-blown novel, have received glancing and
rather patronizing notice; Defoe, enormously productive in many genres,
is assigned a category all his own. The fact calls attention to the multiple
possibilities of generic taxonomy. The nature of a text's classification helps
to determine what one can see in it. Considering these writers together
may help us perceive a common solution to formal difficulties that helped
determine the shape of the early novel in England.

In 1709 Delarivier Manley published a work with a title page designating it as *Secret Memoirs and Manners of several Persons of Quality, of
both Sexes. From the New Atalantis, an Island in the Mediteranean. Written
Originally in Italian.* Promptly arrested as a result, along with her printer
and publishers, she was acquitted at the subsequent trial. Her brief imprisonment, however, lent notoriety to her book, which was widely read and
frequently reprinted. Although *The New Atalantis* employs a mythological
frame, fictitious names, and liberal exaggeration and distortion, it focuses
on contemporaneous court scandal, using it as a political weapon with
which to attack the Whig Party. To avoid confusion on this point, Manley
published a separate key to the fiction's proper names. (In later editions
a key appeared along with the text.)

As a basis for audience appeal, then, Manley exploited her work's connection with actuality. By her use of mythological characters she ostensibly
disclaimed literal truth; by her promulgation of a key, she claimed what
she had denied. Undoubtedly, people read *The New Atalantis* in the hope
of being titillated or horrified by news about the great. Yet they would
also have found in it the satisfactions of fiction. It offered stories about

seduction (consummated or narrowly avoided), rape, polygamy, and various deadly sins in action: dark tales, often, but narrated with zest.

The mythological frame of *The New Atalantis* involves three female characters. Astraea, goddess of justice, joins the personified figure of her mother, Virtue, who has apparently suffered much abuse in her travels through the world. The third member of the triumvirate embodies Intelligence, or news, a putative source of information. Intelligence undertakes to inform the other two of the state of modern society. What news she does not know already, she avidly gathers, painting by means of detailed and elaborated examples a picture of a corrupt world, controlled by lust, cupidity, and the desire for power.

In enforcing this view of society, she and others tell many stories—some comic, others pathetic; some circumstantial, others bare; some representing women as victims, others showing them as villains. Manley thus ensures variety: her readers hardly have time to be bored, given the rapidity with which one story succeeds another. Narrative multiplicity rather than detailed development marks many early-century fictions, apparently predicated on the assumption that readers will not long sustain interest in a single set of characters or predicaments. *The New Atalantis* can hardly be said to have "a plot." The frame narrative sketches the beginnings of one, when Astraea explains that she is seeking through the world for information to help her guide a young prince—probably George Augustus, the future George II—to true greatness. Nominally, her need to understand current manners and customs motivates the subsequent investigations by the three females. This vestigial plot, however, receives no real development and concludes in indeterminacy. Astraea, along with her companions and the reader, acquires a lot of information along the way, but the episodes could be multiplied indefinitely, and the book ends in the middle of one of them.

Instead of a single plot, Manley provides many plots. For instance: a great duke has been given responsibility for rearing a young woman named Charlot, left in his charge by a father who has died. He resolves to bring her up as a model of virtue, instructing her in all good principles and protecting her from every source of corruption. For many years, this system works well. In her adolescence, though, Charlot becomes very beautiful, and the duke finds himself consumed by passion for her. Knowing that her principles will make her refuse any sexual advance, he works out ways to corrupt her as carefully as he had previously thought through her education in virtue. He tells her that she is now an adult, calls her attention to lascivious books he has previously kept from her, loads her with jewels, and procures for her a court position. Early in her time at court, he goes off to war; she, in his absence, confides to a benevolent but cynical countess that she feels attracted to him. When the duke returns, he rapes Charlot, who has continued to resist him despite her own passion. He then secretly establishes her as his mistress in a country house and urges her to invite the countess to keep her company. Subsequently he falls in love with the countess and seduces her. Charlot flees and spends the rest of her life in misery.

Each stage of this intricate series of actions requires and receives analysis of motives and behavior, and the action is more elaborate than a brief summary can contain, yet the entire story occupies only seventeen pages. (This is, in fact, one of the longer stories: some, almost equally complicated, take only three or four pages.) Yet, as the summary indicates, it contains the raw material of what we would recognize as a novel. Because Manley's view of her fictional project does not correspond to modern expectations, she contents herself with rudimentary characterizations—almost necessarily, given her enormous cast of characters. She does not always bring her narratives to completion, but stops when she has made her moral or political point. She apparently worries little about plausibility, though her tales consistently emerge from a single view of current social degradation. What she impressively offers is intense narrative energy, expressed in the breathtaking abundance of distinct stories. As the miniature tales multiply, repeating the theme of society in decay but inventing or discovering ever new instances, the reader experiences vicariously the rich possibility that life can offer.

Much of that possibility is dangerous. Near the end of volume 2, Intelligence remarks, "The race of men are arrived to that perfection in arts, sciences, villainy and penetration, that there can be no laws contrived, how binding soever, in intention and appearance, but what they can extenuate" (229). Even legal safeguards no longer work, given the high accomplishments that the race of men turn to sinister ends. Yet because of the vigor and inventiveness that Manley brings to her enterprise, to read about this dire state of affairs produces not despair but a kind of exhilaration, generated by the richness of personality and event that the imagined world provides and by the excitement of allegedly seeing behind the scenes of public life.

As political intervention, Manley's undertaking asserts female authority. Her book's three presiding presences are women; so, of course, is its author. Her embroideries, distortions, and inventions carry her far beyond the facts of literal social scandal, but the key insists on reference back to a realm in which the designation of political party indicates virtue or vice. Not only does *The New Atalantis* instantiate a woman's right to political opinions; it also interprets politics mainly in terms of personal relations, traditionally woman's sphere. Love and lust, avarice and envy play themselves out through their effects on imagined individuals. If men remain the principal political players, their thoughts and motives largely depend on women. As subjects and as objects, women shape the stories of love. Although they figure often as victims of male lust or greed, they serve also as actors on a large stage.

They are not, however, assigned rich inner lives or finely detailed characterizations, and neither are their male counterparts. Manley's reliance on a large number of small stories implies emphasis on happening rather than character, on diverse rather than detailed evidence. Her political purpose fulfills itself through the multiplication of examples, which also fosters expectation of a particular kind of narrative. Other fiction writers would adopt the same general narrative structure to different purposes.

The anonymous *Adventures of Lindamira, a Lady of Quality* (1702) ("Revised and Corrected by Mr. *Tho. Brown*") exemplifies a more common adventure mode of the century's opening years. Manley adopted a fanciful quasi-mythological framework to protect against the dangers of allusiveness; the writer of *Lindamira,* in contrast, claims the justification for this novelistic enterprise in *"the weight of truth, and the importance of real matter of Fact"* (Preface, n.p.). Although the title claims this as an adventure story, the heroine's "adventures" prove relatively tame, consisting entirely of chances and mischances of love. Adopting an epistolary form, the novel constructs itself from Lindamira's letters to a female friend. The imaginary writer's main concern, predictably, focuses on her own love adventures, which involve frustration brought on her by her mistakes in behavior. She early meets the man she wants; it takes a long time for her to learn to act so as to win him. Lindamira's letters also include stories of other young women she meets, all of whom have tales of love to tell.

This early novel calls attention to a problem implicit in narratives centering on women. Given a desire to make truth claims (however implausible such claims seem as a fiction unfolds), the aspiring novelist who proposes a story of female experience is pretty much confined to the subject of love, its misunderstandings and misadventures. The multiplication of stories provides a device to diminish the monotony. Although female stories will continue to be stories of love, no matter how many female narrators appear, the author at least has the opportunity to vary situations and characters. The assumption that readers want adventure, even when they reject the implausibilities of French romance, dictates the common (almost universal) practice of including the stories of many protagonists without lingering on any. As a consequence, early novels that lack Manley's political purpose adapt a less emphatic version of the fictional structure she employs.

To group Manley's fictions with those of Jane Barker, Eliza Haywood, and Daniel Defoe, as this chapter does, under the rubric of *adventure*, draws on diverse meanings of that rich word. Writers of fiction relied on these meanings too. *Adventure*, the *Oxford English Dictionary* reveals, bore the weight of two opposed sets of significance. It designated things that might happen to a person, and things that a person might cause to happen. On the side of what might happen, it means (or meant) "that which comes to us, or happens without design"; "a chance occurrence, an event or issue, an accident"; "chance of danger or loss; risk, jeopardy, peril." But it can indicate also "a trial of one's chance . . . ; a hazard, venture, or experiment"; "a hazardous or perilous enterprise or performance; a daring feat"; "the encountering of risks or participation in novel and exciting events; adventurous activity, enterprise." With or without the engagement of one's will, in other words, one encounters or engages in adventures, which may entail action or endurance or both. Robinson Crusoe deliberately sets forth to seek excitement at sea: he makes a trial of his chance. He is flung ashore on a deserted island without his volition: a chance occurrence, an accident. He purposefully makes his way to the wrecked ship and clambers among its debris: the encountering of risks. And so on. Combining the kind of adventure that happens to one with the kind that one makes happen, Defoe can suggest through his story a wide range of human possibility.

Indeed, the spectrum of meanings for *adventure* roughly corresponds to the possibilities of life experience. Doing or suffering, man or woman, one can figure one's career as adventure. A woman—in life, at any rate—would not have Crusoe's choice of going to sea to seek her fortune, but even as a victim of male dominance she might undergo adventure. The early fiction of the eighteenth century resolutely declares the excitement, for readers and potentially for those who undergo comparable fates in actuality, of many kinds of life happening. Not that it is, or aspires to be, "realistic," despite allusions to truth. On the contrary: the satisfaction of reading about Charlot's career, for instance, or Lindamira's has everything to do with implausibility, heightened by the speed of the narration. These stories do not represent real life; they effectively stand in for life. They gesture at events without inviting readers to believe in them. They offer outline sketches rather than the fully shaded landscapes, conversation pieces, and portraits that nineteenth-century novelists would make familiar.

The New Atalantis and Lindamira, for all their differences, share the characteristics that will also mark the structural arrangements of the other works treated in this chapter. All stress terms that appear in the OED definition: "novel and exciting events," for example, and "enterprise." Both the events and the enterprise can assume many different forms, but in some shape or other they remain constants of the adventure mode. These stories of adventure implicitly value diversity. One effect of their characteristic narrative speed is to allow room for multiplied happenings that develop meaning by their cumulative effect.

The pattern I have been describing does not necessarily preclude reflection. Internal as well as external happenings may constitute novel and exciting events. In Defoe, as we shall see, the adventure of self-imagining coexists with that of making one's way in the world. Most often, though, the reader is invited to take pleasure in a collection of happenings linked more by sequence than by logic and to register the excitement of sheer event.

Jane Barker claims for her tales no political reference and no allusion to the lives of the great, but she writes in the same narrative vein as Manley, stringing together short stories, more thematically various than Manley's, within a loose and unresolved framing tale that sustains itself through three linked works: Love Intrigues, A Patch-Work Screen for the Ladies, and The Lining of the Patch Work Screen, published between 1713 and 1726. The frame story, vaguely autobiographical, involves a character named Galesia, who purports to offer an account of her romantic life. The entire plot of Love Intrigues, a more obviously coherent work than its successors (also considerably shorter than they), concerns Galesia's love for a man named Bosvil, who leads her on but jilts her in the end. In the trilogy's second volume, new romantic possibilities emerge but also come to nothing. Galesia remains unmarried, and by the third volume that fact seems insignificant. She has increasingly come to define herself as a woman of letters, writer of poetry and prose, and contemplator of society.

As the trilogy continues, Barker intersperses into the narrative quantities of sentimental verse and numerous subnarratives, rapidly told tales often passed on to her by unexpected visitors. Some sound like plaintive shaggy-dog stories, never resolved. Others have predictable dénouements. But the most provocative prove unexpected in their development and their resolutions.

A striking example, which will indicate how difficult it can be to categorize Barker's work, is the story of the wife and the mistress. A young man marries a woman of distinction, physically unattractive but possessed of sufficient fortune to serve his needs. He has several children by her, but all die in infancy. He soon begins also to have children by his maidservant, one a year. For reasons unspecified, and unknown to the fiction's other characters, the wife becomes "a perfect Slave" to this servant, doing all the household work in her stead, getting up early from the bed that all three share every night in order to do so. The husband wishes to get rid of his mistress because her three surviving children burden his financial resources. Despite many efforts to persuade her, however, the wife insists that if the servant leaves, she will leave too. Put to the test, she does exactly that. The two women subsequently return to the husband, who soon dies. His widow begs in the streets to support the mistress. Even when the queen offers her a pension on condition that she leave the other woman, the widow refuses and continues begging.

At one point, Galesia's mother serves as the husband's intermediary to persuade his wife to part with the servant. She goes to the house and finds "the Servant sitting in a handsome Velvet Chair, dress'd up in very good lac'd Linnen, having clean Gloves on her Hands, and the Wife washing the Dishes" (145–46). Rarely in eighteenth-century fiction does one find someone washing dishes, an activity normally reserved for servants and therefore invisible. The details of this scene—the velvet chair, the lace-adorned clothes, the gloves that denote idleness, as well as the dish-washing—have the specificity of a kind of literary realism not common until much later. Yet the psychologically tantalizing episodes that account for the scene receive no analysis of any kind. Not even speculatively does any onlooker suggest the wife's motivation for effectively enslaving her-self to the mistress. Indeed, the lack of explicit motive appears almost to constitute the story's point. The reader can interpret as she will.

The same mixture of detailed physical specificity with lack of explana-tion marks many of the interpolated stories. Occasionally a participant will attempt to account for a strange appearance, only to declare the impos-sibility of doing so. A group of people enter a long-closed building called the Devil's Tower. Inside, they find a cauldron of boiling blood, along with an assortment of monsters and phantoms and a vast grist mill that grinds up human beings. The many "strange and monstrous Appear-ances," the narrator asserts, are "not easily to be remember'd, much less to be describ'd" (209). The visitors feel a need for interpretation, frustrated though it is: "nor could any body conceive the true natural Cause of these Productions, whether a subterraneous Fire heated that Red Liquor, which appear'd like Blood, (which Liquor, perhaps, was only Water, so coloured by passing through Red Earth) no body could conclude; tho' every one made their several Conjectures thereon" (209). A natural explanation is thus suggested for an apparently supernatural manifestation, but neither the narrator nor any participant in the scene gives the explanation author-ity. It simply exists at the same level of dubious plausibility as the physi-cal details. The story itself, consisting mainly of a meticulous account of the various appearances the travelers witness, ends without resolution. Members of the group read a threatening inscription on a statue in the inmost chamber; they leave the building and lock it up again; it sinks mysteriously into the earth. The account concludes, "Thus the little Story ended, without telling what Misery befel the King and Kingdom, by the *Moors,* who over ran the Country for many Years after" (210). Is the Moor-ish invasion a consequence of intrusion into the Devil's domain? The reader, again, must decide.

Indeed, Barker's fiction demands a peculiarly active reader, forced constantly to shift expectations. At one point, Galesia reads in a book of proverbs assembled along with illustrative tales. Her reading causes her to reflect on the weaknesses shared by all humankind and on the particular weaknesses and misfortunes of individuals. When we look around, she concludes, "we find nothing but Distress, Distractions, Quarrels, Broils, Debts, Duels, Law-suits, Tricks, Cheats, Taxes, Tumults, Mobs, Riots, Mutinies, Rebellions, Battels, &c. where thousands are slain; nay, we make Slaughter a Study, and War an Art" (273). One might expect this Swiftian catalogue to introduce further contemplation, satiric or melancholy, of actual human experience. Instead, it introduces a long dream in which Galesia, after passing through a terrestrial paradise, finds a scene presided over by the Queen of the Fairies and including grasshoppers with wings made of gold and nightingales that supply the chorus for a song of praise. The pattern thus adumbrated, of reference to the everyday world immediately followed by resort to a realm of fantasy, dominates Barker's work as a whole.

One explanation for the repeated withdrawal from circumstantial realism occurs in the text, when Galesia reflects on the romances of the past, marked, she thinks, by "a Genius of Vertue and Honour," in contrast with "the Stories of our Times," which "are so black, that the Authors, can hardly escape being smutted, or defil'd in touching such Pitch" (253). So it is, perhaps, that Barker supplies tales of adultery with fanciful resolutions, offers stories that speak of nothing but fancy, draws heavily on writers of the past, and tells her stories very fast, often failing to resolve them. She invites the reader's interest in plot rather than character, providing virtually nothing in the way of character development, but she often abandons her plots in midcareer. Galesia herself, who appears in all three books, receives more characterization than anyone else, but the stories she tells claim more attention than does her personal situation. The reader is urged—indeed, required—to take pleasure in many aspects of narrative. Agility becomes a desideratum for reading as the text places in the foreground the fictionality of its own construction. Without flaunting her power to make things happen, Barker's narrator manipulates scene, plot, and character with utter disregard for probability, plausibility, or consistency. The vigorous, varied, lavishly multiplied narratives that compose her novels declare the power of fiction, not to make the reader suspend disbelief; rather, to make disbelief irrelevant. The pleasure these stories provide acknowledges invention, manipulation, ground-shifting, and the wide possibilities of the reader's role. Above all, the stories acknowledge their own fictionality.

The same thing could be said, somewhat less emphatically, of Eliza Haywood, whose early tales (unlike Barker's) attracted huge readerships. They, too, offer much event and little elaboration. Although their emphasis had shifted markedly, they provided some of the same satisfactions as the romances of the previous centuries, dealing with the affairs of princes and princesses. *Affairs,* however, now carries literal meaning. These stories, most of them novella length, insistently focus on sexual matters. Not only do men and women alike, in this fiction, experience desire; they also frequently fulfill it. Unmarried lovers routinely consummate their loves. Even women are not always punished, or are punished ambiguously, for sexual expression. Thus, in *Fantomina,* perhaps the most startling of Haywood's many experiments in narrating sexuality, a well-born young woman, watching a group of prostitutes at a play, thinks that they seem to be enjoying themselves greatly. She pretends to be a prostitute herself and is consequently raped by a young man who, of course, thinks he is only doing what is expected. Fantomina, as she calls herself (the reader never learns her true name), becomes his mistress. When she realizes that he is tiring of her, she leaves him, then disguises herself so effectively that he, failing to recognize her, "seduces" her again. Fantomina repeats the process, self-disguise leading to renewed sexual connection, twice more. She becomes pregnant, however, and is found out by her mother, who confronts the astonished male lover. After miscarrying, Fantomina is relegated to a convent; the tale concludes at this point. Given the purposefulness and ingenuity that this female protagonist has already displayed, there is little reason to think that the convent's discipline will end her escapades. Nor does the reader necessarily want her transgressions to come to an end: they harm no one, and they declare a woman's freedom and power.

Manley and Barker too on occasion represent women as beings of will and ability, capable of outwitting or outdoing men, but Haywood makes such representation a staple of her fiction. Although men frequently victimize women—rape them, seduce them, abandon and betray them—in her early novellas, women seldom accept victimization as the meaning of their lives or the end of their stories. They find their own means of resistance and revenge. In *The City Jilt* (1726), for an extreme example, a young woman is deserted by her fiancé because he prefers to marry someone richer. The woman he chooses proves to have only a contested claim to her wealth, and her husband loses a lawsuit through which he has attempted to win the money. Moreover, his wife turns out to be of low birth and bad disposition, and she squanders his money. In other words, Providence revenges Glicera, the betrayed woman. But she wants more. She manipulates a series of men so successfully that she accumulates great wealth (and appears to have a fine time in the process). She purchases the mortgage on the property of her erstwhile fiancé, who is forced to appeal to her benevolence for enough money to buy himself a commission in the army. Granting his request, she yet steadfastly refuses to see him. He dies in his first battle; she, with enough money to support herself for the rest of her life, publicly announces her aversion to men, sees only those who she knows have no sexual designs on her, and lives contentedly alone.

As these instances may suggest, Haywood devises original and engaging plots, often with female characters actively at their center. Her tales, longer than the vignettes incorporated in works by Manley or Barker, correspond to the other fictions in their narrative speed, lack of characterization, and abundant action. Haywood, too, organizes her novels and novellas principally on the basis of exciting happenings—most of them erotic. Manley's cast of characters draws heavily on members of the court; Barker touches on many social ranks; Haywood shows herself able to manipulate princes and commoners alike as figures in her fiction. Given the lack of social detail, rank makes little difference. *Love in Excess* has a count as its central character; other works revolve around princes and princesses from exotic places. Many of the novellas, though, concern members of the merchant class, and even those of lower rank appear from time to time. Whatever a character's station, Haywood's preoccupations remain the same. She interests herself centrally in the situation of women and in the meanings of love, particularly for women but for men as well.

Love in Excess explores those meanings fully. The title's significance remains ambiguous. Is the "excess" that of multiplicity—too many people falling in love? Or is it excess of degree: too much love? Or too much of the wrong kind of love? Each of these possibilities has its own plausibility, yet the novel (and this is indeed a novel rather than a novella, although a short one: 183 pages in one of its recent printings) celebrates love as the center and source of virtue. Through the speeches of its most admirable characters, it acknowledges the existence of a kind of love that seeks only the gratification of immediate desire, but it posits also a relatively rational love of equals, in which "*sense* elevates itself to *reason*" (224), that seeks always the good of the other. The lovers whose travails supply the plot's backbone, D'Elmont and Melliora, eventually consummate their devotion in marriage and produce numerous promising children, thus rewarded for the love, faith, and hope that have enabled them to surmount many difficulties.

To say that this pair of lovers supplies the plot's backbone, however, true though it is, ignores the fact that numerous subplots concern themselves with other lovers, and with other kinds of love. (Only in Haywood's shorter tales does she confine herself to a single protagonist.) D'Elmont himself, although presented as a paragon, has an abortive love affair and a misguided marriage before he realizes his love for Melliora. Moreover, he is the object of many women's infatuation. Some try to seduce him; one, Violetta, disguises herself as a young man, becomes his page, and dies of a broken heart exacerbated by her guilt over abandoning her father for the sake of her hopeless love. The main standard of moral judgment seems to be fidelity—fidelity to the idea of love even when its object remains unattainable. Exploring fidelity and its alternatives demands multiple situations and characters, which create a sense of diversity almost equivalent to that achieved by Barker.

The subplots, as I have called them, often bear at least tangential relations to the main plot. Even though some of them emerge through narratives related by minor characters, as in Barker's trilogy, the stories such characters tell generally concern the characters themselves and thus remain loosely connected to the central action. But multiplicity and speed of narration remain crucial to the fictional enterprise. Even in this extended narrative, Haywood supplies little detail. We know that D'Elmont is handsome, charming, and brave, but not what he looks like; we see little evidence of his charm; we read of no specific actions that prove his courage. The narrator tells us almost nothing about how the characters spend their time when they are not engaged in the pursuit of love.

The fictions of the three writers touched on thus far in this chapter differ markedly in many respects—not least in their implicit definitions of *adventure*. For Manley, adventure derives from the pursuit of ambition or lust: sometimes lust in the service of ambition. For Barker, adventure takes many forms, from exploring the Devil's Tower to one woman's running off with another. For Haywood, as for the anonymous author of *Lindamira,* the only adventures that matter involve love, and they too can take many forms. Even *The City Jilt,* which provides no representations of love, has love in the background as the standard against which deviations are judged.

Most conspicuously, the works of Manley, Barker, and Haywood share a similar sense of formal imperatives. All three writers assume the primacy of plot and the urgency of speed, telling their stories in what must seem to modern readers a highly condensed form. They do not solicit conviction; they do not invite readers to "identify" with characters. Instead, they offer their fictional contrivances as verbal equivalents of spectacle, frank entertainment (although not without serious purpose as well). In a period when history was still understood as a form of vicarious experience, such fictions provided a shorthand for experience. Their density depends not on complexity of import but on multiplication of example.

Daniel Defoe, almost exactly contemporary with Eliza Haywood, resembled her in his vast outpouring of verbal material. Like Haywood, he wrote for money. Like her, he experimented with many literary genres. But in one crucial way—one way that implies others—Defoe's narratives differ from those of his contemporaries and immediate predecessors. Elaborate and insistent truth claims often precede his fictions, stories that imitate the forms of autobiography or journalism and thus appear to substantiate such claims. Manley and Barker and Haywood invite their readers to take pleasure in fictionality; the anonymous writer of *Lindamira* claims truth but makes little attempt to approximate it; Defoe both promises and delivers some of truth's satisfactions.

The novels for which Defoe is best known—*Robinson Crusoe* (1719), *Moll Flanders* (1722), *Roxana* (1724)—begin with the locale and circumstances of each first-person narrator's birth and continue more or less straightforwardly with year-by-year accounts of what happens next. Typically, a lot happens. Sequentiality matters more than causality in the narrative construction, but important effects are often assigned causes. In the voice of "editor," Defoe insists on his concern with morality as well as truth, and his narrators at least nominally (sometimes very seriously) offer moral reflections on their own careers. In these respects, too, Defoe diverges from the fictional patterns of the other writers so far named in this chapter.

Why, then, ponder Manley, Barker, and Haywood in conjunction with Defoe? Because, I would argue, the aspects of their narratives that unite them matter more than those that divide. Defoe shares with the others a primary interest in what I have been calling adventure: in the sheer narrative excitement of rapidly occurring happenings. He grasps that a lot can happen to a single individual. Whereas Manley and Barker multiply events by multiplying temporary protagonists, providing numerous miniaturized stories, Defoe typically follows a single central character through a series of events, without subplots unconnected to the principal figure. He differs in this respect from Haywood as well, who in her longer narratives customarily introduces minor characters with developed stories of their own. But like the three others, he interests himself primarily in happenings—happenings that could on occasion (as in Haywood too) be internal as well as external but that always succeed one another rapidly.

Robinson Crusoe provides a provocative case in point, since so much of it takes place on a desert island that might by its nature promise a dearth of incident. The novel traces its protagonist's career from boyhood through a series of mishaps preliminary to his shipwreck to his return to Europe and his subsequent trip across the Alps. It contains happenings only tenuously connected to the central themes, but all concern Crusoe himself. And even the least momentous of them generates excitement: finding some shirts, manufacturing an umbrella can seem like—well, an adventure.

The problem facing Defoe's protagonists is not primarily love or erotic satisfaction, the central issue for Haywood. The crucial problem involves shaping a life. Although first-person narratives obviously cannot take a character from birth to death, Defoe's narrators report long careers, beginning retrospectively with their births and proceeding well into their maturity, when the crucial events of their experience appear already to have occurred. The drama of a life, as Defoe sees it, turns on social class—to modern sensibilities perhaps a vague and abstract topic, but to figures like Crusoe and Roxana a matter of utmost urgency.

Crusoe, for instance, specifies his birth to a "good family," with a father who has won a "good estate." His father, who wants him to study law, explains to him that going to sea is an activity appropriate to those without money, who might seek to make their fortunes, and to those with abundant money, who want fame to match their wealth. The father defines himself and his son alike as belonging to a "middle state," in his view the happiest of possible fates. Throughout the adventures that succeed his willful leaving home, Crusoe returns in memory to this conversation, coming to agree that the middle state is indeed the locale of happiness. Before he can hope to achieve it again, he must go through many situations, including that of figuring himself as a "king." He professes always, though, that he yearns to regain the security of the middle condition.

Moll Flanders and Roxana are yet more mobile than Crusoe. Moll, born in prison as the illegitimate offspring of a criminal mother, ranges through extremes of poverty, which drive her to begging and theft. At the nadir of her experience, she finds herself in prison once more, sentenced to death. Yet she eventually achieves financial prosperity, emotional security, and middle-class position. Roxana begins with wealth and family status, loses both as a result of a bad marriage, prospers mightily as mistress to distinguished men (including a prince and a king), and marries a devoted and wealthy merchant, but ends in a condition of misery and unspecified misfortune.

The adventure of such lives consists both in the happenings and in the self-imaginings that precede them. All Defoe's characters, to be sure, take advantage of happenings that have nothing to do with their own imaginings. Roxana finds her way out of extreme poverty by means of her landlord, who proposes that they live as husband and wife, an idea that has not previously occurred to her. He offers as inducements a good deal of property and extensive rationalization to justify the violation of moral norms; Roxana, although quite aware that she is wrong by her own standards in committing adultery (her husband, who has abandoned her, is presumably still alive), accepts his offer. Robinson Crusoe accidentally comes upon and rescues a cannibal fleeing from other cannibals. He turns the man into his faithful servant, although he has not previously thought it conceivable to have a servant (or, for that matter, any human companionship at all—he longs for company but assumes he will never achieve it on the island), and changes his sense of himself and his own position as a result. The ability of these fictional men and women to exploit every possibility marks their fitness for a world of uncertainty.

But that ability also exemplifies the agility of their minds, their capacity to shift both roles and expectations, the power, in short, that enables them to imagine and reimagine their lives. One tends to remember Robinson

Crusoe marooned on his island for many years, but he has a story both before and after that central experience. On his first attempt at an ocean voyage, the ship sinks in a storm, but he gets to safety in a small boat. A friend's father warns him that the hand of Providence is against him and that he will find nothing but misfortune unless he obeys his own father, but he ignores the warning. He sets up as a trader, is captured by pirates and enslaved by a Moor. On a fishing expedition for his master, in the company of another Moor, he decides to escape and begins by throwing his companion overboard. A boy named Xury remains with him. After many adventures, they are rescued by a Portuguese ship. Crusoe sells Xury to the captain as an indentured servant and begins a career for himself as a Brazilian planter.

This listing by no means exhausts the happenings that take place before the final shipwreck. Crusoe experiments lavishly with possible ways of life, flexible in his expectations of and for himself. The same flexibility enables him to make a comfortable and even moderately contented life on a deserted island—and to adapt to new possibilities as the population multiplies. After a group of Spaniards joins him and Friday on the island, he and his servant take advantage of an opportunity to return to Europe. Then the money he has cannily stored after finding it on the wrecked ship comes in handy, and he makes plans for commercial advantage. En route back to England, crossing the Alps, he has various encounters with wolves and Friday sports with a bear. Reporting such facts suggests that neither Crusoe nor his creator has lost the desire to entertain by representing sequences of rapidly occurring events. The narrator even reports, in brief summary, another voyage back to his island, hinting that he had many further adventures, which he may narrate in a sequel. Defoe displays narrative energy as marked as Manley's, employed for different purposes.

The effect of multiplied happenings has a new flavor in *Robinson Crusoe* because of the stress on a single protagonist. Now notions like identification begin to seem more plausible. Crusoe is represented as having both a physical and a moral life, and a fairly rudimentary but consistent psychology as well. From his own point of view, the most significant event of his life is his religious conversion, the result of various happenings on the island; he reinterprets preceding experiences as all leading up to it. This most powerful of his self-imaginings controls his reading of everything that occurs subsequently. The reader is at liberty to share his interpretation while still enjoying the many irrelevant happenings—or, of course, at liberty to ignore it. The combination of moral and physical experience, with increasingly well-developed psychological life as a concomitant, becomes more elaborate with *Moll Flanders* and *Roxana,* leading to situations, in *Roxana,* where the physical begins to seem a metaphor for the psychological.

Despite his emphasis on rapid sequences of event, Defoe's fiction changes the concept of adventure by its implicit conviction that *life,* as experienced and as imagined, is the fundamental adventure. The fact that Defoe's fictional "histories" cover many years is crucial to their conceptions. Roxana's great adventure is her life. The same assertion holds true also of Robinson Crusoe and Moll Flanders, even given their very different circumstances. These lives depend heavily, as I have already suggested, on their imagining.

Moll Flanders provides a striking instance, with her early, vague, yet powerful imagining of herself as gentlewoman. Both bastard and orphan, she has wandered off with Gypsies, then been abandoned by or abandoned them. At the age of three, she is taken in by the parish, to be reared by a benevolent nurse. When Moll is eight years old, there is talk of her going out to service—being employed in menial tasks in a private household. She weeps bitterly at this idea, insisting that she does not wish to go to service, then or ever. She wishes, rather, to be a gentlewoman. It soon emerges that she means by the word only a woman who works independently for her living, and that she has in mind specifically a woman of dubious reputation who has given birth to two bastards. No matter. Moll's determination to be a gentlewoman differentiates her from others of her kind, brings her the attention of well-to-do people, and shapes the course of her subsequent life.

During that life, she frequently and dramatically shifts roles, inhabiting many social levels. Her capacity to do so depends on reiterated acts of imagination that allow her to conceive herself as belonging at diverse points on the social scale, beggar and thief to rich widow. The excitement of her career consists largely in this social movement, with its sense of possibility. Moll is not fixed by fate. Indeed, she is not fixed at all. An escape artist virtually from birth, she seems hardly aware of the rigidities inherent in the British class system.

The important aspect of Moll's self-imagining, a quality she shares

with Robinson Crusoe and Roxana, is that she conjures up for herself
not a life but a series of lives, each role she inhabits entailing its own
relationships, risks, and opportunities. Crusoe, similarly, has no apparent difficulty seeing himself as Brazilian planter, then slave, then slave
owner and seller. He does not consciously elect these positions; they are
thrust upon him. Nonetheless, he inserts himself into each with gusto.
Even marooned on a desert island—a situation that might seem devoid of
opportunity—he finds scope for different ways of understanding his condition: hapless castaway, manufacturer, forager, lord of the estate, punisher
of the unrighteous, savior of the helpless, slave owner, king. It might be
said that these diverse self-interpretations constitute his entertainment.

Neither Moll nor Crusoe seems a particularly imaginative type. Both
are conspicuously pragmatic in their approach to experience. They do not
survive in the mind as beings of rich or complex interior life because for
both of them, to imagine is to do. (Sometimes almost the reverse proposi-
tion appears to operate: the doing precedes the full imagining.) But one
of Defoe's great achievements as storyteller is to reveal the connections
of imagining and doing. His prolonged attention to the life course of
a single protagonist provides him with the opportunity to explore such
matters. Without, at least in his earlier novels, making the inner life his
primary subject, he acknowledges the presence and the importance of
internal experience. Crusoe's troubled mind over the single footprint that
he discovers in the sand (a phenomenon never explained) and his gradual
development of religious feeling help give him fuller dimensions than his
counterparts in Haywood possess. Moll's self-proclaimed repentance in
Newgate has aroused doubts in many readers: how authentic, exactly, is it
and are her other moral pronouncements? Authentic or not, the proclamation registers her awareness of the need to repent and thus contributes to
her richness as a character.

Roxana, protagonist of Defoe's last and darkest novel, is assigned the
most elaborated inner life, in terms that raise questions about the dangers of imagination closely linked with doing. All too adept at imagining,
Roxana becomes possessed by her vision of herself as cynosure of all eyes,
envied by all observers. Even after she has exceeded the age of fifty, she
prides herself on her appearance and on her ability to manipulate men.
Increasingly avaricious, she amasses vast wealth—the wages of sin—and
dreams of amassing more. In her imagination, she consistently figures

as mistress of rich and powerful men. So compelling is this fantasy, twice realized and never abandoned, that it causes her repeatedly to reject the marriage proposals of the wealthy merchant who would give her a respectable, secure life. The dream of riches and universal admiration also causes her to elaborate what sounds like a modern feminist credo. She does not wish to marry, she claims, because wives are slaves, under their husbands' control; she prefers to manage her own money and life.

In *Robinson Crusoe,* Defoe, through an imaginative tour de force, made the routines of everyday life seem components of adventure by translating them to a desert island. (He also provided more conventional stuff of adventure in the shape of cannibals, shipwrecks, and wolves—but readers remember most vividly the desert island part.) *Moll Flanders* displays the adventure of survival, spiced with sex, crime, and danger from law and outlaws alike. *Roxana* reveals the adventure of possibility. The first-person narrative encourages readers to share the protagonist's constant expectation of triumph succeeding triumph and invites response to the excitement of Roxana's experience. Then, suddenly, Roxana finds herself in an ethical swamp; and the reader, having participated imaginatively in her fantasies, is likewise implicated in moral discomfort.

The life of adventure—and Roxana is in the most literal sense an *adventuress*—hardly prepares its practitioners for moral insight. When Roxana is confronted by an inconvenient daughter, likely to expose her mother's shady past and thus to ruin her prosperous present existence, she declines into ineffectuality and indecision. Her faithful servant and companion, Amy, on the other hand, finds no difficulty in deciding what should be done, on pragmatic rather than moral grounds. Roxana, unable to act, leaves room for Amy to act instead. Although she never achieves certainty about what has happened (she suspects that Amy has murdered the daughter), she takes her subsequent "dreadful Course of Calamities" (329) as heaven's punishment for injuries done her daughter. (The calamities, their nature undefined, afflict Amy as well.) Repentance, she says, follows her miseries, as her miseries have followed her wrongdoing. Her repentance is not, however, delineated in any detail, and the reader must speculate about its nature and quality.

Critical surmise about the degree of irony in Defoe's best-known fictions has abounded from the beginning, encouraged especially by the apparent discrepancy between the claims of moral intent by so-called editors and the protagonists' manifest pleasure in wrongdoing. In *Roxana,* more transparently than elsewhere, Defoe suggests the inadequacy of conventional moral injunctions to deal with complicated dilemmas. Roxana from the beginning of her amatory career (when her landlord rationalizes their adultery by claiming it's just like marriage) knows that she sins. She knows, that is, that she violates the injunctions of the church, and she pays consistent lip service to her awareness of wrongdoing. Yet this recognition seems hardly more than verbal, essentially a social rather than a moral matter. Roxana's imagination does not readily extend to the moral realm. When faced with a choice between honoring her bond to her daughter and preserving her own comfortable life, she can find no basis for decision beyond the self-interest that has always governed her. The revelation of her severe limitation, the bafflement of a woman who has never before been at a loss, gives her poignancy but also reveals a lack in her. Her failure of moral imagination casts a harsh glare backward for the reader on Roxana's ways of imagining her life. Lacking the ability of Robinson Crusoe and Moll Flanders to keep reimagining herself, she conceives her career as an adventure of acquisition, made possible by her manipulation of men. She may disguise herself along the way (as a Turkish dancer, in her most beguiling role; for a prolonged period as a Quaker), but she never alters her sense of self—which proves finally, tragically, inadequate.

The life of the adventuress, or, by extension, that of the adventurer, may not suffice from the character's point of view. More important is the fact that novels like *Roxana* train the reader to feel the insufficiency of such a life. In such short narratives as those of Manley, Barker, even Haywood, one could hardly expect moral analysis or insight (although moral assertion abounds), but more extended stories made possible more kinds of engagement. *Roxana* points the way to subjects beyond adventure.

Because Defoe concerned himself with characters in ordinary walks of life and investigated their responses to their lives' occurrences, his fiction bears a comprehensible connection to later novels likely to be familiar to modern readers. Defoe, however, was not alone in writing extended fictions during the 1720s, nor was Haywood his only peer. Other fiction writers explored different ground. The nature of Penelope Aubin's writing may be suggested by the full title of one of her works, from 1721, two years after *Robinson Crusoe: The Life of Madam de Beaumount, a French Lady; Who lived in a Cave in Wales above fourteen Years undiscovered, being forced to fly France for her Religion; and of the cruel Usage she had there. Also Her Lord's Adventures in Muscovy, where he was a Prisoner some Years. With An Account of his returning to France, and her being discover'd by a Welsh Gentleman, who fetch'd her Lord to Wales: And of many strange Accidents which befell them, and their Daughter Belinda, who was stolen away from them; and of their Return to France in the Year 1718.*

The specific date at the end, a date close to the time of publication, lends an unexpected note of factuality after the summary series of unlikely adventures. The novel itself, although it "explains" its occurrences after a fashion, makes little attempt at plausibility. Thus, for one example, the cave that Mme de Beaumount inhabits for fourteen years consists of several fully furnished rooms. The lady explains that she and the sailors who accompanied her "found this Cave, which doubtless had been contrived by some Hermit in antient Times, and was the Work of past Ages; it was all ruinous, and cover'd over with Weeds, but the Seamen soon clean'd and fitted it up as you see" (35). How they managed this feat is left to the imagination.

Plausibility, however, is hardly a relevant issue. The excitement of fast-paced adventure—adventures of love, but also of survival, and adventures of family dynamics—drives the narrative. If Wales, France, and Russia, the scenes of the action, all lack geographic specificity, the central characters, Mme de Beaumount and her husband, emerge as comprehensibly motivated representations of human beings. Aubin's prefatory justification for her fictional enterprise emphasizes virtue more than truth. Her story, she says, is "not quite so incredible" as the tales of fairies and elves that her contemporaries enjoy; its strangest aspect, she continues, is that the heroine and her daughter "are very religious, and very virtuous, and that there were two honest Clergymen living at one time. In the Lord *de Beaumount's* Story, there is yet something more surprising; which is, that he loved an absent Wife so well, that he obstinately refused a pretty Lady a Favour" (vi–vii). People are likely to doubt the story's truth, "but since Men are grown very doubtful, even in those Things that concern them most, I'll not give myself much trouble to clear their Doubts about this" (vii). Aubin considers herself to be writing in a time of corruption, and her novel aspires to offer a model for change. If it seems "untrue" in relation to the current prevalence of moral laxness, that fact constitutes a rebuke to contemporary mores.

Yet the characters' uprightness is not so exaggerated as to be unin-teresting. Mme de Beaumount, whose Catholic father-in-law determines to effect her conversion (an English Protestant, she has married a French Catholic), suffers imprisonment in a "ruinous old Castle," where she is locked in "like a wild Beast in a Den" (40). At this juncture, she turns to God. She does so, as she explains, because she has no other recourse. "Being left . . . imprison'd, and all alone, faint, hungry, and bereft of all Comfort, I did, as most People do, when their own Prudence can help them no farther; look'd up to God" (44). It seems a reasonable thing to do under the circumstances, and it by no means implies the heroine's passivity. When there is room for enterprise, she proves enterprising.

This novel resembles others we have surveyed, though, in its em-phasis on the rapid succession of unexpected events rather than on the psychology of the participants. Here, too, minor characters appear and tell their stories, despite the fact that so much happens to the protagonists that one might expect any reader to be satisfied without additional love problems and mishaps. The narrative's geographical sweep in itself con-stitutes a bid for the attention of those addicted to tales of adventure. For a twenty-first-century reader, the assemblage of stories retains its capacity to engage attention and to hold it by fast pace and diversified happening. Aubin's self-proclaimed moral purpose does not interfere with her ability to tell a good story well.

All Aubin's many novels look alike in their propensity for multiple actions, their rapid movement, their elaborate summarizing title pages, and their professions of moral purpose. The issue of truth also comes up repeatedly. In the preface to another work published the same year as *Madam de Beaumount, The Strange Adventures of the Count de Vinevil and his Family,* Aubin makes it clear that *Robinson Crusoe* has stimulated her awareness of truth as a source of appeal for the readers of fiction. "As for the Truth of what this Narrative contains," she writes, "since *Robinson Crusoe* has been so well receiv'd, which is more improbable, I know no reason why this should be thought a Fiction. I hope the World is not grown so abandon'd to Vice, as to believe that there is no such Ladies to be found, as would prefer Death to Infamy" (6–7). Although she avoids any direct claim of factuality, by implicitly linking her moral stance to the issue of authenticity, she challenges her readers to believe what she tells them. She also implies that the popular success of *Robinson Crusoe* indicates that readers accepted it as fact. Her tone suggests resentment at that success: Defoe's novel is "more improbable" than hers, yet readers take it seriously.

The difficulty about taking Aubin seriously perhaps stems at least partly from her reliance on romance conventions. Here is a typical description of one of her heroines: "She was tall, and exquisitely shap'd; her Hair was black as Jet, and her sparkling Eyes were full of Fire and Majesty; her Skin was fair, and white as new fallen Snow; and every Feature of her fine oval Face was full of Sweetness: She was in fine a perfect Beauty. She spoke *French, Latin,* and her native Language perfectly; she danc'd and sung exceeding well, play'd on the Lute and Harpsicord, and us'd her Needle with as great Dexterity as if she had been Minerva's favourite S[c]holar" (*Lady Lucy,* 2). In language and in substance, the description relies entirely on stereotypes. The exquisite shape, the sparkling eyes, the snow-white skin, the female accomplishments: all characterize the heroines of romance. If Defoe made the most elaborate claims of factuality, the other novelists thus far treated all resemble him in attempting to repudiate the fantastic events and conventional narratives that mark earlier romance. One can feel plot affinities to romance in certain stories told by Manley, Barker, and Haywood, but their large enterprise is clearly different from that of their predecessors. Aubin's enterprise is different too: in her explicit stress on morality, her fast-paced action, and her multiplied plots. Still, she draws conspicuously on the devices and concerns of an earlier period. Her fictions may not have seemed to a contemporary audience excitingly new enough.

Aubin's contemporary Mary Davys resembled Aubin in her focus on love and her attention to morality. Her best known novel, *The Reform'd Coquet* (1724), conspicuously announced itself "A NOVEL" in large caps on its title page. The list of subscribers to the first edition included the important poets John Gay and Alexander Pope. With a heroine named Amoranda, "a little Angel for Beauty" (5), the novel concerns love adventures, but it creates an atypical context for them. Amoranda, young, beautiful, and accomplished, like her counterparts in other fiction, complies with the wish of her uncle by admitting into her household an elderly tutor to guide her in morality. This tutor turns out in the dénouement to be young, handsome, and in love with his charge. It emerges that he has operated in the background of some of her adventures, including the most dangerous one, in which she is threatened with rape in an isolated spot with no apparent possibility of help. At that juncture she cries out, "Why has Nature denied us Strength to revenge our own Wrongs?" (111). In expressing her desire not for a male rescuer but for a personal capacity to resist, she strikes an unusual note: virtually all novelistic heroines of the period yearn for and expect a man's help. Amoranda, indeed, has the same yearning; but she also has a moment's awareness and resentment of her sex's built-in disabilities.

Unlike most "adventure" novels from the early eighteenth century, *The Reform'd Coquet* does not rely on a multiple plot. It contents itself with Amoranda's travails alone, making them varied in nature and instructive in effect. Lively in style and inventive in happening, the book remains entertaining. So, in a milder way, does *Familiar Letters, Betwixt a Gentleman and a Lady* (1725), which narrates adventures in a new key. This almost plotless work consists of a series of letters between two young people of different sexes, connected not by love but by friendship. The premise is itself astonishing in an era when such correspondence would be virtually inconceivable, a severe violation of propriety. The letters themselves occasionally reiterate their writers' disinclination for matrimony, but their substance consists mainly of reports about the very small adventures of everyday life, sometimes represented with a surprising degree of visual detail. Thus Artander relates his visit to an old lady in the neighborhood. Nothing more dramatic happens than his slipping on a piece of bacon and falling into the woman's lap, to her great amusement, but he reports every minute aspect of the scene. "When I first enter'd, I found the Lady in her Parlour, set in an easy Chair, with her Feet upon a Cricket, which rais'd her Knees almost as high as her Mouth; she was dress'd in a black Cloth Gown, over which she had a dirty Night-rail, and a coarse Diaper Napkin pinn'd from one Shoulder to the other" (275). And so on: the description continues for several more lines, giving way to an equally meticulous account of the setting.

The astonishing assumption that such material will interest not only the characters but prospective readers matches the equally astonishing emphasis on trivial happenings. A man marries a young wife, who bears him no children. After three years, he despairs and takes to drink. One night, when he comes home drunk, his wife says she would like to drown herself, and he says, in effect, Go ahead. He awakens to find his wife gone, seeks for her in the pond, and finds her in the arms of their lodger. End of story. Artander tells it for Berina's delight.

Letters with this kind of narrative accumulate; then, suddenly, Artander announces that he is in love with Berina and wants to marry her. Although she resists the idea, the novel ends with his going to visit her, presumably to persuade her. The instrument of romance is the series of narratives of ordinary life. This substitute for love adventures of the sort other novels have made familiar declares a new definition of fictional excitement as well as of romantic persuasion. It suggests that the significance of events resides in the use made of them, in how they function in individual lives. Near-rape in a lonely forest may seem more dramatic than a visit to an old lady, but the two events serve comparable narrative purposes: both constitute steps on the road to romantic union.

The anomalous example of *Familiar Letters* indicates the fluidity of early eighteenth-century notions about what makes narrative. Throughout the century, many novels had titles beginning *The Adventures of . . .* or *The Life and Adventures of . . . .* After the novel had achieved fuller definition—after Fielding and Richardson—such titles often alluded to inanimate objects: adventures of a corkscrew, a bootjack, a pincushion. The prototype of these accounts was Charles Johnstone's *Chrysal: or, The Adventures of a Guinea* (1760–65), a first-person narrative purportedly by the spirit that inhabits a gold guinea. A great popular success, it went through twenty editions by the turn of the nineteenth century and was much imitated.

In the novel's opening pages, the spirit asserts her capacity to know what happens in the mind of anyone who possesses the gold in which she dwells. She then narrates the histories of her many owners to the "adept" who has inadvertently summoned her. The enterprise occupies four volumes: there are many stories to tell. Although they involve men and women from various walks of life, beginning with the miserable miner who first unearths the gold and continuing through a prostitute, fine ladies, a footman, lords, soldiers of various ranks, gamblers, and many others, the diverse stories pursue a common theme. At all social levels, the guinea's spirit has discovered, men and women are motivated—sometimes possessed—by desire for wealth, the source of social corruption.

The authorial preface elaborately disclaims satiric intent. It purports to relate the discovery of the manuscript version of Chrysal's stories, so mutilated by its sojourn in a chandler's shop that its "philosophical parts" have been erased, reducing "the work to the appearance of a novel or romance." It therefore by implication has no serious intent, "for, as to the personal application of any thing in it, to the present times, the least attention to this account of the author will shew the absurdity and injustice of such an attempt; as it was wrote so long ago, and by a person so little acquainted with the world, that all the stories in it must necessarily be the mere creatures of imagination" (1: xxiii). The ironic disclaimer of course directs the reader's attention to precisely the application it denies.

Midway through the first volume, the spirit herself addresses the relation between what she reports and its meaning. "I see you are shocked at the inconsistency, vice, and folly of mankind," she tells her listener; "but this is owing to your recluse life, and want of acquaintance with the world: to an accurate observer, things appear in their proper colours; and, if the picture should be unpleasing, the fault is in the subject, not in the painter, who honestly represents nature as he finds her" (1: 99). Like Henry Fielding before him, Johnstone claims to represent human nature—which he finds, on balance, unattractive. The content of the multitudinous stories here, however, matters less to this chapter than the shape of their presentation. In seizing on the fiction of a supernatural observer with access to many inner lives, Johnstone finds a device that allows him to return to Manley's exuberant multiplicity. Like Manley, too, he makes at least intermittent reference to real-life personages and situations; a key to some of them, allegedly by Johnstone himself, exists.

The more adventure the better: that seems to be the assumption of this and similar novels, as of the earliest eighteenth-century examples of the form. Johnstone initially published a two-volume version of his novel. Given its huge popularity, he enlarged it for later editions and then added two new volumes. These new volumes, however, do not simply append new episodes. They are really, Johnstone says in his preliminary Advertisement, "*a Restitution of the Original, not an Addition of any thing new*" (3: Advertisement, n. p.). The final volumes include material that belongs much earlier in the text, he suggests. He has not put this material in its proper place because he does not want to "incur the least suspicion" of a mercenary design, a suspicion that might attach to him if he changed the text of a work already published, thus impelling readers to buy a new version of something they might have already purchased.

For the reader, though, it is difficult to discern where the new material might "belong." Although the diverse stories continue to be organized by the guinea's transmission from one owner to another, there seems no reason why they should be in any particular place. The stories are infinitely extendable, justified by their entertainment value and by their reiterative morals. The fact that Johnstone draws attention to the question of their placement only emphasizes this aspect of his narrative. He typically supplies quotations and references to earlier volumes to assert connections. The result is a total confusion of chronology and an increasingly strong impression of the arbitrariness of position. Volume 4 ends in medias res, with an episode from the Seven Years' War (1756–63) and a quotation from volume 2. The book, it seems, might have gone on forever.

The "adventures" it contains mingle the trivial with the manifestly significant. Volumes 3 and 4 concern themselves largely with the conduct of the war and discuss matters of strategy and diplomacy as well as day-to-day events in camp. The earlier volumes more often allow themselves excursions that sometimes skirt the comic: the story, for instance, of a poor man who decides his best course lies in being arrested so that he may enjoy the relative comfort of prison. In letters to a foreign correspondent, he relays the news he has gathered on the street. Although the post office opens his letters, officials think the material he transmits of such negligible importance as not to be worth bothering about, until "some miscarriages in public affairs" (2: 51) alarm the people, and the insignificant man is taken into custody. His efforts to counterfeit fear work so well that his captors think he must have done something worse than they know. He is condemned to hang. "But the contemptibility of his station and behaviour proved his safety, and mercy was extended to a wretch beneath vengeance, after he had served the turn, and amused the people for his day" (2: 52).

The story has little relation to the prevalent theme of monetary corruption, although it bears on Johnstone's recurrent allusions to the meretriciousness of government. Still, it exists primarily for its own sake, for the sake of entertainment, as do many, although by no means all, of the other episodes. Some of the stories Chrysal tells seem designed to make the reader uncomfortable. Moreover, the piling up of stories, the multiplied instances of venality, vanity, and greed, has a cumulatively disturbing effect. Because stories of real evil—things wrongly done and wrongly left undone—mingle with merely diverting anecdotes, Johnstone keeps his readers off balance—and presumably keeps them reading, to find out what will happen next, since no clear logic helps the reader predict it.

Given Johnstone's model, many late-century writers eagerly seized on the possibility of such a device for assembling unconnected short narratives about characters of many descriptions. The proliferation of novels relating the adventures of inanimate objects and using such stories as a pretext for narrating disconnected adventures of men and women indicate the period's continuing interest in happening for its own sake. The books using sequences of possession and dispossession as the basis for organizing events often lacked characterization, description, and reflection, except for a rudimentary sort of moralizing, yet they indicated one direction in which the novel might go: toward the accumulation of mini-stories.

This chapter does not trace a progression leading to "the novel" as we know it. It is true that *Roxana* seems more familiar in technique and substance than does, say, *The City Jilt,* but *Chrysal,* published considerably later, seems less familiar. It is also true that the house of fiction had, and still has, many rooms. Neither at its beginnings nor in its fullest development is the novel a single form. Defoe's fictions comfortably coexisted with Haywood's, both alike finding enthusiastic audiences. Remnants of romance continued to attract readers, even as those readers also became interested in stories about people less remote from ordinary experience than the heroes and heroines of romance. Few generalizations about early-century fiction present themselves as compelling.

Looking back at the group of writers treated in this chapter, we may be struck by two facts. One is that most of them are female. This proportion of female to male writers is in a sense accidental; it does not hold at all times throughout the century. Yet women continued to produce a large proportion of published novels. They wrote for an audience popularly assumed to be predominantly female. The novel as genre did not quickly achieve respectability. Linked in many minds to the romances that supplied a conventional staple of female reading, novels were feared by moralists as possible stimuli to erotic fantasy and domestic idleness. Women and the young, most endangered by novels' allegedly pernicious effects, were thought to compose their major audience. It seemed plausible, then, that women should write for women. (They actually wrote for men as well.)

The second striking fact about the sequence of writers treated in this chapter is that with Defoe, suddenly, abundant detail became important. Haywood had offered considerable fullness of erotic detail; Barker and Manley relied on occasional startling physical details. Defoe's truth claims, though, imply a certain regard for verisimilitude, and verisimilitude resides mainly in his detail—highly selective detail at that. Thus we are told a great deal about Roxana's physical possessions—her clothes, her silver plate—but nothing about the cities she inhabits. We know how much cloth Moll steals and how much it is worth, but not what color it is. When Crusoe studies survival on his island, Defoe supplies specific accounts of his carpentry and sewing and of their results; such accounts, indeed, virtually constitute the story. But almost no detail embroiders the narratives of what happens before and after the mariner's sojourn on his island. The details offered in these novels connect their worlds of fiction with life as directly experienced, but they do not suffice to make the narratives that contain them feel "true" in the literal sense that Defoe evokes in his prefaces. The stories rely heavily on unlikely coincidence—possible, to be sure, in real life, but less than probable. And they all have an end in view, manifestly intended to provide specific kinds of pleasure (and, secondarily, to illustrate moral or prudential lessons). Because of their detail, they seem more immediately connected to actuality than, say, Manley's sketchy narrations, but their alleged truth is one more fiction, part of the design of imparting pleasure.

These novels of adventure illustrate with particular clarity the inseparability of form and content in eighteenth-century fiction. Jane Barker wants to tell a great many stories within a manageable compass. (An alternate formulation: she wants to fill a saleable volume as expeditiously as possible.) Or Jane Barker believes that an abundance of short stories will best captivate a reader and that happening matters more than language, character, or theme. Does interest in the stories precede commitment to a form, or does the shape of economical narrative determine the nature of the stories to be told? Impossible to tell, impossible to distinguish. And Defoe: committing himself to telling a life story composed of many individual events implies chronological arrangement, focus on a single character, and rapid narration. The latter set of choices, however, might well have preceded the former.

In any case, both speed of narration and fundamental interest in exciting events (or events, like those on Crusoe's island, *made* exciting; or events given significance, like the small happenings of *Familiar Letters*) mark many early fictions, and the ideas about form and content implicit in them would reappear later in the century in sharply different modalities. First, though, a group of novelists working in diverse keys explored the possibilities of more leisurely and reflective narrative focused, like Defoe's, on a single character, but taking fuller account of social contexts.

CHAPTER THREE

The Novel of Development

OF THE MANY NOVELS produced in the eighteenth century, Henry Fielding's *Tom Jones* is probably the one most people think of when required to rack their brains for an example of the species. The old Tony Richardson movie, with its vitality and sexiness and its unforgettable eating scene, may be partially responsible for this recognition. But *Tom Jones* as a book is also vital and sexy, and it is only one of many robust fictions that follow the career of a single human being richly imagined in a setting of other human beings and imagined as having meaning by virtue of a process of growth.

To emphasize such a process implies certain formal consequences. Attention to process entails a more leisurely pace than Defoe's: novels of development are often very long. Although they may contain sequences of adventure, their stress lies elsewhere. Many are third-person rather than first-person stories, allowing opportunity for narratorial reflection. They do not necessarily focus on the inner lives of their characters. Rather, they direct attention alike to apparently trivial and obviously momentous events and demonstrate how a protagonist accretes knowledge—knowledge of the world and its workings—as a result of these events. Typically, they display a large cast of characters, for their enterprise includes evoking how social life operates and how it exerts its impact on individuals.

Referring to these works as novels of development suggests that they deal with personal change. In a sense they do—but only in a sense. Growth more than change is the point: not radical alteration but something more like self-discovery. Tom Jones learns prudence (an exceedingly complicated virtue) and becomes worthy of his beloved. Betsy Thoughtless, his female counterpart in a novel by Haywood, learns the same lesson, although prudence has a somewhat different valence for women. Prudence equips a character to deal with a world of other people and the impingements of their varied forms of self-interest. It protects and enlightens; it facilitates human exchange but encourages retreat from corruption. Invariably the product of experience, it helps protagonists emphasize and value their best character traits and suppress the worst. The story of its acquisition—a favorite story of fictions of development—can ideally help the reader too negotiate a path through life.

Novels of development in this period usually conclude in marriage, symbolically marking a protagonist's entry into adulthood and marking also a rapprochement between individual and society, the logical culmination of the process of education through experience that the fiction has recorded. This conventionally happy ending determines the comedic form of such narratives and controls the shape of narrated heterosexual romance. Counterparts of Haywood's early accounts of illicit love no longer assume important positions in the central character's story. Although Tom Jones engages in episodes of fornication (to the horror of moralists like Dr. Johnson), he must be rebuked for the practice and educated out of it.

In some respects the novelistic pattern I have sketched will sound familiar. Even now, some such set of fictional arrangements (usually without the fornication) often governs the structure of novels for "young adults." Many great nineteenth-century novels run variations on the same themes, which, with shifting definitions of prudence, might be said to control such diverse works as *Emma, The Mill on the Floss,* and *Great Expectations.* The possible variations are multifarious. Even in the course of the eighteenth century, divergent versions of the model abound. But *Tom Jones* remains the richest exemplar of the form, in many ways paradigmatic—although also unique.

Before, and in a sense preparing for, *Tom Jones,* Fielding had published *Joseph Andrews* (1742), a shorter version of a life narrative in which the acquisition of knowledge about the world defines the hero's growth. The novel originated in a parodic impulse: the character of Joseph, insistent on preserving his chastity, comments on Samuel Richardson's imagining of Pamela, a fictional heroine whom we shall encounter in the next chapter. The fiction's rich development, however, moved away from parody to incorporate not only abundant episode but the engaging figure of Parson Adams, in every worldly sense a fool yet sublime in his absolute commitment to the Christian doctrine he professes.

Defining his form as that of "comic Romance," and elaborating it as "comic Epic-Poem in Prose" (3), Fielding's narrator thus allows himself to deploy characters and invent happenings at a considerable distance from actuality. Yet he implicitly claims referentiality as he explains his interest in "the Ridiculous," which derives, he explains, always from affectation. One of his examples is particularly suggestive: "Were we to enter a poor House, and behold a wretched Family shivering with Cold and languishing with Hunger, it would not incline us to Laughter, (at least we must have very diabolical Natures, if it would;) but should we discover there a Grate, instead of Coals, adorned with Flowers, empty Plate or China Dishes on the Side-board, or any other Affectation of Riches and Finery either on their Persons or in their Furniture; we might then indeed be excused, for ridiculing so fantastical an Appearance" (7). The plight of a poverty-stricken family may be expected to have cogency for a reader because eighteenth-century England would offer many instances of such a situation. The "fantastical" imagined affectations of its hypothetical version in fiction perhaps bear no immediate correspondence to experience, yet they illuminate possibilities of self-delusion that abound in everyday life. Such possibilities repeatedly engage Fielding's interest. He finds them, in the first instance, in the two texts he mocks, *Pamela* and Colley Cibber's *Apology* for his own life, also published in 1740. In both works, the protagonist, in Fielding's apparent view, betrays an exalted sense of importance unjustified by fact and ridiculous in its pretension.

A satiric impulse, then, grounds the comedy of plot and character in this fiction, which develops a fresh understanding of the relation between fiction and fact. Unlike Defoe or Richardson, Fielding provides fictional personages abstracted and generalized from direct experience, rather than equivalents for individualized human beings. His large cast of characters and his slapstick sequence of happenings do not invite confusion about whether they derive from reports of actual life. The innkeepers and lawyers and country squires one encounters in the text are, we might say, caricatures. Yet the narrator of *Joseph Andrews* explicitly claims that he has "writ little more than [he has] seen. The Lawyer is not only alive, but hath been so these 4000 Years, and I hope G—— will indulge his Life as many yet to come. He hath not indeed confined himself to one Profession, one Religion, or one Country; but when the first mean selfish Creature appeared on the human Stage, who made Self the Centre of the whole Creation; would give himself no Pain, incur no Danger, advance no Money to assist, or preserve his Fellow-Creatures; then was our Lawyer born; and whilst such a Person as I have described, exists on Earth, so long shall he remain upon it" (164).

Generalization, exaggeration, and simplification can provide tools for the novelist to comment on without specifically imitating the vagaries of individual personality. In *Joseph Andrews,* Fielding attempts nothing like what we ordinarily call realism. His work corresponds more closely to romance in the idealization of Joseph and Fanny, the nominal protagonists, and in the resolution of the plot, which depends on not just one mistaken genealogy but two implausible past episodes of baby-switching. The saintly character of Parson Adams, yet more fully idealized in its positive aspects, also contains comic deficiencies (for example the parson betrays his vanity in glorifying the sermon on vanity he has composed), but even these, in their absolute consistency and the lack of serious consequences connected with them (they constitute small follies, not vices), belong appropriately to the realm of comic romance.

In the course of Fielding's narrative, Joseph, Fanny, and Adams traverse a stretch of rural England, encountering along the way representatives of various occupations and social classes, many of whom manifest vicious self-interest, failure of sympathy or compassion, or willingness to make use of fellow human beings as sexual opportunities, as butts of ridicule, and even as entertainment for foxhounds. The novel delineates such "bad" characters, too, in broad, simplified fashion. Yet the systematic contrast between the largely powerless good and the invariably powerful—within a limited context—bad comments on actual social arrangements, calling attention to the fact that this novelist achieves what we might call moral verisimilitude. His absolute clarity about moral distinctions grounds all his fancies.

One immediately noticeable difference between Fielding's novels and Defoe's fictions that focus on a single life story concerns plot. As the previous chapter indicated, early fictions by several authors stressed event over character. They did not, however, characteristically emphasize plot. One thing follows another, in novels by Defoe and Haywood and in the mini-fictions incorporated in works by Manley and Barker, on chronological principles. Such novels do not invite the reader to pursue intricate structures of cause and effect.

Coleridge pronounced (and subsequent critics have agreed) that *Tom Jones* (1749) has a perfect plot. Indeed, the narrator's voice frequently calls attention to the cleverness of the arrangements whereby characters misconstrue one another or meet or fail to meet at opportune times. These arrangements often rely on coincidence, although the narrator takes full credit for contriving them. Thus, at the novel's midpoint most of the principal figures happen to show up at the same inn, yet never encounter one another. But the main principles of action are more complex. In the early pages of the novel, Squire Allworthy discovers an infant in his bed. After strenuous efforts to discover the baby's parentage, Allworthy is led (by his sister) to firm conclusions, which for some time govern the reader's understanding as well as his. As the novel continues, the infant, grown into Tom Jones, makes new discoveries about his parents. Each new revelation determines subsequent actions, but the most important disclosure takes place (plausibly) only toward the end of the book. Although numerous other causes for suspense (to the reader and to the principal characters) develop in the course of the action, the uncertainty about Tom's lineage persists as a compelling undertone throughout the plot.

The systematic construction of suspenseful situations, with purposefully delayed resolutions; the enormous cast of characters; the frequent interventions by the narrator—such elements of *Tom Jones* suggest a new understanding of what will give readers pleasure. And giving readers pleasure was an important desideratum for eighteenth-century writers. Dr. Johnson explained his preference for generalization over particularities on the basis of pleasure: "Nothing can please many, and please long, but just representations of general nature" (*Johnson on Shakespeare* 61). Pleasure could not altogether justify authorial choices; instruction was also crucial. But it was widely (and wisely) assumed that most readers read, in the first instance, for pleasure, which could be made into an instrument of instruction.

Fielding and his followers apparently assumed that readers would enjoy various kinds of challenge. Although no one after Fielding in the eighteenth century generated plots of such intricacy as his, others also found ways to arouse suspense and intertwine themes. Fielding also perfected another kind of challenge to the reader: the frequent use of commentary by the narrator. In less elaborated form, such commentary abounded in *Joseph Andrews*. In *Tom Jones*, Fielding consistently incorporates narratorial commentary in his fictional structure and calls attention to it: the first chapter of each of the novel's twelve books consists of the narrator's remarks, often on the nature of fiction writing, sometimes on the nature of character. But the narrator's asides also occur unexpectedly, often putting the reader off balance—as when he announces, after a rather elevated panegyric to Squire Allworthy's virtues, that he has got himself to the top of as high a hill as Allworthy's and doesn't know how he's going to get himself down again. He demands the reader's alertness; demands, indeed, the reader's active participation in the novel's processes. The reader's involvement does not focus, as with Jane Barker's fiction, mainly on developing the agility to switch rapidly from one mini-plot to the next, with accompanying changes of tone. Rather, the reader must negotiate an ever-shifting relationship with the narrator, who provides a vivid presence among the novel's characters.

For this and other reasons, *Tom Jones* constituted a new kind of novel, a work that demanded to be taken seriously even while it provided rich entertainment. Fielding offers his story up as a kind of microcosm of life, populated by members of every social class: serving maids, gamekeepers, barbers, doctors, lawyers, squires of several varieties, clergymen, noblemen and women, soldiers, all assigned identifying characteristics and provided with roles in the action. Human nature is his stock-in-trade, the narrator announces. His characters are, he suggests, instantly recognizable by virtue of the reader's immediate knowledge of how people in the world operate. All impinge on the hero in one way or another, and he on them. The intricacies of the plot, on the one hand, declare the author's skill (the narrator openly makes this claim), but, on the other hand, they also adumbrate the workings of the world, which exists under the control of the great Author of all. Reading the novel, in other words, is reading the book of life in symbolic form.

The third-person narrator allows for another effect uncommon in earlier fiction: the adoption of varying distances from the protagonist.

At times the narrator's enthusiastic belief in Tom's moral worth leads him to a posture of almost complete identification. Berating the reader who should prove incapable of feeling what Tom feels—for example, in moments of sympathy toward the unfortunate—the narrator comes close to suggesting that readers' attitudes toward the hero demonstrate their ethical capacities. But the same narrator can also locate himself at a great remove, purporting, for instance, to assess dispassionately Tom's chances of being condemned to death. The complexities of his tone often qualify his words, making his position difficult to assess. Through his varying stances, the narrator challenges the reader's assumptions about Tom and maintains a control that often depends on keeping that reader off balance.

Yet there is never any real doubt about the fact that Tom is the novel's hero, taking an exemplary place in the fiction in a far less ambiguous sense than do Roxana and Moll Flanders, both of whom display flaws that can alienate even readers captivated by their gusto. Tom, to be sure, also has flaws, and the narrator jokes from time to time about the prevalent opinion in his community that he is born to be hanged. But his good heart, his genuine capacity to concern himself with others, his human warmth—such qualities make it clear that he embodies the kind of rela-tion to his fellow men and women that constitutes an eighteenth-century ideal. Several philosophers of the period (the earl of Shaftesbury, David Hume, Adam Smith) argued that emotion rather than reason provided the necessary substructure for morality. Tom demonstrates what they mean. Although he makes moral as well as practical mistakes (most notoriously by allowing himself to be kept by Lady Bellaston, supported for the sake of the sexual pleasure he provides), his human responsiveness guarantees that he will be led to see the error of his ways. He loves Sophia; he only uses Lady Bellaston. When Sophia reappears on the scene, Tom instantly takes steps to disentangle himself from his unworthy liaison. Concur-rently, he rescues the poverty-stricken family of a would-be highwayman and enables the happy marriage of his landlady's seduced and abandoned daughter: the reader can hardly doubt his commitment to an ideal of hu-man sympathy as the motive for action.

Conversely, Blifil, Squire Allworthy's nephew and presumptive heir, exemplifies moral consequences of narrow self-interest that substitutes for any vestige of sympathy. Proclaiming his adherence to theoretical moral doctrines, he acts, in small matters and large, from regard to self alone. Fielding provides him with no redemptive qualities. A force of pure evil in the plot, he yet succeeds, by elaborate hypocrisies and concealments, in gaining (for a time) the good opinion of his elders. Blifil possesses a kind of worldly knowledge that Tom will never attain, an awareness of the worst in others that comes, the narrator reveals, from the young man's sense of how he himself naturally operates. Given the novel's assumptions about providential order, though, Blifil's eventual exposure is inevitable, partly implicit in Tom's equally inevitable triumph.

As these remarks will suggest, Fielding's novel, far more than its immediate predecessors, concerns itself with fundamental questions of good and evil. Manley claims revelation of court corruption as her motivation, and the tales she tells show people operating on base principles. Barker proclaims the moral superiority of past over present; Defoe's protagonists repent their evil ways; Haywood celebrates fidelity in love. But no eighteenth-century fiction writer before Fielding so systematically explores the moral implications of characters' actions.

Moreover, Fielding (to Dr. Johnson's alarm) investigates *mixed* characters: imagined personages who display aspects of both good and evil, as human beings in the world do. Tom Jones is exemplary in this respect. Thus, when Allworthy suffers an illness declared mortal by the doctors, Tom grieves more intensely than anyone around him. Correspondingly exhilarated when the squire is declared out of danger, he drinks an excessive quantity of wine—from Fielding's point of view a venial sin. The narrator explains that alcohol intensifies the natural character of a man; Tom, accordingly, shows great good humor in his drunkenness. He nonetheless takes fire when Blifil insults him, and attacks physically. Intervention truncates the quarrel; Tom, still intoxicated, wanders into the fields and groves. There he begins thinking of Sophia. "While his wanton fancy roved unbounded over all her beauties, and his lively imagination painted the charming maid in various ravishing forms, his warm heart melted with tenderness" (222). He throws himself on the ground and rhapsodizes about how completely Sophia possesses his soul. As he rises to carve her name on a tree, his lowborn erstwhile mistress, Molly Seagrim, sweaty, dirty, carrying a pitchfork, comes along. Within a few minutes, he has retired into the woods with her.

The narrator comments: "Some of my readers may be inclined to think this event unnatural. However, the fact is true; and perhaps may be sufficiently accounted for, by suggesting that Jones probably thought one woman better than none, and Molly as probably imagined two men to be better than one. [Molly has, and Tom knows she has, another lover.] Besides the before-mentioned motive assigned to the present behaviour of Jones, the reader will be likewise pleased to recollect in his favour that he was not at this time perfect master of that wonderful power of reason which so well enables grave and wise men to subdue their unruly passions, and to decline any of these prohibited amusements. Wine now had totally subdued this power in Jones" (223).

Tom has gotten drunk; he has attacked another young man; he has violated his own declared devotion to Sophia by making love to another. The narrator explicitly or implicitly condones all these actions. The drinking results from Tom's selfless delight in his patron's recovery; the attack on Blifil comes in response to an insult; the infidelity to Sophia—well, the drinking explains that, and, after all, one woman *is* preferable to none; and the narrator's tone in describing "that wonderful power of reason which . . . enables . . . men to subdue their unruly passions" implicitly mocks reason as the ideal governor of conduct and hints at sympathy for the passions that reason enables a man to subdue. In other words, although Fielding assigns flaws to his hero, he keeps suggesting that these flaws aren't very important; on occasion he even raises the possibility that the flaws are actually virtues.

This fact does not indicate a spirit of iconoclasm: in many ways, Fielding is highly conventional. Rather, it calls attention to a hierarchy of moral failings, and Fielding's technique invites the reader's awareness of the hierarchies that govern us all. By suggesting a slightly unorthodox set of values, the narrator invites every reader to question familiar assumptions. Exactly how bad is drunkenness? Is it a sin to make love in the woods to a willing woman? What relation, if any, obtains between courage (immediately after the Molly episode, Tom stops a runaway horse) and lust? Are passions categorically wicked or only dangerous?

In his introductory essays, the narrator offers fuller clues about his own moral scheme and the relation between his ethical and his literary convictions. Chapter 1 of book 9 ("Containing Twelve Hours") provides a good case in point—it is more complicated than most of its counterparts, but only the more revealing for that reason. It begins with reflections about the particular kind of "historical writing" that the narrator considers himself to be engaged in. He appears to worry about the possibility of unworthy imitators of his own project; for this reason, he claims, he introduces the reflective essays, which are harder to imitate than are the chapters of storytelling. "To invent good stories, and to tell them well, are possibly very rare talents," he continues, "and yet I have observed few persons who have scrupled to aim at both; and if we examine the romances and novels with which the world abounds, I think we may fairly conclude that most of the authors would not have attempted to show their teeth (if the expression may be allowed me) in any other way of writing; nor could indeed have strung together a dozen sentences on any other subject whatever" (423).

It is not unusual for eighteenth-century novelists to proclaim their contempt for novels and romances in general, implicitly announcing their own superiority to other workers in the same genre. Less customary are the criteria of invention and narrative skill: most critics of prevalent fictional modes focus on the works' alleged moral failures. Moreover, Fielding's narrator uses a metaphor, that of showing one's teeth (and calls attention to it by his parenthetical apology), suggesting that the writing of bad novels constitutes an act of aggression or, if not aggression, perhaps merely competition. Remarkably, he goes on to weave a verbal web that indissolubly links morality and narrative skill.

He achieves this connection by an unpredictable series of steps. First he reflects on the general contempt accorded to fiction despite its potential usefulness. He grants that dull writers in particular are likely to be offensive, possessing only "enough of language to be indecent and abusive" (424). The remedy for such abuse of English is more widespread knowledge of the necessary qualifications for writers of fiction. First of all, a novelist must possess genius, by which the narrator means "that power, or rather those powers of the mind, which are capable of penetrating into all things within our reach and knowledge, and of distinguishing their essential differences"—the powers, in other words, as he goes on to specify, of invention and judgment (424). Invention, properly understood, does not imply making things up. Rather, it means finding things out: "a quick and sagacious penetration into the true essence of all the objects of our contemplation" (424). This quality pairs well with judgment, which discerns the differences between one thing and another.

The fiction writer must also possess learning, derived from books and also—the narrator emphasizes this point—from conversation. Conversation alone supplies the writer's knowledge of the characters of men ("men" presumably including women). It must be widespread conversation, with all ranks of men, for the follies and virtues of one part of humankind help to illuminate those of another.

The most important point, however, is reserved for the final paragraph, which begins, "Nor will all the qualities I have hitherto given my historian avail him, unless he have what is generally meant by a good heart, and be capable of feeling" (426). The good novelist, in other words, must resemble Tom Jones in a most crucial respect. Here Fielding articulates once more his central moral principle, connecting it with a collection of qualities usually considered in isolation from morality. Looking back over the mini-essay from the perspective of the last paragraph, we can see that conversation, for instance, of the sort here recommended depends on human capacity not unrelated to a good heart and the capability to feel. Given that good heart, the would-be "historian" can make appropriate use of the learning garnered by reading and by direct experience. The good heart stands behind good writing and guarantees the absence of licentious utterance. The fundamental desideratum for human excellence, it is also, Fielding claims through the voice of his narrator, the desideratum for literary excellence.

Tom, like the good writer, learns from conversation: interchange with all ranks and conditions of men and women. Tom, too, develops increasing powers of insight and discrimination. But obviously Tom will not turn into a novelist. Rather, we are to understand that the good novelist closely resembles the good man (or woman): good novels depend partly on the good characters of their authors, or so the mythology of this particular novel would have it. The reader potentially participates in the same dynamic, engaged (like the ideal novelist) in the educative process of reading, vicariously participating in wide conversation, enabled imaginatively to understand and discriminate along with Tom, urged to make judgments even about Tom, and encouraged always to manifest the feelings of a good heart. In other words, this novel of development intends to contribute to the reader's development: not to impart a set of doctrines but to facilitate an active process. That process, crucial to growth, shapes the novel's method as well as its subject. Introductory essays like the one just described often insist, tacitly or openly, on connections among character, reader, and writer, usually in relation to the story of development. The high ambition of this lengthy work depends heavily on its demonstrations of the reader's implication in a human project involving also the characters and the writers of fiction.

To conceive such a project implies belief that all human beings share desires and needs and other characteristics. Faith in a single, constant "human nature" marked the thought of many eighteenth-century writers, and Fielding certainly shared it. It is thus important to his literary enterprise that he refrain from giving his characters much individuality. As the name Tom Jones suggests, the hero of this novel is imagined as a type of the true-born Englishman, his thoughts and feelings those one can readily predict. His thoughts do not go very deep; his feelings rarely exceed the predictable. The large population of minor characters in the novel yet more obviously make up a group of types, often defined by their social roles: innkeeper, doctor, lawyer, soldier, country squire, recluse. Squire Allworthy's name tells us virtually everything we need to know about him; Sophia's name (from the Greek word for wisdom) tells us a great deal. Such imagining of character implies no lack of capacity in the novelist. It declares an important belief, the very ground of the fiction, which offers a "bill of fare," as the opening chapter proclaims, of human nature.

The fact that Fielding wishes to tell a story about human nature rather than about individual idiosyncrasies dictates aspects of the plot as well as the characterization. The pleasure of reading this novel comes partly from its sheer multiplicity of events and personages, its piling up of happening and predicament, escape invariably followed by further predicament, and the ingenuity and wit with which Fielding maneuvers all the characters and all the predicaments into a coherent, satisfying arrangement. Despite the fact that the characters act on the basis of universal human nature, the turns of the plot are by no means predictable. Everything is believable, in the sense that the events could plausibly take place. Sophia might well fall from her horse and lose a hundred-pound banknote; Tom, meeting up accidentally with a company of soldiers, could plausibly decide to join forces with them, lacking, as he does, any immediate principle of action other than leaving home. But one never knows what will happen next. Fielding demonstrates great inventiveness in the popular sense of that word, as well as in the special sense that he adduces.

The resolution of the action, though, is predictable in the extreme, despite the fact that it violates probability. A series of dramatic occurrences brings Tom and Sophia together and eliminates their elders' objections to their marriage. Sophia reproaches Tom with the Lady Bellaston affair; Tom insists that he is now reformed. Sophia says, in effect, that time will tell: she'll wait a year and see. A moment later, she has agreed to marry Tom the next morning. This woman who has defied her father to the extent of sneaking out of her house at midnight now professes that she cannot disobey him. The novel's concluding summary reports the couple's happy marriage, promising children, and idyllic country life.

The predictability of this resolution derives from a familiar pattern: the design of fairy tale and romance. Everyone knows the fairy tale arrangement that tests a young man, often a youngest son, by subjecting him to a series of trials. Once he triumphs, by virtue of character, over the obstacles placed in his way, he wins the princess and lives happily ever after. The romance pattern resembles that of fairy tales, with a more heavily emphasized erotic element: a man loves a woman who demands of him prolonged devotion and elaborate demonstrations of heroism. Given full demonstration of the devotion and the heroism, she rewards him with marriage. Both archetypal plots, though "unrealistic" in rendition and details, correspond to the universal pattern in life by which the young, inevitably, succeed the old, winning their place in society by demonstrating their capacity to fill it. Inasmuch as *Tom Jones* is indeed a novel of development, it must declare the hero's maturity by assigning him a woman—the woman he wants—and a position. The novel emphasizes its central concern with growth (or perhaps more precisely, education) by confirming the universal logic of social development, even at the cost of violating the logic of its own plot (by which Sophia would require Tom to prove his moral solidity, despite the fact that he has already demonstrated other admirable qualities of character).

Such attributes of *Tom Jones* as its type characters, its avoidance of psychological depth and particularity, and its romance structure separate it from the mode we customarily think of as the realistic novel. Fielding might claim for it the deepest sort of realism, the kind that transcends particularities to get at the essence of things. Such a claim would call attention to the arbitrary nature of casual conceptions of realism—and even, often, of quite sophisticated conceptions. What one means by realism depends, as I observed earlier, on what one means by reality, and the notion of reality is hardly a simple matter. The plot of *Tom Jones* speaks loudly of contrivance, plausible in many details, but artificial in construction, and constantly displaying its own artifice. The novel's awareness of the nature of social interchange, in contrast, corresponds precisely to actual operations of the human world.

A final aspect of *Tom Jones* that links it firmly with its immediate fictional predecessors is its inclusion of stories introduced by minor characters. The most notorious is that of the Man on the Hill, a misanthropic recluse whom Tom rescues from would-be robbers, whose account of his past life has no immediate bearing on anything else that happens in the novel. Sophia's cousin Mrs. Fitzpatrick also recounts the story of her adult life, and Partridge has a predilection for introducing mini-stories that have no relevance to anything except his own fantasies. The pattern resembles that of *Love in Excess,* but it seems surprising in a novel so carefully plotted as Fielding's. Apart from the immediate significance of any individual tale, the incorporation of these narratives reminds the reader of how intimately every human life connects itself with, recognizes itself through, story. Their presence here also reminds us once more that the novel as a genre did not progress straightforwardly from one avatar to the next. It developed, rather, as Tom Jones himself does: by moving forward, then backward, incorporating lessons from its past and experimenting with new possibilities.

After *Tom Jones,* Fielding wrote *Amelia* (1751), another novel of development, but one that charts new territory. Unlike Fielding's earlier fiction, it does not focus on the experience of a young man in his teens, nor does it end in marriage. Its female hero displays a wife's heroism, supporting and helping her imprudent husband, Captain Booth. Most of the action concerns the captain's development. Grown man though he is, married though he is, he has important lessons still to learn. The most crucial is that of Christian doctrine. At the outset, Booth is something of a freethinker; at the end, he reaffirms the Christian values he was taught as a boy, which he has consistently neglected. He also strongly reaffirms the marriage that has been his secular salvation.

Although the pattern of development here is important, it does not involve the reader as openly as does *Tom Jones.* The narrator's interventions, less elaborate than before, tend to concentrate on immediate ethical issues raised by the plot; they do not call attention to the operations of the fiction as fiction. The darker vision of the world in *Amelia* suggests the immense difficulty of learning to make one's way through it. Although Providence continues to preside, men and women face widespread active malevolence—not just the machinations of a Blifil but the systematic depredations of those in powerful positions who are concerned only to consolidate and demonstrate their power. A novel, presumably, can offer warnings; and warnings, as the incident of Amelia's escape from seduction at the masquerade indicates, can forestall disaster. But the travails of direct experience provide the most potent, as well as the most dangerous, educative possibilities.

The plot of *Amelia* is also resolved improbably but not in the fashion of romance. Booth inadvertently reads a pious text; it instantly converts him. An implausible coincidence places an observer at the pawnshop where Amelia desperately seeks funds; that observer unravels past crimes against the Booths and brings about the restoration of their money. This is essentially a religious pattern, an expression of faith that God finally brings justice, even in a corrupt social world. The previous elaboration of the plot, in other words, to demonstrate ever more persuasively the operations of evil, entails Booth's progress in worldly knowledge, but in a sense it comes to nothing: the ending declares that Booth needs not worldly but heavenly knowledge, and it allows the Booth family to escape from the corrupt urban world into the presumed innocence of the country. The inchoate aspects of this powerful fiction suggest that Fielding was feeling his way toward new novelistic developments. His death, however, cut short the possibilities.

Eliza Haywood produced, in her *History of Miss Betsy Thoughtless* (1751), the most ambitious novel of female development. After publishing much amatory fiction during the 1720s, Haywood had fallen silent for a time. In the 1740s she began writing a new kind of novel, more like other works being published during the same period. Earlier she had produced short novellas; now her novels were long. To a considerable extent, though, they indicated continuing preoccupations.

As the character's name and the book's title suggest, *Betsy Thoughtless,* even more than *Tom Jones*, provides "typical" characters. Betsy's name also indicates the specific moral flaw that her education must remedy. Her thoughtlessness includes an exaggerated sense of her own erotic power, developed early in her career; self-blinding vanity; and a dangerous lack of concern for the consequences of romance, whether these entail marriage (she has not considered seriously what marriage means or involves) or seduction (which would ruin her chances for respectable life). Like Tom's, her education is prolonged and complicated; like his, it includes real suffering, though more extended and more serious in Betsy's case. But this is very much a woman's story. Because she is female, Betsy has in life only the possibility of making her way by means of a man. Because she is female, the most important knowledge she must acquire concerns men, and her position in relation to them.

Betsy Thoughtless provides a large cast of characters and many events, but it does not supply a plot so carefully constructed as Fielding's or a narrator whose interventions cover so much ground. Its moral purpose is rather narrowly construed. Ostensibly, it teaches the necessary subordination of women to men and the importance of finding a good—that is, virtuous, as opposed to only sexy, rich, or agreeable—husband. Like other novels by women in this period, though, it opens the possibility of a more subversive reading. The development it lays out for the reader, in other words, is ambiguous: either it teaches the reader received doctrine for females, or it teaches the necessity of seeming to support received doctrine. It does both by means of an intricately organized plot that places Betsy's difficulties in the context of other female life stories.

Female life stories, as I have already suggested, centrally concern a woman's relations to men. The life experiences of the other women Betsy knows, several of which impinge directly on her own, involve, variously, perfect virtue and love of retirement (the female exemplifying these traits dies young); complicated treachery toward a husband, including adultery (this wife ends up exiled to Jamaica); promiscuity and betrayal (Jamaica is also the fate of this betrayer); promiscuity leading to the life of a prostitute (an uncertain resolution for one woman's career); and self-discipline leading to prolonged happy marriage. Virtue, in every case, consists primarily in chastity, although the text explicitly disavows the idea that this is the only definition of female virtue. Betsy, despite her many errors, successfully preserves her own chastity, and the narrator intervenes frequently to remind the reader that, despite mistakes that lead her into dangerous sexual situations, the heroine has a pure heart and remains essentially innocent.

The female plot, if partly defined by the social circumstances of eighteenth-century life, can only with difficulty follow the pattern of traditional romance, which assigns a woman enormous power over her lovers and shows them compliant to her demands. Betsy, in her vanity, believes in her limitless power, only to discover its limits. The exemplary male who courts her, the man whom, as she eventually discovers, she truly loves, leaves her because of his sense of her moral inadequacy and soon finds a better-behaved young woman. The man she first marries pretends to yield to her power during the prolonged courtship period, but domineers over her once they are bound in matrimony. Betsy discovers repeatedly the predatory sexual nature of men in general. Although Haywood's novel reaches the traditional romance ending of presumably happy marriage, it attains this resolution only after severely chastening Betsy.

The structure of *Betsy Thoughtless* in a general sense resembles that of *Tom Jones:* the novel pursues the career of a young person in the process of learning prudence by varied encounters with the world. The machinations of others and the consequences of inexperience impede the protagonist's course. The narrator intervenes to comment on the action. The fiction's goal involves instructing readers about the process as well as the desired consequences of learning. Less openly than *Tom Jones,* the writer aspires also to entertain. In other words, Haywood conforms to the pattern Fielding had established for the fiction of development.

Her differences from Fielding, though, are more instructive than her similarities. When we think of Betsy's path as compared to Tom's, it is difficult to avoid a sense of constriction. Tom goes forth to see the world; Betsy stays in one place, London, with a brief and disastrous excursion to Oxford, until she seeks seclusion from her brutal husband in London's outskirts. To be sure, London virtually defines "the world." But Betsy's opportunities for experiencing it are limited by the rules governing young women. She has an elaborate, and largely unspecified, social life; she goes to the dressmaker; that's about it. For mainly frivolous reasons, she wishes to postpone marriage. Her brothers and her mentors, though, insisting that marriage offers the only possibility of safety for a woman like her (a woman, that is, determined to pursue her own sense of pleasure and possibility), pressure her into a disastrous match. Tom can readily escape his liaison with Lady Bellaston; for Betsy there is no escape but death from a marriage that brings satisfaction to neither participant. Her dreadful husband conveniently dies, but not until Betsy has declared her intention of spending all her days and nights in his sickroom. She forces herself to feel grief; she occupies a full year in mourning—in contrast to Tom's rapid transition from penitence to marriage—before she allows herself a second marriage, to the man she loves.

The differences extend to the narrator's role. Haywood clearly attempts to duplicate Fielding's debonair manipulation of the reader, at least to the extent of providing chapter titles that reveal consistent awareness of the reader's position. Thus, book 1, chapter 3: "Affords matter of condolence, or raillery, according to the humour the reader happens to be in for either." Or 1: 17: "Is of less importance than the former, yet must not be omitted." But she never develops a full narrative persona, and her interventions to comment on reported events betray a certain anxiety. The narrator's observations characteristically pursue a few themes. They express uncertainty about a character's motivations or deep thoughts; or they insist—and insist, and insist—on Betsy's essential virtue despite her rash behavior; or they offer moral reflections. For example: "There is an unaccountable pride in human nature, which often gets the better of our justice, and makes us espouse what we know within ourselves is wrong, rather than appear to be set right by any reason, except our own. Miss Betsy had too much of this unhappy propensity in her composition" (294). The note of uncertainty emerges frequently, even in moral reflections: "Some of my readers will doubtless think Mrs. Munden entirely justified in making a secret of the above-mentioned letter to her husband, as she did so in regard to his peace; but others again who maintain that there ought to be no reserve between persons so closely united, will condemn her for it;—for my part, I shall forbear to give my vote upon the matter" (543). It is yet more manifest in the proclamations of Betsy's essential innocence, so frequent and so emphatic that they suggest the narrator's concern lest her readers lose sympathy for the protagonist. Haywood's narrator never comes close to announcing her absolute authority, as Fielding's narrator gleefully does. Her relation to her imagined readers is more tentative and wary. Not infrequently she actually comments that she doesn't understand a character's motivation, as though the character had a mind of her own.

More troublesome is her apparent awareness that the reader has a mind of her own. The sense of formal complexity that *Betsy Thoughtless* creates derives partly from its atmosphere of uncertainty about reader reaction. To be sure, the novel also displays formal complexity at the level of plot, skillfully manipulating a series of interlocking actions not only to bring about Betsy's fate but also to provide monitory exempla. The admonitions they provide are by and large not particularly useful to Betsy herself, either because she does not need them or because she is for a long time incapable of understanding them in reference to herself. The life course of Flora, the stepdaughter of Betsy's guardian, Mr. Goodman, and thus effectively a foster sister of Betsy's, reveals the emotional consequences of promiscuity and treachery; Betsy feels no inclination toward either. Flora injures Betsy by sending a slanderous letter to the man Betsy loves, motivated ostensibly by her own lust for the same man (though probably also by her envy of Betsy). She later succeeds in gratifying that lust, but her love affair with Trueworth ends in her complete humiliation, repudiated and denounced by the man she wants because he has uncovered a further piece of treachery. Betsy learns rather early not to trust Flora. She actually sympathizes with the other young woman at one stage in her downfall; but since she herself feels no temptation to sins of sexuality or betrayal, she learns from Flora only to be careful whom she trusts.

The more important lessons here, in other words, are intended for the reader rather than for the other characters. Flora and her mother and Betsy's school friend Miss Forward, who falls to prostitution, emphatically reiterate by their slides toward disaster the dangers of sexuality for women—a somewhat surprising message from the author of *Love in Excess*. Haywood in the 1750s changes the locale of her fiction from a fantasized France to an England with the mores of her own environment: thus she leaves no room for condoned female sexuality. She continues to acknowledge the force of female desire, but now she acknowledges also the practical impossibility of gratifying it except in marriage and the moral danger of violating social dictates. *Betsy Thoughtless* presents an unemphasized but obvious contrast between the fate of Miss Forward and that of, say, Trueworth—the novel's male paragon, but quite willing to take advantage of Flora's sexual lavishness and able to walk away from the sexual connection without consequences—or Betsy's older brother, who brings a mistress from France (another figure of unbridled desire) and lives openly with her; then after she absconds can promptly and easily make a splendid marriage. Women pay for open sexuality; men do not. Betsy knows this; the reader is instructed.

If several female characters suggest morals for the reader, three others serve as positive models for Betsy. From them, she has much to learn, and eventually she does so. Lady Trusty provides a voice of social as well as moral wisdom; Harriot, Trueworth's first wife, and Betsy's friend Mabel exemplify discretion, modesty, and wisdom in the persons of young women. Betsy herself conspicuously lacks these qualities, but experience teaches her their importance, and Mabel helps to solidify her new moral commitments. Again, the reader presumably profits by the lesson implicit in the fact that these women's characters facilitate their great earthly happiness. (Harriot, however, dies young—as she must, to make it possible for Betsy finally to marry the man she has loved all along.)

Each of the characters mentioned in the preceding paragraphs has a full life story of her own, but Haywood designs these stories so that all significantly affect Betsy. She reveals, in other words, considerable expertise in conceiving and manipulating a meaningful plot structure. Her complicated relation to her readers also contributes to the novel's provocative sense of tension.

The surface narrative offers a body of moral doctrine straight out of contemporary conduct books. Betsy, blinded by her vanity, makes an unwise marriage to a man who has never cared for her. He soon exposes himself as domineering, unscrupulous, avaricious, and emotionally cruel. Betsy consults Lady Trusty about what to do and hears that she must submit and comply, while yet somehow maintaining her own rights. She tries to do what she has been told: she never speaks ill of her husband, and she makes every effort to control her thoughts and feelings as well as her behavior. When Mr. Munden commits adultery with her brother's cast-off mistress, however, Betsy leaves, consults a lawyer, and sets up separate living quarters. Soon, though, her husband's serious illness draws her back to him, and she conscientiously attends him until his death. Her good behavior throughout the miserable marriage, her attentive nursing, her faithful mourning, and, apparently, her choice of a rural retreat rather than the corrupt city—all make her worthy at last of virtuous Mr. Trueworth.

But a number of undercurrents suggest a different message. In a striking dialogue with her brother Francis, Betsy defends herself against his reproaches for squandering her chance to marry Trueworth. She justly declares herself impeccable in virtue. Francis finds this defense irrelevant. "'What avails your being virtuous?' said Mr. Francis:—'I hope, —and I believe you are so;—but your reputation is of more consequence to your family:—the loss of the one might be concealed, but a blemish on the other brings certain infamy and disgrace on yourself, and all belonging to you'" (384). Betsy seems as shocked by this statement as a modern reader might be. She asks her brother whether he would rather "be guilty of a base action" than be suspected of baseness. He says of course not, continuing, "But virtue is a different thing in our sex, to what it is in yours;—the forfeiture of what is called virtue in a woman is more a folly than a baseness;—but the virtue of a man is his courage, his constancy, his probity; which if he loses, he becomes contemptible to himself, as well as to the world" (384). Female chastity, in other words, really doesn't matter in comparison to courage, constancy, probity; on the other hand, it matters hugely. Although Betsy continues to contest her brother's position, Francis insists that "one publick indiscretion" by a woman damages her family more than twenty private sins.

This view of women as rather dubious properties of their families pervades all the Thoughtless brothers' decisions and helps account for their eagerness to get Betsy married—thus making her, of course, the property of a husband. She verbally endorses this role: "Is not all I am the property of Mr. Munden?" (557). The rhetorical question to herself emerges in the context of a moment of complete realization of the nature of her past follies, now the cause for intense self-reproach. To accept oneself as property constitutes appropriate self-knowledge for a woman.

At a much earlier point in Betsy's career, she entertains herself by manipulating several lovers. Even Mr. Goodman is amused by her maneuvers. He comments that "it was a pity she was not a man, she would have made a rare minister of state" (136). This recognition of an impossible alternative underlines the novel's emphasis on the difficult condition of women, forbidden public use of their talents, allowed only a brief period in which they can cultivate an illusion of power (but even in that period susceptible of restriction from the family whose property they are), then made property to a husband, with no recourse from his dominion.

The story of Patient Griselda (Chaucer tells it in the Clerk's Tale), who endures unspeakable indignities from her husband without complaint, makes sense only in a theological context. If a husband can be seen as a type of God, his wife's mortification and endurance embody imperatives of Christian conduct. Mr. Munden, however, is anything but a type of God. In the novel's most shocking (and most unforgettable) moment, he dashes out the brains of Betsy's pet squirrel, announcing in effect that that's one less mouth to feed. This egregious act of violence epitomizes his power and his brutality in exercising it. Betsy's patience and submission in her marriage testify to her developed capacity for self-discipline—yet one may question precisely what kind of instruction the reader is to receive from it.

Much in the text encourages a reading that would understand the message of the conduct books as a counsel of necessity rather than morality. Even Lady Trusty, writing to Betsy in her premarital condition, emphasizes the vast dangers of a world that "affords but too many wretches, of both sexes, who make it their business to entrap unwary innocence, and the most fair pretences are often the cover to the most foul designs" (206). It's miraculous, she continues, that Betsy has survived intact. "I see no real defence for you but in a good husband," she concludes (207)—this despite the fact that she deplores early marriage. Of course the stress in her sentence lies on the adjective. A *good* husband might indeed supply a real defense against the traps that beset Betsy, but given the nature of the world as described by Lady Trusty, one can readily conclude that a good man is hard to find.

Nominally, this novel accepts as given an order of things that makes women the property of men, surrounds women with dangers, denies women moral dignity as well as autonomy, and burdens women with an impossible array of imperatives, while making all allowances for the self-indulgence of men. Yet the book sets forth this state of affairs so clearly and forcefully that it allows readers to suspect that, at the very least, it does not endorse the order it describes. Moreover, the crucial dialogue between Betsy and her brother, in which she attempts to refute central male assumptions, gives at least mild voice to female protest about the existing order. The tension that informs *Betsy Thoughtless* stems above all from the conflict between an apparent effort to reject and an apparent compulsion to accept a tyrannical system clearly viewed.

Alertness to the hints of female disaffection in the text may, of course, be a product of twenty-first-century awareness rather than its eighteenth-century equivalent. The explicitness of Betsy's resentment (which may, however, be explained by her general, reproachable rebelliousness) and the care with which the system is laid out make me think otherwise, but it is hard to know, given the lack of straightforward records of how novels were read in the eighteenth century. In any case, Haywood's attentiveness to details of the specifically female situation obviously differentiates her sharply from Fielding. The story of Tom Jones is presented as a story of English life, purporting to contain the whole of a society. The story of Betsy Thoughtless is self-consciously about a *woman*'s life, based on an understanding of the enormous differences between male and female experience. Its emphasis on those differences lends it energy and purpose and helps to determine its techniques.

Another female narrative, published a year after *Betsy Thoughtless,* appears at first glance dramatically different from Haywood's novel, but what it has in common with the slightly earlier work helps to define more clearly the female novel of development. Charlotte Lennox's *The Female Quixote* (1752), approved for its morality by Fielding, Richardson, and Johnson, casts itself as broad satire. It tells the story of a young woman, reared in isolation, whose reading, confined to French romances, convinces her of her own role as heroine and determines her interpretation of the events and people she encounters. Disillusioned at last by virtue of the instruction of a wise clergyman, she eventually settles down to a sensible and presumably happy marriage with the man intended for her by her father, the man who has courted her throughout the novel.

The novel conforms to the broad outlines of the fiction of development, carrying Arabella from her birth to her marriage, the sign of her maturing into conformity with her society's standards. It offers a more straightforward plot than *Tom Jones* or *Betsy Thoughtless:* Arabella encounters no one who has an individual story of any fullness, although Sir George invents a romantic and tedious story for himself. Yet *The Female Quixote* does not resemble a Defoe narrative, if only because of the constant intertextual references to romance. It also continues the concern for the individual functioning in society that is apparent in *Tom Jones* and *Betsy Thoughtless,* although Lennox pursues the subject in very different ways. Within the broad context of a development narrative, she turns established conventions on their heads.

Arabella, like Betsy and Tom, must learn prudence, now clearly defined as understanding of accepted social limits. Unlike that of her fictional predecessors, though, her learning is, rather, a process of unlearning. The structure of *The Female Quixote* accordingly follows a sequence through which a young woman comes to reject everything that books have taught her.

From her books, Arabella has learned of female power. That consists mainly, as one might expect, of power over men in the period of courtship, but the romances she has studied enormously prolong this period. Arabella has also acquired a vision of female "virtue," involving not only chastity but also more conventionally male attributes such as courage, dignity, and heroism. She believes that women provide the fundamental sanctions for admirable conduct, constantly judging male behavior and bestowing approval and disapproval that can mean life or death. She thinks that women possess the obligation to help and befriend one another, and she is prepared to judge herself and others by the place in "history" that they can expect to assume.

"History" belongs in quotation marks here because what Arabella means by history corresponds essentially to what others recognize as romance. By no means, though, does she ignore the difference between truth and falsehood: she values the records she has found in romance precisely because she believes them true—true accounts of what has happened in the world and valid guides to conduct.

All this she must unlearn. She must learn, instead, that women have relatively little power or importance in the world and that they rarely figure in historically significant action. She must learn that women have not only no place in history but no real histories of their own: nothing happens to a good woman. They possess no capacity to act boldly, no right to determine the rules. They can aspire only to make a good marriage—meaning one with a compatible man who will provide protection and companionship, and perhaps a modicum of wealth.

Arabella herself does not need wealth. She is rich already, and beautiful, and smart—none of which matters, except to make her attractive to a man. When she gets rid of the false knowledge she has acquired, she humbly asks the man who has courted her whether he still wants her, and she then settles down to the marriage she has earned.

Not only Arabella's education in prudence but her relation to society differs from, for instance, Betsy's. I described the plot of *The Female*

Quixote as straightforward, but its complexities of tone make it seem more complicated than its action alone would indicate. Although Johnson and Richardson saw it as orthodox, although the heroine at the end appears to accept the social order, much of her misguided belief system emerges through her penetrating comments on the society she encounters. Lady Trusty, in *Betsy Thoughtless,* speaks sharply of the predators who lie in wait for young women; Betsy herself protests the incompatible standards for men and women. Fundamentally, though, Haywood's novel accepts as given—if not entirely just—the social system that exists. Arabella, influenced by her novels, sees all the workings of society as corrupt. Men and women alike, she perceives, waste their time in meaningless activity—paying visits, playing cards, dancing, that sort of thing. No one performs or appears to believe in heroic action. Backbiting and malicious gossip permeate what passes for conversation. Social role rather than merit provides the ground for making distinctions. Although each of these observations in fact describes the literal nature of eighteenth-century life, Arabella's indictment is universally taken as a form of madness. Presumably she forgets it, or suppresses it, when she elects social conformity at the novel's end. Although the man she marries is no social butterfly, he does not exist outside the realm of conventional social intercourse. He feels embarrassed, shamed, and outraged by Arabella's premarital social deviations. We can expect him to demand compliance of his wife.

But what of the reader? Even more insistently than *Betsy Thoughtless,* *The Female Quixote* raises troubling questions about the anticipated or desired reader response. One way of formulating the problem is to inquire what kind of pleasure the novel provides. The answer must surely be plural. The book supplies, in the first place, the pleasure of the ludicrous: the ridiculous situations created by Arabella's romance-based delusions. A gardener is chastised for attempting to steal carp from the garden pond; Arabella intervenes because she believes him a prince who has disguised himself for love of her. Arabella commands her literal-minded (and rather simpleminded) maid Lucy to report her history and is then forced to try to explain how to make something of nothing. Her lover's father attempts to influence her on behalf of his son; she convinces herself that the father is trying to seduce her. She burdens her lover with a huge pile of folio romances—immense books—and orders him to read them, then is outraged when he fails to do so. Such episodes—and there are many more—may be expected to amuse virtually any reader, and they form the ground of the novel's appeal.

Beyond this obvious point, matters become murky. How are we to feel at a comment like this: "Sir *Charles* [father of Arabella's lover] in his Way, express'd much Admiration of her Wit, telling her, if she had been a Man, she would have made a great Figure in Parliament, and that her Speeches might have come perhaps to be printed in time" (311)? This echoes Mr. Goodman's remark in *Betsy Thoughtless* about how, were she a man, Betsy could have been a minister of state, but with greater elaboration and consequently more emphasis. Or how should a reader react to the wise countess who, trying to reform Arabella, suggests that the word *Adventures* offends decorum when applied to a woman, since nothing much happens to a good woman? "And when I tell you, pursued she with a Smile, that I was born and christen'd, had a useful and proper Education, receiv'd the Addresses of my Lord —— through the Recommendation of my Parents, and marry'd him with their Consents and my own Inclination, and that since we have liv'd in great Harmony together, I have told you all the material Passages of my Life, which upon Enquiry you will find differ very little from those of other Women of the same Rank, who have a moderate Share of Sense, Prudence, and Virtue" (327). The summary indeed characterizes much female experience. It may delineate a life of quiet contentment—or one of quiet frustration. Like the comment that Arabella possesses the capacities of a member of Parliament, it can be seen as conveying at least a faint aura of resentment about the situation of women. The pleasure provided by such passages may be defined as another version of comedy, or it may be the pleasure of covert protest.

Lennox's chapter titles indicate her awareness of the ambiguities of reader response. For instance: "Containing what a judicious Reader will hardly approve"; "A Dispute very learnedly handled by two Ladies, in which the Reader may take what Part he pleases"; "In which will be found one of the former Mistakes pursued, and another cleared up, to the great Satisfaction of two Persons, among whom, we expect, the Reader will make a third." Such titles constitute arch jokes about the discrepancies between the importance Arabella assigns to trivial matters and the likely reaction of the reader, but they also convey consciousness of the problem implicit in constructing a novel largely around the trivial. Arabella's version of history gives women great importance, but any eighteenth-century writer would know that the history of a woman's romantic life would hardly be thought momentous by serious readers.

The reader faces yet another problem of response in reacting to Arabella's comments on society. "I am of Opinion," Arabella observes to her cousin Miss Glanville, "that one's Time is far from being well employ'd in the Manner you portion it out: And People who spend theirs in such trifling Amusements, must certainly live to very little Purpose" (279). She observes that people in polite society not only lack impetus toward and capacity for heroic action; they also appear to lack serious motivation of any kind. They don't care much about anything. Is the reader to take such indictments seriously, or should they be dismissed as Arabella's peers dismiss them? Similarly, when Arabella jumps into the river and almost drowns, after offering a version of Sarpedon's great speech from the *Iliad* to impel her female companions to do the same, she seeks heroic action or sacrifice. She makes herself ridiculous and, the wise doctor suggests, approaches sin in her carelessness of her own life. But her motivation, however misguided, reveals a praiseworthy desire to act significantly on her own behalf. Foolish though she may be in believing every unknown man a potential rapist, her further folly of believing a woman capable of inhabiting heroic history may win at least some sympathy from the reader. At many points, Arabella's extravagances appear ambiguous in their meaning, expressing the misguided judgments of a girl deluded by her reading, but also conveying sharp criticism of things as they are.

The structure of the novel, in other words, is one of satire wrapped in romance: an unusual arrangement. The impossibility of living out a romance role in a modern world obviously suggests a critique of romance —but more covertly, perhaps, also a critique of the modern world, which allows so little psychic room for women. Already in the 1750s, fiction of development was sufficiently established as a form that it was possible to ring changes on it. *The Female Quixote* both parodies the form (by using reading as a form of obfuscation and making *un*learning the crucial action) and employs it seriously (by telling of a progress from solitude to socialization, from isolation to marriage: a process of growth). Although its narrative method seems relatively crude and sometimes even tedious (notably when Arabella summarizes at length, as she does repeatedly, the plots of her favorite romances), its conception shows great sophistication.

Even before Lennox's novel, the possibilities of parodying the novel of development had become apparent. John Cleland's *Memoirs of a Woman of Pleasure* (popularly known as *Fanny Hill*) appeared in 1748–49, making explicit allusion to *Pamela,* the novel it directly parodies. *Pamela,* published in 1740, relates the rags-to-riches career of a servant girl whose beauty and virtue enable her to marry a rich, well-born man. *Fanny Hill* tells the same story in a different key. Pornographic in content, though not in language (an early prosecution of the author failed because the book demonstrably contained not a single bawdy word), this novel too reports the development of a poor but beautiful girl who finally makes a good marriage. The first-person narrative emphasizes the theme of development, especially toward the novel's end. Fanny's last lover, an older man, teaches her a great deal. She summarizes, in a crucial paragraph: "From him, it was that I first learn'd to any purpose, and not without infinite pleasure, that I had such a portion of me worth bestowing some regard on: from him I received my first essential encouragement, and instructions how to put it into that train of cultivation, which I have since pushed to the little degree of improvement you see it at: He it was, who first taught me to be sensible that the pleasures of the mind were superior to those of the body, at the same time, that they were so far from obnoxious to, or incompatible with each other, that besides the sweetness in the variety, and transition, the one serv'd to exalt and perfect the taste of the other, to a degree that the senses alone can never arrive at" (174–75).

This is, to be sure, not a typical paragraph. Most of *Fanny Hill* dwells in lavish explicit detail on the delights of sex. Fanny's panegyric to the pleasures of mental cultivation hints that the mind and the body work harmoniously together, but the novel as a whole celebrates body rather than mind and depends on a conception of "virtue" quite alien to Pamela's more conventional one. (Fanny's virtue consists in fidelity rather than chastity.) Still, Cleland draws heavily on the literary conventions of the novel of development in constructing his pornographic tale.

Fanny Hill does not usually figure in such respectable company as this chapter provides it. But the work belongs, at least in passing, in a history of the eighteenth-century novel, both because it inaugurated a stream of similar, although considerably less pornographic, fictional memoirs of women gone wrong and because its relative crudity of construction exposes with special clarity the narrative principles of the novel of development. In particular, it calls attention to the often submerged sexual element in the development narrative. The Catholic church apparently agreed with Fielding's view that Pamela exploited her sexuality: Richardson's novel spent many years on the index of prohibited books. Tom Jones's love affairs, Betsy Thoughtless's inadvertent close association with scandalous women, Arabella's predilection for believing men likely to rape her: all suggest that sexual activity composes an inevitable part of human growth. *Fanny Hill* makes the point inescapable.

Another variation on the novel of development emerges in picaresque works. The picaresque, by definition, follows a rogue's career. Tobias Smollett's *The Adventures of Peregrine Pickle* (1751) exemplifies the form, contemplating the title character from birth to marriage, a progress marked by his incorrigible lust and vanity and his often sadistic mockery of others. The practical joke, in particularly crude form, is Peregrine's modus operandi. He especially likes tricks dependent on chamber pots. He also enjoys tormenting lustful women, despite—or because of—his own rampant sexuality. He squanders a vast inheritance, mainly on his own pleasure and prestige, although he also does good to the unfortunate. Indeed, when he is ultimately imprisoned for debt, inside the prison he shares his financial resources with those in worse condition: his warm heart, like Tom Jones's, declares his ultimate virtue.

That virtue, however, is often difficult to discern along the way. The narrative conveys real delight in the "pranks" that occupy much of Peregrine's life, and it allows no lasting consequences to punish his indiscretions and misdeeds. To be sure, he spends some painful time in debtors' prison, but he is duly released, to acquire an even larger inheritance than the one he has misspent. He offends Emilia, the woman he really loves, by his self-loving crudeness, but in due time she forgives him and marries him instantly after she agrees to do so. (He also offends numerous other people, but his offenses do him no harm.) Sometimes he fills the role of social critic, punishing the vain, superficial, gullible, and profligate, but on other occasions he exemplifies most of the sins he punishes. By and large, he gets away with all his extravagancies. Still, he eventually professes to see the error of his ways, and by the time he marries he has clearly learned at least the importance of managing money wisely: prudence of a sort. One can perhaps assume that the upright Emilia will help to keep him in line.

The novel's interest largely depends on its often rambunctious high spirits, which reflect Peregrine's own, and on its overwhelming tumult of event. Among its episodes are a good many that come from lives other than Peregrine's. The incorporation of other people's stories emphasizes the enormous variety of human experience and contributes to the book's powerful sense of vitality. In two important instances, the technique raises crucial questions about the relation between actuality and fictionality.

For more than a hundred pages of the 781-page World's Classics edition of *Peregrine Pickle* an unnamed "Lady of Quality" tells the story of her life—a story of sexual indiscretion, despite the fact that she is and has long been married. A passion for this lady "had begun to glow within [Peregrine's] breast" (432); for this reason, he requests to hear the story. After hearing it, he decides to withdraw from pursuit of the lady, partly because he realizes that she wouldn't wish to divide his heart with Emilia, partly because the reported "extasy of passion" (539) experienced by her previous lovers makes him nervous. He concludes that they should just be friends.

Only to this extent is the memoir integrated within the larger narrative. The lady in question was, in fact, a real lady: Lady Vane, wife of William Holles, second Viscount Vane. The experiences she relates correspond in part to known circumstances of her life, and her memoir was accepted as authentic by contemporaneous readers. She may, indeed, have written it herself and asked Smollett to insert it in his novel. It amounts to an apologia for her sexual misconduct, on the grounds of her husband's alleged impotence and her own warm heart (implying charitable impulse as well as sexual susceptibility).

Later in Peregrine's story, we encounter another extended narrative about an actual person, Daniel MacKercher, identified in the text as "Mr. M ——." The story occupies forty pages or so, and it is told in the third person by a clergyman. Again, its details conform to historical fact. It reports a career of exemplary active benevolence, with some sequences of adventure in the course of the hero's efforts to help others. Unlike Lady Vane's account, it offers virtually no plausible analogies to Peregrine's experience, except for the fact that this generous, brave man too has ended up in debtors' prison—not because of his own extravagance but as a result of others' machinations.

The novel also provides shorter vignettes about various fictional persons. In short, Smollett populates *Peregrine Pickle* with abundant stories as well as abundant characters. At one level, they seem products of the sheer love of life manifested alike by Peregrine and his creator. But the inclusion of extended stories about actual human beings suggests more: a desire, perhaps, to convey emphatically a version of Fielding's claim that he writes "history" even as he writes fiction. If it is impossible to tell the difference, on the page, between an actual life story and a made-up one, the novelist's claim to represent human nature justifies itself. The preoccupation with human nature, although never made explicit by Smollett, belongs to him as well as to Fielding, and it is useful for him to demonstrate that real life can be as extravagant as fiction, and fiction undistinguishable from biography or autobiography.

The point is particularly important because *Peregrine Pickle* apparently makes virtually no attempt at realism. Its characters are differentiated by wild idiosyncrasies that essentially define them: the captain who can employ only naval idiom and who organizes his household like a ship, the man who pretends to be deaf in order to hear the scandal that confirms his misanthropy, the henpecking wife. Its events, in their sheer multiplicity, their concatenations, and their frequent unlikelihood, correspond to little in the way of ordinary experience. The lack of serious consequence for blatant misbehavior suggests a world quite removed from that of most people. Even Peregrine's combination of sadistic and humanitarian impulse is fairly unlikely. Yet the "real life" stories abound in comparable unlikelihood. Unlike most conceptions of realism, which assume a writer's efforts to intensify plausibility, Smollett's assumptions about how fiction should be constructed seem to rest on the notion that fiction, on the contrary, should demonstrate the implausibility of life itself.

By the 1760s the conventions of the story of development were so firmly established that a novelist might find room to play with them. Sarah Scott's *Millenium Hall* (1762) provides a loose narrative frame within which a series of female "histories" play themselves out. The individual stories report the earlier lives of women from the group now gathered in a kind of female Utopia at Millenium Hall. Short though the narratives are, each packs into a few pages the material of a novel. They provide ironic glosses on the idea of "development" as it applies to women. No matter how well a woman behaves, the stories suggest, her learning of the world will entail suffering that educates her in the inadequacy to her needs of existing social arrangements.

Scott manages an astonishing range of variations on this theme. The story of Mrs. Morgan, however, which makes part of the first narration by Mrs. Maynard (who tells all the tales to the male narrator of the frame story), exemplifies the others in its emphasis on the subject's female orthodoxy (all the women are or become models of conduct-book behavior) and its inventiveness about ways in which men can make trouble for women. Born into the Melvyn family, the future Mrs. Morgan enjoys a loving upbringing, guided by her mother. Lady Melvyn, intelligent and virtuous, devotes considerable energy to making her weak-minded and weak-willed husband appear more competent and forceful than he is. She dies, however, and, like many other eighteenth-century heroines, Miss Melvyn suffers at the hands of a cruel stepmother, who convinces Lord Melvyn that his daughter has had an affair with a local farm boy and that she must forthwith be married to the detestable Mr. Morgan. The girl's only alternatives are to be cast out in disgrace from her family or to marry a man whom she can neither love nor respect. After much pondering and prayer, she decides that she cannot allow herself to be disgraced because her alleged misconduct would provide a bad example for other women, and she believes it her moral responsibility to serve as a model for others. She therefore marries an elderly, avaricious, cruel, suspicious man who forces her to abandon her closest female friend, makes her live in intolerable circumstances, and subjects her not only to his tyranny but to his sister's. She never speaks ill of him; she obeys all his commands; when he suffers a stroke and becomes bedridden, she nurses him devotedly. Eventually he dies, making her his heir. His money allows her to buy the building that will become Millenium Hall.

In both form and substance, *Millenium Hall* ingeniously adapts the practices of its predecessors. Like *Love in Excess*, it employs speedy narration, relying heavily on summary rather than detailed rendition. Like *The Female Quixote*, it imagines an outsider's perspective on society. With the moral clarity of Fielding's novels, it insists that moral principle should govern social as well as individual arrangements. In the course of the frame narrative, which concerns the accidental advent of two male travelers and their gradual conversion to the principles of Millenium Hall, we learn of manufacturing, financial, and governmental measures worked out by the group of ladies and of their multifarious forms of practical benevolence. Anything men can do, women can do better, more efficiently and more virtuously: that appears to be the book's moral. But the women it depicts remain deferential to men, and those whose stories we hear have in effect paid their dues to society before they retire from it.

By reiterating in various forms her depressing story of female development, Scott both creates entertainment and enforces a harsh message. The condensed, vivid tales tell of women hoping for but failing to achieve marriage; of women who marry only to find disaster; even, in one peripheral instance (the retrospective story of a dead mother), of a woman engaging in extramarital sex—an act that precludes, for its female performer, the possibility of subsequent alliance with any man, including her original partner. They keep even a twenty-first-century reader's attention by their speed, their variety, and their often horrifying substance. They also justify the startling political act of choosing to absent oneself from the existent social world. Scott's novelistic project demonstrates how conventional forms can serve highly individual purposes.

In several directions, then, novels of development continued the process of narrative experimentation that accompanied the earliest eighteenth-century embodiments of the genre. Neither the novel of development nor any of the other subgenres that emerged during the century was only one thing. Instead, all continued to manifest the variety associated with a sense of large possibility.

CHAPTER FOUR

Novels of Consciousness

DURING THE SAME PERIOD that produced novels like *Tom Jones* and *Peregrine Pickle,* which made happenings in the world the center of interest, writers of fiction also created work focusing more intensely on internal than on external event. The world (and "the world": the eighteenth-century imagining of a frivolous, often corrupt, but severely judgmental society) remained important in such fictions, but the consciousness possessed and experienced by an individual or individuals operating in relation to it became central to the novelistic action.

In an era of slow, difficult travel, spatially separated friends and lovers resorted to copious letter writing to preserve their connection. Novelists seized on the familiar letter as a plausible device for conveying consciousness, and many—though by no means all—of the century's fictions of consciousness took epistolary form. The epistolary novel, in other words, constitutes a subspecies of the novel of consciousness, because personal letters, assumed to be intimate communication, could plausibly express their writers' hidden thoughts and deep feelings. Novel readers and writers alike would know that young women of the upper classes frequently engaged in lengthy correspondence with one another, that letters between those of opposite sexes carried a heavy erotic charge, and that men as well as women often prided themselves on their epistolary skills, on occasion publishing collections of their own letters. Thus the idea of extended written exchanges full of intimate revelation would seem familiar. It was possible for Samuel Richardson, like Rousseau after him in France, plausibly to maintain the pose of "editor" for letters he had invented. Letters had a flavor of authenticity.

Although its use as a fictional device restricts the freedoms of narrative, the epistolary form provided a ready pretext for revealing mental and emotional process and for penetrating beneath surfaces of privacy. In the practice of the most skilled devisers, the artifices of fictional correspondence proved instruments of great subtlety and force. Epistolary fiction readily adapted to telling love stories, providing psychological insight, or offering social commentary. It demanded of its readers alertness to the implications and the ambiguities of individual points of view. It facilitated the novel's development.

Assemblages of fictional personal letters might concentrate on letters written by a single person (*Pamela*), present both sides of a correspondence (*Familiar Letters, Betwixt a Gentleman and a Lady, History of Lady Julia Mandeville*), or offer letters from several different correspondences (*Humphry Clinker*). Fictional correspondences involved men and women alike. They ranged from the claustrophobic (*Clarissa*) to the expansive (*Humphry Clinker* again provides the best example). Always they relied heavily on the sense of immediacy implicit in the concept of the familiar letter.

Epistolary fiction implies special challenges to the reader. For one thing, there is the matter of dependability. Convention had it that personal letters between real individuals exposed the correspondents' souls, providing, in effect, windows into the bosom. Alexander Pope, who published (although with considerable obfuscation of the fact) his own correspondence, boasted in that correspondence of his full self-exposure. Later in the century, though, Samuel Johnson in his life of Pope, writing with his customary bracing realism, pointed out that all men conceal a great deal from themselves; what they conceal from themselves, they will hardly expose to others. People contrive attractive versions of themselves for their intimate friends, Johnson pointed out, and virtually anyone who thinks about the matter will concur.

Recognition of the contrivance implicit in real letters readily carries over into the reading of their fictional equivalents. Such recognition implies suspicion about the dependability of narration conveyed by letters.

Is Pamela, for instance, altogether the good girl she wants to be seen as? The question occurred to even the earliest readers of Richardson's first novel, in some of whom it fueled an impulse toward satire. It is by no means a foregone conclusion that epistolary narrators cannot be trusted. The possibility of their deviousness, however, keeps the reader alert.

Moreover, a certain faint discomfort inheres in the reading of even invented private letters. The epistolary novel puts the reader in the position of voyeur, reading what is, according to the fiction, not intended for eyes other than those of the original recipient. Even readers fully aware of the letters' fictionality may feel overtones of the forbidden in the process of reading them. The fascination of reading over someone's shoulder helps to make the fiction imaginatively compelling. At the same time, it may heighten a reader's slightly uncomfortable self-consciousness.

Epistolary novels can generate special awareness of the processes of reading and writing. Novels are by definition products of writing, but we don't always think about this fact. Reading a novel couched as correspondence, we can hardly do otherwise. The imagined writers of the letters are specifically imagined as writing, often also as reading. The letters are produced, as it were, before our eyes. As a result we may become more aware of ourselves as readers, as well as vividly conscious of the novel's characters as writers—and perhaps of the novelist behind the characters.

Like the other classifications I have suggested (the novel of adventure, the novel of development), the epistolary novel does not define an exclusive category, nor does the novel of consciousness. Pamela, a striking case in point, is both an epistolary novel of consciousness and a story of development, as well as of romance. The epistolary novel as a subspecies of the novel of consciousness differs from other categories, though, in implying an identity between form and theme that originates in form. In the novel of adventure and the novel of development, theme loosely implies form: one happening succeeding another to delineate adventure; a structure of causality to convey processes of development. Because the form of personal letters implies intimacy and demands attention to voice (the particular note of a correspondent putting words on paper) and consciousness (the actuality behind the voice), it implies emphasis on consciousness: form thus entailing theme.

By the time Pamela was published, to wide acclaim, in 1740, many fictions in letters had preceded it. *Pamela* itself, however, grew directly from its author's earlier publication of a handbook of model letters. Samuel Richardson, by profession a printer, had a canny eye for commercial possibility. His model letters not only instructed their readers in how to apply for a job or apologize to a superior; they frequently adumbrated narratives that might lend themselves to full fictional development. Such a sketch for narrative occurred in one of the models for a servant girl in sexual danger from her master. Its expansion into an ambiguously compelling narrative inaugurated Richardson's novelistic career and spawned numerous imitators.

Reading *Pamela* the novel has from the beginning implied reading Pamela the character—a demanding and perplexing enterprise. Fielding, parodying Richardson's creation in *Shamela* as well as, more subtly, in *Joseph Andrews,* saw Pamela—a fifteen-year-old servant girl who avoids her master's attempts at seduction and eventually marries him—as a consummate hypocrite, using her virginity as bait in order to rise in social class and achieve financial security. Eliza Haywood also joined the considerable group of writers who felt impelled to satirize Richardson's work; she published *Anti-Pamela,* a bawdy adaptation of the original story, in 1742. Others have accepted Pamela essentially at her own valuation: a pious and sensible young woman who finally receives the widespread praise she has earned. And many have wavered in areas between these extremes. Richardson provides abundant data about his heroine, but interpreting the facts remains challenging.

In Richardson's fiction the matter of social class possesses a kind of importance difficult to grasp in a more democratic era. From the beginning, Pamela reveals a powerful apprehension of what the social difference between her and her master implies. Indeed, she uses her understanding of this difference as a weapon against him, repeatedly pointing out, to him directly and to her parents in her letters, that he "demeans" himself by stooping to making advances toward a servant. But she also increasingly suffers from her inability to bring any social leverage to bear against Mr. B. Mrs. Jewkes, his Lincolnshire housekeeper, believes herself justified in any course of action if ordered by her master to pursue it. Not only his tenants and servants but his social peers take for granted the utter authority of high rank. When Mr. Williams appeals to neighbors on Pamela's behalf, Sir Simon Darnford finds his concern incomprehensible. "Why, what is all this, . . . but that the 'Squire our Neighbor has a mind to his Mother's Waiting-maid? And if he takes care she wants for nothing, I don't see any great Injury will be done her. He hurts no Family by this" (134). From Sir Simon's point of view, Pamela's family doesn't count: "Family" means family of social status and property. Mr. B's absolute control of his household goes largely unquestioned. His assumption of a right to mastery is equally absolute. When Pamela's father dares to doubt a series of lies Mr. B is telling him, the well-born liar feels outraged: "Pr'ythee, Man, consider a little who I am; and if I am not to be believ'd, what signifies talking?" (96). Rank, in his thinking, determines and guarantees authenticity. Either he must be believed—believed even when he lies—or talking is useless.

Nonetheless, the servant girl challenges the aristocrat's authority. Claiming, and manifestly believing in, her possession of a soul as important as that of a princess, Pamela plots to win allies, to open paths of communication, to make her escape. In her letters and in the journal she keeps during her Lincolnshire captivity, she ventures to criticize the rich and well-born—not only her master but his friends. Even after the possibility of marriage glimmers before her, as the novel's central crisis approaches, she bursts out (on paper) in disapproval of "the Lordliness of a high Condition." This is what it would be like if I married him, she reflects. His mother spoiled him in the first place, and he has to have his own way. All that pride of birth and fortune does for people, as far as she can see, "is to multiply their Disquiets, and every body's else that has to do with them" (242). The section of the novel that concerns events after the improbable marriage has actually taken place abundantly confirms Pamela's vision here, although her account of the nature of "Lordliness" appears to arise from the moment's irritation.

Despite her sharp perceptions of what is wrong with Mr. B and his friends, Pamela takes her prospective and then actual rise in social class as an unambiguous good. She has a clear notion of the dangers implicit in sacrificing her chastity for money alone, but no worries about what might happen to her if she marries to her financial advantage. Her image of herself as cipher, or zero (an image employed again later by Clarissa and Evelina in their accounts of themselves), adding no value when placed on the left side of a figure but serving to multiply when located on the right, conveys with startling literalness Pamela's belief in the power of rank and wealth. With these attributes added to her by marriage, she can

imagine herself exerting force in the wider world as well as in the sphere
of intimate relationship.

This capacity to imagine and reimagine herself lies at the heart of Pamela's fascination for generations of readers, and her self-representation
in letters brilliantly renders her imaginative grasp. If fiction in letters
almost inevitably focuses on consciousness, it allows for infinite variations in the nature of the consciousness represented, and the shifts in
individual consciousness play a large part in the drama created by epistolary forms. Richardson artfully displays Pamela's turns of feeling, which
occur not only between one letter and another but within the record of a
single episode, given the letter writer's commitment to providing a full
rendition of her experience.

Pamela's account of how she contemplates suicide offers a brilliant
example of the technique. The girl has escaped the room in which she is
held captive by squeezing out a window and jumping to the ground, but
her subsequent efforts to get beyond the walled Lincolnshire estate result
in a crippling injury to her ankle. Cut and bruised, discouraged, she thinks
of drowning herself in the pond. She has already flung her outer clothes
in, to supply searchers with a false clue. Now, as she contemplates the
impossibility of escape and the certainty of further abuse from her captors when they find her, death seems her only recourse. She records her
vacillations: her decision to throw herself on God's mercy by committing
suicide, confident in her innocence; her imagining of how remorseful the
other servants, as well as Mr. B, will feel when they see her corpse; her
construction of what her master will say ("Now do I see she preferr'd her
Honesty to her Life, . . . and is no Hypocrite, nor Deceiver; but really was
the innocent Creature she pretended to be!"; 172); her fantasy of "Ballads
and Elegies" made about her (173), though she professes to hope for no
such notoriety. These incentives to self-destruction give way to a dream
that if she continues to live, her master will prove more merciful than his
servants have been, and then to meditation on the power of God to touch
his heart, which leads in turn to religious reflections about the wickedness
of forestalling God's purposes for her life and the horror of the pain she
would cause her parents by killing herself. Finally she addresses herself
as "presumptuous Pamela" (174), thus acknowledging fully the theological
prohibition of suicide, and she drags herself away from the "guilty Banks"
(174) that have tempted her.

Pamela resembles many other novels of the period in its ready reference to theological doctrine. Robinson Crusoe explains many events of his life as "providential," demonstrating God's special dispensation for individual mortals. The narrator of *Tom Jones* frequently suggests the intervention of Providence and makes explicit the novelist's imitation of divinity in his disposal of fictional characters. Clarissa comes to rely entirely on God in her great distress. What is notable in the suicide scene, though, as in Richardson's other religious allusions, is the degree to which a psychological matrix embeds the heroine's pious thoughts. The biblical prohibition against suicide informs Pamela's consciousness in essentially the same way as does the custom of making ballads about dead maidens. Her ability to fancy her master feeling sorry when she's dead and her imagining of her parents' destructive grief alike belong to the knowledge of custom, probability, and story that inhabit every mind—along with, in the eighteenth century, vivid memories of biblical language and teaching. The commitment to personal letters as fictional structure, with its necessary implicit stress on the activity of the verbalizing consciousness, allows naturalization of the religious. Although religious awareness at times controls Pamela's actions, it by no means always dominates her responses. The fact does not prove her a hypocrite; it reveals her as a plausible exemplar of conflicted sensibility.

The central issues between Pamela and Mr. B concern desire and will. Early in the novel, Mrs. Jewkes, proclaiming her loyalty to her master, announces to Pamela that "if your Desire and his Will come to clash once, I shall do as he bids me, let it be what it will" (109). She has formulated the clash incorrectly: at issue, in fact, are Mr. B's desire and Pamela's will, which proves much stronger than his, given the force of his desire. His desire, her will: at the outset, they seem at odds; eventually, they contribute to a single end.

Although Pamela shows herself astute as well as virtuous, Richardson makes her attentive to aspects of experience that might be expected to interest a fifteen-year-old girl. Preoccupied with clothes; alert to sexual hints; interested—though not excessively interested—in money; insistently concerned with what others ("the world," as she formulates it) think of her, a concern that dictates some of her decisions; eager to do the right thing and to be perceived as doing right; alternating between self-satisfaction and self-doubt, Pamela is represented as plausibly indeterminate—another reason, no doubt, for the continuing debate about her character, which is often expressed in terms of crude alternatives. Such indeterminacy belongs to her stage of life.

The novel marries her off shortly past its midpoint, catapulting her into a state where her fate is fixed by her choice of husband. Her mind now moves less freely, especially in relation to her master (the term she intermittently continues to use for him). Richardson allows her some faintly rebellious parenthetical written comments on Mr. B's ordinances for her conduct, but she does not speak them. The fiction becomes less compelling as Pamela's responses turn more conventional. The novelist devises for her a prolonged comic interlude with Mr. B's headstrong sister, Lady Davers, in which Pamela, given her security in marriage, defies aristocratic power; but on the whole he can find relatively little dramatic substance in his heroine's verbalizations once she has dwindled into a wife. The epistolary form, in other words, does not adapt itself well to a settled psychic state. Were Pamela an actual person rather than a fictional character, we might say that her apparently settled condition must depend heavily on repression. Richardson, however, suggests nothing of the sort. He only subsides into reliance on copybook maxims. His novel may not serve as a useful model for actual correspondence, but its last sections surely model the thoughts and behavior of the virtuous eighteenth-century wife.

I have spoken of the psychological accuracy of Pamela's earlier characterization, of her "plausibility" as a representation of a teenage girl. This is not to say that Richardson, any more than Fielding slightly after him or Defoe before, has written a realistic novel. His use of letters creates an atmosphere of verisimilitude, and his imagining of Pamela draws on knowledge of adolescent female psychology, but his plot is pure fairy tale: a new version of "Cinderella" in which the unmarried Pamela feels in constant danger of finding her coach reconverted into a pumpkin, and the prince bestows stockings instead of treasuring a shoe. After the novel's account of the marriage, rejection of realism takes a new form. Rather than draw on traditions of fairy tale and romance, Richardson resorts to a moral idealism that refuses to acknowledge the failings of actual people. Both before and after the marriage, then, *Pamela* supplies wish fulfillment rather than a version of actuality.

This is not a derogatory comment: desire for wish fulfillment often motivates the reading of fiction. It is important to realize how effectively

Richardson mingles precise perceptions of the life of the poor (the servants' helplessness against their master, the struggles of Pamela's parents . . .) and the tyranny of the rich with the kind of fantasy that might satisfy poor and prosperous alike. Drawing on and answering to both knowledge and desire, *Pamela* makes a complex appeal to readers past and present.

It also exemplifies important resources of the epistolary form—this despite its occasional awkwardness in deploying it. Pamela's notorious five letters written, in blatant defiance of plausibility, on her wedding day illustrate Richardson's intermittent clumsiness, as does the sudden intervention of the "editor" to summarize a sequence of events that he can find no way to record in letters. Yet the letters do a lot of work for the novel. In the first place, they allow the voice of a servant girl to dominate a piece of fiction: no small accomplishment in a period when class and virtue were still often conventionally assimilated to each other. Although Pamela exerts little obvious control in the world she inhabits, she can control her story in its telling. More and more, that story proves to exercise power over its readers within the text: not only the parents to whom it is nominally addressed, but the would-be seducer who gradually yields to its force, and eventually a wider circle of readers and auditors. Letters, as I suggested earlier, always give prominence to the uses and the using of language. In Pamela's case, they also create plot, shaping meaning as they interpret action.

The letter form emphasizes the tie between Pamela and her parents, the addressees of virtually all the letters and the imagined recipients of the Lincolnshire journal that its writer has no immediate hope of being able to send. Since the girl's rise in rank provides the narrative's central thrust, Richardson needs to underline the fact that Pamela remains always loyal and devoted to the poor parents who have reared her: she does not consciously aspire beyond her station. The fact that she tells them everything not only provides the novel's narrative material; it also establishes her innocence and virtue. She has nothing to hide; she seeks rather than rejects her parents' guidance. Her use of letters facilitates the reader's perceptions of these facts.

The notion that Pamela has nothing to hide calls attention to what may be the most important function of the epistolary form in this novel—for readers have always suspected that the letter writer's claim of full self-revelation in fact conceals aspects of desire unknown to their possessor.

The letter form is peculiarly well adapted for conveying ambiguity of this sort. Crucial to Richardson's accomplishment is the fact that every personal letter by its nature conveys a single, limited point of view. Mr. B is a man of complicated schemes. Pamela cannot possibly know all his machinations, any more than she can know all that goes on in his heart and mind. She cannot see as he sees, nor can she see like Mrs. Jewkes or the servant John or even Mr. Williams, her would-be ally and savior. Although her point of view controls the information available to the reader, not even the reader will altogether share it. And once the reader realizes the limits of Pamela's awareness, gaps open in the text. The possibility that Pamela does not completely know herself becomes manifest. The story we read includes stories never verbalized—includes, at any rate, multifarious possibilities of interpretation.

In *Clarissa*, his mammoth second novel (1747–48), Richardson draws out such possibilities in detail, supplying letters from four major and several minor correspondents so that the reader witnesses the clash of interpretations and can hardly avoid the obligation to choose among or try to reconcile various systems of meaning. The novel's plot, summarized, sounds simple, predictable, almost clichéd. The valued daughter of a severely dysfunctional family, Clarissa, threatened by the prospect of an intolerable coerced marriage, is tricked into running away with Lovelace, a practiced seducer. Friendless, in a hostile environment, unable to escape (although she tries), Clarissa never succumbs to Lovelace's tricks or appeals but eventually falls victim to his rape. After an interval of quasi-madness, she recovers her poise, steadfastly refuses Lovelace's offers to marry her, and finally succeeds in finding a place of refuge. Her family rejects her efforts at reconciliation. Her slow, pious dying reforms Lovelace's friend, Belford, and edifies all who encounter her. Lovelace, after her death, suffers his own interval of madness and then rushes upon his death in a duel.

It is not immediately obvious why Richardson needed so many words to tell such a story. Various scholars have produced condensed versions for classroom use, leaving out letters that repeat narratives previously supplied, that do not obviously further the plot, or that offer the viewpoint of characters with little bearing on the main action. Such versions, however, miss the point. *Clarissa* in shortened form is another novel. The essential experience of reading the remarkable book that Richardson wrote depends not only on the carefully developed texture of the letters as they pile up, the distinctive voices of their writers (and the sense of texture diminishes as letters are removed), but also on the slow, subtle sequence of often incompatible narratives. Each letter provides its own little story. If two writers individually narrate the same events, their stories will differ though the reported happenings are identical. The reader faces not the problem of figuring out what has "really" happened but that of grasping what a given happening means—what it reveals of character, what it conveys about the order of society and of the universe.

In this claustrophobic novel, Clarissa is mainly confined to small spaces: sentenced to remain in her bedroom at home, imprisoned in a whorehouse, locked in a bailiff's attic when arrested for a trumped-up debt, too weak to leave the room that provides the site for her prolonged dying. She sees few people. Even Lovelace, man of the world though he is, has few companions and engages in little social intercourse. Yet the novel opens with invocation of "the world" by Anna Howe, Clarissa's intimate friend and correspondent, who alleges that Clarissa's merits have made her "the public care" (39) and that "My mamma, and all of us, like the rest of the world, talk of nobody but you" (40). Clarissa's private story appears to implicate society at large. No participant in the drama feels much interest in the nature of the social order, yet the letters that dwell on individual experience and interpretation expose a system in which those newly possessed of landed estates value property over feeling and an older aristocratic class assumes the primacy, the absolute right, of individual desire. The disorder in Clarissa's family stems from the avarice and envy of her siblings, which infect even their elders. That disorder speaks of a social system lacking meaningful loci of authority. The church and its doctrine mean much to Clarissa but apparently little or nothing to most of those around her. The king receives no significant mention. Clarissa offers a wistful vision of the world as originally all one family, but even she must acknowledge the actuality of "politics" as something more complicated and devious than family. The aristocracy, far from embodying virtue, as once it had been thought to do, serves as an object of envy for Clarissa's brother and his kind and as a site of utter privilege, devoid of responsibility, for such as Lovelace. Richardson employs fictional letters to render the lineaments of a corrupt society.

As in *Pamela*, though—and, indeed, as the epistolary form implies—

Richardson directs primary attention to the consciousness of his characters. Lovelace, a consummate performer (he boasts of himself as a veritable Proteus, capable of endlessly changing shape), offers letters as performance, manifestly concerned to preserve whatever pose he has chosen: impervious, triumphant rake for Belford's benefit; desperate lover for Clarissa. His poses shift as the story develops. By the time he finally professes his ardent wish for Clarissa to marry him, his determination to deny the possibility of her death, and his consuming grief when that death occurs, the reader may believe that his feelings have caught up with him, that he "really" feels what he claims to feel. Yet it is impossible for him entirely to avoid the posturing that has become doom rather than talent. A sense of exaggeration clings to all he says. If Lovelace experiences authentic feeling, he contaminates it in articulating it.

Lovelace's inability to stop posing burdens him. "He was out each day," his cousin reports; "and said he wanted to run away from himself" (1049). More explicitly, Lovelace writes to Belford, "But, although I put on these lively airs, I am sick at my soul!" (1109). He cannot forego the lively airs; he cannot deal with a sickness of the soul. Clarissa, who has available to her a language of religion that conforms precisely to the kind of feeling she consciously cultivates, develops—as it were, before the reader's eyes—awe-inspiring integrity. Early in the narrative, Anna accuses her of hiding feelings or of remaining unaware of dangerous emotion. The reader is likely to share Anna's suspicions: Doesn't Clarissa feel more for Lovelace than she is willing to acknowledge? By the end, by well before the end, it is hard to entertain suspicion. Clarissa has achieved transparency. At any rate, she has convinced all onlookers that such is her achievement.

Yet not long before her death, Clarissa uses deliberate deception to ward off Lovelace's approaches, writing a carefully ambiguous letter that she knows he will find impossible to decipher correctly. The episode may lead the reader to recall how often before Clarissa has employed deception as a weapon of self-defense. There is a flavor of mortality about a lie, as a much later fictional character (Marlow, in Conrad's *Heart of Darkness*) would observe. Clarissa's deceptions, necessary instruments for mere mortals, declare the distance between heavenly perfection, the focus of her aspiration, and actual possibility. It gratifies the needs of other people to see Clarissa as an "angel." She herself must experience the gap between her otherworldly desire and her earthbound experience. Human feelings cling about her heart; only with death will she give up the emotions that belong to the world. Richardson believed it important that he had not imagined her as a perfect woman; he endowed her with flaws. The flaws are negligible but crucial nonetheless, since they declare the omnipresent stain of what in theological terms is called original sin.

That is to say that this novel has metaphysical as well as social implications. *Clarissa* uses the intimate, personal form of the familiar letter to comment indirectly on large issues, yet accomplishes its commentary without ever neglecting to reveal the individual consciousness of the novel's primary letter writers. Clarissa reflecting on the nature of Christian obligation is very much Clarissa: she emerges not only as pious but as self-concerned. Her Christianity is a conviction but also an instrument of defense; she uses it against the world—"the world" meaning, as it often does in the eighteenth century, the realm of human corruption, which impinges painfully on the virtuous heroine. In Richardson's revisions of the novel, intended largely to coerce the reader into sharing his own point of view about the characters, he stressed the very different impressions of and uses of Christianity by increasing numbers of persons in the text: not only Mrs. Sinclair, the old bawd dying in terror of hell but unable to repent, but also, for instance, Mr. Brand, the parson sent to investigate Clarissa's behavior after her escape from Lovelace, whose piety always generates the most negative possible interpretation of what he sees.

Even Lovelace has Christian doctrine intermittently on his mind. In a compelling dream, he sees Clarissa ascending to heaven as he himself is dragged to hell. He writes Belford—Belford, whose sense of things has moved distinctly toward the theological as he contemplates Clarissa's final situation—that he has always believed in Christianity, has always planned to reform eventually. His dying words, "Let this expiate," suggest repentance and realization, if not reform. His inability fully to commit himself to a theologically sanctioned way of life focuses the reader's sense of his psychological as well as moral inadequacies: he cannot live as a Christian partly because he is too eager to be seen as a triumphant rake.

Clarissa and Lovelace, of course, dominate Richardson's text. Clarissa's struggle to live as a Christian, and Lovelace's incapacity even to make the effort, provide a context for understanding the novel's many other characters, all professing Christians, most of them far from any notion of

Christian practice. So it is that the novel's theological concerns turn back on its social preoccupations. Eighteenth-century British society claimed to operate by Christian standards. The doctrine of the Church of England provided an official state religion. Yet all segments of society—the Harlowes in their preoccupation with money and property; the landlady and her friends who readily succumb to Lovelace's blandishments; the whores and rakes who are Lovelace's companions—illustrate the failure to allow Christian principles truly to control behavior. Clarissa inhabits a secular world. She is not altogether alone in it: such figures as Mrs. Norton, the housekeeper who once guided her, and the Smiths, with whom she finally finds refuge, indicate the possibility of less strenuous but comparably devout ways of life. But the secular dominates.

Richardson does not make *Clarissa* into a religious tract. The investigation of Christianity as practiced or denied is only one element in a novel of large purposes, involving the social and the metaphysical but above all, the personal. The novelist's choice of the epistolary form emphasizes his concern with individuals, with the nuances of personal voice and personal awareness, of self and of others. Both Clarissa and Lovelace, despite their extensive self-analysis, lack full self-knowledge. To make such a statement about fictional characters may seem inappropriate, but the difficulties—perhaps impossibilities—of self-knowledge are a central subject of *Clarissa*. Richardson's scheme of providing an exhaustive series of personal letters allows him to trace subtle gradations of attitude, showing how a correspondent's outlook imperceptibly shifts from day to day. Lovelace assumes his own self-knowledge, confidently describing himself over and over again to Belford. Yet the more he proclaims his nature, the more the reader is likely to feel his increasing uncertainty, confronting a woman who fascinates him but whom he cannot comprehend. Clarissa's character as a virtuous, pious woman challenges Lovelace's assumptions about the female and the feminine. More important, it challenges his assumptions about himself as the always dominant, always triumphant, always confident rake. He is not, however, able to discover or to define for himself any alternative identity. He can only continue to bluster, as he insists on announcing who he is.

Clarissa, on the other hand, accepts as obligation the Protestant discipline of self-examination. She doesn't proclaim, she doesn't insist, but she considers it an important moral exercise to know herself as fully as possible. With the plethora of letters she produces, she provides a view of how subtly the mind changes not only from day to day but from hour to hour. She thinks she should, she thinks she should not marry Lovelace. She thinks that she *can,* then that she cannot, then that she can. Her friend Anna Howe tells her that she feels more for Lovelace than she has acknowledged. She examines herself more rigorously, but she can find no love in her heart. Yet the reader sees what Anna sees: that Clarissa continues to conceal from herself emotions she considers reprehensible. Her letters, taken all together, convey a persuasive pattern of vacillation, confusion, and ambivalence. Only after she rejects the value of all thought and feeling focused on mortals does she attain the clarity of absolute devotion to the divine. Even then, though, the reader may suspect that her obsessive writing of letters to be delivered posthumously (to members of her family and to Lovelace), despite the piety and ostensible submissiveness of their messages, expresses a refined version of Pamela's fantasies by the pond: they'll be sorry when I'm dead, and I'll make them even sorrier. Thoughts and feelings cling to the earthly; Clarissa cannot fully acknowledge this fact that she exemplifies. Even as she approaches her death, she does not and cannot fully know herself. The reader, moreover, may actually have the illusion of knowing more about Clarissa than she knows, of having penetrated more deeply than Lovelace into her heart. Only the enormous bulk of letters makes such an illusion possible.

Richardson, in short, exploits fully the potentialities of the epistolary form: the sense of intimacy it creates (as readers, we "know" more about Clarissa and Lovelace, and even Anna and Belford, than they know about themselves); the sense of ambiguity (we vividly experience the vagaries of point of view and are brought to understand the consequences of individual myopia); the exhaustiveness with which letters can record experience; the impression of immediacy they generate, making us aware of ourselves in close contact with what individuals feel and think from moment to moment. Reading *Pamela,* we may feel intermittently conscious that commitment to story in letters has narrative limitations. Reading *Clarissa,* we may be brought to think that the form possesses no limitations: all restrictions seem to convert themselves into advantages.

The story told by the letters is the one that Clarissa herself wants to tell: even this fact becomes part of the narrative. As she nears death, the heroine asks Belford to serve as guardian of her story and to guarantee its transmission to posterity. She says explicitly that this story can be told simply by compilation of the letters that have passed. Belford accepts the responsibility of gathering and disseminating them. He is, by this time, altogether under Clarissa's influence, a highly partisan potential editor.

By including the fictional account of how these letters come to exist in print, Richardson calls attention to Clarissa's moral dominance of a story in which Lovelace's utterances take up much space. Although many points of view figure in the individual letters, Clarissa's wins. Her confidence in giving the charge to Belford derives partly from her assumption that the Christian position must compel credence from every reader. For most actual readers, though, the vivid encounter with multiple voices works in a more complicated way. Lovelace, made psychologically credible although morally detestable, exerts real force in the text, his wit, energy, style, and verve attractive even as he employs them to corrupt ends. To the degree we are attracted by Lovelace—attracted against Richardson's conscious will, as his successive revisions make clear—to that degree we participate in and comprehend Clarissa's extent of yielding to him. The epistolary form draws us into the drama that stems from the incompatibilities of individual perspective.

No one in England after Richardson manipulated the epistolary mode with equal brilliance and complexity. (In France, Rousseau and, after him, Pierre Choderlos de Laclos produced epistolary novels of comparable richness to *Clarissa;* both were heavily influenced by Richardson.) *Sir Charles Grandison* (1753–54) followed *Clarissa* in Richardson's work—yet another dramatic meditation on point of view. Examining the situation of an idealized British man, this epistolary novel presents several different love stories, inviting the reader to ponder the morality of love as it plays itself out in various forms. Although the novel was less popular than *Clarissa* in the eighteenth century and remains less widely read, it too demonstrates the psychological, moral, and aesthetic possibilities of fiction in letters.

As the eighteenth century continued, Richardson remained the most powerful influence on epistolary novels, but most such works seem sadly lacking in comparison with his. Yet fictions less accomplished than *Clarissa* can also expose the special resources of their chosen form, and novelists far less accomplished than Richardson could find epistolary fiction rich in possibilities. Early in her literary career, Frances Brooke published *Letters from Lady Julia Catesby,* translated from the French of Marie-Jeanne

Riccoboni. Three years later, in 1763, she produced *The History of Lady Julia Mandeville*, an original work in letters, its author identified on the title page as "The Translator of Lady Catesby's Letters." The novel went through seven editions by the end of the eighteenth century. Brooke followed it, six years later, with a longer and less popular epistolary novel, *The History of Emily Montague*.

In *Lady Julia Mandeville*, Brooke's didactic intent manifests itself even more obviously than Richardson's in *Clarissa*. She employs the novel's letters as a means to promulgate a system of domestic and national politics, shamelessly flattering the current king (George III), whom she presents as the ideal monarch. Both nation and family, the novel insists, profit by clear hierarchy and patriarchal benevolence. The doctrine of noblesse oblige guarantees that no conflict of interest will mar relations among social classes. The novel's hero, Henry Mandeville (who opens the fiction with the words, "I am indeed, my dear George, the most happy of human beings," only to suffer a tragic fate), and his father reiterate aspects of the novel's ideology most insistently, the son observing the idyllic course of existence on Lord Belmont's estate, for happy peasants as well as contented aristocracy, and the father frequently congratulating himself for having spent his son's potential inheritance on educating rather than indulging him. The father, identified only as "J. Mandeville," also comments frequently on national affairs ("Happy Britain! Where the laws are equally the guard of prince and people; where liberty and prerogative go hand in hand, and mutually support each other . . ."; 181), and he articulates a Rousseauvian theory of education: "It has always appeared to me, that our understandings are fettered by systems, and our hearts corrupted by example: and that there needs no more to minds well disposed than to recover their native freedom, and think and act for themselves" (100). The commitment to political and personal virtue reiterated by father and son dictates many of their actions and helps to precipitate the disastrous dénouement, in which Henry and his beloved, the eponymous heroine, both perish.

More specifically, Henry dies because of his gratuitous misconception of Lord Belmont's plans for his daughter, Lady Julia. He rushes into a duel with his supposed rival, and in it rushes upon his death, despite the rival's attempts to avoid injuring him. His misconception stems from the course chosen by his father and Julia's, who have conspired in the children's infancy to marry them to each other and have kept secret not only their plans but Henry's entitlement to a large inheritance. Thinking himself impoverished, Henry believes himself an unsuitable aspirant to Julia's hand. His guess about what her father would think suitable convinces him that he has no hope.

The conviction the two fathers share, that patriarchal hierarchy supports the best system of government, in other words, brings about the devastation of both their lives (Julia dies of grief after her lover's death). Letter after letter has proclaimed their smug belief that all is right in the existent social order, pervasive harmony marred only by the misguided selfishness of individuals whom they may pity but will not associate with. It is an irony never emphasized in the text that the father's authority yields destruction.

In the light of the plot resolution, the formulaic and often mechanical-sounding utterances that compose many of the nominally "personal" letters of this fiction take on a new kind of meaning. They constitute a form of emotional avoidance. The fathers produce resounding utterances about their systems of education or their concern for the welfare of peasants or their admiration for the king; they do not respond to or even recognize the immediate emotional plight of their children. Ignorance precipitates the disastrous events at the end, a son's ignorance mirroring a father's. The education the father has so emphatically provided does not address the needs of actual people.

For this narrative of failed possibilities, the epistolary form functions brilliantly. It is appropriate that the novel rarely supplies reciprocal letters; most of the letters in the text exist with the answers to them unrecorded, thus corroborating the pervasive impression of missed communication among these people who constantly write to one another. Many of the letters, concerned with external rather than internal matters, function not only to promulgate a body of opinion but to display their writers' discomfort with the personal. The same discomfort appears to pervade the consciousness even of the young lovers, who can express their feelings only in highly theatrical terms.

One letter writer alone avoids the difficulty with direct communication that most of the letters convey. Lady Anne Wilmot probably derives, like other sprightly eighteenth-century female characters, from Richardson's Anna Howe, in *Clarissa,* whose lively letters tease Clarissa herself and

report the writer's teasing of her mother and her lover. Lady Anne, however, is a rich young widow. Married by her parents to a man she dislikes,
she has led an unhappy connubial life, cut short by her husband's convenient death. She is in no hurry to marry again, though she has a suitor
whom she means sooner or later to accept. The novel's other characters
confide in her, and she comments on their behavior in letters to her
lover. "Lord! these prudes—no, don't let me injure her—these people of
high sentiment, are so 'tremblingly alive all o'er'—there is poor Harry in
terrible disgrace with Lady Julia, for only kissing her hand, and amidst
so bewitching a scene too, that I am really surprised at his moderation"
(61).

Like the others, as this quotation suggests, Lady Anne uses indirec-
tion to convey meaning. Her characteristic disguise consists of frivolity, a
proclaimed refusal to take anything seriously. As she explains to her lover,
she early realized that only two "characters" for a woman allowed her to
"take a thousand little innocent freedoms, without being censured by a
parcel of impertinent old women" (74). She might choose to act as a *"Bel
Esprit"*—a woman of wit and style—or as a Methodist. Lady Anne has,
of course, chosen the former role. The scene between her and Lady Belmont in which the older woman asks Anne's intentions toward her lover
provides splendid comedy, as the virtuous elderly woman inquires with
what view the lady allows a lover's addresses, and Anne responds with an
elaborate, comic, protofeminist defense of the "unconnected life," which
she declares "the pleasantest life in the world" (133). But Lady Anne, unlike
her elders and unlike the novel's central lovers, also has available to her a
direct language of feeling. When she is ready to accept her lover, she can
straightforwardly do so, with only minimal teasing along the way.

Lady Anne's voice reports the lovers' deaths and their aftermath.
Someone has to do it, and she is the only person left alive who is not directly related to the dead couple. But it is important also that she can talk
about her feelings in an open and at least relatively unpretentious way.
Her role at the novel's end calls sharp attention by contrast to the kind of
language that has previously dominated many of the epistolary exchanges.
It suggests that Brooke has consciously employed the novel-in-letters as
a means to explore problems of communication and the nature of the
obstacles to free human exchange. Convention provides a ready mode
for letters and conversation alike, but conventions can also make real

interchange impossible. Lady Anne, in her refusal to adopt meaningless social conventions—even while she lives scrupulously by her society's moral conventions—exemplifies a kind of possibility unavailable to the novel's other characters.

The History of Emily Montague may have proved less popular because less harrowing to the emotions. It, too, contains a sprightly female character —named Arabella Fermor, presumably with reference to the woman who inspired Pope's *Rape of the Lock*—whose attitude toward love contrasts with more soulful expressions of emotion from the heroine, but the contrast lacks the importance it has in the earlier novel. Not only do the various romances propounded all end happily; the obstacles the lovers face are minimal. Letters seem unimportant *as letters;* they only provide a means of telling the story.

In this respect, *Emily Montague* resembles many other works of its period. *Fanny Hill* presents itself in the shape of two long letters; *Memoirs of Miss Sidney Bidulph* adopts the same technique. Letters in such fictions serve no real purpose beyond vague justification for a first-person narrative. Brooke's novel at least offers different voices, and the epistolary form provides the author with an opportunity to supply social and geographical details about Canada, the site of the novel's early action: one character writes letters almost entirely for the purpose of setting forth information about the New World. (The novel, it should be remembered, appeared before the American war for independence; Canada and what would become the United States belonged to a single geographical unit, all alike remote colonies of Great Britain.)

Only a few years later (1771), Tobias Smollett published a work of epistolary fiction that made letters as travelogue into a device for psychological revelation as well as political and moral commentary. *The Expedition of Humphry Clinker,* although it bears few obvious resemblances to the other epistolary novels we have considered, represents a high achievement of the epistolary form. If it lacks the psychological density of *Clarissa,* it provides instead an intricate texture of individual reaction, not primarily to private problems of love and sexuality but to the manifestations of a complicated and various social world. From one point of view, it could be said that Smollett reveals not the slightest interest in the operations of individual consciousness. From another, one can see consciousness as his primary subject.

The form of consciousness at issue hardly resembles that of Pamela or Clarissa or Emily Montague—or, for that matter, Lovelace or Emily's lover, Rivers. A varied cast of characters, male and female, inhabit the novel and generate its letters. All belong to a single family, in the eighteenth-century sense of the word—not only those related by blood, but the servants who attend them. Indeed, the novel's titular character (who appears for the first time almost halfway through) is himself a servant, although a fortuitous revelation at the end converts him into Matthew Bramble's illegitimate son, thus arguably of somewhat higher social class than he at first appears.

The individual letter writers differ from one another in sex, social class, age, personal preoccupation, and language, their idiosyncratic forms of orthography (which often generate obscene puns) calling attention to the fact that they have not even common assumptions about the basis of communication. They share participation in a journey—or "expedition," as the title has it, connoting travel with a specific purpose. The real purposes of this particular expedition remain unstated (Matthew Bramble claims that the trip is intended to show his niece Lydia the world), although the expedition's effects on its participants are manifest. The letter writers also have in common precisely what divides them: their powerful self-interest. Male and female, young and old, servant and master, all are totally focused on their own immediate concerns—which often diverge comically from those of their companions. Thus Jery, Matthew Bramble's nephew, concerns himself primarily with maintaining his pose as a sophisticated Oxford graduate; his sister, Lydia, sees herself as a heroine of romance; Matthew's sister, Tabitha, tries to sustain both her amorous and her avaricious hopes; the servant Win Jenkins seeks romance and status. Matthew focuses mainly on his own health; secondarily, on his outrage at what he sees. As in Brooke's novels, the letters we read receive no answers. And the figure announced by the title as the central character writes no letters.

This summary should suggest how unconventional is Smollett's use of a conventional form. The fact that the titular hero writes none of the letters in this epistolary novel condenses the oddness of the procedure here. Humphry is not altogether voiceless: his speech is reported by several of the other characters in the letters they write, and it's apparent that he has made an impression on all of them—ranging from Win's amorous attachment to Bramble's amused skepticism (about Humphry's piety and preaching). But not only is his social position anomalous (he first appears as a bare-bottomed hostler, whose semi-nakedness offends Tabitha); he is characteristically self-deprecatory, always ready to see himself in the wrong, always eager to put himself at the service of others. It is not initially easy to discern why he should be honored in the novel's title.

The letters that make up the text do not function, as do Pamela's, for instance, to solicit the reader's identification with, or even necessarily sympathy for, the characters who write them. On the contrary, they often expose the most unattractive sides of their writers: Bramble's hypochondria and testiness, Jery's vanity, Win's upward striving, Lydia's shallowness, Tabitha's lack of human kindness. None of these figures is a knave, exactly, although Tabitha sometimes comes close, but most of them are more or less fools. No plausible heroine presents herself, nor can the reader feel altogether at ease with the idea of Humphry (who rescues others but frequently displays comic excess; who preaches the gospel, with some dubious effects; who initiates no heroic action and delights in proclaiming his devotion to his master) as titular hero. The novel, in other words, eschews obvious forms of novelistic appeal. It offers no adventure. Although the action ends in three marriages, none of the romances stirs much interest. The book's narrative thrust is minimal, and its letters often seem peripheral to any conceivable narrative intent. What is going on here?

One thing that is going on is a reimagining of epistolary possibility. A quarter-century had intervened between *Pamela* and *Humphry Clinker*. The connection between the fictional familiar letter and an emphasis on consciousness still held firm, but consciousness now had different implications. Pamela's consciousness and Clarissa's, even Lady Julia Mandeville's, focus resolutely within, on the thoughts and feelings that constitute their responses to life. The stimulus might be relatively small: Mr. B pretending not to know Pamela in her country clothes, for instance. The response, and the contemplation of the response, could occupy many pages. Through Pamela's reflections on such episodes, the reader comes to understand—or at least to arrive at an interpretation of—who she is. The structure of *Humphry Clinker*, in contrast, suggests greater concern with the objects of consciousness, with the pressures and the implications of a world outside the self. At one level, the novel presents a travel narrative.

The travelers record what they see, with various kinds of emotional response. Thus Lydia perceives London as full of wonders; Bramble sees a chaos of physical and moral corruption.

The travelers, of course, also see other people, and people of many varieties: the sick and the well, the trickster and the honest man, the greedy and the vain, the fortunate and the deprived, the brutal and the unconcerned. As my list may hint, moral corruption predominates. As the "expedition" proceeds northward, corruption appears to diminish—and Matthew, accordingly, believes himself to have recovered his health. The human scene holds the greatest interest in the novel, which dwells not at all on landscape and hardly at all on architecture. The social world is what matters.

This is not to say that the letter writers necessarily look outward rather than inward. Jery and Lydia interest themselves in their own reactions—and predominantly petty reactions at that—as much as Pamela does, although they do not analyze their feelings. I have already suggested the degree of self-concern that shapes all the letters and shapes, likewise, what their writers see and understand around them. Even Matthew Bramble, who comments extensively on what he sees, hears, and smells in the various settings of his travels, acknowledges explicitly that his "illness" (which may be largely imaginary) colors his perceptions: he sees without him evidence of his internal sense of something awry. But the figure of Humphry, the man who never writes letters, provides perspective on all the others.

If Humphry is a hero—entitled to have a novel named after him—he is a hero of a new sort. Naive, often foolish, misguided, he frequently gets into trouble. His predicament when the travelers first encounter him, so impoverished, as a result of illness and misfortune, that he cannot buy clothes, indicates his utter lack of worldly wisdom. His frequent rescue operations often cause physical discomfort to the recipients of his generosity, yet the generosity matters more than the errors. Unlike most of the other characters, he is genuinely and almost completely concerned with the needs of others. Matthew Bramble shares with him a spirit of compassion, a capacity and willingness to help the unfortunate, but this "sensibility" (the novel's repeated term for it) is accompanied by extreme irascibility, which can obscure the softer sentiments and on occasion substitute for them.

Bramble's more mixed responses to other people perhaps reflect his position in the class system: he believes himself to have the right to express negative judgments and feelings. Conversely, Humphry's lowly social status arguably inhibits him from indulging, or perhaps even experiencing, anger. But *Humphry Clinker* by no means criticizes the class system. Humphry is duly rewarded for his virtue and for his illegitimate connection to a gentleman: he receives a farm. Characters can rise slightly, but only slightly, in the social scale. Wealth and privilege do not entitle their possessor to tyrannize: the brutal country squire gets his comeuppance at the hands of Lismahago, Tabitha's bizarre suitor. Rank implies responsibility: the squire who has squandered his money must be educated in estate management. But the social order is a given, not an appropriate subject for criticism. Humphry is a "hero" not because his lack of corruption reflects some natural superiority of the poor over the rich—Win, after all, another servant, has little interest in anyone but herself—but because his emotional responsiveness exemplifies a high human attainment. Its sources are irrelevant.

Humphry embodies the responsive capacity labeled "sensibility"; so does Matthew Bramble, who has the wherewithal for financial benevolence, which Humphry, of course, lacks. But sympathy fails in Jery, Tabitha (who has feeling only for her little dog), Lydia (sentimental, but minimally aware of others), Lismahago, and most of the people they meet. The "world" evoked by this novel is corrupt, often cruel, controlled by individual self-interest. The letters written by the novel's central characters show self-interest in less obviously destructive form. Personal letters presumably record relationship. The fictional letters here assembled reveal little awareness in the writers of the nature or the needs of their correspondents (Matthew Bramble on occasion negates this generalization: he, after all, possesses sensibility). They write for their own sakes, not for the sake of another. Letters appear to exist more for self-display than for communication. The situation is not, as in *Lady Julia Mandeville,* one of avoidance; rather, these correspondents, most of them, possess limited emotional ranges.

In *Humphry Clinker,* then, the epistolary form is employed for purposes almost directly opposed to those it served in novels like *Pamela* and *Clarissa.* In those works, letters seemed the ideal medium for conveying the nuances of emotional vacillation; in *Humphry Clinker,* characters are not in touch with such vacillations, or they experience feeling without analyzing it. The change does not constitute a historical progression: novels of the *Pamela* sort, with protagonists deeply interested in their own emotional situations, continued to be written. But the change calls attention to the range that novels in letters could exploit.

For all that range, epistolary novels do not exhaust the possibilities of the novel of consciousness. Two final examples—*A Sentimental Journey* (1768) and *The Cry* (1754), both anomalous works—will suggest other directions of the form, indicating how eighteenth-century novelists experimented with ways in which consciousness might be explored.

In *A Sentimental Journey,* popular but perplexing even in its own time, Laurence Sterne developed an early approximation of stream of consciousness. His method differs from that employed by James Joyce and his followers, though, in that Sterne seems always to imagine consciousness as engaged with other people. Yorick, the first-person narrator of Sterne's novel, allows the movements of his mind and heart to determine the shape of his story, but he remains always aware of the effect his divagations may have on the imagined reader, of whom he is teasingly conscious.

Sterne had many imitators, although none who could successfully achieve the provocative mixture of tones that he so brilliantly created, making comedy an intimate component of melancholy throughout his fiction, mocking his own persona and the fine sentiments he utters, while also inviting the reader to enjoy a familiar aesthetic of sentiment. Although, unlike many sentimental novelists (see Chapter 5), Sterne makes no point of the fact that his novel is fragmentary and disjunctive, he begins his story in mid-episode, ends it in the middle of a sentence, locates his preface six pages after the beginning of the narrative, and moves from one event to another without necessarily bothering to resolve one situation before describing the next. The absence of apology or explanation for this apparent lack of orthodox form only emphasizes its eccentricity. Sterne's disjunctiveness works to stress the nature of individual movements of feeling and attention. Yorick, his persona (whose language and attitudes sound suspiciously like Sterne's own, as revealed in his personal letters), shifts attention rapidly. The narrative stems from, is constituted and limited by, his consciousness: the novel's true subject.

Often in eighteenth-century fiction—in *Humphry Clinker,* for one example—*sensibility* figures as a term of praise. Yorick offers a panegyric to sensibility that epitomizes Sterne's way of proceeding. Here is a slightly truncated version of it:

> Dear sensibility! source inexhausted of all that's precious in our joys, or costly in our sorrows! thou chainest thy martyr down upon his bed of straw—and 'tis thou who lifts him up to HEAVEN—eternal fountain of our feelings!—'tis here I trace thee—and this is thy divinity which stirs within me. . . . I feel some generous joys and generous cares beyond myself—all comes from thee, great—great SENSORIUM of the world!—which vibrates, if a hair of our heads but falls upon the ground, in the remotest desert of thy creation. . . . Thou giv'st a portion of it sometimes to the roughest peasant who traverses the bleakest mountains—he finds the lacerated lamb of another's flock.—This moment I beheld him leaning with his head against his crook, with piteous inclination looking down upon it—Oh! had I come but one moment sooner!— it bleeds to death—his gentle heart bleeds with it. [117]

Sensibility, in this representation, belongs to heaven and is equated with the fundamental creative force. It seems, indeed, virtually identical with God, who, according to the Bible, numbers the hairs of our heads. Still, here as in other contemporary allusions, sensibility is fundamentally a force of feeling, providing the principle of sympathy that governs the writer, with his generous joys and cares beyond himself, and the principle that stirs within the peasant grieving for a bleeding lamb.

Immediately after this sequence, Yorick goes on to imagine the peasant walking away "with anguish" but living a life full of joy, in a happy cottage, with a happy sharer of it, and surrounded by happy lambs that sport about him. The fancifulness of this evocation underlines the fact that the peasant himself, as well as the dying lamb, belongs entirely to Yorick's imagination.

It is difficult to know—as it is difficult to know in virtually every episode—how seriously the reader should take this. On the one hand, the celebration of sympathy in particular and of the capacity for feeling in general expresses attitudes implicit in all the period's fiction of sentiment. On the other hand, one must note the factitiousness of the situations that arouse emotion here. Yorick's imagination dictates the scene of peasant

and lamb. It is Yorick who makes the peasant arrive a moment too late
to save the dying animal. For purposes of indulging his sensibility, the
sentimentalist *needs* the peasant to arrive too late: he couldn't feel so much
if the animal failed to die.

The panegyric to sensibility immediately succeeds a scene with Eliza,
the mad young woman whom Tristram Shandy also, in Sterne's earlier
novel, encounters and weeps over. Yorick has sought her out for the
sole purpose of weeping. He sits down next to her and wipes away her
tears with his handkerchief, then "steeps" the handkerchief in his own
tears—"and then in hers—and then in mine—and then I wip'd hers
again—and as I did it, I felt such undescribable emotions within me, as
I am sure could not be accounted for from any combinations of matter
and motion" (114). These emotions, Yorick goes on to explain, make him
positive that he has a soul.

The question about how seriously we should take this recurs. The
undescribable emotions sound familiar in their undescribability; allusions
to the impossibility of fully expressing what can be fully felt abound in
eighteenth-century fiction. But Yorick's emotions differ from those in
other sentimental writing in the deliberateness with which he summons
them. Weeping is, quite explicitly, a source of pleasure for him. He seeks
Maria in order to weep over her; he imagines the peasant for the same
purpose. In the course of the novel, he indulges in comparable other
imaginings, summoning up, for instance, a highly elaborated vision of a
prisoner in the Bastille in order to mourn over it. At the least, the repeated
maneuver must raise questions about the moral force of sensibility. The
power Yorick associates with divinity causes an imaginary peasant to weep
over an imaginary lamb, but it does not enable him to rescue the lamb,
any more than Yorick can (or tries to) help Maria. And since weeping
constitutes emotional gratification, as the novel makes abundantly clear,
its purpose is, after all, selfish, not really "generous" at all, except in the
most theoretical sense. Passages like the praise of sensibility sharply reveal this truth, while leaving ambiguous Sterne's awareness of the ironic
implications of Yorick's panegyric. It's partly funny, partly pathetic. The
precise balance remains difficult to ascertain.

Eighteenth-century readers took the novel's sensibility and its praise
of sensibility altogether seriously. Various publishers assembled collections of especially sentimental passages from both *A Sentimental Jour-*

ney and its predecessor, *Tristram Shandy* (1759–67). They presumably
wished especially to separate the sentimentality from the smut of the
two works—for contemporaneous readers also took seriously Sterne's
abundant sexual hints and felt troubled by a clergyman's indulgence in
the bawdy (or near-bawdy). It is difficult, though, to divide the sex from
the sensibility, especially given Yorick's avowed belief that the two go
together. *A Sentimental Journey* abounds in vignettes that entwine sexual
innuendo with sentimental proclamation. Yorick feels the pulse of a shop
girl. Her husband comes in and appears not to mind. By the time Sterne
has finished describing the pulse-taking, the account seems almost pornographic. Another girl goes with him to his hotel room. When he attempts to fix her shoe, she tumbles backward upon the bed. He declines
to report what happens next but later strongly suggests that nothing at all
has happened, except for a kind of emotional massage. At the novel's end,
he finds himself compelled to share a room at an inn with a woman and
her maid. The woman demands elaborate precautions against indecency,
which Yorick willingly follows. But then he reaches out and touches the
maidservant's—here the narrative concludes, in mid-sentence.

Such episodes summon the reader's imagination in new ways, adapt-
ing the technique of emotional suggestion familiar from other sentimental
fiction to call attention to the fact that our imaginations may operate in
less conventionally acceptable fashion than other novelists appear to assume. The author takes no responsibility for what our imaginations may
provide, nor does Yorick. *A Sentimental Journey* strongly suggests, though,
that the sexual is only a logical extension of the emotional.

It thus either undercuts or reinforces the assumptions of more conventional fiction. In an obvious sense it undercuts: decorous eighteenth-
century fiction rigorously excludes the notion of sexual impulse in "good"
characters, whose thoughts at least nominally focus on higher things.
More subtly, though, Sterne's technique reinforces the implications of
orthodox fictions of feeling by emphasizing to an even greater degree
the reader's necessary participation in the activity of creating emotional
meaning. He attempts to draw the peruser of his novel into its emotional
drama, which concerns primarily a man's relation to himself.

With the ironic eye Sterne casts on his own proceedings, he also
complicates the pattern he provides for aesthetic contemplation. The most
obvious "pattern" of *A Sentimental Journey* is no pattern at all. The apparent

rejection of order in the novel's arbitrary sequences, the book's refusals to explain, and its truncations frustrate the reader, but the novel achieves more than frustration. It speaks vividly of how consciousness operates. Indeed, it celebrates the ways of the mind and the heart as the most interesting literary material conceivable. Yorick takes himself with great seriousness. He also laughs at himself constantly. He implicitly invites readers to pay comparable attention to themselves, not only feeling deeply and valuing feeling—the invitation of all sentimental writing—but also grasping how ludicrous are all human pretensions.

Paradox and ambiguity, those forces of antistructure, provide the principles of structure for *A Sentimental Journey*. Each episode contains the seed of its own undoing or precedes the commentary that will undo it—without refuting it. Yorick arrives in France, eats dinner, and feels pleasure in his own capacity for feeling. Conscious of benevolent impulse, he imagines bestowing wealth upon an orphan child. Then a poor monk enters the room. His aspect declares his virtue, a point elaborately emphasized. Yorick, however, for reasons unknown, has decided at the moment of seeing him to give him nothing. The monk speaks of his poverty and of the needs of his convent. Yorick answers him contemptuously. The moment the monk leaves, the Englishman feels great remorse.

The episode of the monk continues, becoming more complicated, but this initial sequence suffices to indicate Sterne's technique. Yorick's nature includes contradictions that he cannot understand and hardly attempts to analyze. He enacts them in his every encounter. He is generous, he is selfish, he has virtually no control over his impulses. Inevitably, an episode of selfishness must follow his self-congratulation for benevolence; inevitably, he will demonstrate his generosity after he realizes his selfishness. Neither quality cancels its opposite; neither quality—*no* quality—exists in isolation.

Yorick meets an old officer at the Parisian theater and praises the wisdom of the observations he utters. Then he observes, "I thought I loved the man; but I fear I mistook the object—'twas my own way of thinking" (63). In other words, what purports to be love of another turns out to be love of self. As the encounters with the monk raise the possibility that all Yorick's impulses—to help or not to help—are equally arbitrary, so the exchange with the French officer casts its shade on all exchanges between Yorick and his fellow man. When he "loves" Maria and wishes to live with her and her pet goat, does he really express love of himself and his own sensations? The novel deliberately induces such questions and insists on their undecidability—indeed, finally, their meaninglessness, since all human feeling is mixed, every action, closely examined, infused with ambiguity and paradox. Such is the glory, such the pettiness of the human condition.

Yorick/Sterne manipulates his reader in every account of every transaction, violating normal expectation, demanding constantly shifting responses, inviting sympathy and mockery at once. He appears to require from the reader excessive reactions comparable to his own violent weeping over Maria, but he also appears capable of mercilessly mocking such reactions. Disconnections that refuse reader satisfaction abound; the narrative offers no completion. Even the inset stories break off inconclusively. Yet the infusion of ironic commentary into sentimental rhapsody guarantees that the ready tear will not suffice as sympathetic reader response. To achieve full sympathy with Yorick would demand of the reader mental and emotional agility comparable to the protagonist's. The code of notation Sterne employs is ultimately impenetrable: that's its point. At once celebrating and deploring the intricacy of the human psyche, mocking the orthodox structures of fiction and the conventional educational purposes of travel, playing games with language, Sterne in *A Sentimental Journey* complicates the aesthetic of feeling that governed much of the period's fiction by reminding us that feeling is just as complicated as anything else—not predictable, not automatic, though deeply valuable, declaring (if we are to believe Yorick—and that's a real question) the existence of a soul. The book's aim is enjoyment, its inlets of enjoyment multifarious; but it insistently makes us wonder about enjoyment's precise components—one of the many questions it raises about the incomprehensibility of consciousness.

A Sentimental Journey is widely taught, thus still frequently read. *The Cry*, by Henry Fielding's sister, Sarah Fielding, remains virtually unknown. Sterne, as I have already observed, had many imitators; Sarah Fielding, as far as I know, had none. She too found an innovative structure for revealing and, as it were, annotating consciousness, but the model she offered failed to invite duplication.

"The Cry," in this novel, does not designate a single verbal utterance. It refers, rather, to a group of people, a kind of chorus commenting on what they hear. What they hear, in Fielding's fable, is the voice of Portia (secondarily, that of Cylinda) as she tries to render the shape of her consciousness reacting to a sequence of events. The events resemble those in many other eighteenth-century fictions: a young woman (Portia herself) loves a young man without having explicit knowledge of his feelings; a wicked brother, who has been spoiled by an overindulgent mother, plots against the man; a wicked woman tries to undermine Portia; finally the good couple marries, to live happy ever after. The Cylinda plot, less stereotypically, concerns a woman misled by her own intelligence and her secular education into leading a sexually loose life with a series of partners. Cylinda cannot, of course, by eighteenth-century standards be allowed to marry, but she finds lasting happiness in the company of Portia and her husband.

The commentary provided by the Cry takes predictable shapes, for the group is composed not exactly of ordinary citizens, but of those adhering to Error and opposing Truth. They are not only clamorous; they prove unanimous in their clamor, despising the good and preferring what Fielding, like her brother, calls "affectation": the structure of individual and social pretensions by which people get along in the world. In fact, the members of the Cry articulate the assumptions of large segments of society. Theirs is, in fact, the voice of "the world," exposed in all its pettiness, self-seeking, and malice.

The introduction reveals clearly the author's intention to concern herself with consciousness, as well as her awareness that she proposes to attempt something new in fiction: "Thoroughly to unfold the labyrinths of the human mind, is an arduous task; and notwithstanding the many skilful and penetrating strokes which are to be found in the best authors, there seem yet to remain some intricate and unopen'd recesses in the heart of man. In order to dive into these recesses, and lay them open to the reader in a striking and intelligible manner, 'tis necessary to assume a certain freedom in writing, not strictly perhaps within the limits prescribed by rules" (1: 14). She devises, therefore, an innovative scheme of representation. It subordinates plot and character, in the usual meanings of those terms, to the communication of a message—a message equally innovative.

Her narrative problem, as she herself understands it, concerns the difficulty of communicating directly to the "mental perception" of the reader. Citing her brother's definition, in *Tom Jones,* of invention as "discovery, or finding out; . . . a quick and sagacious penetration into the true essence of all the objects of our contemplation" (2: 1), she translates it into simpler terms: "having eyes and opening them in order to discern the objects which are placed before us" (2: 1–2). Then she emphasizes her own focus on "the mind's eye": "In order . . . clearly and distinctly to convey his images, the poet is obliged to make use of allegories, metaphors, and illustrations from outward objects, and from things visible, to deduce the evidence of things not seen" (2: 3).

So it is that *The Cry* is organized by an allegorical scheme: a quasi-trial presided over by Una, Spenser's figure for Truth, with the Cry filling the role of collective plaintiff and Portia as defendant. Portia tells her story, which includes the stories of others, to the accompaniment of frequent violent interruptions from the Cry. At the end, Una approves of Portia's narrative and her behavior.

This arrangement provides the novel's structure, but it offers no suspense and little narrative thrust. Una from the beginning endorses Portia. She frequently rebukes the Cry, who are intimidated by her authority. Although she occasionally shows signs of doubt about Portia's behavior at specific moments, the tale Portia tells almost instantly eliminates any misgivings. Since the Cry have from the beginning been associated with Error, readers can hardly wonder what side to be on.

Nor do the stories Portia relates hold much obvious narrative interest. So manifest in their moral nature, and so totally separated from one another in all points of behavior are the "good" and the "bad" that one can feel no uncertainty about which is which. Portia purports to doubt whether she will ever be united with her beloved Ferdinand, but the reader cannot sustain comparable uncertainty: everything in the tone and substance of the narrative foretells the happy ending. Cylinda's much more rapidly narrated story, less predictable, creates more suspense, but it has less narrative importance. It exists mainly to demonstrate Portia's magnanimity and to illustrate the difference between proper and improper education for women.

Despite what may appear to be large narrative flaws, *The Cry* generates reader involvement by its unique didactic project: not only, like so many other works of the period, to inculcate moral uprightness and Christian piety by means of positive and negative example but also to offer psychological arguments for choosing good rather than evil. Hence the extended length of Portia's story, the substance of which a few pages might have communicated. This heroine, however, does not content herself with telling what happened. She also attempts to convey what every happening felt like: not only how she felt at a given juncture but what emotional state dominated the other participants in the action.

Portia's propensity for psychological analysis emerges early, when she attempts to explain her feeling for Ferdinand and how it developed. The Cry accuse her alternately of too much and too little sexuality. Either she must be wanton or she chooses to pursue "Platonic love." Either Ferdinand must have made love to her passionately or by failing to make love to her at all he betrays his lack of interest. Portia calmly, and at length, responds. She declares her disapproval of Platonic love as an unrealistic idea that leads women insensibly into corruption, and she insists that sexual passion invariably and appropriately composes part of love between the sexes. Then she explains how Ferdinand made love to her: by treating an indigent woman with enormous respect; by bestowing charity generously; by manifesting his virtues. The Cry, of course, cannot understand, but the reader has been initiated into Portia's steadily enacted conviction that no relationship is merely personal.

This defendant-heroine invents two new terms that become central to her psychological argument: *turba,* for the discordant mass of conflicting feelings that plague the followers of Error—both consistent followers, like the members of the Cry, and those who choose badly in a given case; and *dextra,* to designate the internal harmony of one who chooses aright. Through one anecdote after another, Portia insists on the crucial link between doing good and feeling good. She never quite argues that one should choose the path of virtue *because* the choice produces the highest pleasure, but her many small stories, like her large narrative, enforce just such an argument. She glosses Cylinda's autobiographical account as well, to point out the operations of the turba as this other young woman repeatedly makes bad decisions. Invariably, in her narratives and in her immediate responses, Portia emphasizes feeling rather than moral judgment.

If *The Cry* offers relatively little narrative excitement, it provides, in unexpected ways, considerable psychological interest. It also implies social commentary, also in an unexpected way. The format Fielding chooses for her novel is remarkably bare. The book proceeds by a series of numbered scenes, with characters listed at the beginning of each scene. It provides no setting, only successive utterances. The arrangement is not quite what it would be in a play intended for stage representation, because the novel's intermittent narrator frequently intervenes with commentary, almost always directed to what the participants feel at a given moment. Thus, for an arbitrary example: "The Cry had a great mind to have thrown out some trite joke at old maids; but as they could not make themselves believe, that *Portia* was likely to be in the number, it was so small a gratification of their spleen, it was not worth indulging; and thus *Portia* proceeded" (1: 66).

Not only does the novel lack setting, it renders no social world. Neither in the plot, if it can be called that, of Portia's trial nor in the biographical and autobiographical accounts orally rendered do we encounter social gatherings, business or professional contexts, or even plausible representations of domestic environments in any fullness. Yet the Cry's presence provides a constant reminder of the world of other people and how it operates, and the Cry's role implies harsh criticism of prevailing social standards. Like Una, the Cry allegorize an abstraction: the alienating pressure of society. If Una, as Truth, exemplifies dispassionate judgment, the Cry represent passionate misjudgment. They condense the impression of the social world on an individual yearning for and trying to achieve internal harmony.

The external world presses on the individual; the individual must resist. Characters like Tom Jones and Betsy Thoughtless learn this truth, an important component of their achieved "prudence." Portia knows it from the outset. Sarah Fielding's representation of "the world," like her representation of distinct persons, simplifies in order to focus on the most salient characteristics for her argument. That argument, although it directs attention primarily to psychology, depends on a perception of society as intrinsically hostile to the deep needs of every separate self.

Concern with the social world remains throughout the novel unmistakably secondary to focus on personal consciousness, although also crucial to that focus. *The Cry* is a novel of consciousness conceptually different from other examples of the form considered in this chapter—and equally different from fictional explorations of consciousness that followed it. Its form encapsulates its difference. All aspects of that form—allegorical personages, disjunctive scenes, structure based on a legal trial, absence of full narrative development and of suspense as a significant element, frequent didactic interventions—distance the reader in almost Brechtian fashion from the experience of the text, forbidding not only identification with any character but also full imaginative participation in the narrative. The novel urges the reader to think rather than feel: to think, specifically, about the nature, the causes, and the value of feeling.

Fielding, in short, makes no attempt to render consciousness, as Richardson and Sterne in their different ways vividly do. Instead, she contemplates consciousness. Through Portia's account of her own experience and her commentary on that of others, *The Cry* enforces the view that attention to the operations of consciousness may enable a woman (or, presumably, a man) to sustain the self against a hostile world and to use self-assessment as a resource for autonomy. The novel embodies a fresh view of the importance of consciousness and a fresh way of rendering it.

Sarah Fielding's novel is unique in form and content; Sterne's became a prototype for other attempts in the same mode; the epistolary novel appeared throughout the eighteenth century in many avatars. All confront the same issue: that of personal consciousness as impinged on by a world of other people. They demonstrate varied expedients for narrating interior life, in the process developing important structural possibilities for the novel.

CHAPTER FIVE

The Novel of Sentiment

THE PARTICULAR FORM OF consciousness that we encounter in *A Sentimental Journey* attracted such interest in the eighteenth century that it generated a novelistic subgenre of its own. For several decades, the sentimental novel, or novel of sensibility, intended to arouse as well as to render sympathetic feelings, flourished in England (as well as on the Continent). Sentimental novels assumed the individual and social importance of sensitivity to the troubles of others. In addition to representing heroes, and occasionally heroines, of extraordinary responsiveness, they also commented on social institutions.

One of the best-known examples of the form—better known, perhaps, for its apposite title than for its substance—occupies ninety-four sparsely printed pages in the Norton paperback edition. In that brief span it treats of seduction, prostitution, military service in India, depopulation, impressment into the army, place-seeking among the wealthy, and many other social and personal evils. *The Man of Feeling* (1769), a product of Henry Mackenzie's youth, exemplifies the kinds of issue and the kind of protagonist that would abound as this subgenre flourished. Harley, the eponymous hero, is, from a worldly point of view, a fool. He understands nothing about how things are done; he lacks a canny eye to his own advantage. In these respects he resembles other figures glorified by the novel of sentiment.

Mackenzie did not originate the form: well before he wrote, Sarah Fielding had produced *David Simple* (1744) and its sequel, *Volume the Last* (1753). Like Mackenzie's Harley, David Simple is a naïf, unfamiliar with the ways of the world and astounded and appalled by the corruption he discovers. He too could be called, from a worldly perspective, a fool: he doesn't know how to take care of himself. David's last name betokens his nature. For eighteenth-century readers, it would denote not only possible foolishness but purity, authenticity, moral clarity, a character unmixed with corruption. (Such overtones of the word *simple* emerge clearly in a work like William Collins's "Ode to Simplicity.") The potential for foolishness and the possession of purity naturally accompany each other since the morally unmixed character can hardly function effectively in a morally mixed society. From the viewpoint of worldly wisdom—a viewpoint that at least some readers might share—the protagonist's lack of success betokens lack of brainpower.

Like Harley after him, David travels through London. Harley's half-hearted quest involves a search for financial security and position; David's whole-hearted pursuit focuses on finding a friend—someone who can offer and receive love and emotional support. Unlike Harley, David gets what he wants: not one friend but three, one of whom becomes his wife.

The naïf makes a stock figure in classic satire, because his wide-eyed perspective illuminates evils taken for granted by those more fully accustomed to things as they are. Sarah Fielding's novel, like Mackenzie's, contains abundant satiric elements, indicting a financially oriented society. It takes potshots at operations of greed, vanity, and selfishness in the marketplace, and it demonstrates how thoroughly the ethos of the marketplace pervades both heterosexual courtship and homosocial attachment.

One does not automatically associate satire with sentimentality. Indeed, the two literary modes may seem to emanate from opposite impulses: sentimentality celebrates tender feelings; satire rejects tenderness for often lacerating criticism. Yet satire assumes a crucial place in Fielding's literary program and in the work of other so-called sentimentalists, a fact that may alert us to unexpected complexities of the sentimental stance. Sensitivity to the misfortunes of others may imply awareness of institutional as well as individual sources of misfortune. Pity can—and in this fiction often does—entail blame.

Modern commentators on sentimental fiction of the eighteenth century have raised a question that also concerned eighteenth-century moralists: what moral purpose does such fiction serve? Mackenzie himself, late in his life, worried in print about the possibility that sentimental fiction exhausts the ethical impulses it arouses. To be sure, it encourages compassion, what we would call empathy. But, deliberately stimulating emotion, it may let the reader weep over fancied sufferings rather than encourage that reader to take action to ameliorate real suffering in real people. The sentimental world—so the indictment goes—is self-contained. Its fictional representations solicit the reader's tears rather than arouse awareness. After all (this point emerges from twentieth-century critiques), sentimental novels reinforce the social status quo by depicting with apparent approval an order in which the poor suffer and the prosperous alleviate the suffering of their social inferiors by benevolence rather than think about the causes of social inequality. David Simple, like Harley, like Henry Brooke's Fool of Quality, like many other sentimental heroes after him, bestows money on those whose stories touch his heart; his sense of obligation often ends there. The awareness of the novelists who create these characters, however, may extend further. Before investigating this possibility more fully, though, I want to call attention to another problematic aspect of sentimental fiction.

The typical structure of these novels raises formal as well as moral issues. Characteristically, the sentimental novel operates through a disjunctive pattern, the logic of its narrative not readily apparent. David Simple is less egregious in this respect than many works that followed it, but since its plot (David is betrayed by his brother; he leaves home in search of a friend; after many frustrated attempts he finds three friends; he marries one of them, and the four friends live together in harmony) proceeds largely by means of the stories David hears of other people's lives, the narrative sequences are often arbitrary. Despite the considerable length of some of these autobiographical tales, many others consist only of short summaries. They arouse sympathy in David but do not necessarily generate comparable sympathy in the reader unless the reader's imagination fills in the details, as David's presumably does. A narrative code seems to operate by which a woman's brief story of an unkind husband, for example, stands for many comparable instances and a multitude of detail.

The pattern of multiplied brief narratives lacking detail or emotional development in some sense recalls the narrative arrangements of Manley's

New Atalantis. Its effect differs sharply, though, from that of the earlier novel because of the stories' fundamental repetitiveness. Characters and situations of course vary from one tale to the next, but every story reports human misery. Like the stories told in *New Atalantis,* these provide ways of understanding the world—but the world as reported in them is narrow. Manley's miniature tales relay episodes of corruption, but they offer much more emotional variety than Fielding's. It remains worth noting, however, that the same structural principles persist past the middle of the century.

Sentimentality, in modern usage, connotes a demand for excessive emotional response, and a novel like *David Simple* may appear to conform to this definition. "Show, don't tell" is a fundamental dictum for creative-writing students. Dramatized action, we tend to believe, affects the imagination more immediately than action narrated after the fact. *David Simple* prefers telling to showing: after-the-fact narration, often severely truncated. Indeed, it apparently assumes the essential identity of showing and telling or assumes, at any rate, that a story told will have effects comparable to those of an event or series of events witnessed. The novel allows characters to tell about themselves and demands extravagant reactions from other characters, surrogates for the reader in their consumption of other people's misery and their responses to it. The sheer multiplication of misery may make it difficult to take it seriously. In *Volume the Last,* David changes from consumer to sufferer, but the piling up of distress (children die, spouses die, the wicked prosper while the good decline into destitution and illness) becomes yet more dramatic. The reader may feel manipulated, coerced into sympathy by the abundance of unfortunate happenings. To be sure, sentimentality, according to current ways of thinking, *always* manipulates.

But *David Simple* and, even more emphatically, *The Man of Feeling* and Frances Sheridan's *Memoirs of Miss Sidney Bidulph* (1761) enjoyed popularity in their own time, and we have no evidence that anyone felt manipulated. To take sentimental fiction on its own terms, we must abandon some familiar assumptions. Above all, it is necessary once more to give up expectation of even approximate realism. Sentimental novels do not aspire to render the world of actuality. They attempt, rather, to illuminate that world by creating images and actions that condense implications of actuality. In this respect, they operate like satire, and it becomes less surprising that satire and sentimentality so frequently mingle in these fictions. Both modes proceed by and depend on exaggeration. To realize this fact implies a new way of looking at a kind of fiction less immediately available to modern sensibilities than is, for instance, a work like *Robinson Crusoe.*

David Simple begins like any novel of development, with the protagonist's birth. Within the first twenty pages it narrates, in summary form, his school experiences with his brother Daniel, his father's illness and death, Daniel's machinations (including the suborning of two servants) to forge the father's will, the servants' subsequent unhappy marriage, David's gradual realization of his brother's disloyalty, his flight from his brother's house to his uncle's, the discovery of Daniel's forgery, with David's consequent reinheritance, and his uncle's death. This extraordinary speed of narration provides the first clue that the story aims to effect no suspension of disbelief. It supplies only a cursory sense of plausibility to the quest for a friend (with whom to share his money) that David now embarks upon. The technique resembles that of a fable more than that of novels on the model of *Tom Jones.*

As my summary of the novel's summary narrative may suggest, emphasis in this early part of the fiction rests more on guilt than on suffering. David regrets his father's death but quickly finds Christian consolation. Briefly "moved" by his uncle's passing, he comforts himself by reflecting that it's better to die than to endure the infirmities of old age. His brother's coldness troubles him greatly, and the discovery of fraternal treachery precipitates David into illness, but his emotions receive no prolonged emphasis. As he begins his search for a friend, the story continues to stress moral insufficiency rather than details of feeling. Stockbrokers, businessmen, literary critics, young women seeking husbands: all, like Daniel, allow self-interest to control them. David rapidly encounters a broad spectrum of humanity, but all value money above virtue and value their own desires—most especially the desire to seem important—above human obligation. (The world here sketched strongly resembles the one represented in *Chrysal,* that tale of a guinea's adventures investigated in Chapter 2.)

In other words, satire dominates this part of the novel. As David cries out after enduring a bout of conversation at a party, "What Hopes can I ever have of meeting with a Man who deserves my Esteem, if Mankind can be so furious against each other, for things which are of no manner of Consequence, and which are only to be valued according to the Use that is made of them, while they *despise* what is in every one's Power of attaining; namely, the Consciousness of acting with *Honour* and *Integrity*" (86). The outburst conveys the novel's satiric standard and the nature of its satiric targets. Not until roughly a third of the way through the book does David hear Cynthia's story—Cynthia being the first of the friends he discovers—and the satiric tone largely disappears as he listens to a long sequence of harrowing autobiographical tales.

The "bad" characters who provide satiric targets and the "good" ones who suffer and tell about their suffering resemble one another in their un- mixed natures. As names like Orgueil (Pride) suggest, they often approach the allegorical. Someone like Betsy Johnson, whom David expects to marry until her self-seeking is unmasked, may *appear* gentle and loving—but she only manipulates appearances for the sake of her self-interest. Mr. Orgueil, who sees compassion as weakness, enjoys laughing at the fol- lies and vices of humankind, and he perceives nothing else. With him as a guide, David too finds nothing else, until he encounters Cynthia, all virtue, and then Camilla and her brother Valentine, who suffer one form of anguish after another but remain pure in heart and action. On occa- sion, sufferers make mistakes: Isabelle, for instance, who has no narrative function beyond telling her intricate tale of suffering, which is also a tale of her errors in judgment. But they never do anything evil, and the evil characters never do anything really good.

The world of this novel, in short, bears little resemblance to that of actual experience, and sentimental novels typically construct just such unreal worlds. Assessment of their moral effects must take this into ac- count. If it is true that the compassion generated by sentimental fiction is self-contained, making the reader weep for the characters but not act, it is also true that those objects of tears only superficially resemble any victim one is likely to encounter. Such a novel as *David Simple* invents characters and actions equally remote from real experience. The charac- ters have relentlessly illustrative histories and altogether generic traits: a man is selfish, and all his actions declare his selfishness; a woman is self- seeking, and everything she does announces the fact. Even David and his friends, who possess the richest histories, lack psychological complexity. The actions narrated and performed or endured by the characters may be individually plausible, but their multiplication duplicates rather than varies a pattern: readers are unlikely to believe that any single person would suffer as much as, say, Isabelle suffers.

The representation of unmixed characters and unmixed actions results in an apparent absence of moral substance. Figures of unalloyed virtue or vice may seem to invite a moral response, but their lack of human complexity makes ethical issues so straightforward as to become irrelevant to real experience. One can readily agree that readers will not be moved to reformative action. Perhaps, though, the criterion of inciting moral action is inappropriate. We do not ordinarily apply such a measure to a novel like *Robinson Crusoe,* despite its didactic interludes; why insist on it for Fielding's fiction? Arguably, the appropriate standard would be aesthetic rather than moral.

The aesthetics of the sentimental have been largely neglected. If Fielding's morality is relatively simple, her aesthetic, I would argue, is complex. The subject, it might be added, is also complex. I will touch on only a few aspects of how sentimental novelists create their aesthetic effects, beginning with a crucial formal choice. The most familiar of sentimental tropes, the so-called trope of inexpressibility, appears everywhere in sentimental fiction, abundantly in *David Simple* but equally often elsewhere. It is a formal device of considerable import. Over and over the narrator tells us that she cannot convey in words the feeling elicited by a given story or provoked by a given event. Sometimes she adds that only those who share David's natural goodness will understand what he felt. Here is one of many instances: "The Raptures *David* felt at that Moment . . . are not to be expressed; and can only be imagined by those People who are capable of the same Actions" (170). Henry Fielding uses the same stratagem; it survives, with ironic variations, even into Jane Austen's work ("What did she say? Just what she ought, of course. A lady always does.").

The overt or covert assertion that the proper reader—that is, the appropriate reader for a given text but also the well-trained reader—will understand without words by its insistence that communication depends on more than the verbal calls attention to an important dynamic of sentimental fiction. *David Simple* must operate on the reader's mind by means of language, but language should work less to utter than to suggest. The insistent pattern of reiteration—actions duplicating in their import previous actions, characters duplicating themselves in every word—evokes the possibility that pattern matters as much as substance. Such patterns as those the sentimentalist invents rarely occur outside the pages of fiction, but the sensitive reader will respond to them, as to other literary and artistic patterns, by feeling rather than action. The feeling may center in identification: the reader capable of experiencing David's "Raptures" will presumably feel some version of them, as David does, in response to the account by Camilla that he has just heard. A range of feelings is possible, though, and a wide range is solicited: horror, distaste, outrage, amusement, approval, and so on. The immediate emotional response matters, in terms of the sentimental project, more than any action it might generate. "Good" characters within sentimental fiction feel a great deal; good readers will enjoy—and the idea of enjoyment is crucial—comparable feeling. Such feeling provides aesthetic pleasure: the pleasure of recognizing, reacting to, and sharing in the harmony of human experience and the emotion that responds to it.

To be sure, sentimental novelists also appear to assume that right feeling guarantees right action. David, the model of appropriate emotional response, frequently feels sympathy: capacity to experience vicariously the pain of others. The reader enjoys aesthetic contemplation not only of suffering but of the sympathetic feeling and action that alleviate it. We imagine and ponder the situation of a wealthy protagonist entering a world of suffering, folly, and vice as both learner and actor. Inasmuch as we identify with David, we presumably ourselves experience vicariously the value of both sympathy and benevolence.

It seems not altogether implausible that contemplation of the sympathizing hero and of the causes for sympathy he encounters will make the reader more responsive to human need, hence by extension more active. No more than other novelists, though, do makers of sentimental fiction focus on action as their aim. They create fables of goodness and badness that may sharpen readers' responses to the good and bad behavior they directly encounter, but despite their insistent moral rhetoric they interest themselves more in emotion than in behavior. Emotion of various sorts, from the indignation that provokes satire to the tenderness of compassion to the exaltation of benevolent action, supplies an end in itself. The ethical justification for cultivating feeling includes its relevance to charitable or reformative action. The aesthetic justification is the claim of moral beauty in the capacity for as well as the exercise of emotion. Such beauty derives, again, from the harmony of stimulus and response.

This aesthetic principle is perhaps less alien to twenty-first-century readers than the system of notation through which it is instituted. The most puzzling aspect of eighteenth-century sentimental fiction two and a half centuries after its writing may be its curious withholding of elucidating or corroborative detail, to which I have already alluded, a withholding that accompanies massive accumulation of ostensibly heartrending episodes. A crucial aesthetic tenet of such fiction demands sparseness in the narration of emotion. Novelists refuse to tell us just what the seduced maiden feels or how it feels to be falsely accused of incest. Despite the density of narrative in *David Simple,* derived from multiplication of stories rather than thickness of detail, every individual account is strikingly bare. A character telling her own story will report what she felt at every juncture, but she will not attempt to dramatize her feeling. Both the immediate auditor and the reader must fill in the details. Even in David himself, the consistent focus of authorial attention, we find no psychological intricacy. The narrator may stress his intense feeling: "His Mind was in so much anxiety, it was impossible for him to spend one Thought on any thing but the Cause of his Grief" (19). But we do not learn his thoughts on the cause of his grief, or what shape that grief takes. Grieving, he goes to his uncle, who "was quite frighten'd at the sight of him; for the one Day's extreme Misery he had suffered, had altered him, as much as if he had been ill a Twelvemonth" (21). How, exactly, is he altered? What are the precise components of his misery? The reader must invent answers.

One may readily assume that the appropriate answers are stereotypical. If a novelist does not allot the seduced maiden individual responses to her plight, the reader can fill in on the basis of other novelistic accounts of other seduced maidens. David's grief over his brother's treachery, its nature unspecified, must resemble the reactions of the betrayed in previous fictions. But although the system of extreme understatement allows all feeling to be clichéd, it also leaves room for other possibilities. Engaged readers are at liberty to invent, to imagine, or to perceive afresh. They do not have total license: given the novelistic emphasis on harmony of response, readers may feel themselves guided toward what would in the period have been thought appropriate. We cannot plausibly speculate, for example, that David's suffering over his brother's betrayal derives from his need to consider Daniel his moral superior, since Fielding's novel supplies no evidence of such a need. On the other hand, we might fancy that he suffers because he does not wish to believe treachery a human possibility, or because he is embarrassed by his own gullibility, or because he feels ashamed for his family. His grief may partake of shame, embarrassment, or violated faith. Readers can always or intermittently refuse the implicit invitation mentally to elaborate rendered feeling, but opportunities abound, in this fiction, for their imaginative participation.

Henry Fielding, in his introduction to *David Simple,* praises his sister for her knowledge of the human heart. But Sarah Fielding does not use language to convey subtle emotional or psychological meaning. She assumes, instead, that the sympathetic reader, the reader with a David-like capacity for imaginative identification, will provide the subtleties out of personal experience. The withholding of language for elaboration matters to this literary undertaking as much as the outpouring of language to pile story upon story. The aesthetic effect depends on both. Presumably the establishment of David as richly "sympathetic" will encourage readers to seek in themselves capacities comparable to the hero's, and such encouragement might ultimately have an effect in the world. More immediately, the demand to fill in the blanks implicates the reader more fully with the text: an aesthetic goal.

Such a goal persists in the profusion of sentimental novels that followed Fielding's early efforts. Later novels perfected further formal devices to generate the desired effects: most important, the reliance on ostentatiously fragmentary narrative constructions. Mackenzie's *Man of Feeling,* for instance, multiplies narrators and ruthlessly truncates stories. The novel's initial narrator reports finding the manuscript of Harley's story, torn into fragments, being used as gun wadding by his shooting companion, a curate. The manuscript's author, the curate explains, was a silent man whom the villagers called "The Ghost." This Ghost's account of Harley, the Man of Feeling, although tattered, contains many stories told to Harley by various people he encounters. The stories, however, like the individual episodes in Harley's life, often fail to reach resolution, because of the flaws in the manuscript.

The putative tears in the wad of paper that the nameless first narrator appropriates refuse satisfaction to the reader in ways even more conspicuous than Fielding's. Thus Harley, setting out on a journey to London, encounters a beggar with his dog. The beggar's account of himself reveals him as something of a rascal, but Harley nonetheless gives him a shilling. At this point chapter 14 ends, to be followed immediately by chapter 19. We do not know the beggar's response to Harley's charity or Harley's reflections on the relation between rascality and human appeal. Later, Harley encounters a needy prostitute; he not only feeds, listens to, and bestows money on her, he helps reunite her with her father. The father tells his story; Harley gives him advice—and chapter 29 is forthwith succeeded by "A Fragment" concerning Harley's relation to the baronet from whom he seeks patronage. Despite our presumably greater immediate interest in Harley's relation to the prostitute and her father, we learn nothing more about that.

The refusal of narrative completion in a sense duplicates the refusal of psychological detail, as obvious in Mackenzie's fiction as in Fielding's, by likewise urging the reader's imaginative activity. The novel's notorious ending offers an especially egregious example. Harley returns from London and lapses into a vague illness. All along, we have been told, he has loved a neighbor's daughter, but he has never acknowledged his love. Now he has reason to think that she intends to marry someone else. She comes to visit him; he articulates, rather indirectly, his love; she indirectly suggests that she loves him too—and he drops dead. The faint promise of real psychological substance is definitively evaded.

This deliberate frustration of normal reader expectation reminds us that stories, after all, need not have beginnings, middles, and ends—a lesson also vivid in A Sentimental Journey and even more conspicuous in Tristram Shandy (see Chapter 9). The ending of A Man of Feeling logically concludes a sequence of comparable frustrations. In episodes like the encounter with the prostitute, Mackenzie builds narrative interest but denies narrative resolution. He maintains a precarious balance: on the one hand, he must offer enough story to keep the reader reading; on the other, he does not wish to risk the story's providing its own satisfaction. The novel's extraordinary compression depends on its rejection of normal narrative development as well as of ordinary rhetorical development. Thus, Harley meets a misanthrope who launches on a long and effective diatribe against urban corruption. This too, however, breaks off before it concludes. The novel consistently avoids completion—except, of course, in its ending, which provides the ultimate completion of death (a far more typical ending than marriage for sentimental novels, which often tease with the promise of romance only to deny its fulfillment). Harley's death at this particular moment, though, paradoxically registers as yet another denial, because it frustrates development of the potential narrative of romance.

In an obvious sense, Mackenzie's method of constructing a fiction contrasts with Sarah Fielding's. Fielding offers highly condensed stories, but they always resolve themselves, and they multiply until the reader may feel virtually inundated by narrative. The stories' duplications—forms of misery vary, but always misery persists and proliferates—enforces the message that human beings typically endure fates of suffering. Mackenzie's stories, far less numerous, often remain sketchy and usually remain incomplete. The reader experiences not narrative excess but narrative deficiency.

Yet the two forms of novelistic construction generate similar effects. Excess and deficiency convey the same message: one can tell the story again and again or hardly tell it at all, but the available possibilities remain accounts of injustice and resultant unhappiness. The ending doesn't matter, *The Man of Feeling* says; all endings have the same meaning. If the prostitute goes home with her father, the father may die, leaving her bereft; or he may lose his money, leaving her destitute; or she may be captivated by another unworthy man: such possibilities outweigh those of living happily ever after. If Harley dies, he escapes all the ambiguities of marriage—a state that, enduring as long as life itself, contains infinite possibilities of unhappiness. The many unrealized possibilities of truncated narratives brood over Mackenzie's fiction, inviting the reader to feel in response to what doesn't happen, as well as to what does.

What kind of feeling is available to the imagined reader? Above all, frustration at the refusal of narrative satisfaction. David and Harley experience the world as a place of bafflement, its only compensations those of intimacy. Readers, invited into narrative intimacy, endure uncomfortable analogues for the characters' emotional predicament. The novels by their structure prevent the reader's emotional fulfillment. The tales of suffering they offer do not meet normal expectations. As the books reject narrative gratification, they tacitly reproach the reader's desire for endings that would supply easy pleasures.

The tone of the narrative, the tone of Harley's experience, also exerts its pressure on the reader. Like that of *David Simple,* it presents itself most obviously as the emotional atmosphere that eighteenth-century thinkers would label "melancholy." Harley feels melancholy because of what he

can't do (like many late-century fictional male protagonists, he is often passive) and because he knows himself to have failed to meet other people's
expectations, as well as because of what he sees and hears in his travels.
He witnesses and endures essentially the same world as David.

To call the dominant emotion of these novels melancholy may raise
further questions about the books' aesthetic effect. Like the feeling we
know as depression, melancholy colors the world all miasmal gray. If,
as I have argued, sentimental fiction pursues an aesthetic of feeling, it is
not readily apparent why inducing such dark feeling should have either
aesthetic or moral value. In fact, though, Fielding and Mackenzie, like
other writers of sentimental fiction, complicate the issue by complicat-
ing the tone, offering something more than melancholy and tentatively
promising possibilities beyond frustration.

Closer to our own time, Samuel Beckett made a distinguished career
from his renditions of depression. His unrelieved narratives do not induce
comparable feeling in the reader because his exuberant linguistic power
declares possibility even while his characters deny it. Fielding and Mackenzie do not exert the same kind of linguistic force, but at least faintly
they demonstrate an exuberance of defiance. David Simple defies a society
of alienated, self-seeking individuals by creating his own mini-society, his
happy community of four. In *Volume the Last,* when natural forces and
the envy and selfishness of others assail that community, David and his
friends remain strong and assured, even while grieving, confident that
they have made the best choices they can and that they will find sanction
in the afterlife if not in their present existence. Harley lacks comparable
assurance, although he never suffers to a degree approaching David's—or,
for that matter, to a degree approaching the old soldier's.

That soldier, who has endured the oppression of a country squire and
his steward and the injustice of the rich, who entered the army in order
to take the place of an only son who had been impressed by a gang of
ruffians, and who has been publicly whipped because of his benevolence
to a poor Indian—that soldier is less prone to weeping than Harley. He
manifests his grief at the revelation that his son has died, but he proceeds
manfully forward, as he has done all his life. The manipulative beggar who
gets a shilling from Harley although he has revealed his rascality (he tells
false fortunes that make people happy to gain a livelihood) remains cheerful despite his neediness. "What signifies sadness, sir?" he asks Harley,

"a man grows lean on't" (12). Even the prostitute, although she collapses from hunger and exhibits great emotion as she tells her story and when she encounters her father, has found expedients for survival. Harley's dark tone, in other words, does not supply the novel's only emotional note. It constitutes an appropriate response to a radically corrupt society, but not the only possible response.

These sentimental fictions operate partly by suggesting alternative emotional reactions. Sometimes the alternatives emerge, as in *A Man of Feeling*, through the varied modes of response exemplified by minor characters. Sometimes, as in *David Simple* and *Memoirs of Miss Sidney Bidulph*, they constitute commonsense possibilities that may contrast with the unfailingly cheerful acceptance of suffering protagonists. At one extreme we find faith and persistence; at the other, melancholy and frustration. By demanding contemplation of as well as participation in feeling, these novels invite readers to speculate about the utility of diverse emotional reactions. Although they limit affective possibilities by the conventions under which they operate—one could not, for instance, seriously expect Harley to erupt in rage at his aunt's pressure to conciliate the rich—they leave room for awareness that possibilities exist.

The *utility* of reactions, of course, hardly matters here. The aesthetic of feeling that controls these novels thrives in conjunction with ethical demands implying rejection of practical considerations. Until late in the eighteenth century the cult or culture of sensibility, which grounds the novel of sentiment, flourished in England, gathering strength particularly in the century's second half. Although some of its manifestations seem in retrospect foolish, it had respectable philosophical antecedents, and it implied principles of action as well as of contemplation. A biblical text much pondered in the period enjoins believers to love their neighbors as themselves. Both parts of this injunction provoked speculation. How, exactly, and why are we to love ourselves? And what can cause us to love our neighbors to a comparable degree, or in a comparable way? Most thinkers concluded that self-love is a fundamental principle of human nature—indeed, the basic force for survival. But it can be corrupted; it is possible to love oneself too much, or in the wrong ways.

A crucial test of corruption might be the degree to which self-love interfered with love of others. The ideal human condition, the condition to which one should aspire, would involve an appropriate balance between love of self and love of one's neighbor. If such balance is achievable, it may depend on the fact that other-love involves as fundamental a human impulse as self-love. So, at least, some philosophers maintained. Anthony Ashley Cooper, third earl of Shaftesbury, argued early in the century that the desire for community was fundamental to human nature. We have, he claimed—and thinkers as important as David Hume and Adam Smith followed him in this respect—a "natural" sense of sympathy with others. Adam Smith developed the argument most fully, in his *Theory of Moral Sentiments* (1759). He defined the nature of sympathy: a kind of identification with the other that comes from imagining oneself in another's situation. Thus we sympathize with the man on the scaffold because we recognize how we ourselves would feel in the same predicament. And we sympathize with those in less extreme circumstances by virtue of the same capacity.

It is apparent, though, that human beings have varying degrees of sensitivity to the feelings or the condition of others. A high level of sensitivity characterizes those said to possess "sensibility," roughly definable as emotional responsiveness. David Simple, reacting to the pain of Cynthia's history or to the situation of a woman with an uncaring husband; Harley, responding to the mistreated old soldier—both reveal their sensibility in these and many other episodes. In *The History of Emily Montague*, Frances Brooke delineates her protagonist's emotional dilemma by poising her between a fiancé with little sensibility and a male friend rich in it. Predictably, the heroine rejects the fiancé in favor of the more sensitive male. Sensibility, in other words, constituted a moral virtue (and a source of attraction) in men as well as women. Such philosophers as Hume argued for feeling, rather than reason, as the foundation of all morality; sensibility thus provided a plausible starting point for right action.

In life as well as literature, some sought to display their sensibility by weeping and fainting and blushing and reacting extravagantly to scenes of poverty or illness. Sensibility was understood as a capacity intimately connected with the physical nature of nerves. Essential to its existence was its operation on the body as well as the mind. Thus a propensity to blush and weep might be taken as evidence that the weepers, full of sensibility, loved their neighbors as themselves.

The backlash against sensibility at the century's end partly reflected the conviction that displays of feeling could and often did substitute both for genuine feeling and for action. Mary Wollstonecraft, whose novels rely heavily on the rhetoric of sensibility, argued strenuously (particularly in *A Vindication of the Rights of Women*) against what she apparently believed to be a typical female commitment to sensibility as a way of life. Such a commitment, she maintained, in effect reifies weakness as the innate possession of women. It encourages, for instance, the social view that women do not deserve serious education and the assumption that men reason, women feel. The man of feeling, however, also attracted Wollstonecraft's scorn. Yet her novelistic practice suggests that the language and plot of sensibility may prove indispensable to a narrative undertaking even if one disapproves of the habit of sensibility. In *The Wrongs of Woman, or Maria* (1798), for instance, her final, incomplete novel, Wollstonecraft used the pathetic story of Jemima, a servant at the asylum where Maria, the heroine, is confined, to indict a discriminatory, unjust set of social arrangements. Maria's unfinished story, which involves her exploitation by one man and her sentimental susceptibility to his manifestly unworthy successor, and which reveals the impossibility of a woman's achieving justice through the law, exposes the evils of a system that bestows virtually unlimited privilege on men while depriving women of fundamental rights.

In the novels we have been considering, sensibility registers genuine emotion, not social display. Inasmuch as it stimulates not only compassion but indignation, it conveys and elicits social criticism. Sensibility's indignant response to perceived injustice accounts for what I have called the satiric element in sentimental fiction and links the stories of individual travail and feeling to perceptions of society's inadequacies. In *David Simple, The Man of Feeling,* and *The Wrongs of Woman,* such perception focuses on obvious targets: the excessive privilege of the wealthy, the mistreatment of common soldiers, the exploitation of women. But the social criticism of sentimental fiction might extend to less well-canvassed topics as well. *The History of Lady Julia Mandeville,* which conforms to the conventions of the sentimental as well as the epistolary novel, offers one example: its indictment of patriarchy, although never overt, inheres in its plot. The woman novelist pursues a daring enterprise in declaring the wrongs potential in the social license accorded to fathers, who, however well-meaning, the book suggests, can cause untold destruction.

Yet more surprising is the implicit criticism of mothers offered by one of the century's most provocative sentimental novels, Frances Sheridan's

Memoirs of Miss Sidney Bidulph (1761). "I know not, Madam," Dr. Johnson remarked to the author, "that you have a right, upon moral principles, to make your readers suffer so much" (Boswell, 276). It is impossible to calculate the exact degree of irony in this comment, or the irony's precise target, but the observation suggests, at any rate, that the moral and the aesthetic might diverge; the aesthetic, it also suggests, depends on the reader's suffering, as well as the characters'.

Sidney suffers extravagantly. A friend of her brother's, Orlando Faulkland, woos her, and she reciprocates his love. A carelessly read letter, however, convinces Sidney's mother that Faulkland is unworthy since he has allegedly seduced and impregnated a young woman whom, according to Mrs. Bidulph, he is morally obligated to marry. At her mother's behest, Sidney marries instead a Mr. Arnold, whom, she claims, she learns to love. He, however, commits adultery with Mrs. Gerrarde, who subsequently tricks him into banishing his wife. Sidney falls into poverty; Faulkland in effect rescues her by means of an elaborate plot that exposes Mrs. Gerrarde's machinations. Reunited with her husband, Sidney lives happily with him and their two children until Mr. Arnold unexpectedly dies. Then she suffers her children's serious illness and her own, as well as the rigors of extreme poverty. Faulkland proposes again, but she insists that he marry Miss Burchell, the young woman he supposedly seduced. He ultimately does so; Sidney is saved by the fortuitous arrival of a rich uncle. Eventually, in tragic circumstances, Sidney and Faulkland actually marry, but Faulkland shortly afterwards commits suicide, having discovered that his previous wife is still alive.

This summary of a complex narrative sequence in fact barely hints at the intricacies of the plot. Not only is the Sidney-plot more complicated than the summary indicates; the novel also, like other sentimental novels, contains interspersed stories of other people's careers. Like other sentimental novels, too, *Memoirs of Miss Sidney Bidulph* is radically fragmentary, ending literally in mid-sentence, refusing the satisfaction of completion. (It is, however, coherent in construction—indeed, rather tightly plotted—up to its truncated ending.)

The first-person narration of Sidney's misfortunes takes the form not of "memoir" in our current sense of the word but of a journal kept for the benefit of and intermittently mailed to an absent female friend. It is, in other words—to borrow Richardsonian phraseology—writing to the moment, not an account composed in distant retrospect. On occasion, when Sidney's sufferings are especially acute (when her husband dies, when she herself undergoes serious illness), Patty Main, Sidney's devoted servant/friend, writes the journal. The letters of others are occasionally interspersed.

Like the two "letters" that compose *Fanny Hill,* this journal has little formal plausibility, with its allegedly verbatim accounts of many extended oral utterances. It simply provides a pretext and a means for the heroine to tell her own story. Sidney is more reflective than Fanny; her account of herself entails psychological complexity. Not only the protagonist but her mother; the villainous Mrs. Gerrarde; and the vicious "female rake," Miss Burchell, have more than one dimension. The book makes us witness the mother's good intentions and her rather pathetic claims of authority as well as her damaging assumptions. The evil women mingle good with their evil. The most important man in the narrative, Sidney's persistent lover, Faulkland, also provides a subject for extended analysis. Sidney's husband, Mr. Arnold; her brother; and her rich uncle, Mr. Warner, receive less penetrating characterizations, but they too emerge vividly as players in the complicated drama. In its subtlety and depth of characterization, its tonal range, its intricacy of plot, and its rather astonishing message, *Memoirs of Miss Sidney Bidulph* is an accomplished and readable novel.

As my account of the characters will have suggested, Sheridan employs a less spare rhetoric than that used by other sentimental writers. In many respects, she fills in the story she tells. Like other novels of the period, this one lacks physical detail, but it contains abundant social, psychological, and moral reflection. It comes closer than the sentimental fictions previously discussed to filling modern expectations for a novel. It too, though, relies on the unstated for much of its meaning, and it utilizes at will devices familiar from less ambitious sentimental novels.

Given actualities of eighteenth-century British life, a novel dealing with the contemporary scene and focused on a woman would, as we have seen already, have to differ in conspicuous ways from one with a man at its center. Neither David Simple nor Harley fills an especially "masculine" role in the novel he inhabits, but Fielding and Mackenzie can plausibly send their protagonists wandering through the world, to observe and to discover the way things are. The naïf onlooker who feels wide-eyed astonishment at the workings of society can be accorded freedom to experience those workings in various contexts. A woman, however, cannot normally wander. (Frances Burney, at the end of the century, devised a fairly persuasive pretext for allowing a heroine to travel alone through England, but she spends a great deal of space in that massive novel, *The Wanderer,* asserting and reasserting her protagonist's respectability.) If the woman is married, she acts according to the will of her husband; if unmarried, she stays home. Sidney Bidulph, whose father is dead, adheres closely to her mother until she marries a man of her mother's choosing. Although she has had little experience outside the home, she is not naive in the way of David and Harley. Her brother thinks her a fool, though, and the novel brings us to see that Sidney has in fact behaved with considerable folly in her failure to recognize and attend to her own interest. Yet she also functions intelligently and courageously, confronting unexpected occurrences with common sense and aplomb. She makes a complicated heroine.

Although Sidney's situation and the story that develops around her both differ sharply from their equivalents in other sentimental novels, Sheridan manipulates certain conventional devices to good effect. She demonstrates unexpected flexibility in employing fairly hackneyed topoi, showing that old tactics can serve new purposes. Like other writers of sentimental fiction, she embeds in her larger narrative stories that elicit the sympathies of "good" characters as well as, presumably, those of the reader. In *Memoirs of Miss Sidney Bidulph,* some of those stories have surprising import.

Interspersed through the novel are three especially important mini-narratives, reporting the experience of Mrs. Vere (daughter of Lady Grimston, a friend of Sidney's mother); telling of an episode in the life of Patty Main's brother; and relating the story of Miss Price, a destitute young woman with an imprisoned father whom Sidney is able to help. Two out of these three stories have shapes familiar in eighteenth-century fiction. Mrs. Vere, widowed at the time when Sidney encounters her, has married against her mother's will. Enraged by her own weak husband's connivance in the marriage, Lady Grimston manages to deprive her daughter of her rightful share of the paternal inheritance. Mrs. Vere bears a stillborn child and comes close to death from illness. Her mother, moved by the daughter's arrangement to free her from a lawsuit, although Mrs. Vere herself suffers financially from the transaction, nominally forgives her but remains cold and disapproving many years after the fact.

The girl who marries without a parent's consent figures frequently in the period's fictions. The inevitable suffering of such a girl provides a sentimental staple. Ordinarily, the reader is invited to weep at the suffering, to regret the disobedience, but to give emotional assent to the power of romantic love. The relevant parent in these stories, however, is customarily a father. Lady Grimston, a strong mother, does nothing illegal, but her tyrannical rule of her family causes suffering as great as that a father might produce. Sidney reports that her own brother has suggested a resemblance between their mother and Lady Grimston. Although she rejects the analogy, the embedded story supports it: both women assume their right to control a daughter's destiny; both indirectly precipitate disaster. The tale underlines the criticism of mothers implicit in the larger narrative. More important, it furthers the subversive message that existing social assumptions, which grant parents hegemony over daughters, are both irrational and dangerous.

The story of Miss Price, also in a familiar mode, centers on the experience of a poor country clergyman's family. The widowed clergyman, Mr. Price, tutors a rich young man. After the young man comes into his estate, he invites his erstwhile tutor, along with that tutor's daughter, to come to London for a visit. When they accept the invitation, their host tries to seduce or actually to rape the young woman. She escapes, but the angry young rake thereupon has her father thrown into prison for debt. Although she attempts to support herself and him, she has little success. She must see her father lapsing into illness and weakness and know that her acceptance of unwanted sexual overtures would liberate him. In this dilemma, she is rescued by Sidney, who, now prosperous because of her uncle's generosity, can buy Mr. Price out of prison and arrange an appropriate marriage for the girl.

The story clearly functions in the larger narrative to demonstrate Sidney's possession of the requisite moral equipment for a sentimental heroine: sympathy and willingness to express it in action—especially important, of course, when she comes into money. It also provides a typical frisson, offering the thrill of sexual material without any real salaciousness. As in *Pamela,* nothing terrible actually happens, but the narrative flirts with terrible possibilities. Beyond these obvious effects, though, this story, like the one about Mrs. Vere, implicitly indicts the established social order. The would-be violator of the young woman also violates the sacred role of the clergy and the obligation of student to teacher. His willingness and ability to overturn established hierarchies emphasize the precariousness of the social order as protection for its members. Although established arrangements assign authority to the clergy and to the teacher, they provide no corresponding power. Money alone is power: the rich wastrel can do what he pleases. Only when Sidney summons the authority of her own money (and she has to work by means of her uncle) can she effect any semblance of justice.

The temptation to read this story, the last in the sequence of narrative interludes, as critical of society may be intensified by the nature of the second interpolated story, which bears little resemblance to any other tale of its kind that I have seen, although it conforms in broad outline to patterns of sentimental fiction. The story comes by way of Patty Main, who reports an episode in her brother's life. Educated as a surgeon, young Main loves a young woman who reciprocates his feeling, but whose family objects to him on social and financial grounds. The young woman falls ill and is diagnosed with breast cancer. Her doctors recommend mastectomy, an operation at this time performed without anesthesia and with a high incidence of mortality. The victim assents to the surgery but asks to postpone it briefly and requests that Main be present for the event. In his presence, she announces to her family that she is now twenty-one, therefore in possession of her own money, and that she has made a will leaving everything to her lover. Overwhelmed with tears at this evidence of her generosity, the young man nonetheless remains able to inspect the breast bared for surgery. Over the protests of the other doctors, he announces that he thinks their diagnosis wrong and that he can cure the ailment without use of the knife. The more famous doctors leave indignantly; Main pursues his treatment; in a few weeks the girl is cured, then allowed to marry the man who has saved her life.

The quintessentially female ailment calls attention to this story as a fable about the female situation. Yet again, authority is the issue. The young woman's brother, the surviving male relative with authority over her, misuses his authority as parents so often do, by valuing money above love. The male doctors, also symbols of authority, pursue a destructive course in the service of their own prestige. Both the knowledge that would have been commonly held in the period of the novel's writing and the language of the text itself strongly suggest that the misguided operation would have resulted in death. The wisdom of love triumphs over that of authority.

Along the way, obviously, readers can weep over the pathos of the girl's situation or admire her courage and poise or deplore the obstacles placed in the way of true love—all familiar sentimental responses. But it is apparent that Sheridan is using sentimental vignettes for purposes beyond that of arousing feeling.

This is not to say that she abandons the sentimental project in designing the novel. The action is clearly intended to elicit sympathy, and the key device of reliance on the unspoken operates frequently. And despite the psychological richness of the characterization and the lingering detail of the narrated events, the novel's aesthetic effect depends heavily on a system for suggesting what is never stated.

The function of the unspoken in *Memoirs of Miss Sidney Bidulph* differs from its use in other novels I have discussed. Partly because of the first-person narrator and the fiction that she writes to a single, intimate reader, the writer cannot use the tactic of claiming that there's no need to express a feeling, since only those of comparable sensibility will understand. Instead, the omnipresence of the unspoken becomes part of the plot, not as a trope of inexpressibility but as an explanatory element for often disastrous developments. Sometimes characters refrain from speaking important facts as part of a pattern of deception. Thus both Mrs. Gerrarde and her niece, Miss Burchell, lead hidden lives of sexual indulgence, about which they never speak. Their speech conforms entirely to social convention; their desires do not. The hidden life centers on unacceptable feeling; the surface conformity only pretends its socially acceptable counterpart.

The crucial importance of this dichotomy becomes apparent when one realizes how consistently, in this novel, surfaces and depths are at odds. In a sequence commenting on this issue, Faulkland takes steps to solve the problems created by the adultery of Mr. Arnold with Mrs. Gerrarde. As he reports in a richly comic pair of long letters (duly transcribed by Sidney for the benefit of her friend), he absconds to France with Mrs. Gerrarde, placating her by constant allusion to her fine feelings. He professes to consider her a woman of sentiment. By insisting on this characterization, he lures her into performing the sentiments attributed to her. They have nothing to do with her genuine feelings, but Faulkland knows he can count on the habit of performance. By means of it, he tricks Mrs.

Gerrarde into writing a letter to Arnold that reveals the baselessness of her slanderous allegations about Sidney.

This plot twist is a *jeu d'esprit,* bringing about vital events, but holding a notable place in the action partly by virtue of its exuberant narration, which effects a salutary shift of tone. It also connects sensibility to hypocrisy, in the person of Mrs. Gerrarde, warning the reader not to take for granted the authenticity of claimed feeling. And it provides an emphatic example of the discrepancy between surface and depths.

Depths are the realm of genuine feeling—and feeling, the novel insists, need not have positive value. *Sidney Bidulph* abounds in examples of unacceptable emotion, usually more or less concealed, sometimes almost impenetrably concealed. Mrs. Gerrarde and Miss Burchell provide key instances, but there is also Mr. Arnold, who, beneath a surface of extravagant decorum (before their marriage, he indicates his disapproval of Sidney's reading Horace in Latin and his preference that she occupy herself in completing a needlework rose) conceals his own lustfulness. Sidney's brother, Sir George, and his wife, Lady Sarah, make some effort to hide their greed and pride beneath surface propriety. The most complex concealer of feelings, though, is Sidney herself, who never speaks her penetrating judgment of her mother (as impulsive, dangerously unworldly, literal-minded, and narrow), her love for Faulkland, or her immediate suspicion of Miss Burchell.

Judgment is not the same as feeling, but the reader may strongly suspect that Sidney's judgments of her mother, which she articulates in her journal although never in her speaking voice, accompany feelings that she will not articulate even in the relative privacy of the written word. Pondering this matter, we may conclude that Sidney doesn't even know that she has unacceptable feelings toward her mother. Certainly her protestations to Cecilia indicate strongly that she doesn't know her true feelings toward Faulkland. Her uncle quickly concludes that she loves Faulkland despite her repeated refusals of his overtures, but she does not become fully aware of her love until far too late. Erotic love for Faulkland, in her mind, would be as unacceptable as negative feelings about her mother; therefore, she must not, cannot, feel it.

Sidney could hardly be called a hypocrite. Her concealment of feeling stems not from a desire to pretend, but from the inability to acknowledge in herself emotions of which she would not approve. Her unwillingness

to approve distaste for her mother or love for Faulkland reflects her in-
ternalization of her society's rules for women, those rules she impeccably observes, the rules that lead her to disaster. Like other characters
in Sheridan's novel, she leaves unspoken the most important things she
has to say. In conceiving her characters thus, Sheridan both exploits and
challenges a commonplace convention of sentimentality. Not all feeling is
positive feeling, she reminds us, and not all verbal withholding enforces
community. The assumptions on which much sentimental fiction rests
become highly tentative in this novel.

Nonetheless, *Memoirs of Miss Sidney Bidulph* is unquestionably a piece
of sentimental fiction, as Dr. Johnson's comment on it suggests. Almost
from start to finish, it is a tear jerker. It invites readers both to identify with
the suffering character, Sidney herself, and to identify with the impulse to
benevolence, conspicuous especially in Faulkland, but also in Sidney, her
mother, and assorted friends. And it offers a putative moral that reinforces
the common association between sentimentality and piety.

That moral calls attention to the loudest questions raised by this disturbing book. The preliminary framework articulates the moral clearly.
In it, a young man visits his friend's elderly mother, in company with
the friend. The three of them weep at hearing the play *Douglas* (a famous
contemporary tragedy by John Home, who was sometimes referred to
as "the Scottish Shakespeare") read aloud. Their reaction precipitates a
discussion of poetic justice, during which the old lady asserts strongly
her view that all things of this earth are changeable, that one should not
become attached to anything here below, and that what seems injustice on
earth is part of God's unknowable plan. "We may wish to see nature copied
from her most pleasing works," she observes; "but a martyr expiring in
tortures is as just, though not as agreeable, a representation of her, as a
hero rewarded with the brightest honours" (7). She offers the manuscript
of Sidney's journal (it turns out that she is the Cecilia to whom it is addressed) as evidence that the good may suffer in this world.

If the moral of *Sidney Bidulph* instructs its readers to believe in God's
mysterious ways and not to cavil against apparent injustice, such a doctrine gives tacit permission to the reader to indulge in vicarious suffering
without worrying about any need for change in the order of things. The
novel ends with an apostrophe: "Gracious Heaven! how inscrutable are thy
ways! Her affluent fortune . . . now proved the source of new and dread-

ful calamities to her, which . . . cut off from her even the last resource of hope in this life, and rendered the close of her history still more . . ." (467). A line of ellipsis marks concludes the account, giving way to the editor's apology for being unable to recover more of the manuscript. He refers to the text he has published as "this fragment," and it is exactly that: a prolonged fragment, which could be infinitely continued by the multiplication of miseries that would render the close of Sidney's history still more . . . more harrowing, or more titillating, or simply more of the same. The invocation of "Gracious Heaven!" of course intends to remind the reader once again that the suffering is all acceptable because it's part of God's plan.

Yet this final reference to heaven has an unsettling effect because by this time, 467 pages into the book, we have abundant reason to believe that Sidney's nature bears more immediate responsibility for her misfortunes than does God. Her brother suggests, unkindly but accurately, that she has brought her troubles on herself. She has accepted her mother's original misreading of Faulkland's letter, although she knows that her mother is impulsive, moralistic, careless, and unduly influenced by her own past. She agrees to marry Arnold although she does not feel drawn to him. She refrains from telling her husband that she knows of his adultery. She neither expresses nor acts upon her misgivings about Miss Burchell, and on the basis of her excessive scruples she refuses Faulkland's new proposal after her husband's death. Each of these acts or refusals to act has disastrous consequences. Each derives from her determination to be A Good Girl: to impress her mother and to adhere to the doctrine of the conduct books expected to guide the behavior of an eighteenth-century woman. She objects explicitly to being treated like a baby, as Lady Grimston and her mother plan her marriage, but she will not take full responsibility for her own thought and action.

The criticism of established authority suggested in the interpolated tales thus becomes more complicated in the main plot. One can blame "authority" for Sidney's mishaps: authority in the form of her mother and in the form of accepted doctrine for female behavior. Yet her total acceptance of authority presents a deeper problem. The novel does not attach blame to her, given the pressures that urge any young woman toward compliance. By demonstrating her intelligence and clarity of mind, though, it suggests her unused capacity to see through the rules that bind her, to follow her own choices to less dreadful conclusions than those she entails by internalizing other people's decisions. She does not see herself as having real choices, but the novel suggests that alternatives always exist, unavailable to someone educated to believe in the necessity of female docility.

Dr. Johnson's comment hints that the suffering generated by *Sidney Bidulph* constitutes a kind of pleasure; his explicit doubt concerns the morality of indulging in it. He may have in mind the moral passivity attending this sort of indulgence—moral passivity in the reader that somewhat resembles Sidney's own. This novel's aesthetic design, far tighter than that of most sentimental fiction, depends on the fateful series of causes and effects composing Sidney's successive decisions. In *The Man of Feeling*, one episode follows another chronologically, by no principle of causality. Sidney's refusal of Faulkland, in contrast, implies her acceptance of Mr. Arnold, her mother's choice. Her effort to make a good wife to Arnold, in the most orthodox eighteenth-century mode, means that she must conceal her knowledge of his adultery. And so on: each conventionally virtuous decision brings unforeseen but retrospectively inevitable negative consequences. Those consequences compose the novel, creating the design that makes the reader, in Dr. Johnson's terms, suffer so much. The aesthetic principle of seeking to generate feeling remains the same as in other sentimental fiction, but Sheridan associates with it the goal of provoking thought as well as feeling. Sidney suffers largely because she refuses to operate on the basis of her own judgment. The reader too has the possibility of judging, of looking beneath the surface, of thinking as well as feeling. The novel raises large questions and opens new possibilities for sentimental fiction—possibilities not fully pursued in the eighteenth century.

Sheridan had introduced into the middle of her dismal series of events a long comic sequence, Faulkland's epistolary account of his triumphant tricking of Mrs. Gerrarde, but that sequence stands alone. Oliver Goldsmith, in *The Vicar of Wakefield* (1766—three years before *The Man of Feeling*) made comedy an intimate component of melancholy, inviting the reader to enjoy the familiar aesthetic of sentiment, but also gently mocking his own persona and allowing questions about the fine sentiments that the Vicar as first-person narrator proclaims. Those sentiments are irreproachable. In every crisis, Primrose adjures his family to count their blessings.

He remains unfailingly pious and refuses to be discouraged; whatever happens, he understands, must be God's will. A Christian hero, he uses his time in debtors' prison, despite being beset by calamities, to preach to his fellow prisoners. Yet so striking is his inability or refusal to grasp the actualities of his family's dynamics that his pious sentiments sometimes seem a mode of avoidance rather than acceptance and he becomes for the reader at least briefly a figure of fun. The technique foretells Dickens. It may also foretell, in the very period of the sentimental novel's triumph, the end of sentimentality as a dominant narrative mode. The mixture of satire and sentiment so common in eighteenth-century fiction is mutually reinforcing, since attacks on the status quo and sympathy for those who suffer from the existing state of things readily coexist. Comedy, in contrast, always risks undercutting sentiment: any balance struck must remain precarious.

The Vicar of Wakefield traffics in pious sentimentality, raising the stakes for its readers by claiming biblical authority for the doctrine it upholds. Parson Primrose believes that God watches over his children, and Providence indeed takes good care of him—at least in the long run. First, however, he must undergo a horrific series of disasters. From prosperity he descends into extreme poverty. His oldest son leaves to seek his fortune, is not heard from for three years, and reappears in prison, apparently about to be hanged for murder. His older daughter, seduced and betrayed, pines away after her rescue by her father and is said to have died. The modest house the family now inhabits burns to the ground, destroying their remaining possessions and severely injuring the Vicar, who is nonetheless taken off to prison. Finally, though, the younger Primrose daughter marries a rich and powerful baronet; the older daughter turns out really to have been married all along (to a scoundrel, but never mind); the son is not hanged; the daughter is not dead; the Vicar gets out of prison; his original prosperity miraculously reappears. All these events, in fact, seem more or less miraculous, but such are the operations of Providence.

The difference between Goldsmith's and Henry Fielding's invocations of Providence is instructive. Providence presides over Tom Jones as well as The Vicar of Wakefield. When Tom finds himself in prison, charged with murder, and then learns that he has committed incest with his mother, his situation, equivalent to Primrose's at its most desperate, entails the extra pain of knowing that he is responsible for his own misery. But a convenient witness reveals that he is not guilty of murder, and he has not actually committed incest, either. The happy ending of *Tom Jones* comes about with the same insouciance that marks the resolution of *The Vicar of Wakefield.*

The experiences of reading the two novels, however, feel nothing alike. Fielding's novel has its sentimental moments, but it is not, like Goldsmith's, a sentimental novel. It does not make suffering its dominant subject, nor does it characteristically indulge in elaborate accounts of distress. The assumptions and mood that dominate *David Simple* govern individual sentimental vignettes in *Tom Jones,* like the account of Mr. Anderson, the needy would-be highwayman Tom helps, and his afflicted family, but the narrator's jaunty tone largely prevents even a temporary belief that Tom's stretches of misfortune will harm him or will last long.

Providence produces the people and events that bring about a happy ending for Tom, but "Providence" often seems another name for the narrator, who, as he frequently reminds us, arranges the novel's happenings and constructs its characters—always, to be sure, with due attention to "human nature." The design of the novel, with the aesthetic satisfactions it provides, thus corresponds to the design of the universe. In Goldsmith's work no such correspondence exists. The first-person narrator, who is also the victim and the beneficiary of Providence, cannot be privy to heaven's workings, and the novel's design does not match the plan that governs the fates of its characters. Primrose, as narrator, writes in retrospect but offers no hints along the way that everything will come out all right. Although we are apparently intended to believe that the eventual good fortune of the Primrose family rewards their virtue, the happy resolution depends on a rapid series of implausible coincidences. The Vicar points out, accurately, that life in fact abounds in coincidences ("To what a fortuitous concurrence do we not owe every pleasure and convenience of our lives"; 188), but his observation only emphasizes the unlikelihood of the multiplying happy events that resolve *The Vicar of Wakefield.* The novel's sentimentality reveals itself both in the emphasis on misfortune and suffering and in the ease with which both are wished away.

Other forms of sentimentality also make their appearance. Goldsmith revels in happy family vignettes, everyone rejoicing together over simple rural pleasures. His villains reform easily: the trickster who bilks both the Vicar and his son comes to understand that the virtuous prosper, whereas he, as a deceiver, repeatedly proves his cleverness but never makes any money (an observation that hardly corresponds to most readers' knowledge of the world). This con man becomes the agent of salvation for the unhappy family. Even Thornhill, the seducer of country maidens, shows signs of amendment at the end. He is learning to play the French horn, and Olivia, whom he has inadvertently married, anticipates his reformation and will presumably live with him when it is achieved, the villainy of his attempts on her conveniently forgotten. The hardened criminals in the prison yield quite readily to the Vicar's preaching, with only a few holdouts. In other words, the novel depicts an unrealistically benign universe.

Although the Vicar's sermons insist that the miserable will find their reward in heaven, Goldsmith constructs his plot so that the deserving all receive rewards on earth: one version of sentimentality. (Another version, we may remember, illustrates the sermon's doctrine: David Simple and Harley suffer here below, and the reader of their stories presumably enjoys both weeping over them and knowing that the good will find recompense hereafter.)

The comic thrust of Goldsmith's novel, however, qualifies its sentimentality. The Vicar, like David and Harley and even Sidney Bidulph, is something of a fool, his folly registered by his blindness to what lies directly before his eyes. The gross of worthless green spectacles that Moses, the Vicar's son, is conned into accepting as recompense for the family cow provides an appropriate emblem for Primrose's consistent failures of perception. His fondness for self-quotation reflects his belief in his own percipience; but he, like Moses, is easily tricked, receiving no compensation at all for the horse he has gone to the fair to sell. He cannot see that the fine London ladies Thornhill brings to visit are actually whores, even though Sir William (in disguise) provides frequent ejaculations of "Fudge" to call attention to the nonsense they speak. The Vicar condescends to his wife and daughters and fails to understand the clues Olivia offers to her imminent sexual danger. He misinterprets Burchell, the disguised Sir William, and blames where he should feel gratitude.

In each of these incidents, the reader presumably sees more than the narrator and consequently feels superior to the Vicar in his blindness. The novel's comedy derives largely from this disjunction. In other sentimental novels, the protagonist's role as fool allows him (or occasionally her) to penetrate the structure of false appearances that provides the ground for much social functioning. Primrose's "foolishness," which, like that of the other sentimental heroes, derives from his unawareness of certain kinds of customary social behavior, leads him not to penetration but to acute astigmatism. We laugh at Primrose (and Moses, his surrogate). The naïveté of the hero as fool does not generate satiric awareness, only immediate comedy.

Yet Primrose also functions more forcefully as hero than do other sentimental protagonists. Feeling the responsibility inherent in his authority as paterfamilias and as pastor, he does not hesitate to act vigorously for his family's or his congregation's welfare. His generosity toward his "fallen" daughter attests to his practice of what he preaches; his sermons in prison, despite his own desperate immediate situation, demonstrate Christian heroism. If his self-satisfaction, approaching smugness at times, makes him readily vulnerable to mockery and to suspicion of his motives, none of his flaws allows one to dismiss the courage and dedication he demonstrates. His role in the novel resembles that of Parson Adams in Fielding's *Joseph Andrews*—another clergyman who often proves ridiculous, but whose faith and magnanimity redeem him from criticism.

Because the reader must acknowledge the Vicar's genuine goodness, his multiplying afflictions arouse sympathy, and the novel invites a sentimental response: at least metaphorical weeping over the sorrows of the protagonist and his family; relief and delight at the cavalier happy ending. Unlike *Sidney Bidulph, The Vicar of Wakefield* conveys no criticism of existing social arrangements. It recognizes the existence of corrupt persons but treats corruption as an individual matter. Sidney's goodness, female goodness, consists in compliance. Goldsmith's fable of goodness represents its protagonist as God's active agent—fallible, even ridiculous, but on the side of the right and therefore to be rewarded.

The fable also represents its protagonist as its author. Primrose tells the story in retrospect (unlike Sidney, who narrates her life's events without knowing their outcomes), but he offers no hints about how matters will turn out. Nor does he show any awareness of his own inadequacies, as displayed along the way. His sense of superiority to his son, Moses, remains, despite the fact that he himself has proved even less astute at driving a bargain, and he still condescends to the women in his family. The novel's structure thus contains its own ironies. The neatness of the story is partly the construct of an "author" who has used it to prove what he knew all along. And how much can we trust this particular storyteller?

Parson Primrose transcends his weaknesses—his vanity, condescension, overconfidence, and smugness—by devotion to a high calling. Yet Goldsmith's comic exposure of his failings creates textual instability. Although eighteenth-century readers readily accepted the Vicar as hero, subsequent critics have frequently considered *The Vicar of Wakefield* a novel whose rich irony undercuts even the clergyman's religious devotion, exposing it as an expedient for retaining dominance. To make one's hero also the object of comedy is a dangerous strategy. Dickens's highly successful mixture of comic and sentimental effects carefully separated the two. Although Oscar Wilde could laugh at Little Nell, she and Little Dorritt and other sentimental figures in Dickens's novels did not invite laughter—laughter was solicited elsewhere in those works. Goldsmith's novel by no means marks the end of purely sentimental fiction, which survived through the nineteenth century. But it perhaps registers awareness that the emotions connected with weeping are not the only ones that provide pleasure for a reader.

Comparable awareness can hardly fail to inflect twenty-first-century readers' responses to novels that solicit participatory melancholy. Irritated by the single note such novels strike, we may feel tempted simply to throw them aside. To take these works seriously, however, invites reflection on critical issues that remain important. Even a book as short and as deliberately sketchy as *The Man of Feeling* can challenge our comprehension of our own feelings. If we refuse to react sympathetically to Harley's narrated experience, does that fact not say something about us as well as about the text? Do we believe sympathetic feeling an appropriate result of reading? Do we resemble or diverge from our forebears in our understanding of the sources of literary pleasure? Do we think that a work's overt claim on our emotions bears on its literary value? On its extraliterary effects? In its self-conscious program for generating aesthetic response based on both experiencing and reflecting on emotion, eighteenth-century sentimental fiction declared its ambition and demanded serious critical response.

One might think that novels of pure sentiment would have become harder to write after *The Vicar of Wakefield,* yet the influx of sentimental fiction continued without abatement. That mammoth work *The Fool of Quality, or the History of Henry Earl of Moreland* appeared between 1765 and

1770, issued in five volumes. Its author, Henry Brooke, followed Rousseau-vian theories in imagining the education of his protagonist, who learns from his every experience, literary and direct, and who bursts into tears at the slightest provocation. The eponymous Henry is educated through his emotions, and the promise of equivalent education presumably lures the reader. Samuel Jackson Pratt, writing as "Courtney Melmoth," provided a sentimental portrait of a virtuous man in *The Tutor of Truth* (1779), although his other works were more miscellaneous in subject and at-titude alike. Mary Robinson's *Walsingham, or the Pupil of Nature,* at the century's end (1797), as its title suggests, assumed the educative power of nature—but to no benign end. The novel begins with a letter from its eponymous protagonist: "You tell me to bear my misfortunes with resig-nation. . . . The magnitude of my sorrow overwhelms the faculties of rea-son" (1: 1). It continues to narrate a bizarre train of misfortunes, reported in Walsingham's self-pitying voice. Unlike earlier sentimental fiction, *Walsingham* provides an elaborate (if implausible) plot. Its dénouement turns on an extended program of cross-dressing, out of which the author engineers a huddled-up happy ending. Unlike many of its predecessors, this novel has no clear ideological or aesthetic purpose. It speaks of the erosion of a form. Nonetheless, one can readily multiply titles of late-century fiction that attempted to duplicate Sterne's sentiment without his irony or to follow the models of writers like Mackenzie and Sarah Fielding.

By the end of the century, though, critics as well as moralists often felt considerable skepticism about the interest as well as the value of sen-timental fiction. In 1796 William Beckford published a spoof of the form entitled *Modern Novel Writing.* His comic version of the sentimental, with a heroine named Arabella Bloomville, mocks not only the predictable and often fatuous substance of novels of sensibility but also the heavy reliance on the fragmentary. Here is a characteristic sequence: "She by degrees recovered her wonted serenity of aspect, and cast a languishing look of pathetic meaning towards the Countess, whose charming cheeks were already bathed in tears. To the amazement of all present, at this instant, upstarted Lord Mahogany [thus introduced for the first time], and with a frown declared, that the prevalence of sedition was become abominable, especially in this happy country where the poor are equally protected with the rich. . . . Having uttered this with an indignant tone of rage, he overturned the silver tea urn on Lucy Melville's favorite lapdog" (19).

Beckford's parodic mode of inconsequentiality does not much resemble Mackenzie's or Sterne's, but it calls attention to the attrition of the sentimental genre. Devices that had once fulfilled serious purpose had become mechanical instruments, references to rather than participants in a tradition. Sentimental fiction would continue to flourish in the nineteenth century, but largely without the complex moral implications of such writers as Sarah Fielding and Mackenzie and Sheridan.

The sense of purpose that marks the early sentimentalists appears largely to vanish in those who succeeded them, and by the century's end many novelists and commentators on social custom raised loud questions about the value of cultivating sensibility, in life as well as in fiction. Most of the questions concerned the morality of sensibility. Was it not merely self-indulgence, or hypocrisy, or fashionable pose? The quality of responsiveness that had once defined the man or woman of sympathy as the quintessentially moral being now could seem a mark of weakness rather than strength. Sensibility came to be understood as a matter of manners rather than morals—and manners without morals, as many novels revealed, were meretricious indeed.

CHAPTER SIX

The Novel of Manners

A STRIKING ABSENCE OF visual detail marks most of the novels discussed thus far. *Robinson Crusoe,* which tells us about every item salvaged
from the ship, every piece of clothing Crusoe manufactures, every aspect
of his fortifications, makes a rare exception. Although Richardson's works
dwell on subtle shades of psychological development; although Fielding
can report in mock-heroic style individual aspects of a pitched battle
among women, in general novelists fail to tell much about how things or
people or places look. *Moll Flanders* provides little sense of the cityscape
Moll inhabits. *Roxana* offers a relatively full account of its protagonist's
most important costume, but most of the items that surround the central
characters remain shadowy. Elaborations of plot and character abound;
elaborations of physical appearances do not.

During the final decades of the eighteenth century, a new subgenre
evolved as women writers in particular experimented with novels focused
on social detail. Physical appearances may remain shadowy (although
appearances of significance to the novels' social analysis sometimes receive a good deal of attention), but social behavior is rendered with sharp
particularity. Manners become a subject of consuming interest.

The previous chapter suggested that when sensibility became a matter
only of manners, it lost significance for the society. Yet manners could be
seen as momentous, reflections of important values. The history of the

word *manners* itself suggests issues involved in the activities that word designates. *Manner* in its most basic sense (the *OED* cites a usage from 1275) merely indicates a way of doing something. Concurrently, however, the word indicated a "customary mode of acting or behaviour, whether of an individual or of a community; habitual practice; usage, custom, fashion." At the same time (citations for both these senses date from 1225), the collective plural, *manners*, referred to "a person's habitual behaviour or conduct, esp. in reference to its moral aspect; moral character, morals." By the sixteenth century, a more abstract meaning had evolved, including "morality as a subject of study; the moral code embodied in general custom or sentiment." Meanwhile, as early as the mid-fourteenth century, more familiar meanings emerged: "the modes of life, customary rules of behaviour, conditions of society, prevailing in a people"; and "external behaviour in social intercourse, estimated as good or bad according to its degree of politeness or of conformity to the accepted standard of propriety."

In this series of definitions, the idea of manners assumes both moral and social significance, despite the neutrality of *manner* as merely a way of doing something. Moral meanings preceded social ones. In the twenty-first century, we associate manners with the social, but generally not with the moral. In the eighteenth century, both levels of meaning operated. The idea of *pleasing* links them. As Lord Chesterfield's famous—or infamous—letters to his son make clear, one practices good manners in order to make oneself pleasing to others. Consideration for one's company dictates speaking in low and harmonious tones, preserving graceful postures, avoiding controversial subjects, offering delicacies at table to others, and so on. The prescriptions are endless, and rule books abound: books recommending what to avoid and what to do for women in search of a husband, men wishing to elevate their social standing, and anyone concerned with propriety.

Since even the most trivial rules justify themselves in terms of the individual's effect on others, concern for manners shades readily into moral obligation. Morality, after all, involves responsibility to and for one's fellow man and woman. We customarily think of it as implying more important matters than a prohibition on picking one's teeth with the knife, but inasmuch as picking your teeth may annoy your neighbor, you refrain from such activity for the sake of that neighbor, thus registering at least a minimal sense of human responsibility. Frances Burney's Evelina, one of the first (1778) heroines of manners, has to learn an esoteric code of behavior at public and private "assemblies," or dancing parties. This code mainly involves a set of prescriptions about dancing partners: she must dance with the man to whom she has engaged herself for the evening and with no one else; with no one at all if she has said she plans not to dance; never with someone to whom she has not been formally introduced. When Evelina laughs inappropriately at a man whose high style strikes her as ludicrous, she marks herself as a "poor, weak girl." The verdict registers doubt of her capacity for good judgment about issues more important than her mockery of a fop. Focus on comparable matters of social behavior accounts for much of the content of Burney's novel.

This focus also helps account for the novel's form and for the form of other novels of the same general species. The idea of manners in all its complexity largely shapes the plot of *Evelina*. In many respects, that plot appears to conform to the conventions of romance. Evelina, though not quite Cinderella, is a "nobody" who succeeds in marrying the Prince Charming her society provides. The ascent from inconspicuousness to prominence that shapes the central fantasy of *Pamela* also governs that of Burney's novel.

Evelina, however, provides a cast of characters who do not correspond to the personages of romance. Burney's contemporaries found the novel's greatest interest in its "low" figures: boisterous, sadistic Captain Mirvan; Evelina's vulgar, assertive grandmother, Madame Duval; the low-bred Branghton family, which includes Evelina's cousins; and egotistical Mr. Smith, a would-be suitor. By their behavior these characters help shape the plot as one of manners. The novel supplies a full spectrum of manners defined along axes of form and content. Understood as social forms, manners are simply conventions, often arbitrary. Understood as moral content, manners express awareness of the needs and desires of others. The novel's mannerly ideal combines moral awareness with conventional compliance. Lord Orville epitomizes this union; Evelina, who demonstrates her awareness from the beginning, gradually learns the conventions sufficiently well to approach the same ideal. The Branghtons and Madame Duval embody failure at both the conventional and the moral level. Such well-born men and women as Lord Merton and Mrs. Beaumont use conventions for their own purposes, but lack moral substance. Other characters locate themselves at various points along the continuum, and the plot works itself out by means of its demonstrations about manners.

In an epistolary moment of heartfelt utterance, Evelina exclaims to her guardian, "But, really, I think there ought to be a book, of the laws and customs *à-la-mode*, presented to all young people, upon their first introduction into public company" (83). That *really*, an unusual intensifier for Evelina, conveys the sincerity of her desire and suggests her desperate need. Understanding of the laws and customs of society seems at this early point in her London career the primary desideratum. She is right in thinking so. On the basis of her apparent ignorance of these matters, she can be insulted, neglected, or dismissed. Lacking her imagined book, she is unable to conceive how she can progress in a world made incomprehensible by its customs. From the point of view of a twenty-first-century reader, it may seem refreshing that Evelina, at a dance, complains about the fact that the men stroll about, looking as though they thought all women at their disposal. The eighteenth-century girl, though, must learn not only that the absolute assumption of male dominance governs much social activity but also that one must not say so.

Issues of manners determine many of the plot's meanings and many of its actual events. The two melodramatic interviews between Evelina and her true father do not directly relate to the pervasive concern with manners, but they are rare exceptions in a sequence of occurrences that reveal and often stem from diverse social codes. In one salient instance, Evelina finds herself forced to accompany her vulgar grandmother and the Branghton family to the opera, although she had planned to go with more cultivated company. The Branghtons know neither how to dress appropriately nor how much they will be expected to pay for opera seats. They have never heard an opera, and they comprehend nothing about its principles. The textual emphasis on such ignorance initially appears to reflect Evelina's social snobbery, and perhaps her creator's. As the narrative continues, though, the reader comes to realize the willfulness of the Branghtons' ignorance and the pervasiveness of their reverse snobbery. Evelina's cousins consider themselves practical-minded realists in their wariness of financial exploitation, their ridicule of their social superiors, and their mockery of all who claim to enjoy music sung in an incomprehensible language and accompanying a ridiculous plot. They cause the heroine acute discomfort, not only because of her embarrassment at being seen with them but because they understand as pretension her pleasure in the music and ridicule her for manifesting that pleasure. When Sir Clement Willoughby appears in the gallery where Evelina is sitting, she sees him as a savior and, as she thinks, makes her escape with him. She actually "escapes" into a situation of extreme danger, alone in a carriage with Sir Clement, who apparently hopes to seduce or even to rape her. The upper classes can prove at least as menacing as their social inferiors, since their code of manners—concerned with "pleasing" only those securely located at their own social level—allows predatory behavior toward unprotected females.

Because of their own social circumstances, the Branghtons predictably lack knowledge of even the basic principles of upper-class decorum. One can hardly fault them for that. But Burney *does* fault them, and the opera episode suggests why. The Branghtons may justifiably not know how to dress for the opera. Evelina, however, has the knowledge they lack and attempts to impart it; her cousins do not wish to learn. Especially, they do not wish to learn from her. They feel superior to her, and constantly display their superiority, because she has not seen the sights of London that they, as city residents, know well. Although capable of being awed by the notion of a lord, the Branghtons more customarily display their cocksureness. Like most of the novel's characters, they approve of the manners they have and reveal no desire to refine them. The "bad manners" that make them talk constantly about money, complaining not only about the price of opera tickets but about the extra coach fare incurred by picking up Evelina, reflect their lack of awareness of and consideration for their cousin's feelings. The social indictment—they don't like opera, they don't know how much it costs, they interfere with others' enjoyment of it—becomes a moral indictment: they don't care about other people. (They don't, in fact, even care about one another: the Branghton siblings quarrel almost continuously.)

The moral indictment of Sir Clement Willoughby is far more serious, despite—or because of—the fact that he knows and practices the manners of the aristocracy. This indictment in itself reveals how much more than snobbery operates in the novel's moral scheme. Within the code of every social level, possibilities for choice remain. The moral judgments that *Evelina* suggests respond to individual choices.

The manners of the upper classes allow for, indeed depend on, considerable pretense. At her first assembly, Evelina realizes that the men who approach her use language with no necessary relation to what they think. Lord Orville himself, who speaks of the honor of her company, thus declares, to her mind, his hypocrisy: what honor can her company possibly bestow? Sir Clement and the fop Lovel, however, misuse language far more seriously than does Lord Orville. The nobleman employs social forms to create ease between people. The other two men use more extravagant language to proclaim their importance and assert their dominance in individual social situations. Moreover, their manners alter according to their perceptions of their interlocutor. Sir Clement is always linguistically excessive, but his "freedom" in talking to Evelina comes largely from his judgment of her as a "nobody."

In parallel situations at different amusement parks, Evelina finds herself separated from her party and in sexual or social danger—once from a boisterous group of men, once from two prostitutes whom she has inadvertently approached. Sir Clement frees her from the first predicament; Lord Orville comforts her in the second. But the two men behave very differently. Sir Clement takes her away from her tormentors only to lure her into a dark alley where, he explains, they will be unobserved. When she insists on returning to her original companions, the Braghtons and Madame Duval, he shows himself astonished by the company she now keeps and displays "unrestrained curiosity." Evelina comments, "He seems disposed to think that the alteration in my companions authorizes an alteration in his manners. It is true, he has always treated me with uncommon freedom, but never before with so disrespectful an abruptness" (201). Lord Orville, in contrast, conducts himself toward her precisely as he has always done: "Whatever might be his doubts and suspicions, far from suffering them to influence his behaviour, he spoke, he looked, with the same politeness and attention with which he had always honoured me" (238).

Sir Clement's manners, on balance, are more attractive to Evelina than are those of Mr. Smith, an associate of the Branghtons who also appears to have romantic intentions toward her. In other words, Sir Clement, despite his predatory intent, does not inhabit the lowest reaches in Evelina's moral hierarchy. But the superiority of Lord Orville's manners to Sir Clement's marks the superiority of his character. Assuming courtesy as a moral obligation, Lord Orville employs it toward everyone—even toward young Mr.

Branghton, who is implicated in damaging his coach and who afterward seeks his business for the family firm of silversmiths. If his politeness masks doubts and suspicions, or even negative judgments, he will never let such discomfiting possibilities manifest themselves. Politeness, rather than any recorded wit, intelligence, or vividness of personality, makes Lord Orville the novel's Prince Charming.

Sir Clement's consistent failures of concern for Evelina's desires—as he says in a climactic conversation with Lord Orville, "Let Miss Anville look to herself" (346)—make him reprehensible, despite his energy and verve. He employs the upper-class repertoire of conventional courtesy only in the service of self-interest. His egotism is less gross than Mr. Smith's, because more dexterously masked, yet he inevitably reveals it. "Your principles, excuse me, Sir, are well known," Lord Orville says to him (346)—"principles" meaning "lack of principle." Failure of consistency in good manners implies absence of principle in more serious matters. Sir Clement is less a libertine than Lord Merton, whose high rank apparently makes it possible for him not even to bother to mask his licentiousness. He is less completely frivolous than Lord Orville's sister, Lady Louisa, who never bothers with even the forms of politeness unless she judges a companion to be of social importance. But he is quite bad enough. All along the social spectrum, manners supply a moral gauge, an index to other forms of merit.

The reader is tacitly invited to measure Evelina, too, by her social behavior, and Lord Orville himself measures her the same way. In his confrontation with Sir Clement, the latter brings up Lord Orville's earlier judgment of Evelina as "a *poor, weak, ignorant girl*," and the lord responds that he did not know at the time "how new she was to the world" (347). Her newness to the world accounts for the anomalies of her behavior. As she spends more time in London, she increasingly learns to conform to the standards of polite society, preserving decorum even while in the company of her vulgar relatives. Although she judges her grandmother rather harshly, she behaves toward her with unfailing politeness. When she first notices the Branghtons' sad, poverty-stricken roomer Mr. Macartney, she is offended by their discourtesy toward him and therefore makes a point of conducting herself graciously to him. Her "graciousness," indeed, extends to rescuing him from despair, by means of both financial largesse and emotional support. This rescue, too, demonstrates the continuity between social and moral excellence. Evelina's interest in and compassion for others displays itself in the help she offers Mr. Macartney, in her efforts to intervene in the race between two old women, and in her rescue of her grandmother from a ditch, but also in her commitment to good manners.

A crisis in the developing romance between Lord Orville and Evelina, hence a crucial plot nexus, occurs when Lord Orville apparently lapses dramatically from good behavior, or, as Evelina repeatedly terms it, "propriety." That word sits squarely on the borderline between manners and morals, referring to proper or appropriate action in either sphere. Lord Orville's ostensible failure responds to a bold choice on Evelina's part, when she reacts to her relatives' improprieties toward Lord Orville by writing him a letter of apology, despite the social ordinance forbidding epistolary exchange between a man and a woman not related by blood, married, or betrothed. She takes this step because her sense of personal obligation overrules her social scruples. In response, she receives a letter signed by Lord Orville that thanks her for initiating a correspondence and implies that she has confessed her love for him. Evelina falls into melancholy because of her shock at such behavior in a man she has idealized. Her guardian, Mr. Villars, points out, too late, that she should simply have returned the letter to its writer without comment. Society, in short, provides a rule for responding to rudeness, as well as rules forbidding it—but Evelina fails to remember the right rule at the right time. Only when she learns that the letter was a forgery can she allow her esteem and affection for Lord Orville fully to reemerge.

Lord Orville's apparent lack of social propriety makes him for the moment romantically unacceptable, despite his rank and wealth. Paradoxically, Evelina can use her own difficulties in maneuvering within social rules as a ground of romantic appeal. Lord Orville overhears her making an appointment to meet the unfortunate Macartney, thus violating yet another social prohibition for young ladies. When Lord Orville uses the word *appointment,* he makes her realize what she has done and precipitates one of several utterances by her about her inadvertent and frequent "mistakes." Like other similar remarks, this is transparently a plea for help, and Lord Orville responds accordingly. Indeed, Evelina's professed helplessness and need for guidance is a fundamental basis of her attractiveness. When Lord Orville summarizes her character, shortly before he proposes to her, he emphasizes her "modest worth, and fearful excellence" (347). The adjectives bear at least as much weight as the nouns: Evelina's proclaimed sense of social inadequacy has helped her to get her man.

These episodes should suffice to suggest how vital a part manners play in the design of *Evelina*. Burney's piece of fiction can appropriately be labeled a novel of manners not just because its action takes place in a social world, with the rules of decorum constructing its environment. More important, manners make motives. To be sure, they restrict the possibilities for women, in particular. Lord Orville can arrange appointments as he likes. He can ask a woman to dance, or to marry him; Evelina has only the power of refusal. But as poetic conventions, limiting permissible paths of creativity, enrich a poem by their pressure, social conventions create ways to operate—again, for women in particular—even as they constrict. Without her professions of social incompetence, Evelina would have less romantic opportunity. Burney makes the complex paradoxical relations of social inhibition and possibility her primary subject, thus inaugurating the full-blown novel of manners.

Inasmuch as manners play a vital part in such novels as *Evelina*, the novels illuminate how vital a part they play in society. Men and women in the higher reaches of society necessarily operate within a frame of decorum, these works remind us, as they urge us to assess the ways in which, the degree to which, that frame impinges on lives occurring within it. No apparent desire to overturn existing conventions informs Burney's novelistic examination of them, but her meticulous investigation of how society works exposes possibilities of inequity and falseness as it examines a hierarchical society with highly codified rules.

Burney renders manners and customs with precision, as she also renders her heroine's mixture of repugnance and desire for the social world she encounters, and the nuances of her recurrent embarrassment. All evoke real experience, not only plausibly but persuasively. Both the psychological and the social details of *Evelina* seem grounded in actuality—a fact that allows Burney to construct her fairy tale plot on a solid base. The structure of romance incorporating data from the literal social world: this combination characterizes many novels of manners and helps to account for their appeal.

Evelina locates its concern with manners in the foreground of the action, making it easy to argue for the issue's central importance. Burney's later novels ostensibly focus on other subjects—money, its uses and dangers, in *Cecilia* (1782); the difficulties of female independence in *The Wanderer* (1814)—but all fit under the rubric of the novel of manners because, whatever their other concerns, all manifestly assume that only within the sometimes Procrustean framework of social decorum can even a fictional character operate, and all investigate the ways that young women may use manners to their own purposes. "Manners," in these as in most novels of manners, does not necessarily designate the realm of etiquette so important in *Evelina*. The more relevant meaning is customarily one of the earliest senses: "usage, custom, fashion."

Camilla, Burney's third novel (1796), worries over what it might mean to establish one's own sense of fashion rather than conform to conventional modes. Published during the politically tumultuous final decade of the century, it shows no awareness of politics. It concerns itself primarily with the difficulties and dangers of growing up, not only through the career of the eponymous heroine but through the various fates of her siblings, her remoter relatives, and her friends, male and female. Although it seems to recommend total conformity and compliance as the proper course for a woman, it raises questions about the viability of such a way of proceeding. Despite a cast of characters almost Dickensian in proportion and a considerable number of intersecting plots, the novel manages to examine the inner life of its protagonist and to convey the conflicts implicit in conformity.

Although concern with manners may seem in *Camilla* only an adjunct to more momentous matters, that concern helps account for the disjunctive quality of Burney's novel, which proceeds by a series of lurches, sudden shifts corresponding to the frequent reversals of feeling in both Camilla Tyrold and the object of her love, Edgar Mandlebert. No external obstacle prevents their marriage. Edgar loves Camilla as Camilla loves Edgar. Yet Edgar changes his mind abruptly and repeatedly, about whether Camilla merits his love and about whether she reciprocates it; and Camilla tumbles over and over from hope to despair in interpreting Edgar's feeling for her. The violent changes in how each understands the other correspond almost invariably to alterations in social self-representation—that is, manners.

Crucial to the intricate narrative is a character named Mrs. Albery, a woman, as we are told repeatedly, of impeccable reputation who holds a high place in fashionable society precisely because of her refusal to abide by social convention. She will not, for instance, allow people to apologize to her: apologies bore her. She doesn't want anyone to dress for dinner. She dresses always to suit herself, not in accordance with social expectation. She prefers men to women for company, yet no scandal touches her. Her male counterpart (and constant companion) is Sir Sedley Clarendel, whose ostentatious rudeness makes part of his elaborate system of affectation. Both Mrs. Albery and Sir Sedley, in other words, deliberately and flamboyantly reject the complicated codes that govern their peers. Mrs. Albery proclaims her own "freedom" and appears to lead a life of pleasure. She constitutes a potent temptation for Camilla, a young woman new to the intricacies of social life.

For readers of a later era, Mrs. Albery's appeal is obvious. Her unconventionality feels refreshing in the context of a depicted world so strictly subservient to its own regulations. When she walks through a crowded scene at a dance, casually dressed and doing needlework along the way, one feels inclined to applaud: her daring declares the possibility of escaping the inescapable. She could hardly fail to appeal to the inexperienced Camilla, even if she did not add to her attractiveness by her display of enthusiastic interest in the girl. Even straitlaced Edgar can say nothing against her morals. Why, then, should Camilla decline her offered friendship?

A telling exchange between Camilla and Edgar focuses on this question. Edgar has acknowledged that no stain sullies Mrs. Albery's reputation; Camilla responds that moral character is all that matters. Edgar, however, suggests that character and reputation do not suffice, asking whether Camilla "account[s] as nothing manners, disposition, way of life." Such characteristics, she replies, are not absolutely nothing, "but taste settles all those things, and mine is entirely in her favour" (198). As the action of the novel demonstrates, Camilla follows a dangerous course in considering the approval or disapproval of "manners, disposition, way of life" only a matter of taste. Her temporary conformity with Mrs. Albery's way of life and her effort to adapt Mrs. Albery's manners to her own use endanger her happiness and, finally, her moral uprightness. (She falls not into sexual looseness but into dubious financial dealings.)

Another unconventional female, Mrs. Berlinton, more immediately challenges Camilla's sense of propriety but nonetheless attracts her. Beautiful, rich, fashionable, young, Mrs. Berlinton is married to an off-stage

tyrannical husband, but she considers it as much her right to pursue sentimental friendships with other men as to immerse herself in the poetry
of William Collins. Such behavior puzzles but fails to alienate Camilla
—partly because Mrs. Berlinton offers her the uncritical love that she
receives from no one else. Camilla does not appear to feel, as the reader
may, the tedium of Mrs. Berlinton's repetitive effusions and shallow self-
justifications. On the contrary, Mrs. Berlinton seems to her the antithesis
of the boring: "She possessed all that was most softly attractive, most
bewitchingly beautiful, and most irresistibly captivating, in mind, person, and manners." Her behavior, like Mrs. Albery's, promises freedom
from social restriction, exciting Camilla even as she worries about the
possibility of sexual impropriety, or apparent impropriety, in her new
friend. The description of Mrs. Berlinton just quoted continues, in the
narrator's voice, "But to all that was thus most fascinating to others, she
joined unhappily all that was most dangerous for herself; an heart the
most susceptible, sentiments the most romantic, and an imagination
the most exalted" (486). Her inner qualities present dangers to herself;
her mind, person, and manners, as it turns out, make a combination that
endangers Camilla.

The excitement that Camilla feels in the presence of these two women,
let me reiterate, depends largely on the manners that they adopt, or partly
invent. Their unconventionality emphasizes the import of conventional-
ity. Manners are a form of self-representation, but to follow an elaborate
system of etiquette that prescribes the response for every situation may
make the practitioner feel as though she were disappearing. Camilla endures considerable pressure to "disappear," particularly from her parents,
who urge the importance of concealing all crucial emotions. If she allows
anyone to see that she feels romantically interested in a man, she risks
not only social disapproval but the repugnance of the man in question.
As Evelina at her first dance intuits, the discipline of propriety is one of
false appearances: of systematic concealment.

It is true that, despite their flouting of social expectation, both Mrs.
Albery and Mrs. Berlinton exist within structures of self-imposed rigidity.
The freedom they claim for themselves is largely illusory. Moreover, the
moral shoddiness implicit, from Burney's point of view, in their rejection
of conventional manners finally exposes itself. Mrs. Berlinton, unwilling
to accept any externally imposed discipline, becomes a slave to gambling.

Mrs. Albery reveals her moral insufficiency in her treatment of Camilla, whom she urges to coquetry and fails to protect. Refusing to allow its readers to rest in the appeal of the two characters, the novel firmly, and rather harshly, judges them. Yet the presence of these figures constitutes a daring authorial move in a novel so centrally concerned with manners. In *Evelina,* Burney differentiates sharply between characters represented for the reader's admiration and those who merit disapproval. Readers will have no more difficulty than Evelina has about deciding that Mr. Smith is low-bred and unattractive, in contrast to that paragon, Lord Orville; or that Madame Duval has a meretricious character, whereas Mrs. Selwyn, despite her sharp tongue, possesses a warm heart. (Indeed, the sharp tongue, typically directed at Evelina's male persecutors, frequently provides grounds for approving of Mrs. Selwyn, even though Evelina considers it the mark of an "unfeminine" woman.)

The two female characters who lure Camilla are likely to lure the reader as well. They provide alternative models of female possibility, indicating that despite the power of social pressure, women can imaginably make their own rules and live successfully by them—"successfully" at least inasmuch as society accepts them although they reject its code. In a novel that tells a central story of repression, they seem to open things up, to promise the existence of options. The promise, though, turns out to be false: Burney opens a door only to close it. Like other novels of manners, *Camilla* tells us that social conformity is the only acceptable course for a young woman.

Edgar's reliance on codes of behavior as a basis of revelation emphasizes the point. When he tells his tutor of his love for Camilla, the older man warns him not to be too hasty in proposing. He must make sure first, Dr. Marchmont says, that Camilla has the stability of character to make a good wife and that she will marry Edgar for love, not for money. Women pretend to feelings they don't have, explains the tutor. Their relatives urge them toward falsity in the interest of gaining security. Edgar must watch Camilla closely over a prolonged period in order to ascertain her character from her behavior.

Since, given the rules of eighteenth-century upper-class etiquette, Edgar essentially can see Camilla only in social settings, what he sees when he watches her behavior is her adoption of one set of manners or another. On a prolonged visit to Mrs. Albery, Camilla follows the implicit and explicit promptings of her hostess and becomes flirtatious and apparently fickle. Keeping company (because she does not know how to disengage herself) with the vulgar Mrs. Mittin, she behaves in a way that leads observers to conclude that she and her companion are either crazy or dishonest. Edgar, a fortuitous observer at the end of this episode, accepts neither conclusion, but he sees that Camilla has placed herself in a compromising situation. Her manners, in other words, lack the "delicacy" that he considers a desideratum for his wife. Camilla accepts the attentions of an elderly peer, a roué, in order to avoid those of a young man who doesn't interest her. She rejects the peer when he tries to propose to her: she has assumed that his interest in her was essentially paternal. Edgar overhears her rejection. She thinks she has demonstrated that she loves only Edgar; Edgar thinks that her conduct betrays her avidity for attention. And so on: whatever manners Camilla adopts prove subject to misinterpretation. In concealing real feelings, manners may appear to reveal them. Hence many of Camilla's misfortunes.

Edgar, like Camilla, makes many mistakes, although, unlike her, he is only lightly penalized for them. His mistakes are all errors of interpretation based on external appearances of social behavior. As Marchmont points out to Edgar, Camilla's father has reared her with great attention to theology and morality, teaching her only the best moral principles. But, Marchmont continues, Mr. Tyrold is himself unworldly. He cannot teach his daughter the ways of the world; he has not instructed her adequately in social behavior. And failure to understand society's behavioral demands amounts to an unacceptable flaw in a wife—at least in a wife for someone blessed, like Edgar, with wealth, intelligence, personal attractiveness, and appropriate education. Well-nigh perfect himself, Marchmont implies, Edgar deserves a perfect wife.

So Marchmont enjoins Edgar to watch Camilla, and Edgar watches. His feelings repeatedly lead him toward an immediate proposal. This novel figures erotic impulse as a form of sensibility and of response to sensibility. Thus, Edgar often finds himself moved by such aspects of Camilla's personality as her spontaneous kindness to the needy, and he feels overwhelmed by his recurrent desire to guide and protect the girl. Compelled, though, by his understanding of the reason/feeling dichotomy, he attributes to infallible "reason" his need to watch—after all, his tutor, by definition, speaks for reason—and to dangerous "feeling" his desire to abandon watching for marriage.

Readers may be drawn to sympathize with Edgar in his painful internal conflict, but they can hardly fail to suffer vicariously with Camilla, the victim of Edgar's close attention, as well as of surveillance by her malicious cousin Indiana and Indiana's yet more malicious governess, Miss Margland. All three employ the ordinances of polite behavior as their standard of judgment. All demonstrate the punitive consequences of deviation from those ordinances.

The omnipresence of personal surveillance comes to seem a metaphor for the function of manners in polite society. If manners, considered as adjuncts to morality, reveal their possessors' concern and consideration for others, as adjuncts to society they provide testimony of compliance. And compliance proves, Burney tells us over and over, a hard discipline. Only slightly less socially inexperienced than Evelina, Camilla finds it difficult to distinguish between the imperative and the merely fashionable. Would it be bad manners not to get a new dress in order to conform to the ordained costume for a social gathering? How inappropriate is it to borrow money from a man who may have an amorous interest in her? She tries to conform; she makes mistakes; Edgar sees them, and so, often, does Miss Margland. Disaster succeeds disaster as a result of poor judgment intimately connected with social ignorance.

But her desperate self-accusation and her mother's eventual indictment of her make no allowance for ignorance. Camilla finds herself in a situation of metaphysical distress, enduring a vision of final judgment by which she must be utterly condemned. Her social sins have turned into moral ones, leading her into disastrous debt, frustrated love, and shamed isolation from her family. Edgar, judging her from without—as society, of course, judges everyone—has given her up. Her mother, judging her inner life as well (she has yielded too much to her feelings, Mrs. Tyrold says, indulging reprehensible sensibility), condemns her for the pain she has caused her family. Camilla implicitly accepts all negative judgments of herself, resolving henceforward to be guided entirely by her family: both her family of origin and the husband she happily accepts. Social behavior has turned out to have ethical as well as social meaning; Camilla consciously abandons the effort to fathom its demands. Other people can accomplish this task for her—at the cost, to be sure, of her abandoning all pretense of, all hope for, autonomy. Of Burney's four novels, *Camilla* has the ending most somber in its implications because it suggests even more clearly than *Evelina* does how much a woman must give up for the sake of security.

After Burney, one must wait for Austen to find the full-blown novel of manners again. Yet the function of manners as formal elements by no means disappeared from late-century fiction. In intricate ways, social behavior provided markers for both moral and emotional substance. Even works primarily concerned with romance or politics rather than social matters might use manners as a means of characterization. When the subject of manners recedes from centrality, the specificity notable in Burney's treatment of the matter also recedes. The very word *manners* can suffice to indicate a character's nature and to predict the attitude of others toward that character.

Before considering the kind of notation that occurs in fiction not primarily focused on manners, it is worth contemplating another work—sharply different from Burney's—in which manners occupy a central position and are delineated with striking exactness, although also sometimes referred to in general terms. A particularly subtle and complex use of manners as markers occurs in Elizabeth Inchbald's *A Simple Story* (1791), which establishes the problem of interpretation as central to its narrative and then frequently represents social behavior as a basis for interpretation. In a telling episode, less important for the plot than for the structure, Miss Woodley, the heroine's faithful friend, and Sandford, the Catholic clergyman who has been Lord Elmwood's tutor and who disapproves of the heroine, disagree. Miss Woodley proposes to warn the heroine, Miss Milner, that her lover, Lord Elmwood, has declared his intention to leave her forever if his judgment assures him of her unworthiness. Sandford, not wanting the warning passed on, observes that Lord Elmwood probably wished for secrecy in the matter. Miss Woodley points out that she has not promised secrecy and that it would be only kind to protect Miss Milner from the consequences of her actions. "'There now!' cried Sandford, 'there is how you judge of this matter.—You judge of things as they are in reality, not what they are by construction; the only way to judge of any thing'" (137).

It is a curious comment, this announcement of the practical, or perhaps the moral, superiority of judging "by construction" rather than assessing "things as they are in reality." Implausible though it may seem, it establishes an issue that unifies the novel's two disparate sections and provides a principle for understanding the apparent shifts in characterization that have baffled readers. Both actors within the text and readers outside it must indeed judge by construction—by the special circumstances, the complicated contexts of every episode—in order to grasp what is going on and why it matters. In this convoluted process of interpretation, social behavior provides a vital set of clues.

It is perhaps worth noting at this point that one might make precisely the same assertion about *Evelina, Camilla,* and Burney's other novels— and, for that matter, about such a work as Austen's *Emma.* When manners assume an important structural position in a work of fiction, they customarily provide a basis for interpretation. They may, as in *Camilla,* prove misleading; they may, as in *Evelina,* signal either social hypocrisy or moral substance—or both. In *A Simple Story,* it is most often tiny deviations from a norm that point to the crucial "constructions" made by individuals in the service of personal agendas.

Early in the novel, the narrator's voice intervenes to declare the importance of manners as indices to character, contrasting them explicitly with the undependability of words. Miss Woodley, the novel's pattern of unmarried female virtue, saying that she will not forgive, expresses forgiveness by her aspect; Mrs. Horton, a devout landlady, begging heaven to pardon an offender conveys in her tone of voice her sense that the sinner does not deserve pardon. But interpretation, of course, cannot always depend on such simple oppositions. Miss Milner, quasi-heroine of the novel's first volume, is left to the guardianship of the young, attractive priest Dorriforth, whose manners, we are told, "sometimes appear even like the result of a system he had marked out for himself, as the only means to keep his ward restrained within the same limitations" (25). Quite apart from the ambiguity of *appear,* the statement leaves uncertain what hides behind those good manners. As for Miss Milner's behavior in general, it turns out that she feels tempted to treat her guardian with levity but refrains because of the effect of his politeness. In both cases, good manners tell the observer something about their possessor, but hide something else.

It is after the two are declared lovers (Dorriforth, having inherited the title Lord Elmwood, is released from his priestly vows) that manners become of paramount importance in assessing them. There have been previous hints of how tiny social gestures matter: Dorriforth's calling for his hat and leaving the house as a mark of resentment; Miss Milner's

opening a window and leaning out as a sign of embarrassment. Miss Milner, concerned about Lord Elmwood's feeling for her, repeatedly plays the
wrong cards in a game; Lord Elmwood, after inquiring about her health,
solicitously urges her to eat and even feeds her chicken. It is easy enough
to interpret such bits of action.

After Miss Milner and the new Lord Elmwood agree to marry, they
watch each other for signs. The engagement period proves a time of tension, with the young woman obsessed by the project of testing her fiancé's
love for her and the man increasingly concerned lest she turn out to be
an unsuitable match. Each examines the other's behavior to ascertain
emotional truth. The reader is consistently invited to engage in equivalent
examination. Sometimes the narrator provides explicit hints about the
meaning of a tiny bit of behavior; sometimes she reports it with no commentary. In either case, the text solicits the reader's sharp awareness, as
the signs become increasingly ambiguous.

Even when the narrator reveals directly that Miss Milner engages in
pretense, the text entangles the reader in minutiae of her social behavior.
She decides that hauteur rather than affection will serve her purposes; the
reader knows why she acts as she does. At the same time, we know nothing about what lies behind Lord Elmwood's behavior: "cold, polite, and
perfectly indifferent" (157). Miss Milner, responding to his coldness, gives
up her own assumed chilliness for assumed levity, engaging in a constant
round of social visits, appearing to be in high spirits, singing and laughing. We know that anxiety provides the underpinning of such behavior;
we do not know any details. Miss Milner has an accident, but "the gaiety
of her manners" persuades Lord Elmwood that nothing has happened
(159). He betrays signs of chagrin at the presence of a former wooer of his
fiancée; she realizes that she must not appear to notice his concern. The
intricate texture of deception, detection, falsity, and truth generates narrative tension as it creates tension in the depicted household. When Lord
Elmwood ordains that they must separate, that tension only heightens.
The two lovers alike adopt flawless manners: manners "perfectly polite,"
but "not tinctured with the smallest degree of familiarity," behavior "polite,
friendly, composed, and resolved" (165). When Miss Milner finds herself
in other company than Lord Elmwood's, her behavior remains the same,
although her looks and her voice show less self-command.

It seems profoundly appropriate that Sandford's decision to marry the lovers rather than allow them to part rests entirely on his interpretation of minute appearances. The night before the surprise wedding, he has addressed Miss Milner, in unprecedented fashion, as "my dear," when he notes the pain in her looks. In the morning, Miss Milner refuses to join Lord Elmwood at his final breakfast before he leaves for the Continent, until Miss Woodley assures her that she "may go with the utmost decorum" (176). At breakfast she blushes, Lord Elmwood places a chair for her, she almost drops her cup and saucer, Sandford claims to have lost his gloves—and finally she allows herself to weep, at which point Sandford commands them to marry instantly or part forever. Neither says anything. Lord Elmwood gazes "as if enraptured"; Miss Milner sighs "with a trembling kind of ecstasy"; Sandford makes a speech in which he announces that he can tell by her looks that she will intend to keep her vows. When Lord Elmwood actually asks Miss Milner to marry him, she conveys her response "by the expression of her face" (178).

Facial expressions, trembling cups and saucers, blushes: perhaps the testimony such clues offer is no less dependable than that provided by verbal protestations. In any case, language plays a relatively small part in the drama of these improbable lovers. They interpret each other largely on the basis of nonverbal evidence—involuntary behavior and conventional behavior. When Lord Elmwood gets up to place a chair for the woman he declares himself to have rejected, he performs an utterly routine ritual of politeness; yet the circumstances and the text assign it great importance. Nothing is too small to take seriously: such is the import of *A Simple Story*.

Critics customarily neglect the undefined middle of Inchbald's story, the first two chapters of volume 3, which summarize seventeen years of Lady Elmwood's life and report her death. The text itself seems to encourage one to ignore it, or at least to pass over it as fast as possible. It adopts the purposeful narrative technique of telling rather than showing that we have seen before, especially in sentimental fiction. The narrator reports events of high drama in a distant tone of summary. The married lovers live happily together for three years; they have a daughter; Lord Elmwood goes to the West Indies to tend to his estate; he is delayed there by illness; Lady Elmwood commits adultery; when her husband returns, she flees, leaving their daughter behind; Lord Elmwood returns the child to its mother; Lady Elmwood pines away, over ten years, and finally dies, in the loving company of Miss Woodley, Sandford, and her daughter Matilda, deliberately leaving no will.

Most eighteenth-century novels in which a woman sins sexually punish her by death. Inchbald's story here, though, differs from the norm in some significant respects. Lady Elmwood does not become pregnant as a result of her adultery; she is allowed loving companionship thereafter; and on her deathbed a priest virtually promises her salvation. Moreover, the narrator provides excuse if not justification for her sin: her husband neglected to inform her of his illness, wishing not to trouble her. Instead, he temporized about his time of return, leaving her to feel that he had in effect abandoned her.

This episode echoes the novel's inaugurating event, when Miss Milner's father dies in her absence because a well-meaning friend, from a desire not to distress the young woman, has concealed from his daughter the fact of her father's illness. Both acts of concealment are conventional behavior, arguably performances of "good manners," which dictate the honoring of female delicacy. Lady Elmwood, however, might respond more positively to being treated as an adult. Her self-will and lack of discipline lead to her bad behavior, and the narrator does not condone those characteristics, nor is the reader invited to. In her ten years' subsequent penance and her education of her daughter in a discipline of deprivation, she demonstrates her painful achievement of greater wisdom.

The novelist's decision to pass quickly over the years between Lady Elmwood's marriage and her death emphasizes the work's tendency to treat small happenings more emphatically than large ones. Seduction, adultery, and flight are neglected; a girl's fondling of her father's hat receives detailed attention. Toward the last part of volume 3, momentous events occur again: kidnapping, near-rape, precipitous rescue. These too are narrated in summary fashion, necessary preliminaries to a happy ending that depends on nuances of expression. And that happy ending itself—the presumed marriage of Rushbrook and Matilda—is not narrated at all. Instead, the narrator leaves it up to the reader whether Matilda will respond positively to Rushbrook's proposal.

In the concluding volume, the theme of interpretation receives increasing emphasis. Lord Elmwood appears to have changed his nature. Is he really changed, has he become heartless and cruel, or is he trying to cover up a broken heart? Various characters venture various hypotheses, although everyone fears him. Unquestionably, the nobleman has suffered. The loss of his wife, whom he passionately loved, has marked him. In his interaction with the world thereafter, he, like his wife before him, uses manners and mannerisms as protective devices.

In a small episode, almost a nonepisode, related in considerable detail, Lord Elmwood reads in a newspaper of his wife's death. He lays down the newspaper for several minutes. He rests his head on his hand. He leaves his chocolate untasted. He walks two or three times across the room, sits down again, and quietly resumes reading the paper. The narrator comments at length, reproaching the hypothetical man or woman of sensibility who finds this behavior heartless. The commentary concludes, "And who shall say, but that at the time he leaned his head upon his hand, and rose to walk away the sense of what he felt, he might not feel as much as Lady Elmwood did in her last moments" (193). This characteristically convoluted and indeterminate statement suggests the possibility that small actions betray large meanings. It does not, however, unequivocally offer an interpretation. Long before the narrator invites the reader to decide what happens at the end, that narrator has repeatedly ventured hypotheses rather than explanations of characters' behavior. The narrator, it seems, knows no more than the reader. The necessity of interpreting behavior applies to both, and the possibility of mistake exists for both.

The first two volumes of *A Simple Story* tell of lives lived in an enveloping social context. Dorriforth's relation to society during his time as an unmarried priest remains rather obscure, but Miss Milner, from start to finish, exists within a rich social texture. She has friends and admirers; she goes to auctions and parties; she visits at other people's houses and receives visitors at her own. Her occupations are those conventional for her age, sex, and social class. When Dorriforth becomes Lord Elmwood, he enters into the same social world, although his participation is never so wholehearted as his ward's. But he too visits and is visited, goes to the opera (or, more significantly, doesn't), fills a place at dinner parties. A structure of social expectation exists in the background of each individual's drama. Lord Elmwood's plan to travel on the Continent, like his earlier plan to enter a marriage of convenience with the pious but vapid Miss Fenton, conforms to conventional expectations. Even unconventional Miss Milner finds herself unable to leave a masquerade that provides her with no enjoyment because it would be "bad manners" to abandon her companions. Although the text does not emphasize the existence of an elaborate world of other people, it assumes such a world.

Everything changes in the final two volumes. Now there hardly seems to be a "world" at all. Lady Elmwood flees into utter isolation. Her society consists solely of Miss Woodley, Sandford, and Matilda; each of them has only the society of the others, although Sandford preserves his connection with Lord Elmwood for the sake of the good it might ultimately do. After Lady Elmwood's death, the others hardly enlarge their social spheres. They replace their melancholy retreat in "a lonely country on the borders of Scotland, a single house by the side of a dreary heath" (188) with a great country house, but the two women live as anxious outsiders with severe restrictions on their mobility within that great house. They have contact with the servants, but with no one outside, except for the occasional unwelcome incursion of Rushbrook.

Matilda and Miss Woodley have no independent financial resources, no familial status, and, as females, few rights. But Lord Elmwood, in all these respects their opposite, is depicted as leading a life of almost comparable isolation. Although he enjoys off-stage hunting expeditions, visits, and visitors, the reader sees him as always alone, except for servants, Sandford, and Rushbrook. He has, at any rate, retreated into spiritual isolation comparable to the physical isolation that his wife sought. Nobody, he clearly believes, has the slightest right to control or even influence his actions or decisions.

The emotional emphasis of the novel's final volumes is on confinement, literal or metaphorical. Even Rushbrook, heir to Lord Elmwood's great wealth, young and attractive, experiences no sense of freedom. Imprisoned by his uncle's expectations and demands, cut off from Matilda, whom he believes himself to love, he feels deprived of possibility. He, like his uncle, has social opportunities beyond those textually depicted, but the reader experiences him as yet another isolate.

The novel's movement toward stress on isolation and confinement bears on the matter of manners, those formulations of social expectation. The novel of manners, one might think, self-evidently concerns the encounter between the individual and society. Evelina's entrance into the world supplies a paradigmatic instance of the kinds of problem and solution typical of such fiction. It is surprising, then, to find a novel that emphasizes the importance of manners, yet places its characters in a condition of social isolation.

Even in the first two volumes of *A Simple Story*, manners function frequently—although not always—as deliberate concealment. The determined politeness Miss Milner and Lord Elmwood manifest toward each other after the man has declared the necessity of their separation is the most important case in point. The forms of courtesy, in this instance, mask passionate love, anger, and despair. They provide not only a convenient but a necessary means to obscure unacceptably complicated, unacceptably contradictory emotions. They perform their appropriate function of "pleasing," making the surface of things smooth to avoid distress for onlookers and actors alike.

When social context virtually disappears, in the final volumes, manners remain, but they no longer seem to have much relation to pleasing. The narrator emphasizes several times that Matilda resembles her father, specifically in her "mind and manners" (207). The assertion strikes one as implausible the first time it occurs, even though the characterization goes on to specify that Matilda's tender heart and melancholy situation, in addition to "the delicacy of her sex," soften the qualities she shares with her father. What she turns out to share most conspicuously is the capacity to use manners as intimidation—not to please, but to frighten—or as a mask for negative feeling. Lord Elmwood behaves politely, but Miss Woodley sees through him: sees that he is now "haughty, impatient, imperious, and more than ever, implacable" (215). Matilda, temporarily angry with Miss Woodley, possesses "too much of the manly resentment of her father" to reveal her feelings when she sympathizes with the older woman's grief. She appears grave and majestic; Miss Woodley is "awed by her manners" (242). Only when Miss Woodley offers to fall to her knees before Matilda does the girl relent. She behaves in comparably majestic fashion to Rushbrook, who feels nonplussed by her dignity and at a loss for the appropriate manners to employ in response.

The separation of manners from their traditional purpose of pleasing declares the sense of isolation the characters experience. They do not feel sufficiently connected with others to wish to please them. Matilda, compliant and tender though she is, can only fantasize about a real connection with her father; she cannot even imagine a real connection with his heir. Lord Elmwood, whose avowed aim in life now consists only of self-protection, will not risk vulnerability by even appearing to be concerned with the feelings of others. Only when Rushbrook is ill does his uncle's tenderness briefly emerge; only when there are no witnesses can the nobleman fleetingly express warm feeling toward his daughter. Manners seem vestigial remains of a vanished social system.

The novel, however, has a happy ending, or at least hints at a happy ending: the novelist's evasiveness about the match between Rushbrook and Matilda prevents certainty. Matilda rejoins her father and travels with him to London, symbolic center of social existence. Lord Elmwood accepts his daughter and presumably returns with her to a more normal, less solitary, way of life. The narrator offers a wise saw about education, endorsing Matilda's education in deprivation over her mother's education in self-indulgence. The proper order of things has been reestablished.

There is a curious textual moment just before the end when Rushbrook reveals to Matilda his desire to marry her. He has previously confessed that desire to her father, who sends the girl to him to determine his fate. He falls at her feet, begging that they should be joined "till death alone can part us." At that juncture, the passage hints, she returns to her father's manners as her resource. "All the sensibility—the reserve—the pride, with which she was so amply possessed, returned to her at that moment" (317). Pride and reserve have been the resources of father and daughter alike as they employ haughty manners to awe others. Rushbrook responds to this final manifestation by announcing his own vulnerability, giving her control over his happiness or misery; it is then that the narrator invites the reader to decide whether Matilda would be capable of dooming her lover to unhappiness. If the reader supposes that she would not, the narrator continues, that reader may also suppose that the two will have a life of sustained happiness.

The emphasis on Matilda's sharing with her father crucial characteristics raises the possibility that she might, like her father, choose in time of crisis deliberately to separate herself from others. The only basis on which we can decide about her future happiness is indeed our supposing. The reminder in effect reinterprets the process of interpretation that the reader, like the characters, has engaged in. Interpretation, after all, is only a form of supposing. We have more or less data at our disposal; on the basis of that data, we arrive at conclusions about character and intent—which is to say we imagine as best we can what the data mean. The process of novel writing is one of directing the reader's imaginings. The processes of living, as this novel depicts them, involve a constant sequence of people imagining one another. The behavior dictated by manners can provide either obstacle or enablement in that sequence.

In Burney's novels, as in most novels of manners, manners are taken for granted as a mode of social functioning. Inchbald by no means takes them for granted. *A Simple Story* explores to unsettling effect some possible uses of manners, demonstrating how even a system socially ordained can be turned to private purposes and function not to smooth but to roughen human relations. Manners provide a social code. Like other codes, they demand to be read. Inchbald examines their reading as she examines other forms of interpretation, and she strongly hints that all readings of other people and their actions, whether the other people are textually constructed or exist in the external world, depend upon forms of supposing, more or less dependable, but never infallible. *A Simple Story* opens with a dying man's efforts to ensure his daughter's goodness by providing her with a virtuous guardian. It proceeds through the revelation that this guardian, Dorriforth/Elmwood, has more dimensions than Mr. Milner could imagine. It ends with a dramatic shift in familial connections and with an invitation to readers, who have been exposed to a series of such shifts, to do their own supposing about the future. The education it provides, like that experienced by both the female protagonists, instructs its students in human unpredictability.

It goes almost without saying that all literary treatments of manners assume some intersection of the personal and the social in any individual's way of utilizing social codes. Burney, especially in *Camilla,* implies the danger of "personalizing" manners, of loosening conventional bonds. At the same time, she shows how social conventions can be experienced as impositions on the individual, the disguise of manners interfering with emotional communication. Inchbald, in contrast, suggests that even the most conventional behavior can effectively be turned to personal ends. The many references to manners in works of fiction that assume social systems of behavior without examining them often lack specificity, and such books do not analyze the personal meanings of social conformity. They nonetheless insist on the moral significance of conventional conduct.

Charlotte Smith's 1788 novel, *Emmeline,* offers self-serving autobiographical details but concentrates on constructing an elaborate, if rather implausible, romance around a young woman thought to be illegitimate and poor (ultimately revealed as legitimate and rich). It supplies a large cast of characters and a dizzying assortment of subplots. The characters and situations multiply so rapidly that the narrative requires readily legible cues about how the reader is expected to assess new personages on the scene. Manners most often provide these cues. Not that the characters' manners are specified: on the contrary, they are cursorily generalized as "vulgar" or "simple" or "charming." Such adjectives suffice to locate the characters both socially and morally.

We might wonder why the adjectives are not applied to characters rather than to their manners. It would seem more direct to call a woman vulgar than to announce that she has vulgar manners. Directness, however, is not a primary desideratum; the point is, rather, to locate persons on a social scale that refers also to a moral one. The particular importance of manners may be suggested by an autobiographical account offered by a subsidiary character. Her mother dies; her grieving father wanders around Europe with some of his children. Ultimately he sees "his elder daughter advantageously disposed of in marriage to the eldest son of an Irish peer." The next sentence explains how this advantageous match comes about: "The beauty of Lady Camilla was so conspicuous, and her manners so charming, that though entirely without fortune, the family of her husband could not object to the marriage" (216). Beauty and manners combined—*charming* manners: that is, manners that can charm someone into becoming a suitor—provide an equivalent to money. Conversely, the storyteller continues, her stepmother, acquired soon after her sister's marriage, has no such attractions: she has money instead. "Her vulgar manners, and awkward attempts to imitate those of people of fashion," the narrator explains, "excited my perpetual mirth" (219). Manners control behavior; behavior determines the impressions others form; such impressions often shape individuals' fates.

In both the instance of the beautiful sister and that of the ugly stepmother, manners appear as relatively superficial characteristics, specifically equated in the first case with physical beauty. The text offers no explicit judgment of the character, only of a pattern of behavior. The point is not that the sister is charming or the stepmother vulgar; rather, that the sister acts in a charming fashion. The stepmother behaves vulgarly and makes matters worse by trying to behave fashionably. Why does the attempt to improve her behavior make her more unattractive? Partly because she doesn't do it well; she doesn't succeed in her effort at imitation—but partly also because of the tacit assumption that manners reflect character, so that endeavors to adopt different manners may amount to efforts to disguise character. When Evelina and Camilla learn conformity to codes of politeness, they express their native compassion and generosity through conventional behavior. The stepmother, by implication, imitates the forms practiced by her social betters but lacks the genuine concern for others that manners should convey.

The assumed nexus of manners and character becomes especially obvious when the manners in question are "simple"—a term that in the eighteenth century, as we saw in the case of *David Simple,* had powerful positive connotations, suggesting purity, lack of contamination, the morally unmixed. Thus a minor character is distinguished: "Her manners, tho' simple, were mild and engaging; and her heart perfectly good and benevolent" (337). Simplicity of manners implies lack of sophistication, absence of fashion and therefore of corruption. The conjunction of simple manners and benevolent heart indicates moral worth. Emmeline herself is marked by her simple manners. Her would-be lover considers them among her attractions: "In Emmeline, he discovered a native dignity of soul, an enlarged and generous heart, a comprehensive and cultivated understanding, a temper at once soft and lively, with morals the most pure, and manners simple, undesigning and ingenuous" (300). Pure morals, simple manners: the two go together. Again, the qualities assembled in a single sentence reflect on one another. A woman of "undesigning" manners will not use her manners, as father and daughter do in *A Simple Story,* against others. And she will almost inevitably possess also a generous heart, a cultivated understanding, and a soft temper, because other kinds of heart, temper, and understanding would corrupt her manners to evil uses.

Other adjectival summations of manners abound in *Emmeline,* economically establishing the nature of one character after another. They sometimes duplicate one another—more than one character has vulgar manners, as more than one possesses their simple counterparts—but they are never filled out with more specific accounts of what the individual's manners are like. To be sure, we witness the actual behavior of many imagined figures in the crowded narrative. Emmeline acts in ways dignified, generous, wise, and pure, but it would be difficult to specify what aspect of her behavior constitutes her "manners." We can readily distinguish a woman trying to display herself as fashionable from a woman making no

particular effort to display herself in any special way, but the difference
between them involves more than one usually thinks of as manners.
Yet the value of the term and its literary ubiquity perhaps depend on its
elasticity. Eighteenth-century conduct books consistently maintain that
true good manners are "natural." They need not be taught, because they
emanate from the heart, from innate concern with the rights, the desires,
and the needs of others. (On the other hand, such books often promulgate
numerous specific rules of behavior.) Eighteenth-century novels corrobo-
rate the fantasy of natural manners. Emmeline has not been systematically educated, as far as we know, in the rules of polite behavior, yet she
behaves with flawless decorum, her simple manners conveyed in her
direct responsiveness to those she encounters.

To speak of simple or vulgar manners, then, or of affected manners,
or fashionable manners, is to employ a kind of shorthand. Each adjective
is designed to call up for the reader a set of behaviors and to remind that
reader of the judgment conventionally attached to them. The reader is
invited to discriminate the nature and the meanings of different kinds of
manners, and the text even provides an object lesson of failure to make
the proper discriminations. Mrs. Ashwood, a rich, husband-hunting vul-
garian whose home for a time provides Emmeline with a refuge, goes to
visit the arrogant mother of Emmeline's persistent suitor. "With that sort
of condescension that seems to say, 'I will humble myself to your level,'
and which is in fact more insolent than the most offensive haughtiness,
her Ladyship had behaved to Mrs. Ashwood; who took it for extreme
politeness, and was charmed on any terms to obtain admission to the
house of a woman of such high fashion" (162). Mrs. Ashwood can't tell
the difference between insolence and politeness partly because self-love
blinds her. The reader is expected to keep just such differences in mind
and to be wary of the possibilities for self-blinding.

To focus on references to manners in a novel like *Emmeline* may seem
perverse, since the work clearly exists almost entirely for its plot. That plot
in its wild complications occasionally suggests serious concern with the inequities of the female lot, but on the whole the story is the point, the story
for its own sake and for the sake of entertainment. Manners are at most
an adjunct to the central plot issues, hardly more than a facile reference
point for character. The fact that they can be used so readily as reference
points, though, calls attention to their structural importance in building

fictions. The meaning of different labels for manners—simple, affected, natural, fashionable—is *known*. Such designations can establish the moral location of characters, from which plot meanings are constructed.

The point may become clearer from one final example, another novel in which manners have only peripheral importance and are described only by generalizing adjectives. Eliza Fenwick's only novel, *Secresy; or, The Ruin on the Rock* (1795), establishes a protofeminist agenda through a fiction rich in Gothic trimmings and sexual titillation. (The book will be treated more fully in the next chapter.) Although its initial evocation of a young woman confined under male tyranny for mysterious reasons recalls dozens of contemporaneous Gothic novels, the work pursues an unusual plot. Its apparent heroine, Sibella, has developed as a sort of child of nature, free from society's corrupting influences. She has pledged her love to a young man, Clement, who for a time in their early youth shared her captivity. Another young woman, Caroline Ashburn, who lives in without approving of polite society (her widowed mother is a quintessential denizen of the social world), makes it her project to rescue Sibella. The plot develops many complications and adds a number of characters. Its most crucial event turns on Sibella's ignorance of society's rules. She has no understanding of marriage as a social institution. Consequently, because she loves Clement, she gives herself to him sexually and becomes pregnant as a result. Clement, although willing to take advantage of Sibella's naïveté, has no particular interest in the sexual liaison—he has plenty of other sexual opportunities in his worldly life—but he yields to her initiative. Sibella's death is the long-range consequence.

The subject of manners comes up often as a means of moral definition. Sibella's uncle—the tyrant responsible for the girl's imprisonment, who believes that women need not, indeed cannot, reason and who sees docility as the crowning female virtue—preserves the punctilio of a past age. Clement finds most women unsatisfactory because of (unspecified) inadequacies in their manners. Caroline's mother takes fashion as her deity; she consequently instructs her daughter to call her "Mrs. Ashburn" rather than "Mother": an unusually specific instance of the kind of manners she practices and endorses. In particular, the matter of Sibella's manners constitutes a recurrent issue. "I wish I could have prevailed on Mr. Valmont to allow his niece a more enlarged education," says a male friend of Sibella's uncle; "Her manners, I think, must be constrained and ungraceful" (172).

Her aunt remarks of the girl, "the child has a fine person, and is—that is, had she any thing like manners, and were not such an absolute idiot, I do think she would be very handsome" (219).

In fact, Sibella's manners are unconstrained and graceful: they are *natural* manners. Growing up outside society, she has not even witnessed the affectations that characterize such women as Mrs. Ashburn, and she knows nothing of the artificial rules governing social behavior. She behaves graciously because of her warm impulses toward others. Ignorance of punctilio shows itself in her as a grace.

Sibella's manners matter little in the plot, but they assume considerable symbolic importance. The artifices of society, fully rendered in the parts of the narrative concerning Caroline, her mother, and Clement, only corrupt. Caroline, forced to live in their context, sees that fact clearly. On the other hand, marriage, like manners, is a social institution. One cannot arrive at understanding of it by nature alone: Sibella's concept of her union with Clement as a marriage demonstrates that truth. And Sibella's ignorance of the institution and its social meanings, as well as her ignorance of Clement's true nature, which is revealed only in his social interactions, leads to her destruction.

The subtlety of Fenwick's fictional argument emerges in the contrasting consequences of social ignorance. Despite her criticisms of existing social practices and of the assumptions that underlie them, she perceives also the importance of society as an arena of social observation and discovery. Marriage as a social institution offers women at least basic protection against male fickleness and irresponsibility. If one considers it, rather, as a sacrament, Sibella's intuitive understanding of it comes closer to truth than, for instance, Mrs. Ashmont's self-seeking concept of marriage as social status. As an institution, marriage belongs to a corrupt world: in an edenic social universe, no "institution" would be necessary. Sibella is both wrong and right in uniting herself with Clement: wrong because he is the wrong man for her and because such a union, from his point of view, entails no commitment; right because her natural goodness leads her to the desire to give to the man she loves. And her manners provide a metaphor for the more dangerous naturalness of her sexual conduct. They are naturally good, in that they derive from genuine feeling for others, but they can be perceived also (as by Mrs. Valmont, Sibella's aunt) as socially inadequate. Both views have validity.

Secresy is in no sense a "novel of manners," nor is *Emmeline*. Both novels, however, call attention to the kind of importance assigned to manners in eighteenth-century fiction. After Austen, the "novel of manners" would continue to flourish, but increasingly it would be considered a relatively frivolous mode, not concerned with serious matters. The true novel of manners in the eighteenth century, represented by such works as *Evelina,* was very serious indeed—and so were the other novels that relied on manners as points of reference.

CHAPTER SEVEN

Gothic Fiction

THE GOTHIC NOVEL—A FORM, unlike the novel of manners, with little ostensible connection to ordinary life—originated in a dream. Such, at any rate, was the claim of Horace Walpole, who dreamed, he said, of a giant helmet and forthwith composed *The Castle of Otranto* (1764). This short work (110 pages in the World's Classics edition) is generally thought to have initiated a genre that continues to flourish, although frequently in debased form; that draws even now on material reminiscent of dreams; and that still attracts large audiences—as it did from the beginning. First published pseudonymously, the novel went through eleven editions in English by the end of the eighteenth century. Walpole acknowledged it, at least by his widely recognized initials, in the second edition, to which he prefaced an explanation of his intentions. His book, he suggested, "was an attempt to blend the two kinds of romance, the ancient and the modern. In the former all was imagination and improbability: in the latter, nature is always intended to be, and sometimes has been, copied with success" (7). By the "modern" romance, he means the evolving genre of the novel, which typically attempted verisimilitude in its representation of character. Walpole wanted, his statement implies, to combine supernatural improbabilities with plausibilities of human nature. His followers, who greatly elaborated the Gothic form, pursued similar purposes.

For all its brevity, *The Castle of Otranto* adumbrated crucial elements of the Gothic mode. The combination of the supernatural with the psychologically believable, although central to much Gothic, is only the beginning. Perhaps equally important—at any rate, omnipresent in later Gothic novels—was the stress on troubled family relationships. The father figure in Walpole's novel attempts to marry, and apparently first to rape, the woman who has been engaged to his dead son; he subsequently murders (accidentally) his daughter. In later works, too, hints of incest and unnatural murders would abound. Walpole set his fiction in a castle. Subsequent experiments in Gothic would likewise often locate their action in castles (usually castles with secret or subterranean passages). Like Walpole's novel, later Gothic fiction would typically concentrate on the plight of young women, usually pursued by predatory men. And many subsequent Gothic works, like Walpole's, relied heavily on servant characters for comic relief that often depended on their extraordinary verbosity.

Most significant for the Gothic mode was its establishment of a special atmosphere. Eighteenth-century commentators would refer to that atmosphere as "terror," but more crucial still was a pervasive sense of uncertainty, not only about what would happen but about what had already happened. Something is out of joint in Gothic fiction, and one cannot always readily discern precisely what. Although most Gothic novels, like eighteenth-century novels of other varieties, end in marriage, the search for an appropriate mate or the effort to secure the one chosen does not organize their plots. Instead, the narrative problem at least tacitly established is how to alleviate anxiety that typically exceeds its announced causes. In *The Castle of Otranto,* the central anxiety, experienced by Manfred, the father-figure, stems from a misappropriated inheritance, but that fact emerges only late in the novel. In Ann Radcliffe's novels, the heroine often announces her anxiety over every tiny obstacle, but she does not really know what is wrong. "What is wrong" frequently turns out to involve family structures, but it may implicate larger spheres as well.

Critical exegesis of Gothic fiction has emphasized the psychological, especially the sexual (all those dark passages . . .), but the form's efflorescence in the troubled late years of eighteenth-century England may tempt one also toward political interpretations. The uneasiness presumably experienced by characters and reader alike perhaps reflects that of a nation recently defeated by its own colonies, torn by political dissension, and frightened and fascinated by revolutionary developments across the

Channel, where before the century ended a king would be guillotined. Walpole evokes ancient political conflicts in resolving his plot; Radcliffe, in *The Mysteries of Udolpho,* alludes to vague political problems in Italy and gets rid of her villain by state execution for political reasons; Sophia Lee makes politics central to her plot in *The Recess.* Even without such direct references, though, disharmonious families may be thought to echo disharmonious countries.

A final characteristic of most, though not all, Gothic is its invocation of supernatural forces. Walpole appears to take them for granted in all their preposterousness, employing for the sake of plot convenience such figures as a talking skeleton and a walking portrait; Radcliffe subjects her characters to harrowing appearances, although she explains them all away in the end; in M. G. Lewis's *The Monk,* the supernatural is lurid and horrifying; in William Beckford's *Vathek,* some aspects of the supernatural teeter on the edge of comedy, despite their horror. Always, though, supernatural appearances provide correlatives for emotional distress, underlining uncertainty and suggesting cosmic disturbance behind it.

Despite its fairly rudimentary plot development, *The Castle of Otranto* demonstrates how confusion and foreboding can generate narrative drive. The novel begins with the inexplicable happening of Walpole's dream: a giant helmet falls from nowhere, killing Manfred's son Conrad on the verge of his marriage. Manfred reacts unpredictably to this catastrophe, evincing little grief but much activity. The reader at the outset may feel undisturbed by the father's lack of grief, though, the narrator having offered scant reason to mourn the death of a young man characterized as sickly, homely, and "of no promising disposition" (15), not even an object of devotion for his own fiancée, the beautiful and virtuous Isabella.

The novel's opening pages provide an incomprehensible prophecy and the death-dealing helmet as precipitants of action. Thereafter, things happen at tumultuous speed. Manfred takes his son's death as license to pursue Isabella. He will divorce his compliant wife, he explains to the girl; Isabella will, he assumes, bear him sons to preserve the family line. When she shows no eagerness to fulfill this assignment, Manfred pursues her through the castle's dark recesses, foiled by the intervention of a fortuitously present young man. Although she escapes, the young man—apparently a peasant of remarkable presence and courage—suffers imprisonment and threatened death at Manfred's hands.

Spectacular moments abound: the walking portrait, the speaking skeleton, the apparition of a giant hand. But much of the plot emphasizes individual characters' conflicts about duty. Manfred's wife, Hippolita, provides the most egregious example, explaining that women have no right to make choices: "Heaven, our fathers, and our husbands, must decide for us." "Have patience," she continues, addressing her sorely beset daughter Matilda and the beleaguered Isabella; "until you hear what Manfred and Frederic have determined" (88). From her point of view, the perception of duty sounds like a simple matter: a woman does what the man in her life commands. But even Hippolita suffers conflicts. What should a woman do when "heaven" and her husband make opposed demands? Manfred orders her to divorce him; the priest tells her such divorce would be a sin.

Isabella and Matilda also face duty's difficulties. Both love the same man, the helpful peasant. Manfred's commands in every instance conflict with their feelings. Manfred himself feels the tug of duty, shaken by the priest's injunctions and by his sense of responsibility for ancient wrongs. His submission to passion rather than duty leads him to murder his daughter—for which he atones by yielding his estate and his sovereignty and retiring to a monastery. (The guiltless Hippolita also ends in religious retirement.)

So a novel that presents itself as mere entertainment ("A Gothic Story," as Walpole designates it) carries moral overtones. Yet it would be hard to say just what moral it inculcates. The language of duty and the rendered conflicts of duty and passion call attention to parental, marital, and filial responsibility, yet the recommendation of such virtues assumes no prominence in the narrative. Theodore, the brave young peasant, appears to wear his virtues of courage, steadfastness, and honesty mainly as sex appeal. A conventional moral vision governs the novel's explicit utterances, but its plot punishes the innocent (Conrad, Matilda, Hippolita) without comment on the injustice involved, and allows Manfred, despite his guilty intentions and his rash murder of Matilda, to live. Moreover, the narrator hints at a certain disrespect for romantic love, that verity of fiction, in an ending marked by tone and action that surprisingly foretell the resolution of *Mansfield Park*. All the survivors think it convenient that Theodore should marry Isabella: a tidy resolution to chaos. But, the narrator tells us, "Theodore's grief [for Matilda] was too fresh to admit the thought of another love; and it was not till after frequent discourses with

Isabella, of his dear Matilda, that he was persuaded he could know no happiness but in the society of one with whom he could forever indulge the melancholy that had taken possession of his soul" (110). Suddenly romantic love seems almost a joke, so inevitable as to be uninteresting, and so does the melancholy that has characterized Manfred and that will mark many a later Gothic hero/villain.

The effect on the reader is to create something like cognitive dissonance, a disparity between what one expects and what is affirmed as actually the case. In this way too, Walpole's early Gothic novel reiterates its sense of uneasiness, that atmosphere it so richly utilizes to establish its force.

The talkative servants who inhabit much Gothic fiction, firmly rooted in the commonplace, indirectly contribute to the reader's uneasiness. They frequently feel fear, even terror; they are more likely to flee than to resist menace. They usually prove more superstitious than their masters. Bianca, Matilda's servant, immediately interprets groans she hears as emanating from the ghost of a dead astrologer who once tutored Conrad and whose spirit, she believes, is conversing with that of his newly dead pupil. Matilda suggests that they say a prayer and then speak to the ghosts; Bianca replies that she would not speak to a ghost for the world. She readily understands Theodore, when they encounter this flesh-and-blood source of the groans, as pining away for love. Indeed, she appears to believe love the root of most human maladies.

Such trivial details matter little in the action of *The Castle of Otranto;* they seem like mild jokes. Walpole himself, however, called attention to the importance of the servants' role. In the preface to the first edition, where he posed as translator of an ancient Italian manuscript, he suggests that "the art of the author is very observable in his conduct of the subalterns," because the servants through their naïveté and simplicity both reveal and help effect action (4). In the preface to the second edition, speaking in his own voice, Walpole argues more fully the case for his domestics, claiming the precedent of Shakespeare for the mixture of tones created by the presence of members of the lower orders in the company of more dignified characters. He speaks of the servants' effect on readers, first suggesting that these domestics "might almost tend to excite smiles." Then he mentions the suspense servants can create. "The very impatience which a reader feels, while delayed by the coarse pleasantries of vulgar actors from arriving at the knowledge of the important catastrophe he expects, perhaps heightens, certainly proves that he has been artfully interested in, the depending event" (8).

As Radcliffe would demonstrate more fully than Walpole, the talkativeness of servants often intolerably postpones important revelations, to an extent that may produce impatience rather than suspense in the reader (the servant's fictional interlocutor typically suffers from both emotions). It lengthens narratives: Walpole's small volume would have been yet more slender without Bianca. But one may feel tempted to seek more serious explanations for the omnipresence of domestics—and to find elucidation in the social facts of the class system. Servants, as Walpole suggests in his first preface, have less serious, less "sublime" reactions than their masters do. And they talk much more, usually less to the purpose. They respond less courageously to crisis. (Some exceptions to this generalization occur in Radcliffe's novels.) The supernatural—real and apparent alike: Radcliffe, as I have said, explained away her supernatural appearances—tests the social order. When forces beyond the natural challenge human nature, the differences that emerge between masters and servants justify social inequality by moral inequality.

The fictional roles of domestics in Gothic fiction, then, despite their role in creating suspense, also deliberately counterbalance the sense of uneasiness so carefully established. The servants' roots in the commonplace, their insistent return to the everyday, even the banality of their superstitions, remind the reader of an ordinary world that continues despite all horrors allied to an imagined other world. They talk too much, a fact linked to their comparative lack of moral discrimination and discipline. Their volubility calls attention to differences between those of high and low rank—differences redounding to the advantage of the high. (Theodore, the noble and attractive peasant in Walpole's novel, turns out to be of elevated rank by birth.) If moral superiority accompanies social superiority, it justifies the social system that creates unbridgeable gaps between the ranks. Thus the existing human order, as rendered in such novels as *The Castle of Otranto,* rests on solid logic. Within the fictional world, this order functions securely even as ghosts and skeletons and massive armor suggest disorder. The servants in this sense provide a ground of stability. Readers should not find themselves too uneasy, after all. Romance may be frustrated, the innocent may die, but the social hierarchy remains.

The servants in their talkativeness also provide, as Walpole hinted in his preface, a kind of emotional relief. Gothic fiction trafficked heavily, or attempted to, in the sublime. Not long before *The Castle of Otranto*, the young Edmund Burke had published *A Philosophical Enquiry into the Origin of our Ideas of the Sublime and Beautiful* (1757), articulating the eighteenth-century implications of a cloudy critical term. The sublime, he explained, was associated with the vast, the powerful, the terrible, and the obscure. A thunderstorm could be sublime, or a rugged mountain. God himself—vast, hidden, omnipotent, terrifying—epitomized sublimity. Because the sublime by definition (Burke's definition, but also the interpretations of earlier critics) aroused powerful emotion, some imaginative writers hastened to evoke it. Supernatural appearances easily lent themselves to the engendering of terror and awe, stereotypical responses to the sublime. In the dénouement of *The Castle of Otranto*, Walpole might be writing with Burke open on his lap, so systematically does he draw on the established vocabulary of sublimity as he describes the novel's final supernatural appearances: "The walls of the castle behind Manfred were thrown down with a mighty force, and the form of Alfonso, dilated to an immense magnitude, appeared in the center of the ruins. Behold in Theodore, the true heir of Alfonso! said the vision: and having pronounced those words, accompanied by a clap of thunder, it ascended solemnly towards heaven, where the clouds parting asunder, the form of saint Nicholas was seen; and receiving Alfonso's shade, they were soon wrapt from mortal eyes in a blaze of glory" (108).

But Gothic novelists often attempted to create sublime effects through character as well as through the supernatural. Manfred emerges as a rather rudimentary rendition of the sublime character, his "sublimity" inherent in his power (absolute within his realm) but also in his reticence. The obscurity characteristic of the sublime (we cannot discern the full contours of the mountain; we cannot see God) may operate within the human realm. That atmosphere of uncertainty so typical in Gothic issues partly from obscurity's operations. In *The Castle of Otranto*, the confusion and anxiety afflicting many of the characters emanate largely from Manfred's refusal to divulge what he knows. His intentions as well as his knowledge remain unrevealed. As a man of few words—many of them peremptory orders—he draws on the power of the sublime in his self-representation. Bianca, with her unstoppable flow of language, contrasts sharply with him, offering the relief of transparency to the tension of obscurity, the relief of the humdrum to the tension of the sublime.

Like novels of sensibility, Gothic fiction not infrequently reminds its readers of the inadequacy of language to intense feeling. "Words cannot paint the horror of the princess's situation," Walpole writes (26). Readers, engaged in reading words, are yet invited to imagine "the horror" without language, as in the fiction of sensibility they are in effect urged to evoke the feelings of characters by direct recourse to their own emotional capacity. This connection to sentimental fiction is by no means accidental. Indeed, one might think of the Gothic as a direct offshoot of sensibility. In *The Castle of Otranto* and its successors, as in *The Man of Feeling*, the goal is to arouse the reader's emotion by narrating the characters' emotional experience. The painful happenings that afflict Isabella or Matilda generate painful feelings in those who encounter them on the page, arousing some version of that sympathy that makes the foundation of sensibility. Moreover, the possession of highly developed emotional capacity marks moral discrimination. Only those who feel deeply, in the logic of these novels, can judge rightly. Thus readers who find their emotions harrowed by the extravagant and often terrifying mishaps that afflict the characters may silently enjoy their affinity to the innocent and virtuous.

Yet the relation between sublimity and sensibility presents real complications. In a general sense, the sublime is associated with the passions, powerful feelings like rage, envy, and lust; sensibility draws usually on gentler and milder emotions—sympathy, above all, and what we call empathy; at its strongest, perhaps shame. Gothic novels typically attempt sublimity, yet rely heavily on sensibility. The tense relation between the two generates much of this fiction's force.

The term *Gothic,* as applied to a particular form of the novel, draws on two eighteenth-century senses of the word: "belonging to, or characteristic of, the Middle Ages" and "barbarous; rude; uncouth." Walpole did not explain his use of the term to describe his story, but his successor, Clara Reeve, did, specifying that her book, *The Old English Baron* (1778), "is the literary offspring of the Castle of Otranto" and that "it is distinguished by the appellation of a Gothic Story, being a picture of Gothic times and manners" (3). Although the time period of the events in some novels remains vague, and some actually set their action in the eighteenth century, specified times lie most often in the distant past. (To remove the narrative further from contemporary Britain, its happenings usually occur on the Continent, especially in Italy, although France and Spain also make their appearances.) And the "sublime" characters of the novels are, by the standards of cultivated eighteenth-century English men and women, barbarous and uncouth. Sublimity as a quality of character appears to depend on *lack* of sensibility—lack of concern for the feelings of others, the concern institutionalized, as we saw in the last chapter, by the system of manners.

The character of Manfred in *The Castle of Otranto* exemplifies such lack of concern, although Manfred is not fully developed as a type of the sublime. Walpole's novel provides an outline version of the most familiar aspects of Gothic fiction that succeeded it, but the outline is by no means complete: subsequent novelists on occasion struck out in quite different directions. Even Clara Reeve, after announcing her intention to follow Walpole as model, confesses that she finds aspects of his novel silly. That is, she is inclined to laugh—as twenty-first-century readers may be too (and she knows other readers in her own time who feel the same way)—at some of the supernatural manifestations. A sword that requires a hundred men to lift it, a helmet so large that its fall forms a passageway in the vault beneath the surface it hits, the walking picture and the skeleton ghost: all these, Reeve says, "destroy the work of imagination, and, instead of attention, excite laughter" (5). Her own ghost, in *The Old English Baron,* is perfunctory. He appears only once, and only to reprehensible characters, although his groans are intermittently audible.

Writing less than fifteen years after Walpole, Reeve demonstrates a new imagining of Gothic possibilities. Perhaps more emphatically even than her alleged model, she dwells on family disorder, both hidden and manifest, and her insistence on reinforcing the class system appears to dictate many of her narrative choices. She doesn't bother with talkative servants, but she makes her protagonist a young man allegedly of peasant origin and acutely conscious of what he cannot do because he lacks the privileges of rank. Only the discovery of his high birth, which occurs well before the novel's end, allows him to pursue the path in life for which his chivalric virtue has equipped him.

That virtue provides the novel's most salient subject. Reeve does not linger on sublimity. Her stalking ghost offers a momentary appearance in the sublime mode, but her interest focuses, rather, on manifestations of sensitivity, sympathy, and courage by her allegedly lowborn hero. *The Old English Baron* virtually functions as a conduct book for men. Like literal conduct books, it implicitly promises that those not born to aristocratic behavior can learn its rules and practice it successfully. Edmund, of course, needs no rules. His noble actions—more heroic, more compassionate, more gracious than those of his avowedly aristocratic contemporaries— occur, apparently, by virtue of his fine instincts. Such actions win him powerful patrons, wealth, and the status to which he is entitled by birth—but which, also, he has earned by highly principled behavior.

The novel exposes the conservative implications often latent in Gothic fiction. Although its subject is disorder, such fiction also expresses a corollary longing for order, which inheres in old ways and long traditions. *The Old English Baron* contains loyal, brave servants—but if they are born servants, servants they remain, and they wish to be nothing more. Members of the upper class experience the "inexpressible sensations" (126) of sensibility; members of the lower classes do not. The class hierarchy reflects and sustains a hierarchy of feeling and behavior. Order runs deeper than chaos: such is the message of all Gothic fiction. And awareness of this message reveals the importance of such fiction's characteristic form, which circles back on itself to create a pattern of revelation more important than its pattern of action. Perhaps a better way to put the point would be to say that the pattern of action exists for the sake of revelation: what has happened in the past matters more than what happens in the present. Thus, the discovery of Edmund's high birth and his father's murder creates the instrumentality for restoring order. And all ghosts lie quiet once order is restored.

A more anomalous instance of Gothic is William Beckford's *Vathek* (1786), which abounds in occurrences of sublimity, most of them manifestations of supernatural malignance. Few of my generalizations about the Gothic mode apply to this perverse tale. Reeve focuses novelistic interest on virtue; Beckford concentrates instead on vice. Unlike Reeve and Walpole, he shows no interest in making his characters psychologically plausible. On the contrary, he creates monsters—a mother and a son—of immense power. The son, Vathek, is caliph of an unnamed Eastern realm. In the first paragraph, we learn of him that "when he was angry, one of his eyes became so terrible, that no person could bear to behold it; and the wretch upon whom it was fixed, instantly fell backward, and sometimes expired" (1). And this is only the beginning. The tale continues to relate one instance after another of the caliph's brutality and the self-absorption that generates it. His mother proves even more casually destructive than he. Their murderous activities reach such a pitch of excess that the narrative, deadpan in tone, frequently topples into a comic register.

At an early point in the story, for instance, Vathek and his mother light a fire at the top of a tower. The caliph's citizens think that the tower is on fire and rush to his assistance, a hundred and forty "of the strongest and most resolute" successfully bursting through the doors and ascending the stairs. Carathis, the wicked mother, recommends sacrificing them. The fire and fumes overcome them as they reach the top: "It was a pity! for they beheld not the agreeable smile, with which the mutes and negresses adjusted the cord to their necks: these amiable personages rejoiced, however, no less at the scene. Never before had the ceremony of strangling been performed with so much facility. They all fell, without the least resistance or struggle: so that Vathek, in the space of a few moments, found himself surrounded by the dead bodies of the most faithful of his subjects; all which were thrown on the top of the pile" (34–35).

In the next sentence, these bodies are referred to as "carcasses."

This scene of bloodshed is typical in its absence of struggle, its remoteness and unreality, and the uncomplicated pleasure of spectators and murderers alike. It invites the reader too to smile at its moral disjunctions—the agreeable facial expressions of mutes and negresses, the praise of the strangling as "ceremony." Yet it provides sly reminders of other possible reactions, through allusion to the victims' fidelity and through the jarring reference to them as carcasses, like the bodies of animals. Such diction heightens the scene's dissonance. After the horrors of the twentieth century, of course, it is particularly difficult to read of mass slaughter—and scenes of mass slaughter abound here—without emotional response quite different from the mild amusement apparently solicited by the novel.

The original reviewers, generally approving, saw *Vathek* as a moral tale. Indeed, mother and son are punished for their evil deeds by consignment—self-consignment, really—to an elaborately described hell in which their hearts burn endlessly in their breasts and they find themselves utterly alienated from all others, including their companions in the nether regions. Yet the narrator manifestly takes pleasure in his hell as simply one more locus of sadistic excess. Nominally, the infernal punishment of the sinners should restore order, in the familiar Gothic pattern. It can be read, however, as the reverse of restoration: as a sustaining of aesthetic and moral subversion, a continuing invitation to contemplate sadism simply as aesthetic spectacle.

Vathek is unusual among Gothic novels, possibly unique, in inviting no sympathy for the victims of "sublime" forces. As I have already suggested, it does not traffic in psychology; it does not pursue Walpole's goal of uniting the resources of the nominally realistic novel with those of the fanciful romance. Beckford makes not the slightest gesture toward realism. His effects depend on an ironic sense of distance. He employs the general form of the Oriental tale, a familiar eighteenth-century mode, heightening it to extravagance and raising its moral stakes. The only remotely attractive figure he represents is a Peter Pan–like young boy who escapes Vathek's malice and lives forever, forever infantile, on a cloud. Beckford implicitly challenges the reader to judge his characters but makes judgment difficult if not impossible within the novel's terms.

Beckford's Gothic perversities met an immediate dead end: no other novelist experimented with the same combination of Oriental tale and supernatural dread, albeit dread tinged with comedy. One other writer, Matthew Gregory Lewis (called "Monk" Lewis after the great success of his novel), provided his readers with sadistic rather than moral gratifications, publishing *The Monk* toward the century's end (1795). I shall postpone consideration of his important fiction, though, and look first at yet another fictional experiment that briefly opened new territory for Gothic.

Sophia Lee's *The Recess; or, A Tale of Other Times* (1783) explores imaginative possibilities in Elizabethan history. Unlike most Gothic fiction, *The Recess* does not rely on even the apparent supernatural. It does not, for the most part, locate the sublime in character. Its servants speak strictly to the point. Yet it develops the possibilities of what we might call "Gothic atmosphere" and demonstrates, without obvious models at its disposal, that the Gothic could serve serious purposes.

If Lee lacked models of "serious" Gothic, she had available to her by the final quarter of the eighteenth century many novelistic forbears working in other subgenres. *The Recess* draws on several of the modes we have investigated in previous chapters. It is in a loose sense—the sense of *Fanny Hill* or *Memoirs of Miss Sidney Bidulph*—an epistolary novel, constructed primarily as two long retrospective letters by two sisters, each writing to and for the other. Each of these letters, like some of the journal-letters of *Sidney Bidulph,* embeds short letters by others. *The Recess* relies heavily on the tradition of sensibility, constructing both its heroines as figures dominated and largely controlled by their emotional capacities. The novel follows the *Robinson Crusoe* model as a tale of adventure—adventure not consciously sought, often painful, but a primary fact of experience nonetheless, even for women of rank and wealth who would traditionally be cut off from daring action. Tracing the lives of two women from birth to death, it thus conforms to the model of fictional life history. Incorporating structures from all these subgenres, Lee succeeds in combining them under the aegis of Gothic, employing the tension of sensibility and sublimity to comment on the role of women in history.

For history is an important element in this novel, despite the fact that much of the "history" the book provides is fictional. That the action occurs in Elizabethan times serves more vital purposes than simple distancing. Lee's story concerns imagined twin daughters of Mary, queen of Scots, by a secret marriage. Matilda and Ellinor, after childhoods passed together in ignorance of their lineage and in seclusion from the world, go different ways, separated by their choices of love object. Matilda bears a daughter by the man she loves, the earl of Leicester, whom she has married; Ellinor never achieves marriage to her beloved, the earl of Essex. Both women endure relentless suffering in multiple forms. Ellinor dies insane; Matilda is at the point of death at the novel's end; Matilda's daughter, her hope for regal reinstatement, is poisoned. No happy endings here. As for marriage, that conventional form of resolution: not only does it figure throughout the novel mainly as a device for achieving political ends; it does not guarantee happiness even when its participants deeply love each other.

Sublimity in this novel finds realization in history, history conceived as a concatenation of irresistible but incomprehensible forces. Obscure, terrible, all-powerful, unmindful of individuals, it possesses all the qualifications of the sublime. To be sure, there is no "it" there: "history" is an abstraction, a retrospective generalization, an unpredictable product of memory, myth, and desire. The reader, obviously, is in a different position from the characters in relation to history. Lee brilliantly exploits the difference by constantly reminding us that what we accept as truth depends on where we stand. Looking back from almost three centuries' vantage point, even eighteenth-century readers would realize that what they see as history—and Elizabeth and James, Essex and Leicester, and many minor figures were all presences in history, all people they would have read about before—is for Matilda and Ellinor only a series of unfathomable happenings. We are all of course caught up in history; this novel insists on how little we can know what that means.

The main experience the sisters share, almost constantly, is the negative one of lacking all control. They may briefly feel that they control someone or something, but soon life forces them to realize that the feeling is illusionary. The recess of the title is an elaborate cavelike series of structures in which the little girls come to consciousness and grow to adolescence. They live with a woman whom they call "Mother," but she tells them finally that she is not their mother. They know nothing of their parents, nothing of why they must live in such circumstances, nothing of any larger world. All children lack control, but for these girls, whose life follows an invariable daily routine and whose capacity for larger awareness is severely limited, the lack is heightened.

Eventually they escape their seclusion. Their surrogate mother dies; they accidentally encounter Leicester, in flight from would-be assassins, and shelter him in the Recess. Matilda falls instantly in love and marries him, then departs with him. The subsequent events defy summary, so numerous, so various, so confounding are they. Matilda finds herself at the mercy of forces she does not understand. She tries to operate by the well-established rules of female propriety, unfailingly loyal and submissive to her husband, but following or not following such rules appears not to have the slightest bearing on her fate. It does not matter whether she behaves well or ill. When she endeavors to calculate her advantage, her calculations seem not to matter either. Things happen at random. Leicester dies; a would-be lover—a coarse and brutal man—kidnaps her and carries her to Jamaica; she gives birth to her daughter; a slave revolt rescues her from near-rape; she spends many succeeding years in prison, along with the infant, who grows to the age of eight or nine, deprived of books but provided by her mother with moral education, before the two are released. And all this represents but one chapter in her tumultuous saga. One unforeseeable happening succeeds another. Many emanate in one way or another from Queen Elizabeth, a constant presence, on- or off-stage.

The queen is the novel's villain, its most powerful character, dangerous because of her power and its erratic applications. Both sisters, who
nominally compose the novel's narrative through their letters, understand
her in terms of their own preoccupations, as motivated by erotic impulse
and vanity. They only weakly grasp national concerns, beyond the fate of
their family as potential heirs to the throne. Understanding Elizabeth from
their own perspectives, without sympathizing with her, they nonetheless
convey the pathos of her situation as a woman alone, afraid to trust a man,
not wishing to yield any power, but inexorably aging and losing both sexual
and other kinds of personal force.

As this paradox of sympathetic revelation and hostile intent may suggest, *The Recess* is emphatically a female book. A large preponderance
of eighteenth-century Gothic novels had female authors, and the fact is
important in understanding their substance: they often focus attention
on the plight of women. *The Recess* is unusual in its formal intricacy—not
only multiple narrators, but multiple narrators with varying points of view
on the same subjects—and it employs an immensely complicated plot.
Throughout its elaborate developments, it emphasizes its concerns with
the female situation. "Ah man, happy man!" Ellinor reflects; "How superior are you in the indulgence of nature! blest with scientific resources,
with boldness, and an activity unknown to more persecuted woman; from
your various disappointments in life ever spring forth some vigorous and
blooming hope, insensibly staunching those wounds in the heart through
which the vital powers of the feebler sex bleed helplessly away; and when
relenting fortune grants your wishes, with unblighted powers of enjoyment you embrace the dear bought happiness; scarce conscious of the
cold dew-drops your cheeks imbibe from those of her, permitted too late
to participate in your fate" (213).

If such observations declare vividly the letter writer's self-pity and
prophetic sense of vulnerability, they also summarize sexual differences
that the narrative stresses. These differences involve character as well as
circumstance. Neither Ellinor nor anyone else in the novel reflects on
the possible reasons why men prove more hopeful and more resilient
than women, but the fact that males are permitted activity while "persecuted" women are doomed to confinement seems more than coincidental.
Ellinor's comments acquire additional poignancy by comparison with an
earlier remark of hers, at a moment of crisis, to Lady Pembroke. "Born

for conflict," she says, "I seem only to exist by that mental action" (189). Mental action alone is customarily available to women, and "that mental action" destroys Ellinor.

Confinement and flight provide the traditional alternatives for the Gothic heroine. Lee's heroines spend much time in both situations, but their "mental action" in the condition of confinement supplies them with considerable resources for managing their flights. Bold in their imaginings, they likewise prove bold in executing them. Ellinor, despite her susceptibility to mental anguish, disguises herself as a man for one extended foray and purposefully risks life and chastity in pursuit of her lover. Matilda exhibits courage and ingenuity in desperate situations. Like other Gothic heroines, the sisters possess great powers of endurance, bearing the strain of massive uncertainty—about their own prospects and about the fates of those they love—as well as actual danger. In short, though doomed to those female destinies of confinement and flight, they never remain passive under restriction. As we first encounter them, young, mysteriously consigned to a more or less underground existence, they are already busy thinking, trying (although in vain) to make sense out of their circumstances. From the moment they accidentally encounter Leicester and scheme to rescue him, they do their best to circumvent restriction. Even when Matilda finds herself imprisoned for many years without recourse, she declines to consider herself helpless: she devotes herself to finding expedients to educate her daughter.

In other words, Lee uses plight as an arena of possibility, demonstrating the female capacity to think and act, as well as feel, within a context of proclaimed dependency and devotion. Although her heroines, as we have seen, may complain about their lot, on the whole they adapt to or manage to improve the situations in which they find themselves. As Ellinor rightly points out, they lack the opportunities available to men—but they make the most of the opportunities they have.

No one within the text appears to notice this fact, and the general failure to grasp female heroism is significant. The novel's formal structure, its pattern of interlocking letters, calls attention to the problem of point of view, most conspicuous in relation to assessment of Leicester's character. To Matilda, her lover and husband is the best of men. Ellinor has her doubts. She sees Leicester as engaged in political calculations, untrustworthy. Until his untimely death, Leicester behaves impeccably, as far as we are told, to Matilda, but little evidence emerges about his motives or purposes. The opposed understandings of his nature simply exist side by side. Readers can take their choice, or can conclude that they lack evidence for evaluation. In any case, they have been forced to contemplate the possibility of radically opposed interpretations.

This matter of point of view returns us to the question of history. History as lived, the novel tells us, is confusion and incomprehensibility. If we have no evidence for Leicester's motives and purposes, neither do we know the intents of other actors in the drama. But we know their names, many of them, before we read the novel; and if we are readers of history, we have previously encountered interpretations of them. To an eighteenth-century audience, it would have been apparent that Lee drew heavily on popular history books of the period. If she invented a great deal in her fiction, she also recorded behavior and events that had been set down—in effect codified—by others.

Turning these declared facts into fictions, she invests them with mystery by interpreting and reinterpreting them as lived experience. Her intricate, moving narrative is calculated to arouse wonder and awe, to make one feel how momentous the course of a woman's life can turn out to be.

No subsequent eighteenth-century novelist followed her lead. Instead, the Gothic novel progressed along the course outlined for it by Walpole, although not without many elaborations and variations. *The Monk* marked its most lurid eighteenth-century development. Lewis, reacting to Ann Radcliffe's *Mysteries of Udolpho* (1794), which will be discussed later in the chapter, differed from Radcliffe in relying heavily on the supernatural, and he employed sex as well as heightened violence as fictional substance. Like Walpole, he flirted with incest. Instead of a father inadvertently murdering his daughter, he provides a son accidentally murdering his mother. Like Beckford, he multiplies violent episodes to a degree that may make one suspect a sadistic sensibility. Like all his Gothic predecessors, he incorporates vignettes of more tender, more orthodox eighteenth-century sensibility. His plotting allows room for digression: he adds Gothic subplots to his primary story of a corrupted monk.

The monk's corruption comes about by supernatural means, but neither he nor the reader knows this important fact until the end. At the novel's opening, Ambrosio, admired and revered by all, preaches to enormous congregations and leaves his monastery only to preach. Within the monastery, he finds himself increasingly fascinated by a young novice who is both physically attractive and devoted to him. The novice, it develops, is in fact a woman, whose face duplicates that of a painted Madonna that also fascinates Ambrosio. She seduces him physically, then leads him to responsibility for ever greater horrors, including rape and murder. It turns out at last that she is not a woman but a demon, dedicated from the outset to his destruction. That destruction duly occurs in physical as well as moral terms: after Ambrosio sells his soul to a devil, the monster seizes him and drops him from "a dreadful height" over cliffs and precipices to an agonizing and prolonged death.

At the novel's opening, Ambrosio appears as a sublime figure. Not yet corrupted, he has become legendary for his piety and severity. All of Madrid flocks to hear his weekly sermon at the cathedral. "There was a certain severity in his look and manner that inspired universal awe, and few could sustain the glance of his eye, at once fiery and penetrating" (20). If his ocular powers remind us of Vathek, he emerges as a less arbitrary, therefore more significant, presence. When he begins preaching, "his voice, at once distinct and deep, was fraught with all the terrors of the tempest. . . . Every hearer looked back upon his past offences, and trembled: the thunder seemed to roll, whose bolt was destined to crush him, and the abyss of eternal destruction to open before his feet!" (20–21). The tempest, thunder, lightning, hell: these signs of power, terror, and mystery associate themselves with the charismatic monk and declare his quasi-divine force.

The reader acquires an initial impression of Ambrosio partly from the perspective of Antonia, young, lovely, and innocent, ready, even eager, to be awed. In other words, the declaration of "sublimity" depends on an outside observer. The novelist who wishes to evoke the human sublime may not choose to give the sublime character much in the way of psychology, for introspection might dispel mystery and terror, those indispensable characteristics of the sublime. Lewis offers no subtle or exhaustive exploration of Ambrosio's mind, yet he brilliantly deconstructs the sublimity he evokes. The narrative focuses on a limited register of the monk's thoughts and feelings as he succumbs to his seductress, then finds himself involved in increasingly vile behavior. Lewis thus suggests the inherent fallacy of assigning any human being larger than lifesize stature.

In *The Monk*, the terror that Gothic novelists had systematically tried

to evoke becomes converted into horror: the horror of an old woman stran-
gled; of an imprisoned mother clutching the corpse of her infant, which
crawls with worms; of a woman trampled into mush by an enraged mob.
The spurious grandeur of the diabolical, like Ambrosio's spurious moral
magnitude, not only yields destruction; it generates sordid misery.

Sexuality is tainted: an effort to elope leaves the suitor sharing a carriage with the ghost of a nun, while his beloved ends up chained in the
dungeon of a convent. Ambrosio lusts after Antonia and therefore rapes
and murders her. The satiating gratification of lust generates only dissatisfaction. Indeed, dissatisfaction marks all Ambrosio's efforts. Although
his self-seeking and malignant intentions prevent his ever becoming a
sympathetic character, the reader is yet compelled to realize the pain he
creates for himself by his efforts to fulfill his desires.

Lewis's novel gradually reveals a strong and rather unexpected sentimental strain. The sentimental note emerges mainly in the sympathy
invoked for Ambrosio's various female victims: innocent Antonia, her
canny and loving mother, and especially Agnes, the most vivid sufferer
from clerical tyranny. Through Agnes, in particular, Lewis explicitly the-
matizes the tension between sublimity and sensibility.

Agnes, Raymond's beloved, has been consigned to a convent against
her will. Pregnant with Raymond's child, although not yet married, she
becomes the object of the prioress's wrath because of her sexual lapse.
That prioress, not unlike Ambrosio, concerns herself mainly with her
reputation; she worries, or says she worries, lest lack of severity disgrace
her in the eyes of "Madrid's idol, . . . the very man on whom I most wanted
to impress an idea of the strictness of my discipline" (199). That idol, of
course, is Ambrosio, who, himself recently initiated into the joys of sex,
feels inclined toward leniency for Agnes. Matilda, his devilish paramour,
urges him instead to redouble his appearance of austerity, lest anyone suspect his own deviation from rectitude. As for Agnes, "she is unworthy to
enjoy love's pleasures, who has not wit enough to conceal them" (199).

Ambrosio follows Matilda's advice, recognizing its perspicacity. But
he is shocked by her "insensibility." Pity, he muses, "is a sentiment so
natural, so appropriate to the female character, that it is scarcely a merit
for a woman to possess it, but to be without it is a grievous crime" (200).
He himself feels sincere pity for Agnes, but he resolutely suppresses it. He
preserves the appearances of sanctity and severity that have contributed

to his high reputation; although he lusts after the women who confess to him, none of them suspects the fact.

Sublimity, as *The Monk* makes increasingly clear, is entirely a matter of appearance, although qualities of character contribute to appearance's successful construction. Such construction, in Ambrosio's case, depends partly on the suppression of pity, the denial of sensibility. Even after he rapes Antonia, the monk feels active pity for her; yet his concern for his own reputation proves stronger than any impulse toward compassion. Lewis arranges his narrative to emphasize that the monk's religious education has encouraged the nullification of many virtues—compassion and "noble frankness" are specified—and the "narrowing" of Ambrosio's native sentiments for the sake of his grand self-representation. The disjunction between real and apparent virtue does not amount to hypocrisy until the liaison with Matilda brings the monk to consciousness of his own base impulses, but the church has deliberately encouraged the potential for hypocrisy.

The most unambiguously sublime figure in this novel is the fiend who lures and dashes Ambrosio to his destruction. He comes attended with an extravagant paraphernalia of thunder, lightning, and whirlwinds, his form enveloped in darkness, his hair composed of living snakes, his "enormous sable wings" images of terror. "Fury glared in his eyes, which might have struck the bravest heart with terror" (369). This elaborately described presence in effect solidifies the book's association between sublimity and evil. Sensibility, the virtue denied by sublimity, operates on a human scale; sublimity claims more. Lewis's novel attempts to have it both ways: on the one hand, it repeatedly invites the reader to sympathetic response; on the other, it offers the titillation—the factitious terror—of the sublime.

For some readers, *The Monk* generates a kind of moral uneasiness comparable to that created by *Vathek*. Here, too, one may suspect rather too much pleasure in lovingly detailed sadism. If Lewis invites sympathy for Ambrosio's female victims, his lavish accounts of their suffering (particularly Agnes's agony during and after her infant's death and Antonia's brutal and prolonged torment in the catacombs of the nunnery) suggests an almost pornographic delight in the spectacle of male-inflicted anguish. For all its power—indeed, because of its power—*The Monk* demonstrates the moral ambiguity often implicit in the project of Gothic.

Ann Radcliffe, probably the most popular Gothic novelist of the late eighteenth century, appears to have felt conscious of the danger in such ambiguity. Perhaps her most compelling novel, *The Italian* (1796), offers a deliberate rewriting of *The Monk*. Radcliffe retains many elements of Lewis's work, including the opening scene in a cathedral where a young man sees for the first time the beautiful woman to whom he will devote himself. Here too we find the monk famed for austerity and virtue and discover the discrepancy between his apparent and actual nature. Here too are hints of unnatural family relations. The Inquisition becomes a powerful presence in Radcliffe's novel, as at the conclusion of Lewis's. The text supplies a proud and wicked prioress, as well as a nunnery equipped with dungeons and with the threat of perpetual imprisonment. But no actual murder occurs—at any rate, no murder of the virtuous characters during the time of the novel's action—and certainly no incest, nor are there literal supernatural interventions, despite many appearances that encourage characters and readers to believe in supernatural presences.

Radcliffe's redaction of her famous predecessor makes the polemical point that suggestion can carry more power than description. By her heavy reliance on a rhetoric of suggestion, Radcliffe staked out new ground for the Gothic. She also accorded the relation of sublimity and sensibility a conspicuous place in her narrative, using indirect means here too to make a significant point.

Like all Radcliffe's heroines, Ellena displays a large quotient of sensibility. She reacts with feeling to every small event; she perhaps exceeds all other Gothic heroines in her frequent outbursts of anxiety; she is drawn by sympathy especially to other women. Her lover, Vivaldi, at least equals her in his subservience to the impulses of sensibility. Anxiety of Ellena's sort does not mark him (although he proves subject to extraordinarily ready doubt about whether his beloved really loves him back), but he shows great capacity for sympathetic identification, and his most conspicuous characteristic is a labile imagination, ready to conjure up false explanations and, in particular, to accept temporarily inexplicable appearances as the product of supernatural forces. As more unmixed novels of sensibility consistently demonstrate, imagination and sensibility go hand in hand since only imaginative capacity enables the kind of emotional identification essential to the response of sensibility.

Here as in Lewis's fiction, sublimity characterizes evil rather than good characters. The monk Schedoni, extraordinarily tall, impenetrable, and severe, epitomizes the erotically tinged but essentially malignant figures who appear in all Radcliffe's fiction. He has the aspect of the sublime; Vivaldi does not. At the novel's conclusion, Schedoni, inevitably, dies, unflinching and unrevealing to the last. (In this respect he deviates sharply from Ambrosio, who pledges himself to the devil in a paroxysm of fear and proves a craven figure at the end.) Vivaldi and Ellena marry, but not before Vivaldi has been chastised for his imagination. Schedoni explains that he has taken advantage of the young man's "prevailing weakness" for his own purposes. That weakness, he elucidates, is "a susceptibility which renders you especially liable to superstition." "The ardour of your imagination," he adds, "was apparent, and what ardent imagination ever was contented to trust to plain reasoning, or to the evidence of the senses?" (397).

Both Vivaldi and Ellena, however, have a tougher side, which exists not in opposition to but in consequential relation with their ready sensibility. Like Sophia Lee's heroines, Ellena endures adversity not merely with stoicism but with active resistance. She uses her wits to fathom and foil her enemies. Thus, confined in an isolated house, alone with a murderous man, she figures out that he plans to poison her and refrains from drinking the milk he supplies. At the mercy of the wicked prioress, who offers her the choice of instant marriage (to a man she has never seen) or immediate consecration as a nun, she repeatedly and determinedly refuses either. Vivaldi likewise resists, insisting on his own innocence in the face of the Inquisition's manipulation and accusation and preserving his capacity for sympathy even in a tormented situation that might excuse self-absorption.

The relation between the capability to resist and to sympathize is never spelled out. It becomes apparent partly by means of Radcliffe's invocations of the natural world. One can easily mock the set pieces of mountain grandeur or pastoral beauty, clearly indebted as they are to eighteenth-century paintings (Radcliffe never went to the Continent, although she locates the action of her novels in France and Italy), but those set pieces serve important purposes. They spell out in visual and psychological terms the contrast between the sublime and the beautiful and suggest the opposed forms of power the two concepts embody.

Eighteenth-century painters, like poets and novelists, had utilized the aesthetic possibilities of Burke's key terms. Radcliffe's reliance on paintings, therefore, would have reinforced her tendency to rely on aesthetic dichotomies. Each of her novels employs oppositions between "sublime" and "beautiful" natural scenes that underline the related human contrasts. The technique is particularly conspicuous in *The Italian,* in which the heroine, abducted, taken on a long carriage trip through the Alps, then confined in an Italian nunnery, gains both comfort and courage from the contemplation of sublime landscape, which calls to her mind the power of God—power that can, she realizes, overthrow the tyrants who keep her captive. Looking out from a turret window at the mountain landscape, Ellena affirms in herself the strength of resistance. She possesses the capacity, the narrator explains, to have her mind "highly elevated . . . by scenes of nature. . . . Hither she could come, and her soul, refreshed by the views [the turret] afforded, would acquire strength to bear her, with equanimity, thro' the persecutions that might await her" (90). Women, in Burke's figuration, have nothing to do with the sublime. Radcliffe manages, without compromising her protagonist's "femininity" (softness, fearfulness, concern with propriety, yearning for relationship), to connect Ellena with the sublime by allowing her to appropriate the internal power it connotes.

The beautiful, in this novel, associates itself often with the domestic —at the level both of scenery and of psychology. "How sweetly the banks and undulating plains repose at the feet of the mountains," Ellena observes; "what an image of beauty and elegance they oppose to the awful grandeur that overlooks and guards them!" (158). She goes on to specify images of cultivation and control in those plains. In the novel's final pages, after Ellena and Vivaldi have married and returned to Ellena's paternal estate, Radcliffe allows herself detailed description of the natural scene, with stress on the blooming flowers it contains, to carry the message that the two young people, who have been agitated victims of the human sublimity embodied in Schedoni, now can repose in the beautiful.

If Ellena has an affinity for the sublime, she also manifests a stereotypically female desire for dependency. Her sustained resistance to the terrifying Schedoni draws on that dependency: she appeals to him as "Father" (he is, after all, a monk), and after she believes him to be identified as her literal father, she insistently dramatizes her need for him. Such tactics do not notably soften Schedoni, although they occasionally appear to disturb him. They help define Ellena as belonging to the realm of "beauty" herself, despite her responsiveness to the sublime.

With her emphasis on the capacity for responsiveness in her male and female protagonist alike, Radcliffe in effect glorifies the feminine "beautiful" in character, even as she delineates one of the most effective sublime characters of any eighteenth-century Gothic novel. Unlike most of his "sublime" predecessors in Gothic fiction, Schedoni is assigned more than a rudimentary emotional life. He possesses recurrently explored interior experience as well as an impressive exterior. The narrator investigates his motivation and the nature and causes of his self-construction as amoral plotter, focusing frequently on his scorn for those who allow conscience or morality to impede them. A towering figure physically, he also towers as an imaginative presence, partly because of his ambiguous role in Ellena's family. Implicitly commenting on Lewis's Ambrosio, he suggests Radcliffe's conviction that family dramas hold more power than do incursions of the supernatural.

Walpole, as we have seen, began the Gothic genre with a tale of family disorder, and his successors followed his cue. Not until Radcliffe, however, did a Gothic novelist perceive the possibility of making hidden intricacies of family life the source of all important disturbance in a narrative. The ambiguity of Ellena's parentage turns out to create much of the suspense in *The Italian*—not because the girl does *not* know who her father is, but because she thinks she *does*. The ostensible revelation of paternity teases the reader with a natural order that feels like disorder, setting up a disturbance that is not alleviated until the novel's end.

Such a novel as *The Italian* implicitly comments on the well-established and perhaps unduly facile convention of eighteenth-century fiction that has sons in particular discover their true parentage and thus solve all their problems. From Tom Jones to Humphry Clinker (and beyond), fictional heroes, after many vicissitudes, discover that social stability and financial security after all belong to them by the generosity of parents, even parents who have fathered them illegitimately. Radcliffe suggests that the discovery of a father may only intensify a child's difficulties. Moreover, she ponders the possibilities of jealousy, rivalry, and other family tensions extending far beyond the parent-child dyad. In *The Italian* both Ellena's family and her lover's create difficulties. Vivaldi's mother, driven by family ambition as well as, the text hints, even darker motives, plots with Schedoni to effect Ellena's murder; defeminized (Schedoni taunts her for thinking like a woman), she is finally virtually dehumanized.

Radcliffe's novels characteristically explore versions of the family map in order to create the mystery and horror that mark the Gothic mode. Her refusal to allow supernatural explanations of even the most startling phenomena underlines her insistence that natural accounts offer not only more plausible but more compelling principles of exegesis—principles likely to strike a chord in the reader. To investigate one more case in point, we might contemplate *The Mysteries of Udolpho* (1794), perhaps her best-known novel, partly because of its lavish displays of apparently otherworldly manifestations, which are ultimately explained away.

The immense, sprawling story, more than six times the length of Walpole's, focuses on the vicissitudes of a young woman named Emily. Orphaned—like most Gothic heroines—early in the narrative, Emily finds herself under the guardianship of a disagreeable aunt who marries a powerful, brooding Italian nobleman named Montoni, possessor of the castle of Udolpho in the Appenines, to which he takes, and where he persecutes, the two women. Montoni's only interest, the text tells us explicitly, is power. His threats when the young woman dares to cross him claim the unimaginable magnitude of his power. He cannot forgive the slightest defiance, nor can he be moved by any appeal to sympathy, an emotion that he fails to comprehend. Emily fears and dislikes him, yet he emerges as a far more compelling figure than, for example, his henchman Morano, whom Montoni intends as Emily's husband.

Montoni is consistently associated with the passions: "His soul was little susceptible of light pleasures. He delighted in the energies of the passions; the difficulties and tempests of life, which wreck the happiness of others, roused and strengthened all the powers of his mind, and offered him the highest enjoyments, of which his nature was capable. Without some object of strong interest, life was to him little more than a sleep" (182). This characterization evokes the ambivalence typically marking Radcliffe's accounts of "sublime" men. On the one hand, Montoni delights in "energies"—an important positive term in this period—and cultivates powers of mind, while repudiating merely "light pleasures." On the other, the phrase "of which his nature was capable" implies reservations about that nature: other natures would have higher capabilities. And this passage immediately precedes the revelation that Montoni spends much of his time gambling: such is the most immediate "object of strong interest." A powerful figure, then, but one who misuses his capacities; a man associated with the "tempests of life," the tempest being a conventional figure for the sublime; a man to be feared, but also, perhaps, to be reluctantly admired. Such contradictory responses are constantly solicited for Montoni, as also for Schedoni, whose gigantic presence invites awe even for his physical nature and whose tumultuous internal conflicts help to make him commanding.

Emily, in contrast, is by instinct all sensibility, a fact that causes her parents worry. After her mother's death, and again when his own death impends, her father elaborately warns her about the importance of strengthening her mind against the potential ravages of feeling. Happiness, he explains, "arises in a state of peace, not of tumult." (Montoni, in other words, will never find it: he prefers satisfactions far removed from happiness. Emily, though, wants and finally achieves happiness.) "It is," Emily's father continues, "of a temperate and uniform nature, and can no more exist in a heart, that is continually alive to minute circumstances, than in one that is dead to feeling. You see, my dear, that, though I would guard you against the dangers of sensibility, I am not an advocate for apathy" (80).

Emily remembers this advice, and other sequences like it, repeatedly during her harrowing ordeal at Udolpho and after her escape from the castle. By remembering it, she indeed proves able to fortify her mind. She behaves with strength, courage, and consistency, in these respects outdoing her lover, Valancourt, whose own great sensibility helps make him susceptible to corruption. The narrator waxes rhapsodic as she reports the final great happiness of the young couple, restored "to the beloved landscapes of their native country,—to the securest felicity of this life, that of aspiring to moral and labouring for intellectual improvement—to the pleasures of enlightened society, and to the exercise of . . . benevolence" (672). With the pleasures of society and of benevolence, the pair has achieved the opportunity to make the best possible use of controlled sensibility. Montoni, off-stage, is executed.

For purposes of plot, obviously, Emily and Montoni need each other: persecutor and persecuted, tyrant and resister. But their mutual dependence goes beyond plot. Burke's exposition of the sublime and the beautiful makes the sublime essentially masculine in its nature, associated with power, terror, and obscurity; the beautiful is feminine, associated with gentleness, openness, and soft curves. Although the two qualities exist independently of each other, Burke makes it clear that human aesthetic desires demand both, the "gentleness" of the beautiful a necessary relief from the terror of the sublime. The design of Radcliffe's novels—and, perhaps less self-consciously, of much other Gothic fiction—depends on constructing ways of implicating the two forms of power.

Hence the great importance of sensibility as a component of Gothic characterization. Even in works like *The Mysteries of Udolpho,* in which admirable characters deplore sensibility's power, the presence of this emotional capacity not only differentiates the survivors from the victims of treachery, terror, or justice. It also provides a sign of individuality. Although sensibility's responses may seem stereotypical to postmodern readers, they declare the interior life, the personal responses of separate beings. Emily and Valancourt belong together partly—perhaps mainly—because both possess the same kind of emotional capability, which differentiates them from such as Montoni and the woman he marries. Sensibility guarantees suffering—guarantees, indeed, suffering often in apparent excess of its causes—but it also guarantees human superiority. Those who can live in a Gothic world, a world marked by the eruption of unanticipated horrors, while still maintaining their emotional responsiveness deserve to survive and *will* survive: every Gothic plot says so.

Not even the considerable variety of fictional arrangements already discussed in this chapter exhausts the eighteenth-century possibilities of Gothic. A final subspecies of Gothic spins variations on domestic themes, focusing attention on heroines who, unlike Radcliffe's, essentially never leave home. Outstanding examples of the mode include Charlotte Smith's *The Old Manor House* (1793) and Eliza Fenwick's *Secresy: or, The Ruin on the Rock* (1795). Both typify the domestic Gothic in eschewing the supernatural in order to emphasize the more routine horrors of families out of joint. Both adapt the conventional Gothic situation of an orphaned girl confined to a sinister castle (the "old manor house," an ancient mansion, is a castle in all but name), although the presiding tyrant in Charlotte Smith's novel is a woman rather than a man. Both writers, unlike Radcliffe, make overt reference to social and political actualities. In *The Old Manor House,* the heroine's beloved fights as a British soldier in the American Revolution, explicitly raising questions about a situation in which rich old men bring about conflict and send poor young men to die in it. *Secresy* concerns itself centrally with prevailing attitudes toward women and their proper social functioning.

Both novels adapt the familiar Gothic structure to new ends. The heroine remains in vaguely sinister confinement, where a tyrant appears to hold all the power. Her lover has freedom to wander the world. (In *The Old Manor House,* however, the lover leaves reluctantly and endures hardship in his "freedom." In *Secresy,* the lover proves himself reprehensible—although the confined girl remains unaware of this fact—when he encounters the temptations of "the world.") The tyrant's power is ultimately overcome and family secrets are revealed.

The "new ends" arguably possess greater importance than the Gothic machinery that effects them. *Secresy,* in particular, with its intricate plot and tragic resolution, demonstrates intense social concerns and an enlarged sense of human relations. It translates the idea of the sublime into a new register. Its confined heroine, Sibella, conforms in few respects to the female figure characteristic of Gothic. Her guardian uncle, who believes that women require no education, should not cultivate reason, and need learn only to submit, has incarcerated her in his castle, attended by two uncommunicative servants (one of whom is literally deaf and dumb). She can roam the grounds, which are secured by a moat, but she can go no farther. Although her situation affords her little physical freedom, she powerfully asserts her mental liberty. She receives an "accidental" education, profiting from the lessons of the boy who for some years shares her captivity, and she makes the most of it. But Sibella is more significantly a child of nature, unafraid of storm or darkness, figuring life out for herself. Her companion, Clement, whom she comes to love, understands from early childhood the uses of slyness and concealment. Sibella, in contrast, espouses openness. She knows nothing of the world's laws and customs, her unworldliness the source of her strength and weakness.

Despite her self-cultivated rationality, Sibella upholds absolutely the law of feeling. Her devotion to an adventitious female friend (Caroline Ashburn sees her only once before initiating an epistolary relationship) matches her commitment to Clement. Caroline shares Sibella's lofty ideals but accompanies them with worldly experience. She acts as mentor both to Sibella and to the virtuous but misguided Arthur Murden, who loves Sibella from afar. Even Caroline's best efforts, however, cannot avert the disasters that befall Sibella and Arthur, ending their lives and allowing the corrupt Clement to survive, lovelessly married to Caroline's wealthy mother.

The most crucial single event in the novel's action is the contrasting "marriage" of Sibella and Clement. Sibella, in her innocence, believes that the sexual enactment of her love constitutes marriage. She knows nothing of the social forms customarily entailed in such physical commitment. At Clement's insistence, they keep their union secret. From this secrecy, as well as from the novel's many other concealments, tragedy ensues.

The plot holds many further complexities, but this much summary will indicate its ideological drive. Most Gothic fiction had supported a conservative agenda, enacting the restoration of hierarchical social order. *Secresy* restores no order. Its ending offers only the ambiguous hope of a single enlightened individual, Caroline, continuing to struggle in personal ways for convictions that no one around her shares. The novel does not endorse the class system: the characters within it who prove proudest of their lineage and rank are frivolous or malignantly misguided. The book reveals vivid consciousness of economic power and inequality, implicit condemnation of imperialist exploitation, fierce reprehension of social frivolity and of the social degradation of women. Such aspects of *Secresy* might suggest a political thrust, but its political recommendations remain latent. Instead of imagining political remedies for the evils she deplores, Fenwick evokes the possibility of individual enlightenment and action. She apparently sees that possibility as embodied mainly in women.

The two central female characters, Sibella and Caroline, possess striking "energy" and "vigor," two words insistently recurrent throughout the text. The male characters appear passive, ineffectual, or both. Arthur engages in an elaborate charade involving various disguises and the exploitation of secret passages, but his maneuvers only enable him to see Sibella from time to time and occasionally to exchange a few words with her. Almost dead himself (he has contracted a fatal disease from hanging about in dank caves), he succeeds in rescuing Sibella from her immurement, only to lose track of her at an inn where they stop. Clement has no purpose in life beyond effecting his own pleasure. He follows always the path of least resistance. Sibella's cruel uncle, Valmont, makes elaborate plans and plots—all of which come to naught. The impecunious young Lord Filmar, another elaborate plotter, finds his plots foiled and his economic survival dependent on Sibella's posthumous bounty. No man among the novel's characters achieves much of anything.

To be sure, no woman achieves much either, but the two admirable women embody the principles of energy and openness that this fiction espouses as its only remote hope. In choosing to adapt the Gothic mode to her purposes, Fenwick committed herself to a story of individuals in distress. Her individuals, at least the noble females, function admirably but futilely. They give not the slightest credence to supernatural appearances, which in this narrative are altogether factitious, manufactured by Arthur Murden. Yet Sibella, at any rate, succumbs to the "something wrong" that even the false supernatural suggests. In this instance, the indicated discontents are ideological as well as familial, but the Gothic framework does not encourage ideological resolution. Fenwick's rhetoric of suggestion, unlike Radcliffe's, conveys social unease rather than stimulates terror.

Not even the strongest individual can resolve social discontents. Fenwick evokes a new version of the sublime, associated not with powerful men but with the lofty words of women. "I feel within the vivifying principle of intellectual life," Sibella declares. "My expanding faculties are nurtured by the passing hours! and want but the beams of instruction, to ripen into power and energy" (74). Her claim of potential power becomes more concrete. When Arthur suggests the possibility of secret escape, Sibella announces, "Did I think it right to go, I should go openly. Then might Mr. Valmont try his opposing strength. But he would find, I could leap, swim, or dive; and that moats and walls are feeble barriers to a determined will" (104).

This is sublimity of the mind, and only of the mind. In the event, Sibella indeed dives into the moat—to be ignominiously removed from it by Valmont's servants. Her power inheres solely in her imagining of it, which endures to the verge of death. Caroline likewise adopts an elevated tone, claiming aspirations that affect others. She writes to Murden, "I would first subdue the fermentation of your senses, teach you to esteem Sibella's worth, pity her errors, and love her with infinite sincerity, but not so as to absorb your active virtues, to transform you from a man into a baby.—You are but two beings in the great brotherhood of mankind. . . . You must be dependent for your blessings on the great mass of mankind, as they in part also depend on you" (285). Caroline's grand visions, however, prove no more efficacious than Sibella's. The failure of all significant efforts by the two noble females creates a strong undertone of despair in Fenwick's novel. Women, who seem the only hope for society, can do nothing. Caroline survives, her will intact, but her actual power dubious. She remains quite alone.

Secresy marks the limits of the Gothic mode, dimly suggesting a desire to achieve something more than, different from, what the form allows. Its rich emotional texture, its subtle characterization, its economic awareness, and its tense plot mark its sophistication as a piece of fiction, and it is unquestionably a good read. In conjunction with the other novels this chapter has treated, it emphasizes the varied tonal and substantive resources of Gothic conventions. Fictional playfulness, sadistic fantasy, historical romance, investigation of the sublime or of the situation of women—the Gothic could develop all these and more. It did so by means of deceptively simple structures, which often appear to duplicate the episodic arrangements of adventure novels.

A deep logic in fact governs the configurations of Gothic fiction. The episodes that rapidly succeed one another are linked by a slow pattern of revelation that supports the action of *knowing* controlling most Gothic novels. Mystery envelops both past and present. It is rarely clear why things happen in the present or what has happened in the past, but the workings of the plot ultimately reveal reasons and facts to elucidate motives and events alike. The reader duplicates the characters' processes of knowing, achieving clarity only toward the novel's end. This advent of clarity corresponds to the restoration of order customarily signaled by marriage.

Gothic novels thus conveyed concerns more serious than generating some version of "terror" in their readers. Their assertion of logic in the face of confusion perhaps expressed the longings of a population facing great political confusion, but they could not fulfill all the needs of end-of-the-century novelists and their readers. The hints of *Secresy* would come to fruition in a new politicized fiction, the subject of the next chapter.

CHAPTER EIGHT

The Political Novel

POLITICAL FICTION ABOUNDED IN England during the final years of the eighteenth century. Unlike the other subgenres we have examined, examples of such fiction do not fall readily into a typical formal mode. Novelists with political purposes freely utilized forms that had developed for narratives of adventure, of development, especially of romance. Formal suggestion thus reinforced ideological purpose by conveying the view that politics can be understood to include all else.

Most eighteenth-century political fiction appeared in the century's concluding decade, when the French Revolution held forth menace and promise, political repression threatened the principle of free speech in Great Britain, and to write or publish radical speculation might entail imprisonment. Unsurprisingly, the novelists who chose to set forth political convictions in fictional guise promulgated radical views more often than conservative ones, which would not require the disguise of imagined characters and happenings. The novels offered visions of ideal political possibility or, more daringly, indictments of society as it currently existed—"Man As He Is Not," the subtitle of *Hermsprong,* or "Things As They Are," to quote the original title of *Caleb Williams.*

William Godwin's *Caleb Williams* remains the best-known and probably the most intricate example of the mode. Published in 1794, it issued from the pen of a political philosopher whose reputation rested mainly on his philosophic work *Enquiry Concerning Political Justice* (1793), an idealistic argument for anarchism that derived, from rational principles, the necessity for rejecting government. Godwin offered varying accounts of his intent in the novel. In the preface to the first edition—withdrawn in response to the publisher's understandable anxiety—the author explained that "it was proposed, in the invention of the following work, to comprehend, as far as the progressive nature of a single story would allow, a general review of the modes of domestic and unrecorded despotism by which man becomes the destroyer of man" (55). This statement occurs in the context of Godwin's slightly earlier assertion that only recently has "the inestimable importance of political principles . . . been adequately comprehended" (55). Together, the two comments imply that political intent controls the novel's formation.

In a retrospective account of the novel's composition, published in Godwin's preface to an 1832 edition of *Fleetwood*, however, the writer implies a different and more complicated authorial purpose. Here he focuses on his plotting of *Caleb Williams*, hinting that he wrote the novel in order to make money and saying that he planned it as "a book of fictitious adventure, that should in some way be distinguished by a very powerful interest" (445)—the nature of that interest never elucidated. He invented the action of the third volume first, then worked backward to the first. Thus he achieved, he says, great unity of plot, "and the unity of spirit and interest in a tale truly considered, gives it a powerful hold on the reader, which can scarcely be generated with equal success in any other way" (446).

The desire to achieve such a "powerful hold" dominates this version of the narrative of composition, which also uses such terms as "overpowering interest" (446). Godwin reports having said to himself "a thousand times, 'I will write a tale, that shall constitute an epoch in the mind of the reader, that no one, after he has read it, shall ever be exactly the same man that he was before'" (447). As he explains having moved from an earlier third-person narrative to the first-person form with which he stayed, he acknowledges that his imagination "revelled the most freely" in "the analysis of the private and internal operations of the mind" (448). Nothing in Godwin's account here alludes to political purpose. Claiming that his own imagination reveled in psychological analysis, he suggests that readers' imaginations might likewise revel, and his stress on careful plotting appears to emanate from a desire to engage the imagined reader—without declared ideological intent.

This was Godwin's last word on the subject of *Caleb Williams*. Earlier, in response to an attack published in a journal, *The British Critic* (1795), he had insisted once more on political intent: "to expose the evils which arise out of the present system of civilized society; and, having exposed them, to lead the enquiring reader to examine whether they are, or are not, as has commonly been supposed, irremediable" (451). But the *Fleetwood* preface appears to indicate that as the novel receded in time from the date of its composition, its author remembered more vividly what we might call his purely novelistic motives.

To think of *Caleb Williams* as one in the long succession of eighteenth-century English novels helps define its compelling quality. Godwin often referred to it as a tale of adventure and indeed patterned it as a perverse adventure narrative. Like Robinson Crusoe, Caleb faces the problem of inventing a life, after being metaphorically shipwrecked by his employer's plot against him. He too needs to discover means of survival; he too must devise expedients for meeting the demands of daily experience; he too must face isolation. But his milieu is England, not a desert island; pursuit by enemies threatens his survival; his solitude stems from his rejection by others, not from the absence of potential companions. With motives less straightforward than Crusoe's, Caleb wants not only to survive but in an obscure sense to triumph.

Godwin's narrative focuses on the mutual obsession of the wealthy, upper-class Falkland, Caleb's erstwhile employer, and Caleb himself, a younger man, originally from the working class, who has served as Falkland's secretary. The "adventure" Caleb first constructs, then endures, originates, he repeatedly tells us, in his "curiosity," which compels him to ferret out the truth about whether Falkland has committed murder. After acknowledging his guilt, Falkland declares his lasting power over his subordinate. Caleb can never escape him, he says, and can never successfully blacken his name. He does not explain the sources of his asserted power, but subsequent developments, as Caleb unsuccessfully attempts to escape Falkland, reveal that wealth and rank invariably control events and generate belief. If curiosity dominates Caleb, concern for reputation compels Falkland—so Caleb tells us, and so Falkland himself affirms.

Caleb experiences first an adventure of discovery, later one of escape, finally one of revelation. The exhilaration attending Robinson Crusoe's repeated triumphs over his environment by no means marks Caleb's experience. On the contrary, as narrator of his own story Caleb insists on his unexampled suffering. He does not ostensibly claim the excitement of adventure. By his narrative's end, he does not even claim to tell his own story. He finishes his "memoirs," he explains, only "that thy [Falkland's] story may be fully understood" (434). Concentration on himself, he suggests, has been his sin.

A reader might readily agree that extreme narcissism, as we call it now, marks Caleb, as well as Falkland and Tyrrel, other important actors in the story. Distortions caused by narcissism generate much of the action. Thus Falkland's concern for how others see him precipitates his murder of Tyrrel after Tyrrel has publicly insulted and disgraced him. Tyrrel's persecution of the innocent girl Emily, which ends in her death, stems from his indignation at her intolerable defiance of his will. Tyrrel's public degradation of Falkland registers his rage that the other man should interfere with the esteem he is accustomed to receive from his neighbors.

If narcissism interferes with clear perception and with ethical action, it might also be expected to misshape narrative. The first sentence of Caleb's story raises such a possibility: "My life has for several years been a theatre of calamity" (59). Beginning with a first-person pronoun, the sentence betrays a melodramatic sense of self, suggests self-preoccupation, and possibly makes the reader wonder why the writer understands his life not as drama but as a setting for drama. If his life is a theater, what is the play?

The rather grandiose tone of this opening assertion prepares for a tale of tragic adventure, but unpacking the metaphor reveals the narrative's affinities also with the novel of consciousness. The "play" unfolded by the events of Caleb's life is a drama of consciousness, a psychological agon. Godwin's acknowledged pleasure in analyzing "the private and internal operations of the mind" has borne fruit. As a result, so has his purpose of exciting "very powerful interest": the interest of ferreting out truth from an elaborate structure of self-justification.

Caleb Williams is an "undependable narrator" not because he proves unreliable as a reporter of events but because the degree and nature of his self-concentration make him susceptible to distortion in his interpretation of what happens, to him and to others. The self-dramatization of seeing his own experience as a theater of calamity prepares for a story in which he becomes uniquely the object of total persecution. Although he often acts ingeniously, effectively, and energetically—*energy* being a term of high praise throughout the novel—Caleb understands and narrates himself as victim rather than actor. Falkland, in his perception, becomes virtually omnipotent. Only in Caleb's final moment of realization, itself characteristically exaggerated, can he see Falkland as victim and reverse his sense of self to insist on himself as murderer.

The brilliance of Godwin's novel consists largely in its capacity to convey at once the truth and the distortion of Caleb's narration. *Things As They Are; or, The Adventures of Caleb Williams,* to use the book's original title, reports on things as they are in the psychic as well as the social world. Caleb's "adventures" occur more compellingly in his mind than in his physical activity. Unlike Robinson Crusoe, he neither has nor discovers any religious faith. His principle of interpretation depends not on God but on his self, and, as he discovers, that principle proves inadequate.

So the reader may be led to suspect the neatness of Caleb's view that curiosity constitutes his besetting sin, and concern for reputation holds the same place for Falkland. We may even feel some suspicion about whether Caleb actually believes this himself. He castigates himself for the curiosity that leads him to study Falkland for every clue about his possible crime, but he sounds almost boastful as he explains that boyish curiosity led him to attend to the activities of the carpenter who lived next door: as a direct consequence, he can devise the means for escaping from prison. Curiosity has guided him to a study of costume, accent, and idiom. As a result, he can disguise himself effectively over and over again, never duplicating a strategy. Curiosity causes him to embark on the project of creating an etymological dictionary, a project aborted by the need to flee his latest refuge, but one in which he takes manifest satisfaction. If curiosity indeed gets him in trouble on occasion, it also often gets him out. It figures frequently as a positive attribute, testifying to the mental agility and intellectual capacity that presumably made Caleb attractive to Falkland in the first place and that are calculated to make him attractive also to the reader.

Falkland's undeniable concern for reputation likewise can arouse ambivalent feelings. It causes him to murder, depriving three men (two of them innocent of any wrongdoing) of their lives, yet it also motivates praiseworthy actions. No evidence links it directly with his heroic concern for the welfare of others, although such concern supplies the most obvious cause for his high reputation, but Caleb himself connects it with Falkland's delicate sense of honor, his chivalric moral code, and his masterful self-discipline. At the very least, the alleged sins of the novel's central figures bear close connections to virtue.

The narrative's most important adventures develop from Caleb's early pursuit of Falkland, to unearth his secret, and from Falkland's more extended pursuit of Caleb, to keep him from revealing that secret. The most destructive result of the second pursuit, Caleb maintains, is his isolation. Every time he devises an adequate mode of existence, Falkland or his agents circulate news of the young man's alleged crimes, and he finds himself ostracized or compelled to flee for fear of imprisonment or even hanging. "Solitude, separation, banishment! These are words often in the mouths of human beings; but few men except myself have felt the full latitude of their meaning" (408). Caleb's belief that no one has ever suffered as he has suffered expresses itself recurrently, and he often insists that his separation from humankind accounts for the greatest part of his suffering. In fact, though, he meets kindness from many strangers: from Brightwel, a paragon of virtue, in prison; from the troop of robbers especially, and for a prolonged period; from the woman who acts as his London agent for publishing fiction; from Laura and her family. True, Falkland's interventions always truncate his out-of-prison relationships in one way or another. He cannot confidently settle into any way of life, nor can he sustain a web of human contact. His suffering is undeniable. Yet we may note also that Caleb fails to allow those who help him a great deal of independent identity. Understandably, he considers them primarily in terms of their usefulness to him. He does not fully *see* them (or, for that matter, Falkland). His horror at a system in which "every man is fated to be, more or less, the tyrant or the slave" (238) is predicated on what has happened to him; he never appears to notice that people like Laura function successfully as neither tyrants nor slaves.

I do not wish to deprecate Caleb's suffering, vividly evoked in the novel. When he announces his belief that "misery, more pure than that I now endured, had never fallen to the lot of a human being" (267), we may note his persistent exceptionalism but still acknowledge that he indeed endures great misery. Yet the novel encourages its readers to note also the degree to which his suffering depends partly on his embrace of his own victimization. Seeing the world as composed only of victims and victimizers, Caleb has no question about his own role. He might be said to exploit (that is, to tyrannize over) the woman in London, who is imprisoned after his departure as a result of her help to him, but he does not see the situation that way.

The conclusion, in which Falkland suddenly emerges as a victim too, on the verge of death and consumed by his own feelings, underlines the degree to which role derives from perception. Now Caleb functions as tyrant, Falkland as slave. Or it might be more nearly true to say that both men emerge as their own tyrants, their own slaves. Caleb makes the original observation about the universality of the two roles as a political comment. By the novel's end, it has become more profoundly a piece of psychological analysis.

Unsurprisingly, given its psychological emphasis, *Caleb Williams* lends itself also to a reading as a novel of development. If the novel's "adventures" have an aspect of perversity, in their stress on obsessive persecution rather than on the excitement of mastery, so does its pattern of "development." Caleb changes in the way that protagonists of eighteenth-century fiction typically change: not by any transformation of character but by the accretion of knowledge. Like Matilda in *A Simple Story*, he is trained in a school of adversity. He "learns" from his suffering, first that he can revenge himself on his enemy, second that he must loathe himself and glorify his persecutor. His utter self-denial at the novel's end ("I have now no character that I wish to vindicate"; 434) testifies to the kind of wisdom he has acquired. He has moved from narcissistic self-absorption to its precise opposite—another version of the same thing. Falkland, Caleb's effective alter ego, undergoes a comparable if slightly less extravagant change, throwing himself into Caleb's arms at the culminating trial scene in order to testify to his erstwhile secretary's nobility of spirit.

The pattern suggests deep pessimism about the fantasy of development that shapes so much fiction before, during, and after the eighteenth century. Caleb in the course of his narrative frequently invokes a malignant fate that dooms him to destruction. No comforting idea of Providence counters this notion of fate. The novel's shape, its almost parodic adherence to the familiar arc of development, hints that "fate" is self-created. Caleb's obsessive focus on Falkland turns into a covert competition for dominion. One man must triumph over the other: everything in their life histories points to such a resolution. Godwin, who had written the dramatic ending of his novel before he consciously arrived at the principles of its justification, ultimately denies to both characters the satisfaction of winning, demonstrating instead how winning becomes losing and how men destroy themselves in trying to defeat one another.

Such a demonstration might provide a plausible foundation for a political novel, but the question of how *Caleb Williams* functions as a political novel remains difficult. The book epitomizes the problem faced by all political novelists of the period: the relation between concern with individuals and awareness of social actualities. Although it is both easy and tempting to discuss Godwin's novel as a psychological study, the book unquestionably concerns itself also with political issues. It focuses attention particularly on the evils of the class system, through such vignettes as the account of Tyrrel's mistreatment of Emily or of his equally egregious persecution of the Hawkinses. Falkland's ability to pursue Caleb depends not only on the wealth that facilitates his hiring of agents but on the rank that makes most men and women certain that his version of events possesses more authority than Caleb's. Tyrrel and Falkland are *structurally* defined as tyrants, regardless of their personal desires.

Caleb's time in prison provides much opportunity for social and political commentary. The virtuous and vicious suffer indiscriminately in a penal setting; the horrors of physical life in prison vie with the moral horror of a system that often dooms the innocent and accords no one the right to a speedy trial. Far more justice emerges within the band of robbers, governed by an honorable leader and a coherent system of rules—yet misusing their energy and prevented by existing social assumptions from returning to life within the law even if they wished to do so.

Inasmuch as rank and wealth create Falkland's power, the issue of social class permeates the novel. Caleb, who frequently offers political reflections, sees the class system as fundamental to the tyrant/slave dichotomy: members of the upper classes everywhere and always tyrannize over their perceived inferiors. To the extent that the novel persuades the reader that Falkland's power derives from his rank, it functions effectively to deliver a political message.

Strikingly, though, it fails to offer or to hint at any conceivable solutions to the problems created by existing social arrangements. The leader of the robber band justifies the group's lawless activities by the injustice of the social system: "Who that saw the situation in its true light would wait till their oppressors thought fit to decree their destruction, and not take arms in their defence while it was yet in their power?" (312). But the war of each against all hardly constitutes an improvement to the status quo. Caleb's idyllic interlude with Laura and her family suggests an ideal of harmonious community as the solution to human problems. As Caleb reflects, "The pride of philosophy has taught us to treat man as an individual. He is no such thing. He holds necessarily, indispensably, to his species. He is like those twin-births, that have two heads indeed, and four hands; but, if you attempt to detach them from each other, they are inevitably subjected to miserable and lingering destruction" (408). Community, then, is an urgent necessity, but the text suggests that it is more or less accidental. Godwin offers no program for achieving it.

Moreover, the power of, say, the novel's denunciation of the class system pales in comparison to that of its rendition of mutual obsession. His rank, to be sure, provides Falkland with instruments of pursuit, but such instruments are only means to an end determined not by political actualities but by personal idiosyncrasy. Theoretically, one might argue that a society consists of an assemblage of individuals and that every political system expresses decisions by a multitude of separate persons. *Caleb Williams*, however, neither establishes nor clearly defends any such position. It makes little connection between the vicissitudes of personality and those of government. Its diatribes against oppression have the force of conviction, but they lead nowhere, seeming finally to amount to expression for expression's sake.

All this is to say that fiction and political argument are not coterminous. Neither in Godwin's novel nor, I would argue, in other eighteenth-century fiction, firmly centered as it is on the careers of individual characters, can a political case be forcefully articulated except by means of speeches or authorial interventions that interrupt narrative drive. A novel may show, as *Caleb Williams* shows, the evil of political oppression, but the effects of such oppression on imagined individual persons will necessarily focus a reader's interest more insistently than generalized conclusions can do. As for political recommendations—well, they can be embodied in utopian fantasies, but rarely in this period do they emerge sharply from the development of fictional action. One reason may be that eighteenth-century novelists do not imagine the possibility of concerted political endeavor. The great political novels of the twentieth century—such works as George Orwell's *Nineteen Eighty-Four* and Arthur Koestler's *Darkness at Noon*—embody imagined personal situations in a context of political maneuvering and conflict. Although a novel like *Caleb Williams* dramatizes such political effects as unjust courts and prisons, it includes no imagining of group action. Nor do other political fictions of the late eighteenth century. Their political imaginings tend toward the abstract and general rather than the concrete and specific.

The limitations of novelists' political imaginations become more apparent in fiction by writers less adept than Godwin at conveying psychological subtlety. As the novelist's conflicting assertions about *Caleb Williams* indicate, his authorial intentions were divided. Charles Lloyd, the author of *Edmund Oliver* (1798), manifests no such division of purpose. Defending a conservative position, he wishes above all to combat the sexual permissiveness that he associates with radical politics. After citing Godwin as a supporter of sexual expression outside marriage (Godwin's liaison with Mary Wollstonecraft was well known, and he had written in *The Enquirer* an essay maintaining the probity of such an arrangement), Lloyd explains in the Advertisement to *Edmund Oliver,* "I think I can perceive, in the introduction of concubinage, . . . and in the character of that indefinite benevolence, which would reject the mass of existence without addressing its operations patiently to parts of that mass, principles, that would destroy the tranquility of society, that, by means of annihilating all the dear 'charities of father, son, and brother,' would at last lead to a callousness that spurns at all affections, to a mad spirit of experiment, that would eradicate all the valuable feelings of man's nature" (vii–viii).

Lloyd's objection to the ideas expounded by such as Godwin appears to be that those ideas rest on destructive principles. In his reference to "indefinite benevolence," he suggests that the ideas he abhors are too sweeping. One should, apparently, focus on individuals rather than on humankind. And one should avoid pernicious notions about women—notions of independence and self-determination—because such views might deprive men of chivalric opportunity. Finally, what's wrong with radical politics is that it would surely prove an enemy of feeling.

I offer this paraphrase of the lines quoted above without perfect confidence in its accuracy. Lloyd's argument seems muddled in structure, if intense in feeling, and I'm not altogether sure what it means. But the passage provides a useful perspective on the clumsy novel it precedes, indicating the author's belief from the outset that political concepts lend themselves to refutation by individual examples. All politics is personal, Lloyd suggests; and the story he tells, about a beautiful woman doomed to destruction by her espousal of free love and about the man who learns to rise above his early infatuation with this unworthy female, demonstrates that "concubinage" leads to trouble and marriage provides salvation. Gertrude, the erring beauty, is, the Advertisement explains, "a woman of warm affections, strong passions, and energetic intellect, yielding herself to these loose and declamatory principles, yet at the same time uncorrupted in her intentions, unfortunate from error, and not from deliberate vice" (x). The Advertisement acknowledges that the novel makes less and less attempt as it goes on to provide persuasive detail, and indeed *Edmund Oliver* often reads more like a parable than like an imagined version of actual existence.

This novel, in itself hardly worth critical attention, makes more transparent the dilemma exemplified by *Caleb Williams,* by pursuing an opposite course. If Godwin allows his psychological interest to dominate his original political intent, Lloyd proves altogether unable to make characters convincing or to exemplify his views in any other way than by having characters make speeches about them. Not, for the most part, literal speeches: this is an epistolary novel, and its inhabitants write long instructive letters to one another. Lacking the kind of character development that might lead readers to the willing suspension of disbelief, *Edmund Oliver* presents a series of lessons in life (good girls have saintly mothers; bad girls suffer in, and from, what we would now call dysfunctional families; the emotional ravages of illicit sexuality even exceed their physical counterparts, and so on) that may possibly enlighten but more probably will simply bore.

As the "lessons" cited above will suggest, the novel's political aspects tend to disappear. It may be that contemporary readers assumed that female expressions of sexuality inherently constituted a political issue. More probably, they understood the entire book as an expression of that "principle of political non-resistance" (184–85) recommended by Charles Maurice, Edmund's mentor (a figure allegedly modeled on Coleridge). He elaborates his theory thus:

Believing, Sir, that no good, however apparently desirable it
may be, that is effected by force can be lasting, as in that case
it cannot have appropriated itself to the minds of men by individual experience; I would desist from meddling with political
bodies, and conforming to a system of complete passiveness,
wind myself into the bosoms of my neighbours; attack the root
of the evil, the selfishnesses of human nature; I would excite
my friends to follow the example, and trusting that the process
of amelioration thus begun, would make a *sure* though slow
advancement, I would consider myself as a co-operator with
infinite benevolence, and should look forward with hope to the
glorious day when all wars and fightings, and their necessary
causes, distinction of rank and person, should be banished
from the earth! [185–86]

As a political program, this presents obvious problems, especially in
its notion that appropriate methods would eliminate "the selfishnesses
of human nature." The leap to a vision of warless society is startlingly
grandiose but, given the hypothetical disappearance of human selfishness,
perhaps plausible enough. No clearly "political" aspect marks any of the
recommendations, although the end point of making war impossible of
course has political bearing.

Lloyd does not endorse this prescription—the book is intended to
mock the Coleridge figure—but neither does he provide any clear alternative to it. Although he lacks the power to create plausible individual
characters, his imagination focuses strongly on the individual, and he can
only conceive of resolving the world's difficulties by the actions of single
persons, not of aggregations. Hence, presumably, his choice of the novel
as a form for conveying his convictions.

The political novels of the 1790s differ from one another less in substance than in method. Some such vague notion of utopian community as
the one Lloyd's character Maurice promulgates recurs regularly, especially,
as one might expect, in radical fiction. Godwin hints that no such destructive isolation as what Caleb Williams endures could exist in the context of
communities dedicated to the common good. Godwin's friend Thomas
Holcroft, in *Anna St. Ives* (1792), elaborates in sometimes excruciating

detail the moral possibilities of a commitment to the good of humankind that subsumes individual desire. A self-proclaimed revolutionary, Holcroft argues for a position virtually identical to that of Lloyd's target, Maurice. So, less explicitly, does Robert Bage, in *Hermsprong* (1796), which represents its eponymous, idealized hero as having been reared in an equally idealized community of American Indians.

Inasmuch as many works share the same glowing vision, quite unanchored to actuality, the period's optimistic political novels also share the same kind of narrative resolution: a vague promise of future bliss for humanity. The penultimate paragraph of *Anna St. Ives* epitomizes the pervasive tone of these resolutions. It is spoken by Frank Henley, son of the steward of Anna's father's estate, who has wooed and won the heiress Anna and has just been reunited with her after both have survived considerable peril. He does not, however, focus on his love. Instead, he reiterates the novel's ideals: "Ours is no common task! We are acting in behalf of society: we have found a treasure, by which it is to be enriched. Few indeed are those puissant and heavenly endowed spirits, that are capable of guiding, enlightening, and leading the human race onward to felicity! What is there precious but mind? And when mind, like a diamond of uncommon growth, exceeds a certain magnitude, calculation cannot find its value!" (481).

Multiplied exclamation points signal the feverish intensity of such utterance, barely coherent, quite unrelated to narrative event, but presumably intended to exercise persuasive or coercive or at least inspirational force on the reader's mind. As this sample will suggest, Holcroft, like Lloyd, has a dead ear for the rhythms of speech. He thinks more like a reformer than a novelist. Yet his inventiveness far exceeds that of his conservative counterpart, generating a plot full of implausibilities yet compelling by virtue of its energy.

The pattern of that plot derives from the novel of education. Education, indeed, provides one of the book's pervasive themes, promising the possibility of a new version of the human race. Thus, when Anna despairs of the existing system, perceiving and experiencing the competitiveness and envy inherent in "the errors of this selfish system," she imagines that in "another century" all will be right. In the meantime, we should live in hope and speak the truth. "We have but to arm ourselves with patience, fortitude, and universal benevolence." She apologizes for taking advantage of friendship to express her feelings, implying that friendship itself should have no claim on noble spirits who judge and act on the basis of truth. "The prejudices of our education" account for the excessive value we place on friendship. The letter to her friend Louisa concludes, "Once more, Louisa, we are the creatures that education has made us; and consequently I hope we shall hereafter be wiser and better" (210). Education has made us weak; the corollary that it could therefore make us strong provides the novel's intellectual foundation.

Holcroft's key terms are *mind, truth,* and *energy.* The paragon Frank judges all he encounters by their possession of or adherence to these qualities. Anna shares his values, although she is, from his point of view (and apparently from the author's), somewhat laggard in accepting their implications. Those who possess the best and highest minds have the right and responsibility to lead the world. No excuse can ever justify a lie. Energy—like the book's other virtues theoretically the equal possession of men and women—constitutes the means to noble ends. Anyone with sufficient "mind" can be led to truth, given the leader's energy and determination. Mind, energy, and truth in concert provide principles of education.

Believing all this, although it remains unclear whence either she or Frank imbibed their convictions, Anna nonetheless falls into error when she decides to marry Coke Clifton, a highly eligible young man of whom all her relatives approve. She understands that he has faulty principles, but because she believes him also to have high intelligence she thinks it possible to reform him. She does not wish to displease her family; she considers it part of her social obligation to fulfill their desires for her as much as she can. The narrative problem is that from the beginning she really loves Frank, whose social standing does not entitle him to be her mate. Because, despite her love, she believes that marriage should not stem from individual desire, she not only refuses his overtures but enlists his help in the project of reforming Coke.

Frank, in contrast, manages invariably to align his principles more closely with his desires. He considers himself and Anna alike superior beings, fit to lead the world. When he refers to the "bliss" he might experience in union with Anna, he immediately corrects himself: "I confess the thought of renouncing so much bliss, or rather such a duty to myself and the world, is excruciating torture" (131). Given that marrying the woman he loves can be figured as duty, it is unsurprising that he claims his happiness at the marriage is "not because I have gained a selfish solitary good; but because I live in an age when light begins to appear even in regions that have hitherto been thick darkness; and that I myself am so highly fortunate as to be able to contribute to the great the universal cause; the progress of truth, the extirpation of error, and the general perfection of mind!" (382). He gets to have it both ways: to acquire the woman he loves—and her fortune—and to rest in the conviction of his virtue in marrying her.

Such quotations will convey the insistent high-mindedness of Holcroft's novel. A twenty-first-century reader is likely to feel that announcements of principle compose rather too high a proportion of the text, but the novelist leaves room as well for exciting plot developments: Frank's multifarious performances of heroic deeds, Anna's abduction and Frank's concomitant capture, the successful escape that includes Anna's climbing a wall with an announcement to her maid that anything men can do, women can do equally well. (In stressing the equal capacities and equal rights of the two sexes, *Anna St. Ives* and the other revolutionary novels differ sharply from *Edmund Oliver*.)

Like many other political novels of the time, *Anna St. Ives* shows signs of strain. In order to engage readers, it must interest them in the individual fates of Anna and Frank while also proclaiming insistently that individuals don't matter. Anna's "education" teaches her that she should not marry a man in order to reform him, but the project of reforming Coke Clifton continues to obsess her even after she has committed herself to Frank. The novel's plot engineers a full reconciliation of desire with duty, but its rhetoric insists that one must elevate duty to the whole of humankind above merely personal desire. The process by which Anna convinces herself that marrying Frank constitutes her duty to the world holds potential psychological interest, but Holcroft implicitly disclaims all concern with the workings of the psyche. Only the general welfare matters to him, although he devises a series of personal adventures to attract his readers. The reader too can enjoy the satisfaction of finding desire and duty identical, but this satisfaction provides little instruction about human actualities. The novel of education or development typically strives to educate readers as well as characters. Holcroft, however, cannot readily find means to instruct if he stoops to entertain.

Despite its pervasive allusions to existing social and political arrangements, then, Holcroft's novel tells us little about the world as it is. In this respect it resembles many of the period's other political fictions. "Realism" has rarely proved a useful designation for the works investigated in this study, but political storytelling often seems, paradoxically, to locate itself at an especially great distance from actuality. Although the very designation *political* suggests direct reference to the ways of worldly power, political fiction of the late eighteenth century tends more toward the visionary than the realistic. Its tone may lack the exaltation we associate with the visionary in poets like Blake and Shelley, but it typically dwells either, like *Anna St. Ives,* on possibilities of an idealized future condition or, like *Caleb Williams,* on grotesquely imagined versions—satiric visions—of the immediate human plight. The narrator's eye often focuses less sharply on the here and now than on the conceivable earthly life to come. Holcroft's plot inventions—his version of the here and now—eschew probability for the sake of significance.

Thus Coke Clifton, representing old, bad, hierarchical ways, must deal with obstacles by incarcerating their creators, whereas Frank and Anna, spokespersons for liberty, implausibly achieve freedom despite the vast power of money, rank, and mercenaries arrayed against them. Wicked, snobbish, plotting Coke succumbs entirely to the power of his rival's ideas: again, at the cost of plausibility. As Frank has earlier, rather daringly, put it, "By his intercourse with Anna his mind is become impregnated with the seeds of truth" (383). Thus Frank feminizes his opponent in the act of praising him. Coke finally exclaims, "And must I submit? Are you determined to make a rascal like me admire, and love, and give place to all the fine affections of the heart?" (480). Yes indeed: exactly so. In spite of his ostensible compliance, Coke's diction reveals his understanding that the contest of power in which he has played a conspicuous role implicates Frank and Anna not only as his victims but as triumphant opponents.

Tension between rhetoric and action echoes that between referentiality and vision. In *Anna St. Ives,* as in *Edmund Oliver,* a rhetoric of social vision contends with a narrative trajectory designed to arouse engagement and suspense. When Gertrude (in *Edmund Oliver*) turns out to be pregnant, when Frank Henley is waylaid by a band of ruffians, the reader will presumably feel suspense about how the dilemma will resolve itself. Yet the texts insistently refer to imposed meanings. The reader's consequent split awareness seems unlikely to produce either political insight or narrative satisfaction.

In the context of such novels as Holcroft's and Lloyd's, the achievement of *Caleb Williams* appears more remarkable. Although Caleb too bursts into political reflection as he contemplates the horrors of imprisonment or the condition of robbers, his outbursts stem plausibly from his situation and his character, and Godwin provides abundant data about both—data emerging from within the imagined character, not from the assertions of another. The psychological and the political vie for dominance, but they do so within the control of compelling narrative. *Caleb Williams* generates that "powerful interest" its creator hoped to achieve without destroying its political impact.

The most entertaining by far of the period's political fictions is *Hermsprong, or, Man As He Is Not* (its author had earlier published a novel called *Man As He Is*), unusually playful in plot and sometimes in tone. It educates its readers and its central female character, Caroline Campinet, by a series of narrative inventions, many of them involving attempts at or approaches to marriage. The range of possible marital arrangements stimulates the imagination. Gregory Glen's fruitless comic pursuit of Miss Bennett inaugurates the narrative. Caroline's father, the detestable Lord Grondale, proposes to marry his daughter's feisty friend Maria, an Anna Howe–like figure of feminist inclinations who leads him on until she has accomplished various worthy nonmarital aims. Harriet Sumelin, the unpleasant daughter of Maria's guardian, elopes to France with a money-seeking clerk. (Hermsprong rescues her, as he rescues many others.) Mrs. Stone, Lord Grondale's live-in mistress, plots futilely to make her lover marry her, then settles for Canon Blick, the arrogant, authoritarian clergyman who toadies to Lord Grondale. Sir Philip Chestrum, heir to vast wealth and born into a family of long and distinguished pedigree, woos Caroline with every expectation of winning her. His commanding mother has told him to marry Caroline, and he thereupon spins elaborate fantasies of their union. Naturally, he remains unaware that he is pusillanimous, stupid, and inflexible. Caroline has no interest in him.

All these false starts imaginatively envelop the possibility of Caroline's marriage to Hermsprong, which tantalizes the reader almost from the text's beginning. Hermsprong, a paragon of courage, compassion, and inventiveness—in short, man as he is not—appears first as Caroline's savior, rescuing her from almost certain death by checking a runaway horse. He remains a mysterious figure, possessed of adequate funds but unequipped with servants or carriage, professing to have walked all over Europe. American Indians have reared him, he reveals. These Indians owe little to historical or geographical research. Their most important characteristic is the negative one of not being European. Accordingly, Hermsprong has avoided European vice and cultivated native virtue. Active and enterprising, he helps the needy, rescues the distressed, and recognizes goodness in whatever form it takes. Gregory Glen, the story's ironic narrator, adores him, and many share this extravagant emotion. Only Lord Grondale and his sycophants loathe the man who appears unawed by and uninterested in rank and wealth.

The union of Caroline and Hermsprong duly takes place, but the wooing does not occur in familiar terms. Hermsprong announces his love with fervor, but also with dignity. He claims from Caroline corresponding dignity. She must come to him as a grown-up, having defied her father simply because her father is wrong. When she temporarily yields to her father's demands and to her pity for his illness, Hermsprong does not plead with her or proclaim his despair. He reveals his intention of leaving the country and returning to America. Caroline, predictably, sees the light and accepts his proposal: the trajectory of romance dominates. Familiar eighteenth-century romance, that is: Hermsprong has turned out, conveniently, to possess English wealth and title as well as American integrity. Yet the novel does not *feel* altogether familiar because, without undue polemic and without the implausibilities of *Anna St. Ives,* it suggests what equality of the sexes might imply and acknowledges that such equality may not prove easy even for the females it presumably liberates.

Nothing in my summary of plot elements suggests much political drive in this fiction, which sounds like, and is, a mixture of comedy and romance. Nothing, that is, unless one understands sexual politics as the foundation or the emblem of every other sort of politics. Bage apparently holds this view. The relations of the sexes have traditionally rested as firmly as those of nobles and peasants on hierarchical assumptions. Sir Philip Chestrum, in his moral, physical, and intellectual weakness, demonstrates the point with comic exaggeration, assuming his complete dominance over a wife even as he operates as the instrument of his mother's manipulations. Hermsprong calls for equality between the sexes (although he behaves in courtly fashion toward older women and rescues a damsel in distress). He rejects all inequality based on anything but merit. Indeed, as he gathers around him the people he values, he adumbrates an idealistic vision of meritocracy.

That vision functions more persuasively than the corresponding ideal in *Anna St. Ives* because it emerges more in action than in assertion. Hermsprong, like other idealistic political heroes in fiction, makes some speeches about his convictions, but these remain relatively brief and infrequent, and they are often refreshingly tinged with irony. His convictions reveal themselves energetically in his practices. It is hardly coincidental that Lord Grondale and his henchmen, working to defeat this upstart, try to convict him of treason. He has been seen in a group of striking miners; the lawyer can *almost* prove that he has read *The Rights of Man*. The political activity of which Lord Grondale accuses Hermsprong turns out to be innocuous. Not so the political action implied by his claim to marry Caroline. Given the benevolence of plot, Hermsprong turns out to deserve a rich wife by virtue of his birth and inheritance; but he claims her on the basis simply of his integrity as a man: a revolutionary idea.

Bage's indubitable political intention in constructing his romance in this way, however, by no means guarantees political effect. The novelist's dexterity in plotting and characterization works against him. *Hermsprong* steadily entertains the reader, by means of witty dialogue, fast-paced action, unexpected plot development, varied characters. The novel constructs its hero as elegant, smart, brave, and overwhelmingly charming. Readers can be expected to want a marriage between him and Caroline because that's the way the romance should go: Caroline should find rescue from a wicked father in a marvelous husband. But the structure of romance inherently contradicts the implications of progressive politics. Typically in romance the hero ventures; the heroine waits. Hermsprong, enabled by wealth and masculinity, travels the world rescuing the needy. Caroline stays home, at the mercy of an arbitrary and unfeeling parent. Urged by circumstance into a position of passivity, she moves from obeying one man to obeying another. The daring—and the importance—of Anna St. Ives's slightly ludicrous claim to physical equality with men becomes more apparent in the perspective provided by Caroline Campinet. Bage's choices conform more nearly to reader expectations. The writer sacrifices some political urgency to the pressures of romance.

But inasmuch as *Hermsprong* utilizes the form of education narrative in conjunction with that of romance, it leaves room for subversive suggestions. The novel trains its readers as well as its characters to understand that appearances of treason need not correspond to substance, that wealth need not breed pride, that a sense of human equality need not lessen the dignity of the person who feels it, that a woman can and should think about what she is doing, rather than simply follow the conduct books. Encasing such sensible but radical suggestions in the sugarcoating of romance, it provides one model for a kind of political novel that might not seem threatening even to timid readers.

At the end, *Hermsprong* provides efficiently for all its characters, in a way that feels familiar from many a romance. It does not, however, dispose of the independent Maria Fluart in marriage. Instead, it summarizes her fate in this fashion: "Miss Fluart, not yet willing 'to buy herself a master,' establishes a little household at Bloomgrove. Once a day she quarrels with Sir Charles [Hermsprong in his new avatar as titled Englishman] about *le bon ton, et le bel usage;* and the greatest vexation she has yet to complain of is, that she cannot vex him. She calls him savage; abuses his antediluvian ideas; and then tells her friend, with half a sigh, she will have a savage like himself, or die a maid" (247–48).

The passage neatly epitomizes the novel's deliberate doubleness. On the one hand, it offers the advanced notion that a woman need not define herself by marriage. The girl who daringly mocked authority does not have to accept it unless she chooses to. Choosing not to, she leaves herself the freedom to "quarrel" at will with even the ideal romance hero. On the other hand, her half-sigh suggests that after all she longs for marriage, and her final remark reinforces the view that Hermsprong embodies the ideal. Bage's skill at having it both ways defines his achievement in this novel.

Sexual politics appeared crucial, predictably, to women as well as men, and women wrote a number of important political novels during the period. Best known of the group, in her own time as well as now, was Mary Wollstonecraft, author of *A Vindication of the Rights of Woman* (1792), which powerfully articulated the current female situation and argued for the urgency, in the interests of men as well as women, of ameliorating it. Both before and after this polemic, she published works of fiction. Her two novels use versions of her own name as title: *Mary, a Fiction* (1788) and *The Wrongs of Woman, or Maria* (1798). Although they contain literal autobiographical components, their most significant autobiographical bearing is their implicit claim that the misery of women is universal. As Maria puts it in her meditations, "Was not the world a vast prison, and women born slaves?" (64).

Wollstonecraft's perceptions do not lend themselves to disguise by romance. She takes a dark view, writing with no apparent hope for amelioration of the inequities she perceives. The political aim of the two novels consists in their attempt to make readers *see* the true nature of women's situation—*seeing* constituting the necessary if not sufficient precondition for change. To enforce her vision, Wollstonecraft writes something of an antiromance. The falsity of the romance plot, like the falsity of sensibility, provides one of her targets.

The Wrongs of Woman, left incomplete at its author's death, provides no clear sense of its formal pattern as a whole. *Mary*, though, deliberately attempts to subvert established fictional conventions. Its protagonist suffers from a father and mother whose commitment to fashion entails parental irresponsibility: the mother reads romances and indulges in fine sentiments; the father ignores his family. Developing into a young woman of deep feeling, self-educated and thoughtful, Mary finds herself abruptly married, at her father's behest, to a rich youth, two years younger than she, who instantly leaves her to finish his education abroad. She takes some pleasure in being able as a result to provide financial help to her friend Ann, but her life offers few obvious compensations for the misfortune of being bound to a man whom she neither knows nor loves. On a trip abroad for the sake of her friend's health, she meets a male soulmate and pursues a platonic relation with him; he subsequently dies. Her husband returns to cohabit with her. "When her husband would take her hand, or mention any thing like love, she would instantly feel a sickness, a faintness at her heart, and wish, involuntarily, that the earth would open and swallow her" (53). The novel's final sentences convey the tone of the whole: "Her delicate state of health did not promise long life. In moments of solitary sadness, a gleam of joy would dart across her mind—She thought she was hastening to that world *where there is neither marrying*, nor giving in marriage" (53; emphasis in original).

Marriage, in other words, constitutes a disaster rather than a goal for Wollstonecraft's protagonist, and everything in the novel's structure supports this view. To be sure, Mary yearns for what she calls "love," but her notion of love does not appear to include the erotic. She seeks love first in the young woman whom she befriends, a woman needy both financially and psychologically, but Ann, although a willing recipient of Mary's "compassion," offers her little emotional return. Henry, her soulmate, also ill, responds more richly, but both Mary's marital situation and his own impending death inhibit him. After his death, Mary finds satisfaction in doing good for others. She lives with her husband as a matter of duty, not desire. The longing for death hinted in the sentences quoted above constitutes her strongest emotion.

Mary's foolish mother, an unattractive character, testifies her folly by her taste for sentimental fiction. She enjoys reading about the woes of imaginary lovers. In imitation of one fictional couple, she plants a rose bush, only to regret that she has no lover to weep with her as she waters it with her tears. Wollstonecraft's marked distaste for novels of sentiment energizes her effort to write fiction of a new sort—but it, too, appeals to sentiment, if not the variety that takes delight in tear-watered roses. Mary's mother indulges false sensibility. Mary herself is possessed by a truer version, the source of her yearning for "an object to love" (8); she, too, in her youth takes pleasure in "reading tales of woe" (8), their nature never fully delineated. Although she differs from her mother in almost every respect, her difference in relation to reading concerns not the substance of what she peruses but the way in which she peruses it: "She entered with such spirit into whatever she read, and the emotions thereby raised were so strong, that it soon became a part of her mind" (11). In this activity as in others, she uses her sensibility as a source of energy and as the basis for empathy.

The summary of how Mary reads belongs to a long sequence defining her character in generalizing and synoptic form. Wollstonecraft writes more effectively as essayist than as novelist. She rarely thinks in fictional terms. The action of her novel, such as it is, illustrates the generalizations that surround it. If the writer finds no other pretext for general reflection, she has Mary write down in her notebook the thoughts that occur to her: Mary becomes the generalizer. Yet the generalized ideas set forth in the text gain their power largely from the somber tone that marks Mary's experience and her reactions to it. Tone, rather than action or character, creates the novel's impact and conveys its political message, the message Wollstonecraft consistently worked to impart: women everywhere and always endure hard fates.

Romance is delusive and meaningless; manners are empty convention; education, for women, can only instruct in misery; adventure belongs solely to men. The established patterns of eighteenth-century fiction are irrelevant to Wollstonecraft's project. Indeed, her project involves their systematic overturning or undermining. The rather schematically rendered plot of *Mary* (the entire novel occupies fewer than fifty pages) debunks all possibilities for women except that of systematic benevolence—in other words, self-subordination. But the plot and the reflections that surround it have designs on the reader. This is not a novel of education or development like, say, *Tom Jones*, but it is, in a clearer sense than any other work we have discussed (with the possible exception of *David Simple*), a didactic novel, intended to educate readers. Everything in Mary's experience tells her the same thing: the world will give her no satisfaction. She knows this from early childhood; she hardly needs to learn it. The reader, however, must be brought by iteration to understand that the misfortunes of female experience, far from accidental, reflect a corrupt and corrupting set of social arrangements.

Given this account of the novel's import, it will not seem surprising that anger pervades the text. Mary herself feels no such emotion, but the condensation and insistence of the novel's implicit polemic carry powerful impact. If the story fills primarily an illustrative function, for that very reason it carries a strong political message. Unlike Bage or Godwin, Wollstonecraft never allows her ideological intent to submerge itself in the pleasures of narrative. Narrative provides a means to the end of simple, forceful statement—statement of outrage and of the justification for outrage. The central character, who suffers so much, protests only weakly (against the imposed marriage, after the fact). Her relative passivity emphasizes the degree to which women's voices are effectively silenced. Mary's yearning for death may express her understandable depression, but it also conveys the impossibility of a satisfying female life on earth.

Wollstonecraft writes stiff, clumsy sentences. She demonstrates no capacity for demonstrative rather than declarative characterization. She appears to feel little interest in details of plot or ramifications of structure. Yet she writes, even in this first effort, effective political fiction because of her clear purpose and her intense passion. As an instance of the political novel, *Mary* suggests how sharply the principles of this subgenre can deviate from those of other forms. For development, this novel substitutes reiteration. Its strength comes not from its manipulation of fiction's techniques but from its deployment of political energy. It does not bother to assert the connection between sexual politics and other kinds of politics; instead, it simply insists steadfastly on the injustice of things as they are in the sexual sphere.

The Wrongs of Woman, fragmentary though it is, shows fuller attention to the demands of fiction without any diminishment of political intensity or any change in message. Published by Wollstonecraft's husband, William Godwin, after her death, it apparently includes roughly a third of the planned work. In approach and in projected length, it conforms more nearly to eighteenth-century fictional norms than its predecessor had done. It shows signs of elaborate plotting, and it conveys character through speech and action more often than by means of summary statement. Like *Mary,* it sets out to demonstrate the unavoidable horrors of a woman's life. Its protagonist begins the action in a madhouse, where she has been unjustly confined by her husband. This Gothic structure quickly becomes a metaphor for the universal female condition. All women find themselves metaphorically confined to madhouse or prison, cut off from the possibilities that only freedom enables.

Maria finds love, or what she believes to be love, within the madhouse, in the person of another unjustly confined inmate, Darnford. She has married unwisely, in order to escape an intolerable family situation, and—as we learn only late in the published section—she has purposely left her husband when she realizes his willingness to prostitute her. Because she has inherited money from a wealthy uncle, the husband cannot tolerate the possibility of her escape. He causes her abduction and confinement; she suffers also the corollary anguish of having her infant daughter torn from her breast. That child, the text asserts, is dead, but ambiguity surrounds the baby's fate, and some of Wollstonecraft's notes for a continuation suggest the possibility that she remains alive after all.

Maria's keeper at the asylum, Jemima, becomes a vivid subsidiary character. She tells her story to the lovers; Maria writes down her own story for the sake, she imagines, of her daughter. These two life narratives make up complete substructures, indicating Wollstonecraft's new interest in constructing a complex narrative. In conjunction, the paired autobiographical accounts demonstrate that women's oppression does not depend on social class. Jemima, the illegitimate child of working-class parents, endures hardships including but extending far beyond the conventional fate of seduction and betrayal. Her "seduction," by her master, approximates rape. No love enters her life at any time as she suffers hard labor, physical pain, emotional rejection, extreme poverty, and other forms of misery. She tells her story because Maria and Darnford treat her like a human being: no one has done so before. Although they promise her a better life if she enables them to escape, the novel offers no assurance that better life is possible.

Maria's upper-class existence contains less physical stress but at least comparable emotional privation. Her account of herself stresses the trials, indeed the horrors, of marriage, which makes a woman into a man's possession. Her husband, a dissipated gambler, allows her little money for household expenses and demands that she turn over to him any funds she receives from her uncle. He transmits to her a sexual disease. For sexual pleasure, he prefers prostitutes to women of his own social class. When Maria flees him, he repeatedly hunts her down. Her confinement for alleged insanity is only the last of many miseries she suffers from and with her spouse.

The patterns of the two interpolated life stories, then, duplicate each other in their trajectories, and those trajectories, determining the stories' structures, enforce their political meaning. Both tales reverse the familiar pattern of development. To be sure, Jemima and Maria acquire the sad wisdom of their experience. That wisdom, however, does not, like Tom Jones's achieved understanding, open new possibilities or point to a coherent and ordered way of life. On the contrary, both women learn increasingly to recognize the shapes of constriction that dominate their experience as their lives become ever less coherent. If Maria still longs for romance, Wollstonecraft's narrative heavily hints that romance means only illusion, which will inevitably be dissipated. The woman from the gentry class, like her working-class counterpart, possesses no real legal rights—no rights that she can conceivably enforce without the help of a man. Stories of women's lives, this novel conveys, eventuate in unhappiness. The careers of Maria and Jemima illustrate a particular sense in which politics is the science of power: for women, lacking all power, effectual action becomes virtually impossible.

Wollstonecraft left notes for alternative resolutions to *The Wrongs of Woman*. Most of her suggestions resolve the plot with Maria's suicide, although one sentimental version has the protagonist brought back from the verge of death to live for her rediscovered infant. Given the stress on female misery in the finished portions of the text, it is difficult to believe that rearing a girl child will produce a happy ending. Like *Caleb Williams,* most political fiction by women examines "things as they are"—to find in existing social arrangements little justification for any fictional pattern involving an upward trajectory.

Other political novels of the period, to be sure (particularly novels by men), imagine the female situation in other ways. Anna St. Ives has and exercises the power of wealth and social class as well as that of verbal skill and physical energy. If Caroline Campinet, in *Hermsprong,* requires a great deal of instruction from a man, her friend Maria Fluart uses her own beauty and wit effectively as the means of getting what she wants. Wollstonecraft's specific ways of imagining women in their social setting make her fictions' dark outcomes inevitable. But those dark outcomes, like the constrictive patterns of what precedes them, enable her to articulate her insistence that injustice pervades the social sphere.

The same somber tone and the same movement from hope to despair, from apparent possibility to acknowledged impossibility, mark the writing of other women who tried in fiction to convey political messages. Wollstonecraft's contemporary and friend Mary Hays supplies two final examples of political fiction by a woman. In *Memoirs of Emma Courtney* (1796), Hays declares her political allegiances by quoting both Wollstonecraft and Godwin. Her second novel, *The Victim of Prejudice* (1799), more fully imagined in fictional terms, reiterates with yet greater force the dreadful, monotonous message that society and all its institutions are so organized as to condemn women to existences that are limited at best, intolerable at worst. Like Wollstonecraft, Hays offers no prescription for reform, not even the vague idealism of such works as *Anna St. Ives.* She insists, though, that her readers understand tales of personal disaster as indictments of social principles and practices.

Much of *Emma Courtney* consists of letters from the eponymous protagonist to the man she loves, who responds only in obscure terms to her overtures, never unambiguously rejecting but never explicitly encouraging her. These missives allegedly adopt the language of actual letters written by Hays herself to William Frend. Their autobiographical basis may help account for the degree to which the novel persuasively represents the pathology of obsession. In its painful rendering of neurosis, it foretells such works as Charlotte Brontë's equally painful *Villette*. Emma half-realizes from the beginning that her love for Augustus Harley will meet with no full return, but she has no power to free herself from her obsession. Over and over she reasons with the object of her devotion, declaring her worthiness of his love, defending the propriety of her declarations. Augustus typically responds with generalities and becomes testy when Emma fails to accept his responses as definitive. He never quite tells her to go away and leave him alone.

This work does not, however, purport to be what we might now call a psychological novel. Hays wishes to demonstrate that Emma's obsession stems from the universally impossible situation of women. The young woman has no real occupation (except, disastrously, serving as companion to Augustus's doting mother) and virtually no available choices. She briefly presides over the education of some young children, a part-time enterprise so little engaging that she never mentions it after the post is offered her and she accepts it. Little or no opportunity exists for her to meet other men or even women who might provide companionship and stimulation. Given her restricted opportunities, everything urges her toward fantasy as her only recourse. The pathos and power of Hays's novel stem largely from the protagonist's compulsive effort to make her capacity for serious political thought serve the purpose of her fantasy.

Emma believes that women's innate capacities equal men's. She recognizes, though, that character "is modified by circumstances: the customs of society, then, have enslaved, enervated, and degraded women" (39). This economical statement explains much about the young woman's subsequent career—her inability to yield her futile hope for full response from Augustus, her inability to discover any course of action that might distract her or utilize her energy to better purpose. As she elucidates her position to her mentor, Mr. Francis, she conveys the mixture of rage and despair that establishes the novel's tone. "Hemmed in on every side by the constitutions of society," she writes Francis, "and not less so, it may be, by my own prejudices [which she understands as also socially induced]—I perceive, indignantly perceive, the magic circle, without knowing how to dissolve the powerful spell. While men pursue interest, honor, pleasure, as accords with their several dispositions, women, who have too much delicacy, sense, and spirit, to degrade themselves by the vilest of all interchanges [that is, marriage for the sake of material advantage], remain insulated beings, and must be content tamely to look on, without taking any part in the great, though often absurd and tragical drama of life. . . . The strong feelings, and strong energies, which properly directed, in a field sufficiently wide, might—ah! what might they not have aided? forced back, and pent up, ravage and destroy the mind which gave them birth!" (86).

If *Memoirs of Emma Courtney* as a novel records the ravages of strong feelings and strong energies with no appropriate outlet, it also deploys melodramatic plot devices in a structure of odd disproportion. For more than four-fifths of the novel, no external happening has much importance. To be sure, Emma's mother dies, and later her father; she moves from one place to another; yet the significant events occur within her consciousness. All that matters is her developing, frustrated love for Augustus Harley. Although it early becomes apparent that the young man will not reciprocate as she wishes, the narrative continues to dwell on Emma's efforts—through letters to Augustus himself and to the wise Mr. Francis and through various systems of rationalization—to come to terms with her own feelings. This concentration on reiterated inner actions gives a claustrophobic quality to the reading experience, locking the reader into the circularities of disturbed consciousness. There seems no hope of resolution and no hope for deviation.

In the novel's final pages, though, a great deal happens. Emma, discovering that Augustus is and long has been married, marries someone else herself, bears a daughter, and learns to love her husband (although with considerable moderation: "rational esteem" and "grateful affection" define her emotion). When that husband goes away from home on business, she accidentally encounters Augustus once more. Thrown from his horse, he is in mortal danger. She nurses him devotedly until his death (in the course of his dying, he confesses that he has long loved her), agrees to care for his one surviving son, then becomes seriously ill herself. Convinced by her delirious utterances that she has never loved him, her husband first pursues an adulterous affair with her servant Rachel, then kills himself, after having murdered Rachel's infant, which he fathered. Emma devotes herself to the care of her daughter and Augustus's son, who love each other; she imagines their eventual union. The daughter, however, dies. The novel we are reading, a first-person narrative, turns out to be the protracted explanation she offers Augustus's son, another Augustus.

To summarize these events takes longer than it would take to summarize fully the happenings in the rest of the book. Yet the dramatic, disastrous series of happenings are huddled together in a few pages, reminding me of the dictum—I think it was T. S. Eliot's, but I have been unable to find it—that plot in fiction is like the meat the burglar feeds the watchdog in order to distract it. Hays seems to have no real interest in the plot she devises, and the plot in its final unfolding has no connection with the novel's political import. The structure of *Emma Courtney* not only bears little relation to any pattern we have seen before; it is difficult to make narrative sense of it.

It makes sense, however, in terms of its narrator's inner life. For Emma herself, nothing has much reality except her absorption with Augustus, partly erotic and partly idealistic, since she has constructed him (with considerable help from his mother) as flawlessly sensitive, noble, and astute. Much happens to her and around her. It hardly matters. What matters is only her idea of Augustus.

Emma's loving aunt, who has largely reared her, offers a deathbed warning about the dangers of sensibility. "Endeavour to contract your wants, and aspire only to a rational independence," she advises; "by exercising your faculties, still the importunate suggestions of your sensibility. . . . I dread, lest the illusions of imagination, should render those powers, which would give force to truth and virtue, the auxiliaries of passion" (27). Of course, her "dread" proves prophetic. Emma indeed allows imagination to make passion dominant, with disastrous results. But the aunt's admonition also suggests how political meaning underlies even this tale of female obsession and distortion. The advice to "contract your wants" expresses the pathos of woman's situation in the world. Men are allowed to want infinitely; want fuels ambition and thus accomplishment. For women, ambition is both inappropriate and futile. Women will not be permitted or enabled to fulfill capacious wants. They must contract their longings. Emma's aspiration can find no focus except a man, and focusing on a man guarantees reliance on "the illusions of imagination." Personal neurosis thus reflects societal deformation.

The peculiar shape of *Memoirs of Emma Courtney* also reflects that deformation. It echoes the distortions of Emma's mind, the novel's subject, and underlines the sense of waste, of "powers, which would give force to truth and virtue" turned to self-destruction. On the novel's final page, Emma meditates hopefully about the future of society. "Moral martyrdom may possibly be the fate of those who press forward, yet, their generous efforts will not be lost" (199). She does not imagine herself as pressing forward. That possibility seems to belong to the young Augustus: only a man can help determine the future of the race. Emma herself has subsided, her life's only clear accomplishment the partial rearing of a young man. The novel leaves a bitter aftertaste.

The *Victim of Prejudice,* published three years after *Emma Courtney,* focuses more sharply on political issues, although it too uses a narrative about a private woman's experience as the means to its commentary. Like its predecessor, this is a first-person account, by one Mary Raymond, who begins her story with her idyllic childhood and ends it when she appears to be at the point of death. Attractive, intelligent, carefully educated, Mary initially loves a youth who has been educated with her under the tutelage of "a sensible and benevolent man" (5) identified only as "Mr. Raymond." Her lover, William Pelham, withdrawn from her company by his worldly father, subsequently enjoys social dissipation and soon makes a worldly marriage. Mary, after many vicissitudes, is brutally raped by an aristocrat who has pursued her at intervals for many years. She has previously learned for the first time of her mother's history. Not only is Mary illegitimate; her mother, who descended from gentility to whoredom, was hanged for murder. The mother's story and the more current, altogether false, story that Mary has willingly lived with the man who raped her provide the basis for the "prejudice" that dogs the heroine through all attempts to live independently and earn her own living. Although she is rescued from the disgrace and misery of debtors' prison, she is by then too exhausted, disillusioned, and despairing to make further attempts at productive life.

Mary's mother, condemned to death, writes a letter about the miserable course of her life. Toward the end, she offers this retrospect: "*Law* completes the triumph of injustice. The despotism of man rendered me weak, his vices betrayed me into shame, a barbarous policy stifled returning dignity, prejudice robbed me of the means of independence. . . . A sanguinary policy precludes reformation, defeating the dear-bought lessons of experience, and, by a legal process, assuming the arm of omnipotence, annihilates the being whom its negligence left destitute, and its institutions compelled to offend" (68–69). She blames "man"—by which she means not humankind but members of the male sex—for her destruction, but more emphatically she blames society and its institutions, which foster prejudice, neglect society's weakest participants, and "compel" the destitute and betrayed to "offend."

Mary's last word on her own life resembles her mother's. "The vigorous promise of my youth has failed. The victim of a barbarous prejudice, society has cast me out from its bosom. The sensibilities of my heart have been turned to bitterness, the powers of my mind wasted, my projects rendered abortive, my virtues and my sufferings alike unrewarded, *I have lived in vain!*" (174). She goes on to raise the possibility that her story might "kindle in the heart of man, in behalf of my oppressed sex, the sacred claims of humanity and justice" (174), but she does not appear to anticipate anything of the sort. Instead, she concludes with a vision of "the fabric of superstition and crime, extending its broad base," to mock "the toil of the visionary projector" (175). Only a visionary projector, she implies, could imagine that the claims of humanity and justice will ever sway "the heart of man."

These polemical passages express the doctrine and the vision of the novel as a whole, a doctrine and vision that remain its steadfast concern through every episode. *The Victim of Prejudice* represents several "good" characters, all primarily associated with Mary's girlhood and early youth. The good remain unfailingly good; the bad never deviate from their badness. Only William Pelham occupies a middle position, weak rather than evil, unable to summon the moral force to resist temptation. The good prove effectual only in confined private arenas. The bad can summon the law to their aid. Sir Peter Osborne, the rapist, knows that he faces no prospect of retribution. "Who will credit the tale you mean to tell?" he inquires of Mary. "Where are your resources to sustain the vexations and delay of a suit of law, which you wildly threaten? Who would support you against my wealth and influence?" (119). He proposes several more rhetorical questions of the same sort, and his suggestions are quite accurate: Mary has no resources except her inner strength, which protects her from falling into vice but brings her no rewards. Sir Peter holds the power; Sir Peter gets what he wants.

The events that take place in the course of the novel add up to a coherent plot, a plot of devolution, but this fiction has less emotional impact than *Memoirs of Emma Courtney* because its episodes are illustrations; its characters, exempla. Although the reader cannot predict all that will happen to Mary, the pattern that the book's happenings will fall into is clear from the outset. Such a first-person narrative as *The Victim of Prejudice* may seem to bear affinities to novels like *Pamela,* which I designated a novel of consciousness. In fact, it differs sharply from Richardson's work. *Pamela* is full of surprises of consciousness. The reader may have the illusion of understanding Pamela better than Pamela understands herself, but the novel also abounds in moments when Pamela suddenly discovers something new about herself—her divided psyche, for instance, which allows her both to wish to escape from her "wicked master" and to wish that no harm should befall him, and which allows her to "dialogue" with her heart even while recognizing that all the time this heart is Pamela. Mary's consciousness, in contrast, is predictable. The heroine invariably reacts in high-minded fashion, and the world invariably refuses to reward her merit. The energy of Hays's novel stems from its single, harsh view of things as they are. Everything else is subordinate.

Political novels seek to expose. They eagerly deploy devices that earlier novels had made familiar; they sometimes disguise their intent by soliciting the reader's interest for plots of love and adventure; but their purposes always center on revealing the urgency of change. In one way or another—I'm thinking of Godwin's divided purpose, for instance, and of Wollstonecraft's reluctance, in *Mary,* to provide much in the way of plot—these works often suggest a necessary disjunction between medium and message. The eighteenth-century novel, with its stress on the individual, does not readily lend itself to political purpose. Yet several of its practitioners, as the century drew to an end, wrenched it successfully to fulfill such an aim.

CHAPTER NINE

Tristram Shandy and the Development of the Novel

PARADOXICALLY, THE MOST ECCENTRIC novel of the eighteenth century best exemplifies the genre's developing resources and the sense of wide possibility that had accrued to it. *Tristram Shandy* (1759–67), a diverting, willful, rule-breaking work that bears few obvious similarities to other fiction of its own period or to anything else before postmodern inventions, nonetheless reveals much about what had happened to the novel in less than fifty years of its early evolution. The Russian critic Victor Shklovsky declared Laurence Sterne's masterpiece "the most typical novel in world literature" (170)—presumably meaning that in his book Sterne consciously deployed the full range of techniques that the form had evolved. *Tristram Shandy* not only works brilliantly as a novel; it also comments brilliantly on the novel as a genre.

The classifications that make sense for other eighteenth-century fiction offer little immediate help in grasping this one. To be sure, the first-person narrative begins at the beginning—begins, indeed, with the process of Tristram's conception—thus promising a novel of development. It delivers nothing of the sort. The first sentence, almost half a page long, instantly complicates subject by tone. It merits full quotation: "I wish either my father or my mother, or indeed both of them, as they were in duty both equally bound to it, had minded what they were about when they begot me; had they duly consider'd how much depended upon what they were then doing;—that not only the production of a rational Being was concern'd in it, but that possibly the happy formation and temperature of his body, perhaps his genius and the very cast of his mind;—and, for aught they knew to the contrary, even the fortunes of his whole house might take their turn from the humours and dispositions which were then uppermost: —Had they duly weighed and considered all this, and proceeded accordingly,—I am verily persuaded I should have made a quite different figure in the world, from that, in which the reader is likely to see me" (5).

This inaugural sentence condenses issues that will dominate the novel as a whole, establishes the idiosyncratic voice that in a sense constitutes the book's subject, and suggests the crabwise motion of much of the narrative. It begins with the plaintive "I wish" and continues by spinning a tiny counterfactual story. Nothing actually happens in the first sentence. Instead, the sentence plays with possibilities. Concerning itself with sexual activity, it yet renders no physicality. It operates through sequences of crucial vagueness. In what sense, exactly, do the parents fail to mind what they were about? How *should* they have proceeded? What kind of "figure in the world" does this narrator in fact make? Although the sentence purports to involve intimate behavior, it eschews specificity. It announces the narrator's awareness of his reader; it suggests a triangular family drama; it claims concern with "the world" as well as the family; it institutes a sense of grievance. All these matters will turn out to be important. Yet the reader may well be left with no inkling of where the novel is going. For all its many pages, *Tristram Shandy* never clearly answers the question of its narrative intent.

In other words, the novel ostentatiously rejects a comprehensible structure. If none of the structural principles that we have examined so far suffices to describe it, neither does the book provide a clear alternate principle. It refuses conventional sequence: a dedication appears in chapter 8. It relies at will on visual aids: the all-black page that signals Yorick's death, the diagram that claims to elucidate the plot, the two chapters consisting of blank pages. Whimsically introducing and abandoning characters, it lacks the kind of character development that works as early as *Robinson Crusoe* made familiar (although its narrator likes to claim, and claims rightly, that he is providing much evidence about character to the attentive reader). Reading it in the context of other eighteenth-century fiction may make us aware of how much we rely on the clues of convention in coming to terms with a new work. In less than half a century, the novel as form had educated its readers in the kinds of expectation they should bring to fictions of several varieties. *Tristram Shandy*, however, violates expectation.

To say that the book lacks structure, sequence, and familiar kinds of character development, however, is misleading. What it offers is far more important than what it lacks, and among its offerings is a vivid cast of characters. Walter Shandy, Tristram's father, and his Uncle Toby, and Yorick, the parson whose death is mourned early in the novel, although he reappears at the end: these men erupt into life on the page, at once unpredictable and entirely consistent. We cannot guess how Walter will respond to any new happening, because Sterne imagines him as full of theories that for him answer all needs. He has theories about noses and names and procreation, about the city and the country, about the procedures of childbirth. His weird combination of learning and nuttiness enables him to interpret his experience and challenges the reader to keep shifting ground with him.

Uncle Toby, the kindest of men, yet obsessed with the details of warfare, usually finds a military reference that in his mind applies to new events. In this general sense, the reader knows in advance how he will react, but the delightful specifics of his responses prove always unexpected. Even a minor figure like Dr. Slop, struggling with the knots by which a servant has secured his obstetrical bag or holding forth to Walter, has a distinctive voice and stance. The human world that Sterne represents contains strongly individualized characters—most of them vociferous talkers. Their rambling or purposeful conversations create much of the novel's texture.

Most of the conversations take place within the Shandy family, dramatizing that family's peculiar yet recognizable dynamics. As Tristram puts it, "Though in one sense, our family was certainly a simple machine, as it consisted of a few wheels; yet there was thus much to be said for it, that these wheels were set in motion by so many different springs, and acted one upon the other from such a variety of strange principles and impulses,—that though it was a simple machine, it had all the honour and advantages of a complex one" (323). Tristram's mother makes claims for herself only in extreme circumstances; his father takes for granted his own rightful dominance; Tristram, the son of the family—well, the son has control of the story being told, a position of strength. He may appear to exercise his control in arbitrary fashion; that fact only reveals his power. Telling a story, in the ostentatiously individualistic way that Tristram tells it, rules the family fate, not by invention but by interpretation. Tristram leaves not the slightest doubt that the conversations and happenings he records occur in and are transmitted by his consciousness, whatever their original provenance. Although he never explicitly tells a great deal about his own character, he emerges as the most sharply etched member of an extraordinary cast because the idiosyncrasies of his imagination, shaping the narrative, reveal an individual, aggressive, energetic, humorous mind, full of odd bits of knowledge.

Tristram's ostentatiously lighthearted book combines its exuberance with melancholy. References to death are never far away. Not only do his brother and the admirable Yorick die in the course of the narrative, but Tristram makes it increasingly clear that he considers himself in a race with death, his outpouring of language an effortful testimony to his persistent vitality. Impotence threatens (and overtakes) him; his recurrent worries about the impossibility of completing his literary project reflect, among other things, the deeper worry about survival. The survival of books seems more likely than the survival of men, and Tristram takes pains to link his own literary production with works that have endured from the past.

Thus *Tristram Shandy* abounds in borrowings, acknowledged and unacknowledged, from earlier authors—Rabelais and Cervantes especially, Robert Burton, Petronius, Montaigne, Erasmus, and many others. The book's unique flavor derives partly from its lighthearted appropriations, adaptations, and imitations, which declare Sterne's participation in a long literary tradition (despite the much-noted "oddness" of his book) and call attention to his enthusiastic manipulation of language and to his delight in the richness of verbal possibility.

The fertile possibilities of incorporation exemplified in *Tristram Shandy* testify not only to Sterne's remarkable gifts—although certainly to those—but also to how complexly the novel had by this time developed as a form. Contemporary critics considered Sterne's work odd—too odd to last, Dr. Johnson suggested, in a spectacular instance of false prophecy— but they did not judge it something outside the realm of the novel. It included bits of the past and allusions to the present, chunks of peculiar knowledge, eccentricities of structure as well as of allusion, strange characters, unmentionable happenings such as the act of procreation, sequences of joyous bawdry; and all this could plausibly be contained within the bounds of a novel. The genre had from its beginning been inclusive and adaptive, making use, as we have seen, of various fictional and nonfictional modes that had preceded it. Sterne calls attention to the vast scope of its conceivable inclusiveness.

This novel wants us to notice its anomalous structure, since that structure provides a frequent subject for the narrator's commentary. He professes to operate by profound structural principles, analogous to those of the universe itself: contemplating the movement of the planets, he explains, gave him the idea for his story's structure, although his way of organizing matters is "a very different story." "The machinery of my work," he avers, "is of a species by itself; two contrary motions are introduced into it, and reconciled, which were thought to be at variance with each other." The two motions are those of forward narrative and of digression. Tristram offers a panegyric to the latter. His interweaving of "the digressive and progressive movements" shows such skill as to be virtually self-sustaining; it could go on forever and will, he proclaims, continue for the next forty years, if he lives so long (63–64).

The principles Tristram announces, however, are by no means transparent. The first volume of *Tristram Shandy* ends with the narrator's vehement assertion that if he thought the reader able to guess what would happen next, he would tear the subsequent page out of his book (70). After all, the best explanation for how the novel organizes itself may consist in the categorical characterization of all male members of the Shandy family as marked by their "excentricity." Uncle Toby, who spends his time modeling and reenacting bygone battles, offers a conspicuous example of the trait (58), but Tristram's father, with his faith in the magical power of Christian names and his exaggerated concern for noses, seems almost equally "original," to use another term Tristram applies. As for Tristram himself, the book he purports to write testifies above all to the uniqueness of his personality. In its unpredictability, its predilection for retrograde motion, and its highly personal choices of subject matter, it declares the liveliness of its ostensible maker's mind and the impossibility of any other mind's duplicating it.

Tristram claims at once a profound understanding of complex ordering and a position that relieves him from any need for order. The novel's
full title is *The Life and Opinions of Tristram Shandy, Gentleman,* and opinions possess primary importance. Because they issue from an eccentric
mind, they take eccentric form, like the novel they inhabit. Defying the
reader to guess what comes next or to follow the pattern that only he sees,
Tristram implicitly asserts the importance of structure even as he taunts
us with our inability to apprehend the principles governing his book. It
is, above all, *his* book, not ours. What we have learned from reading other
novels will not help us with this one, or so the self-satisfied narrator suggests. When, in chapter 40 of volume 6, he purports to diagram the movements of the first five volumes, he provides a series of fanciful squiggles.
He professes to be moving away from the squiggle, toward the perfectly
straight line (426). If the reader finds it difficult to experience the allegedly straightforward movement of volume 6 as different from that of its
predecessors, that fact only attests once more to the narrator's superiority.
He has everything under his control; he can insert any chapter—on buttonholes, on "pishes," on knots, or, of course, on his own activities—where
he wishes (562).

This sampling of Tristram's remarks on his novel's structure suggests the primary importance of fictional form to his enterprise, even
as his comments render opaque his understanding of what such form
entails. Our understanding need not, indeed cannot, coincide with his,
but that realization does not relieve us from the obligation to investigate
the patterning of this bewildering fiction. The models we have pursued
before may after all provide help. Think, for instance, back to the adventure novel. The episodes reported in *The New Atalantis* are at least
as arbitrarily chosen as are those that Tristram supplies. They illustrate
a common theme; they share a dimension of political allegory; but they
hold no other connection with one another, except for the fact that the
same imagined observers perceive them all. By comparison, Tristram's
recurrent concentration on his family's vicissitudes seems wonderfully
comprehensible. *Love in Excess* makes the figure of D'Elmont a presence
throughout its divagations, but it diverts the reader with stories more or
less extraneous to the protagonist. In both these early novels, the crucial
fact is that things keep happening.

So it is with *Tristram Shandy,* although the things that keep happening, many of them trivial (for example, Mr. Shandy's exact way of taking his handkerchief out of his pocket), hardly conform to any ordinary definition of adventure. Inasmuch as this is a novel about *opinions,* though, it locates new territory for itself. We might read it as a record of a mind's adventures, the writing of the book constituting Tristram's ultimate mental exploit. Reading it thus, we would understand the digressions—numerous, various, often extended, and sometimes in languages other than English—as products of an eccentric mind in action, and we would accept eccentricities as the novel's substance.

Tristram Shandy sketches the adventures, too, of minds other than the narrator's. Unlike Robinson Crusoe's adventures or D'Elmont's, the exploits of Sterne's characters lead to no fulfillment. Uncle Toby, possessed by his passion for the military history in which he has played a part, can go on as far as mortality permits, modeling battlefields and reenacting battles. Tristram's father will never stop his fruitless and largely meaningless speculations on names, noses, and heads, on education and women. Corporal Trim demonstrates again and again the concreteness of his imagination; Yorick, while he lives, imagines and reimagines his obligations to others. As these instances suggest, "mind" includes imagination. It also includes emotion, which often drives other mental activities.

Tristram, as narrator and as character, inhabits the story he tells. The novel elaborately demonstrates his mind's operations: its leaps and sallies, its disjunctions and associations, its power to make and to unmake, its need for control. It demonstrates also, with wonderful comic amplification, the impossibility—which Tristram shares with his father and his uncle —of that mind's reaching any conclusion. Like *A Sentimental Journey, Tristram Shandy* ends in mid-career: not in the middle of a sentence, but in the middle of an episode. Like *A Sentimental Journey* too it could hardly end otherwise. Everything that precedes the ending reiterates the unlikelihood of finality, an unlikelihood with which the book extensively concerns itself. Finality, however, is never the point. In fact, the novel tacitly insists, it *should* never be the point. The possibility of understanding the mind's activities as a form of adventure depends on the fact that human consciousness constantly establishes new worlds to conquer. Like Tennyson's Ulysses after them, Tristram and his father and his uncle strive and seek and find and never yield, locating new ground for seeking in the reiteration of their private obsessions.

The novels of adventure we examined shared a predilection for events—rapidly narrated, multifarious events—over plot. *Tristram Shandy*, despite its narrator's suggestions to the contrary, famously lacks plot. It, too, provides instead a great many loosely connected events, mostly consisting of Tristram's memories or associations. The apparent randomness of the memories, ranging from a bishop's extended curse to the circumstances of the rememberer's near-castration, effectively diagrams the putative author's mind. He possesses canonical authority for the picture of a mind that he draws. As he explicitly declares, his understanding of the mind derives from John Locke. Critics have demonstrated in detail how extensively Sterne depends on Locke's *Essay Concerning Human Understanding* as the novelist expounds in action the workings of the intellect. In particular, he relies heavily on the doctrine of association, elucidating in the structure of his narrative the apparent arbitrariness and profound logic by which consciousness moves from one topic to another.

We do not ordinarily (unless we are neurologists) think of memories as "events." *Tristram Shandy* makes it virtually impossible not to think this way. The story of two nuns trying to avoid saying a wicked word, the account of a traveler in France, the bishop's curse, the details of his parents' relationship, the episode of the hot chestnut, as presumably reported by his father—such memories inhabit Tristram's mind and compose his book. They become events for the reader inasmuch as they make up the novel's happenings. Although each is narrated in leisurely fashion, they follow one another at such a rate as to be almost overwhelming, thus approximating, in unfamiliar terms, the method of the traditional adventure novel.

Tristram Shandy in the reading, however, feels nothing like an adventure novel. To demonstrate that it shares characteristics with its very different predecessors does nothing to alter this fact. If it adapts certain techniques shared by such novelists as Haywood and Defoe, it does so to different purpose. Inasmuch as it theoretically duplicates aspects of a book like *Moll Flanders*, it sheds a harsh light on Defoe's accomplishment, making the rendition of Moll's consciousness seem comparatively superficial and merely conventional. Sterne adopts methods of less extravagant novelists only to subvert them. His comic energy constantly undermines the literary past, playing with what others take seriously, exposing falsities of what passes for realism, and proclaiming the inadequacy of convention even while establishing its own conventions.

The conventions with which Sterne and Tristram play extend beyond those of the adventure novel. At least equally important are the established modes of sentimental fiction. Eighteenth-century readers, if they acknowledged enjoying *Tristram Shandy,* consistently testified to weeping over it. Uncle Toby will not kill a fly. "The world is surely wide enough to hold both thee and me," he proclaims (100), offering a sentimental justification for his act of charity. Corporal Trim, reading aloud a sermon on conscience, feels overwhelmed by emotion at an account of the Inquisition because he imagines his brother as the sufferer evoked by the text. Mr. Shandy suggests the inappropriateness of such feeling on generic grounds: a sermon is not a history; generalization, unlike particularity, does not demand intense and personal response. Yet Corporal Trim assumes his place for the moment as sentimental hero.

Are we to laugh or to weep at such junctures? How seriously can we take a fly? Is the corporal ridiculous or magnanimous in translating the general into the particular? Sterne encourages such questions. The text is likely to discomfit the reader who settles on either alternative. Uncle Toby's ability to love all creatures great and small marks both his moral heroism and his lack of discrimination. To share his sentimentality entails abandoning what we usually understand as a sense of proportion. Sterne's delicately balanced tone both mocks and celebrates such abandonment, as it mocks and celebrates the disproportions implicit in commitment to one or another "hobby horse," his term for Uncle Toby's obsession with battles and Mr. Shandy's strong feelings about noses and names.

Tristram, moreover, proves capable of mocking himself, as in the episode of Maria, precursor to the encounter narrated in *A Sentimental Journey.* Tristram hears her story (a different version from the one adumbrated in the later novel) and hears her playing upon her pipe. He sits down beside her. She looks back and forth several times between him and her goat. Tristram asks her what resemblance she finds, explaining his reason for the question in terms that summon up for the reader the carnal associations of *goatishness.* Such an allusion undercuts the evocation of pity, but Tristram immediately returns to the subject of his emotional response to Maria's misery. So moved is he by the "tale of woe" she tells with her pipe that he walks "with broken and irregular steps" to his chaise. The next sentence goes like this: "————What an excellent inn at *Moulins!*" (574). In other words, Tristram cannot sustain the emotion he has generated. He reminds us, even as he solicits sentimental response, of the evanescence, and implicitly of the self-gratification, entailed in such response. The sentimental, with its glorification of emotion for its own sake, supplies not only part of the novelist's method but one of his satiric targets.

The sentimental novel offers Sterne both narrative substance and narrative method. It provides a pattern for disjunction. *Tristram Shandy* need not employ the fiction of a tattered manuscript; it utilizes instead that of a tattered mind. Its contemporary readers were already being trained in making sense of narratives that lack obvious coherence and in understanding lack of coherence as a signal to react with feeling. This novel offers incoherence of a new sort, insisting that disjunction represents a way of thinking—the way most people think—as well as of feeling. Like the novel of sentiment, it implicitly invites its readers to look within, to compare their own responses and means of attaining them to those of the rendered characters, especially that most vivid character, the narrator.

If the adventure novel and the novel of sentiment provide conventions for Sterne to utilize and subvert, so does the novel of consciousness. Tristram's concentration on the movements of his own mind duplicates that of Pamela or Clarissa, although in a different key. This first-person narrator does not employ the familiar letter as ostensible model, although the entire novel feels in some respects like one enormous letter or monologue to the reader. For Clarissa and Pamela, situation provides an excuse for concentration on the self. Tristram neither has nor feels the need for excuse, and he barely establishes any immediate situation, except for his travels on the Continent, the subject also of his later novel. Self-concentration constitutes his predicament. He cannot escape it. Although he takes himself with the utmost seriousness, he also mocks the very self-absorption that makes the book. Wordsworth could be described (by Keats) as master of the "egotistical sublime," in *The Prelude,* for example. Sterne, instead, specializes in egotistical comedy. In *Tristram Shandy* he produces a comic epic of narcissism, an epic of extraordinary self-awareness, the self-awareness constituting both technique and subject. It is, to be sure, an epic without meaningful middle or end, though it insists on its beginning, and an epic whose hero accomplishes nothing—but that fact makes an important component of the comedy.

Tristram does not talk only about himself; his is not that kind of narcissism. He tells extensively about others, narrating at great length, for instance, Uncle Toby's abortive romance with Widow Wadman. He offers a full account of Corporal Trim's equally abortive attempt to tell a story about the king of Bohemia and of his father's series of decisions about the breeches he proposes to have made for his son. All these narratives emanate from his memory. Their ultimate importance depends on what they tell us about how Tristram himself has been shaped. Thus, to mention only one salient example, we must understand Tristram's concern with sexual impotence in the context not only of the window dropping on his penis in his early youth ("nothing was well hung in our family," Tristram explains; 339) but of his father's reluctance to engage in the sexual act and his uncle's mysterious wound in the groin, both the subject of extensive narration. So it is that, speaking of "the disasters of life," he interrupts himself to apostrophize "my dear Jenny," inviting her to "tell the world for me, how I behaved under one [disaster], the most oppressive of its kind which could befall me as a man, proud, as he ought to be, of his manhood" (466). We learn nothing of how he behaved, but behavior, in any case, matters far less—to Tristram and to the readers he trains—than awareness.

The conventions of development also provide an implicit subject for Sterne's reflection. Eighteenth-century novelistic characters typically "develop," as we have seen, mainly in the sense that they acquire through experience the kind of knowledge that enables them to move more successfully through the world. Tom Jones learns prudence; Evelina learns decorum. Neither changes character, but both modify the possibilities of their positions in society. One could hardly describe Tristram in comparable terms. Despite the fact that his story of himself begins with his conception and continues to his adulthood, he learns nothing at all. He hardly seems to move through "the world": so complete is his concentration on the contents of his own mind that he conveys no sense of any society beyond his family, though he encounters others on his sketchily rendered trip abroad. Terms like *prudence* and *decorum* have no meaning in relation to him. Sterne aggressively rejects the implications of the novel of development by demonstrating that an individual's sense of self may have nothing to do with progress. To oneself, the novelistic imagining of Tristram suggests, one simply *is*, the ultimate fact of the universe.

This way of representing the novel's protagonist denies rather than

subverts the conventions of character development. The reader's understanding of the central character and the figures that surround him develops, but the character himself remains quirkily constant. The meaning of
that constancy, however, depends on the well-established convention that
it contravenes. Only in the context of the more orthodox novels that have
come before it does *Tristram Shandy* make the fullest sense.

Conventions of the adventure novel and the novel of sentiment, of
development, and of consciousness supply Sterne with large structural
principles that he can both exploit and challenge. He also drew on conventions of less obviously far-reaching implication. From Fielding, perhaps,
he appropriated the practice of addressing the reader directly and repeatedly. This procedure, too, he adapted to new purposes, in such a way as
to raise questions about his predecessor's use of it. Although Fielding
on occasion expressed doubts about his readers' rectitude or generosity,
although he even attacked his readers directly when he figured them as
"critics," his prevailing tone conveys rather condescending benevolence.
He deigns to explain himself because he imagines readers as requiring
explanation. He acknowledges his financial and literary dependence on
readers' goodwill and acknowledges repeatedly the necessary variety of
readers' consciousness.

Benevolence rarely manifests itself in Tristram's comparable addresses. More typically, he berates the reader: "Madam," who has a dirty
mind; the careless peruser who doesn't pay attention to the full implication of words on the page; the casual reader who assumes that "Jenny" is
Tristram's wife, or his mistress, or who, indeed, makes any assumption
at all. His invocations of the reader remind us that despite his extensive
accounts of what passes in his mind, we cannot after all know everything
in his consciousness. His relationship to Jenny remains hidden unless
he exposes it. His hint about the Shandys' religion does not necessarily
transmit itself even to someone reading his text for a second time. The
reader cannot know whether the bawdiness of references to crevices and
covered passageways belongs to Tristram's awareness or is a product of
readerly interpretation. The relation between the narrator's perception
and the reader's must remain mysterious for both. The narrator's interventions, however, expose clearly the aggression implicit in an author's
sense of his readers—an aspect of the situation much less apparent in
Fielding.

To speak of aggression, though, fails to convey the effect of Tristram's intrusions as narrator. As both subject and teller of his story, Tristram occupies a position importantly different from that of Fielding's narrator, who stands in for the author but does not inhabit the tale of Tom Jones's experience. Fielding's narrator, although he occasionally professes insecurity about his readers, never loses for long his air of superiority. Like Tristram, he reminds us of his control of the story. The control, however, has authority beyond the personal: as maker of the story, he stands in for Providence, for God himself. Tristram, more modest in his claims, often stresses his vulnerability—not only to impotence, falling window sashes, and incurable coughs but to ineptitude and uncertainty. That vulnerability applies to him as character in his narrative but also as reflector on the human situation. "Inconsistent soul that man is!—languishing under wounds, which he has the power to heal!—his whole life a contradiction to his knowledge!" (183). He includes himself in the universal condition of inconsistency, capable on occasion of glorying in the condition, but also of suffering from it.

The position of narrator, for Tristram, provides freedom as importantly as it does control. Two kinds of liberty appear to matter to him: the opportunity to speak his mind on any subject and the latitude to say anything he wishes to the reader. He will hold forth on wigs or staircases or buttonholes or chestnuts; he will scold or mock the reader. More often than not, though, even his scoldings carry such joyous energy that they entertain more than rebuke. For instance: "Now don't let Satan, my dear girl, in this chapter, take advantage of any one spot of rising-ground to get astride of your imagination, if you can any ways help it; or if he is so nimble as to slip on,—let me beg of you, like an unback'd filly, *to frisk it, to squirt it, to jump it, to rear it, to bound it,—and to kick it, with long kicks and short kicks,* till like *Tickletoby's* mare, you break a strap or a crupper, and throw his worship into the dirt.————You need not kill him.————" (202). As is often the case, Tristram here addresses an imagined female reader about her capacity for lascivious imaginings. The initial impulse to rebuke, though, promptly gives way to delight in the possibilities of language—delight that the reader can hardly fail to share. The opportunity for free expression provides a source of pleasure for reader as well as narrator. The entire novel begins to feel like a shared enterprise.

Neither large nor small structural conventions in themselves explain much about *Tristram Shandy*. It doesn't feel like an adventure novel, but neither does it feel like a novel of consciousness, in the sense that had been established in the eighteenth century, or one of sentiment, much less one of development. It does not consistently parody any established mode. Its addresses to the reader do not work like Fielding's. To say that Sterne mocks earlier conventions accounts hardly better for his novel's effect than would the claim that he imitates them. The novel's impact depends on the richness of allusion and the comedy of undercutting. The most obvious aspect of *Tristram Shandy* is its conspicuous unlikeness to everything that precedes it. The deliberateness of that unlikeness becomes fully apparent only when one realizes the fiction's dependence on established models. In its deviations from the century's norms, *Tristram Shandy* invites attention to the nature of those norms: to their value and to their inadequacies.

To its own value and inadequacies as well. The novel's concluding episode begins with a conversation between Mr. Shandy and Uncle Toby motivated by Mr. Shandy's discovery that the Widow Wadman has demonstrated an unladylike concern with the precise location of Uncle Toby's wound. Uncle Toby, as a result, has broken off the relationship. His brother sees in the widow's attitude new evidence of female concupiscence. He holds forth at length on the degradation implicit in the means of human procreation, which, he alleges, "couples and equals wise men with fools, and makes us come out of our caverns and hiding-places more like satyrs and four-footed beasts than men" (586–87). He compares the act of procreation unfavorably with that of killing a man in war, which is far more dignified, he claims, even "glorious" (587). Obadiah, interrupting with a personal complaint, hardly changes the subject. He had brought his cow to Mr. Shandy's bull on the day of his own marriage. His wife has produced an infant; the cow has not, nor is she pregnant. Obadiah's suspicions of inadequacy have fallen on Mr. Shandy's bull, which its owner, perhaps identifying with it, vigorously defends. The final exchange involves Mrs. Shandy and Yorick, neither of whom has spoken previously, although their presence has been noted:

> L——d! said my mother, what is all this story about?—
> A COCK and a BULL, said Yorick—And one of the best of
> its kind, I ever heard. [588]

The reference of "all this story" is purposefully vague. The story in question may consist of Obadiah's account of his cow and the bull with an inadequate cock, or it may include Mr. Shandy's diatribe, or it could allude to the entire complicated narrative that Tristram has constructed, the narrative containing all the other stories. A cock-and-bull story is, idiomatically, a tale of nonsense, one that purports to convey meaning but has no truth in it. Tristram, then, ends his comedy by suggesting its lack of import and importance. He mocks the very substance of what he has achieved, deriding but not destroying it, as he has derided without destroying, or attempting to destroy, a set of novelistic conventions.

Like the story Obadiah tells, Tristram's larger narrative both deals obsessively with the trivial and conveys significant truth. Like the conventions of sentimentality or adventure, its mode of proceeding evades some aspects of experience while conveying others. Thus, the narrative's denial of coherence obscures the coherence that every human being tries to create in understanding what it means to be a particular self in the world. Its insistence on defining characters by their "hobby horses" obscures the noneccentric aspects that imagined personalities ordinarily share with their real-life counterparts. Its extreme self-consciousness interferes with the "natural" flow of event and reflection.

That self-consciousness in some respects constitutes the novel's most salient aspect. If *Tristram Shandy* can properly be characterized as a comic epic of narcissism, its narrator's ingenuity in demonstrating his own self-absorption (this ingenuity serves in a sense as one component of Tristram's narcissism) achieves a level unmatched by any other writer of fiction before Philip Roth. Narcissism lies at the heart of the pervasive joking about novelistic structure, which typically reminds the reader that Tristram must and will have things his own way. Thus, in the middle of chapter 20 of book 3, he inserts a preface. "All my heroes are off my hands," he explains; "—'tis the first time I have had a moment to spare,—and I'll make use of it, and write my preface" (173). His convenience alone governs the preface's placement. Here, as elsewhere, he compels the reader to attend to the act of writing and to him as writer, the latter fact the more important. His governing assumption insists that everything about his processes of thought and emotion merits attention. He may assume, for purposes of entertainment, the guise of fool, but the true fool, in his view, is the reader, to whom, on one occasion, he offers his cap and bells as a bribe to urge close attention to the chapter (170). Paying such attention perhaps makes one into a fool in earnest—but no ready alternative is available. And Tristram will mock his reader frequently, tacitly or explicitly declaring the impossibility of other minds' following his. Thus he comments on the marbled page that he arbitrarily inserts into the text: "Read, read, read, read, my unlearned reader! read,—or by the knowledge of the great saint *Paraleipomenon*—I tell you before-hand, you had better throw down the book at once; for without *much reading,* by which your reverence knows, I mean *much knowledge,* you will no more be able to penetrate the moral of the next marbled page (motly emblem of my work!) than the world with all its sagacity has been able to unravel the many opinions, transactions and truths which still lie mysteriously hid under the dark veil of the black one" (203–4).

The black page occurred immediately after the account of Yorick's death, thus appearing to signify mourning. Now Tristram hints that the page concealed many meanings that we, his readers, surrogates for "the world," have been and presumably will be unable to fathom. As for the marbled page, which signifies his "work" (the book we are reading and the entire realm of his endeavor), we are unlikely to know enough to grasp its import. Tristram claims to control all meaning; he flaunts his possession of superior knowledge; he glories in his capacity invariably to do whatever he wishes. He thus insists on himself as the universal center of interest (the universe in question consisting of his readers: no one outside that circle concerns him in the least).

Tristram makes two chapters—he calls attention to the fact—of what happens during the time that two men pass down a single flight of stairs. Then, as he says, "a sudden impulse comes across me," and he strikes a line across the page and starts a new chapter (253). He has no rule to follow about the making of chapters, and if he had one, he wouldn't follow it. Sounding rather like Humpty Dumpty in *Through the Looking-Glass,* who understands the relation of words and speaker as a question of who should be master, Tristram exclaims, "A pretty story! is a man to follow rules—or rules to follow him?" (253). Thus, with some further elaboration, he constructs his chapter on chapters, which he considers the best of all his chapters. Two pages later, he summons an imaginary critic to help him get his father and Uncle Toby off the stairs. He also comments on the state of affairs between himself and the reader, which he declares unprecedented: no one before him has written as he has done; he will never catch up with his life in the narration of it; his readers will have more and more to read as he struggles to bring work and life into full conformity.

Following rules would interfere with his personal sense of grandeur. He must remain in control: rules should follow him. He also dominates imaginary critics and readers, turning the critic to his own uses and pointing out to readers that they will find themselves doomed to an endless task if they commit themselves to participating in his enterprise. The grandiosity of his posturing provides one of the novel's running jokes but also contributes to its substance.

That substance can be and has been described as one of digression, since the presumably central story of Tristram's life rarely takes center stage. Inasmuch as digression expresses the workings of Tristram's mind, it indeed constitutes his fictional autobiography's dominant concern. The narrator's fascination with every manifestation of his selfhood shapes the text, controls the reader, and accounts for the novel's apparently arbitrary divagations.

The narrator's narcissism conveys itself not only in the structure of the text and the use he makes of that structure but in the relationships he reports himself as involved in. He appears to have genuine sympathy and affection for Yorick, who has died (although he reappears at the novel's end, muddying the book's confusing chronology), and for Uncle Toby, a man himself so kindly and so harmless, the narrative suggests, that it would be difficult to feel anything but affection for him. Tristram also seems to feel superior to his uncle, whose monomania about battles blocks rational perception and judgment. The narrator's posture toward his father most often entails partially concealed irritation. He barely notices his mother. He feels great sympathy and fellow feeling toward an ass; Maria moves him. But his attitude toward Maria and the ass also exemplifies his most consistent position toward others: they constitute spectacles for him, pretexts for emotion. We see nothing of Tristram in a relationship of equals.

Thus he negatively reiterates his narcissism, by the absence of such ties as those Evelina has with her friend Maria, or D'Elmont with his brother, or Caleb Williams (temporarily) with Laura. Other people are real to Tristram inasmuch as they generate emotion in him, but he does not acknowledge them distinctly as separate selves. Locked within himself, he can dramatize that self by representing its interior motions. He can also dramatize the behavior of others—his father, Uncle Toby, Corporal Trim, Dr. Slop, Obadiah, Widow Wadman—but only as eccentrics, comic deviants from an unstated norm.

As I have already suggested, he represents himself also as eccentric and glories in his eccentricity as a mode of domination. For the other characters, too, eccentricity can serve as an instrument of dominance: Mr. Shandy, for instance, tyrannizes by means of his bizarre theories. Tristram, with the power of the word fully at his disposal, makes the reader a victim of comparable tyranny even as he creates the illusion of fellowship with the reader.

To parse a joke entails losing its immediate delight; to parse Tristram's narcissism risks neglecting the comic pleasure it provides. The narrator's intense involvement with the workings of his own consciousness generates the novel's unique enchantment. The leaps and sallies of his mind, the alternations of peevishness and jollity, the exuberance of wordplay, the excursions into bawdiness (with attendant rebukes to the reader for seeing it), the liveliness of imagination—such aspects of Tristram's central subject create much of the immense enjoyment (and perhaps patches of irritation as well) that many readers experience with *Tristram Shandy*. Much of the enjoyment, but not quite all: some comes from the preposterous behavior of characters besides Tristram, as seen through his eyes. At the heart of the encounter with Sterne's novel, though, lies the exploration of mind and sensibility, not by means of systematic introspection but by a precursor of stream of consciousness writing. The quotations included in this chapter (an arbitrary selection inasmuch as many other examples would in every case serve to support the point at hand) provide a reasonable sample of the range of tones and subjects that the narrator turns to his purposes, the means by which he reveals himself.

We respond to such exploration of mind and sensibility not with laughter alone, although laughter is paramount. The implicit project of *Tristram Shandy*, the way in which it, like other eighteenth-century novels, sets out to educate its readers, is to foster self-awareness. Tristram, much of the time, doesn't really look into his mind; he simply spreads it out on the page. He thus offers a model of consciousness. Readers who, in reaction, look within themselves are likely to find comparable incongruities and inconsistencies. They are invited to realize the essentially comic composition of human nature, the degree to which ordinary sanity and rationality depend on the suppression of much that lies within. Tristram traffics in the comedy of self-exposure. He thus fosters the realization that any uncensored self-exposure must have comic flavor.

This last point, about the degree to which a character's narcissistic self-revelation encourages a special mode of reader self-awareness, leads me to the most important convention that Sterne subverts in his remarkable novel, that of realism. Realism in fiction must always be a convention, inasmuch as the perception of action or characters or even rendered cultural context as realistic depends on the reader's tacit agreement to ignore the artifices on which all fictional technique depends. To the degree that realism had developed as an eighteenth-century convention between *Robinson Crusoe* and *Tristram Shandy*, it manifested itself most clearly in social detail (*Tom Jones, Humphry Clinker*) or in its psychological counterpart (*Clarissa*). *Tristram Shandy* virtually ignores the social realm and makes no claim of psychological revelation. Nor does it claim realism in any way comparable to that *Clarissa* employs, with its use of the familiar letter as realistic pretext. On the contrary, Sterne's novel ostentatiously displays its fancifulness. Yet it reiterates in many ways the crucial perception that human beings persistently create fictions of order and declare them real. Tristram in his self-centeredness refuses to follow rules and implicitly insists that rules must follow him. His representation of himself reveals the disorderliness of his mind. One would not ordinarily describe him as a "realistic" character. The attempt to perform and represent the disorder of consciousness, though, suggests a principle of realism more profound than any previously established. If we took seriously the implications of *Tristram Shandy*, we might reflect that even a young woman who has suffered rape would be in actuality far less single-minded than Clarissa, that fictional representations of the interior life typically depend heavily on the following of rules, that the chaos of real inner experience defies rendition and fails to serve the purposes of most fiction—that, in short, fictional realism is all illusion.

That dictum would also apply to *Tristram Shandy*: even such an ostensibly disjunctive and self-willed narrative follows certain rules; even it, especially in its making of comedy, shapes and falsifies the psychic life. It tells a different truth from its predecessors about the nature of that life, and it exposes certain kinds of deviation from realism in previous novels of consciousness. In effect, it raises questions about the procedures of fiction by employing those procedures in fresh ways, not by evading them. It glories both in its fictionality and in its reality.

Tristram Shandy can generate an awareness of literary convention, its limitations and its opportunities, that provides a useful perspective for a look back at some of the novels we have surveyed. It has already become apparent that the categories of classification do not necessarily provide adequate labels for complex works of fiction. To classify *Pamela* as an epistolary novel ignores the fact that it is also an almost stereotypical romance, to say nothing of a rather unusual story of development (unusual in that it extends development beyond marriage). To think of *Moll Flanders* as adventure risks denying the pattern of development that both the protagonist and her ostensible editor claim. Can *Caleb Williams* be understood more cogently as adventure rather than as political fiction? What difference would it make to the critic's perception to reclassify individual books? In fact, all these novels, most of the period's novels, employ multiple systems of convention to multiple narrative purposes. We must come to terms with this fact.

In other words, the variety of literary experience available in eighteenth-century fiction exists within as well as among novels. Each novel reshapes the conventions on which it draws; each employs those conventions in an individual balancing of possibilities. For purposes of convenience, the critic classifies a book in one way or another and thus determines what to make visible about the text—but also, necessarily, what to make invisible. *Evelina* as a novel of manners teaches its heroine and its readers the meanings and the urgency of decorum. As a novel of development, it, like *Betsy Thoughtless,* teaches prudence. Investigating it as a novel of development, we might focus on issues quite different from those we explored in connection with the matter of manners. For Evelina, prudence is almost entirely a verbal matter. The girl has already been trained in the kind of prudence appropriate for a rural village, before she comes to the city. She has few obvious rebellious impulses. Still, she needs to learn a new system of self-control. Specifically, she must learn when to speak, when to remain silent.

In general, Evelina's development tends toward silence. At the beginning, at the earliest dances, she shows a reprehensible tendency to say what she thinks. She learns to confine such saying to paper: in her letters she continues to express her often sharp judgments of the people and the behavior she encounters. In the social settings where she finds herself, though, sharp judgment is unacceptable for a young woman. By the time she comes to inhabit Mrs. Belmont's house in Bristol, where she is surrounded by the fashionable, she finds silence her best recourse. She has also learned, however, the need for verbal self-assertion in contexts of sexual danger. More than once, as she reports her rebuke of an impertinent male, she comments that she had not known herself to possess such spirit. The discovery of her own capacity for verbal self-defense, although only against men who immediately threaten her, marks an important aspect of her growing up.

More vividly even than *Betsy Thoughtless*, *Evelina* represents the special difficulties of growing up that were faced by an eighteenth-century young woman. Such a woman would be expected always to depend on a man—a father or a husband. Evelina's search for a father long preoccupies her. She incessantly proclaims her devotion to Villars, who has assumed the role of father during her childhood, and she announces her need for guidance in many of her encounters with Lord Orville. When finally she meets her true father, she has already pledged her devotion to her suitor: she has a husband in waiting. In her two encounters with Lord Belmont, she lavishly dramatizes her devotion and subordination. He thereupon arranges for her inheritance and presents her with a thousand pounds for her immediate needs.

When an eighteenth-century text refers to a woman as "independent," it customarily means that she has money of her own. By his financial generosity, Evelina's father establishes her relative independence. She remains eager to demonstrate her obedience to the husband she has won and her devotion to the man who has reared her, but she has at least symbolically grown up: found her place in the adult world.

The points of intersection between *Evelina* as novel of manners and as novel of development illustrate that the world in which Evelina must find a place is a social world, with social rules. Learning when to talk and when to remain silent involves discovering how to conform to social ordinances as well as how to protect herself—a truth demonstrating yet again that generic classifications are never sealed categories.

Evelina is both novel of manners and novel of development, as well as romance, and many—most—of the novels we have considered would lend themselves to comparable multiple categorizing. That fact by no means implies the futility of sorting books into categories that cannot altogether contain them. Quite the contrary. To organize eighteenth-century novels into groups by aspects of their plot structures—plots being the skeletons of novels—makes it possible to see affinities that might otherwise remain invisible.

Such organization also helps reveal the importance of conventions to the life of novels. The principles for which I have employed such terms as "aspects of plot" in fact constitute conventions for novelistic practice. Aspiring novelists quickly appropriated and adapted the procedures of their immediate predecessors. *Adapted* is important: rarely did a procedure pass from one practitioner to the next without significant modification. Defoe's methods and Haywood's in some respects resemble one another (and the two writers are so close in time that we can hardly determine precedence), but no one would mistake a novel by one for the work of the other. The difference between them obviously involves their choices of subject and diction, but also their ways of dealing with a subject.

Conventions, then, changed shape in transmission. Early novelists may barely have been conscious of employing conventions at all, in a period when the evolving novel was just beginning to feel its way. Clara Reeve acknowledging her debt to Walpole; Radcliffe deliberately revising Lewis: these are late-century developments. One need not posit that Sarah Fielding thought about Richardson's model of the "novel of consciousness" when she wrote her very different work *The Cry;* but her awareness that a protagonist's thoughts and feelings could lend structure to a fiction surely owed something to her immediate predecessor.

Conventions, for these novelists, were living forms. As new experimenters adapted the shapes that slightly earlier writers had created or altered or appropriated—often from other genres, such as popular biography, conversion narrative, travel book, or drama—they articulated new possibilities for story. New possibilities developed partly from new combinations of convention. Hence the appropriateness of classifying these fictions in multiple ways. Smollett used, in *Peregrine Pickle* and in other novels, the *Tom Jones* story of development as a pattern. He simultaneously wrote a picaresque novel of adventure (as, for that matter, so did Fielding). With our eyes on development, we see how the central character grows into socialization. With a focus on adventure, the novel's delight in tumultuous happenings becomes apparent.

Classification draws maps of affinity that help us see connections and thus lines of development. Defoe, Richardson, and Henry Fielding, but also Manley and Sarah Fielding, established bases for the divagations and elaborations of others. By the 1760s, when *Tristram Shandy* was being written, several distinct subgenres had been established. In less than half a century a new genre had solidified in diverse shapes. Sterne could assume that his readers would recognize the games he played with the novel's evolving traditions, and only the relative stability of the genre's forms made it possible to play such games.

The playfulness of *Tristram Shandy*, then, not only foretells that of postmodernism—as many readers, with varying degrees of astonishment, have discovered. It also testifies to how much had happened to the novel in the few years since its invention as a form distinct from the seventeenth-century romance. The possibility of such a book's existing only a decade or so after the middle of the eighteenth century provides an emblem of the atmosphere of narrative experimentation that governed the period's fiction writing. *Tristram Shandy*, presenting itself as unique, one of a kind, simultaneously shows itself one of many kinds.

Afterword

WHAT CAME NEXT

WHAT CAME NEXT: THE NOVELS of Sir Walter Scott, Jane Austen, Maria Edgeworth, Mary Shelley—immensely readable works of enduring popularity. And after them the Brontës, Dickens, Eliot. We all know the riches of nineteenth-century fiction; their abundance derives partly from that of eighteenth-century novels.

Nothing in the eighteenth century accounts for Austen, any more than anything before him accounts for Fielding, despite the fact that we can discern some of his roots. Austen too has roots, of course, and many of them lie in the works—and the kinds of work—we have considered. The extant letters between Austen and her sister report on some eighteenth-century novels she read, and the novels she wrote provide indications of others. *Sir Charles Grandison* was one of her favorites. *Northanger Abbey,* in its famous defense of the novel as genre, mentions Burney's *Cecilia* and *Camilla,* as well as *Belinda,* a work by Austen's contemporary Edgeworth. The title of *Pride and Prejudice* presumably comes from a phrase in *Cecilia,* a work itself profoundly concerned with the same abstractions in action. Austen both respects and builds on her forebears' contributions.

Burney seems an especially plausible point of reference, for Austen's novels, like hers, invite consideration as novels of manners (as, for that matter, do many of Edgeworth's). The link between manners and morals governs the action of *Pride and Prejudice* and *Emma* and figures in the other novels as well. When Emma carelessly insults Miss Bates, she violates her own standards of manners and of ethics. Not only has she failed at "pleasing," she has actually done emotional harm. Her remorse and efforts at recompense and reformation mark a crucial change in her.

Emma (1816), the only one of Austen's novels to adopt the familiar eighteenth-century strategy of using a woman's name as title, charts the development of a lively, intelligent, privileged young woman—a woman like Anna Howe, from *Clarissa,* or Miss Milner in *A Simple Story,* both of whom, like Emma, require chastising. The eighteenth century offered abundant literary models for the figure of a spirited female operating cleverly within social conventions or daring, at least tangentially, to challenge them. It also, as we have seen, supplied patterns for structuring plot, including those of development and of discipline by manners, the organizational principles most relevant for *Emma*. Emma, handsome, clever, and rich, mistakenly believes that she can be a law unto herself—and, for that matter, a law unto others. She deliberately defies normal social expectations in making a pet of Harriet Smith, a young woman of marked pliability and dubious birth. With some plausibility, Emma considers herself and her father the aristocrats of their village, and she makes edicts about the company she will and will not keep. In her flirtation with Frank Churchill, she enjoys imagining what others will say about her but feels no need to avoid general speculation. On the contrary, so confident is she in her social supremacy that it never occurs to her that gossip might damage her reputation.

Emma knows and practices the forms of politeness. Her insult of Miss Bates is by no means characteristic; indeed, the reader has been made witness to her courtesy in hearing about Jane Fairfax's letters and enduring tedious conversation. She does not, like Evelina, need to learn what is and is not done in various social contexts. She does, however, need to learn that, despite Frank's public assertion to the contrary, she cannot always and everywhere preside. Her lesson in humility, a lesson that extends to the realization that she may not even stand first in Mr. Knightley's heart, instructs her in the complexity and the pressure of "society," understood as the concatenation of other people in which one necessarily lives. Not even Emma Woodhouse, handsome, clever, rich, and well-born though she is, exists outside a social context or can afford not to take that context seriously.

The lesson is different from that learned by Burney's heroines, who might often be said to suffer from an excess rather than a deficiency of humility, but as instruction in the subtle demands of a social world it resembles their learning. Social demands, some of which Emma recognizes from the beginning (for example, the need to arrange card games for her father and to devise means of adequately feeding the participants), lend structure to the novel, which proceeds largely by means of a series of social encounters and comes to its climax in a proposal scene in which Emma says "just what she ought, of course. A lady always does" (431). By this time, however, she has developed a richer sense than she had at the beginning of just what she ought to say and do.

Even this sketchy account of a single aspect of *Emma* may remind us that the novel is also manifestly, like most of Austen's work, one of development. It could equally well be termed a novel of consciousness. Inasmuch as it fits into such categories, it prompts us to realize how Austen builds on what has come before her. Without Richardson, Haywood, Lennox, and Burney, Jane Austen would not be the Austen we know. It is important also to realize, though, how significantly she alters the models she employs.

Betsy Thoughtless develops by a sequential pattern of mistakes suffered from and acknowledged. Her experience consistently chastens her. The process of turning her into a good eighteenth-century wife takes a long time (Haywood's novel is very thick) and involves the gradual accretion of knowledge and prudence. Austen's heroines also experience a series of educational episodes, but typically these young women come to new recognition in a sudden flash of insight: Emma, "most forcibly struck" (376) by Knightley's rebuke of her, or the realization darting through her with the speed of an arrow that Knightley must marry no one but herself; Catharine Morland, in *Northanger Abbey*, realizing that Gothic novels do not after all provide adequate interpretive principles for daily life; Elizabeth Bennet, of *Pride and Prejudice*, forced to acknowledge how wrong she has been about Darcy. Such moments of insight result in deep change, change that goes beyond behavior, although it affects behavior.

Tom Jones learns from experience that he must not act in certain ways. Although Tom claims an accompanying change in consciousness, Fielding provides evidence of no such alteration, nor is either Sophia or the reader likely to demand change of consciousness from a character so little inward as Tom. Emma, in contrast, learns a new generous awareness, manifested in her conduct toward Harriet, Frank, and Jane Fairfax as the novel's action draws to a close. She has experienced a noticeable change of consciousness. Consistently in her novels, Austen renders processes of change that affect characters in profound ways. She writes novels of manners, in the sense that principles of social conduct shape much of the action, but the function of manners in the novels, ultimately, is to permit or enable character development.

The crucial fact that Austen's characters undergo changes extending far beyond the acquisition of "prudence" marks a great difference between eighteenth- and nineteenth-century fiction. The difference partly depends on new understandings of what "character" in fiction means, new understandings derived partly from modes of rendering personality that developed in the eighteenth-century novel and also probably indebted to biographies and autobiographies published before and after 1800. Such works as Boswell's *Life of Johnson* and Rousseau's startling *Confessions,* with their richly detailed texture and their evocations of the mystery of personality, enlarged the possibilities for verbal interpretation of human nature in its particularities.

Austen's sense of "human nature," like Rousseau's in this respect if in no other, included inner experience as well as outward behavior. So it is that *Emma* and the other novels can be read as novels of consciousness, partly in the eighteenth-century sense, partly in a new sense. A striking aspect of the eighteenth-century novels of consciousness we considered, with the exception of Sterne's, is that their conception of consciousness focuses on mental processes moving mainly in logical sequence. Sterne alone conveys an equivalent for what we have come to recognize as stream of consciousness, a kind of awareness that jumps unpredictably from one subject to another by a process of loose association. In contrast, the awareness rendered by *Pamela* or *Clarissa* or *The Cry* shifts by means of processes combining reason and feeling, with rationality a conspicuous component, if not necessarily dominant.

Emma's consciousness, and Elizabeth Bennet's, and even Catharine Morland's, also have strong elements of reason always present. Feeling makes Emma respond powerfully to Knightley's rebuke of her rudeness, but reason tells her how well justified that rebuke is. Catharine has allowed her emotional response to Gothic fiction to shape her interpretation of Northanger Abbey and its inhabitants, but her moment of revelation depends largely on the operations of reason. Like Pamela and Clarissa before them, though, such characters, as they reveal their inner lives, reveal also the power of desire to shape perception. Elizabeth Bennet finds Darcy's letter persuasive because she wants to be persuaded; Catharine succumbs more significantly to Henry Tilney than to the power of reason. Rationality mingles readily with rationalization. Although the kinds of consciousness Austen delineates never approach incoherence, neither do they operate altogether by the laws of logic. Like Richardson and Sarah Fielding, Austen renders inner lives not entirely controlled by the wills of their possessors but reflecting needs and conflicts that might not be acknowledged out loud. Eighteenth-century readers would have recognized the kinds of consciousness that she portrayed.

The eighteenth-century novelists of consciousness we considered invariably employed some form of first-person narrative to communicate the nature of psychic life. Austen, writing fiction in the third person, developed a new technique for such communication: that of free indirect discourse, whereby a character's unvoiced thoughts and interpretations become part of what purports to be objective narration. (Others—notably Godwin—had used the technique before her, but Austen greatly enlarged its capacities.) A brilliant example from *Emma* involves Emma's contemplation of the village square from the doorway of a shop where Harriet is trying to decide among muslins:

> Much could not be hoped from the traffic of even the busiest part of Highbury;—Mr. Perry walking hastily by, Mr. William Cox letting himself in at the office door, Mr. Cole's carriage horses returning from exercise, or a stray letter-boy on an obstinate mule, were the liveliest objects she could presume to expect; and when her eyes fell only on the butcher with his tray, a tidy old woman travelling homewards from shop with her full basket, two curs quarrelling over a dirty bone, and a string of dawdling children round the baker's little bow-window eyeing the gingerbread, she knew she had no reason to complain, and was amused enough; quite enough still to stand at the door. A mind lively and at ease, can do with seeing nothing, and can see nothing that does not answer. [233]

Emma, in a good mood, expects to be entertained. Her musing tells her that not much can be hoped for, but she imagines the possibilities of Mr. Perry, Mr. Cox, the letter-boy, and so on; then she actually sees the butcher, the curs, and the children, and declares herself amused. Only with the final sentence, however, does one see the technique's subtlety. The sentence sounds like the kind of moral pronouncement abundant in eighteenth-century fiction, yet it functions far more complexly if understood as the product of Emma's mind. This is a characteristically self-congratulatory pronouncement: Emma applauding herself for making something out of nothing. Or is it? Perhaps, instead, it issues from the narrator, as an assessment of the movements of mind that she has just evoked. Like the "Much could not be hoped" sentence, it purports to be an objective statement, yet we must recognize that it issues from the particular consciousness that shapes it. Recognition of the ambiguity about who thinks this thought leads to awareness—that awareness reiterated in various ways throughout Austen's novels—that the meaning of any judgment, any interpretation, depends on its source.

In relation to this study's project, then, two aspects of Austen are important: the fact that she builds on patterns that have been established before her and the fact that she devises new ways of executing them. Both these truths are self-evident. Every writer, always, both relies on and transforms what has gone before. Admirers of the nineteenth-century British novel, however, have often failed to acknowledge how crucial to its accomplishment is the achievement of its predecessors. Dickens would not have written in the same ways without Fielding, nor Eliot without Richardson. Trollope inherits from Burney. *Wuthering Heights* and *Dracula* draw on the Gothic tradition. One can feel the connection between Sophia Lee and Sir Walter Scott, that master of historical fiction.

Literary history as a record of reading literary works may heighten awareness of such links. It may also encourage attentiveness to the fact that nineteenth-century fiction, for all its massive and brilliant achievement, does not always innovate in such fundamental ways as the novels of the eighteenth century. Although eighteenth-century novelists too had abundant models, they basically had to devise the forms in which they wrote. Deep knowledge of *Don Quixote* and of classical epic allowed Fielding to conceive a way of relating an imaginary person's life, but no one before him had written just such a life. To realize how fragmentary struc-

ture might reflect a troubled and troubling social situation, thus enabling
the development of the sentimental novel, contributed enormously to the
development of fiction. Eighteenth-century novelists abounded in fresh
ideas.

Not that their nineteenth-century successors didn't. The nineteenth
century produced, among other things, the detective story and the immense enlargement of discovered means for incorporating social observation and commentary as part of a fictional structure. The fertility of
novelists continued to manifest itself. But such fertility did not appear
first in the nineteenth century: a century of previous efforts helped encourage it.

And Austen was by no means the only novelist to pursue lines of
development first laid out in the previous era. Her contemporary Sir Walter Scott took for granted the fundamental interest and the urgency of
narration about a youth's progress toward maturity. In his first novel,
Waverley (1814), he embedded the story of a young man's growth—that
story made familiar by Fielding and his followers—in a highly elaborated
historical fantasy, based on extensive knowledge of fact. Young Waverley
in some respects resembles a stereotypical eighteenth-century heroine.
His predilection for reading romances may remind one of Arabella, the
female Quixote. If he does not, like Arabella, quite believe fiction truth,
he yet absorbs many ideas and ideals from it, driving "through the sea
of books, like a vessel without a pilot or a rudder" (13) and taking aboard
a considerable cargo. Actuality, of course, educates him, as it educates
Arabella; and his creator is at pains to insist that he has masculine virtues
as well as conventionally feminine characteristics. By locating his story of
development in a context of male conflict (as well as female plotting), Scott
partly nullifies gender stereotypes, even as he makes use of them.

Not all nineteenth-century novelistic accomplishments, however, constitute pure gain: there is loss as well. Already in *Waverley,* Scott deftly
deploys immense knowledge of the Scottish past and feeling for the nobility of a long-lost cause. He supplies a complicated, if leisurely, plot and a
large cast of characters. Yet he does not achieve the sense of urgency that
marks Sophia Lee's *The Recess,* that earlier version of historical fiction,
with its brilliant dramatization of the impenetrable confusion attendant
on being caught in history.

Indeed, one may miss in nineteenth-century fiction various versions of the urgency that permeates the novel in its earlier years. A novelist's persona now may still address readers directly, but the question of who, exactly, the reader is and how that reader feels engaged with the text—that previously compelling question seems to have disappeared. "Shall this be a short or a long chapter?" Scott writes. "—This is a question in which you, gentle reader, have no vote, however much you may be interested in the consequences; just as probably you may (like myself) have nothing to do with the imposing a new tax, excepting the trifling circumstance of being obliged to pay it" (115). Like Fielding and Sterne before him, he toys with the imagined reader. He even fancies that reader's comparative powerlessness—but only to juxtapose it with his own. The political allusion neither enforces the narrator's dominion nor comments on the nature of his novel. Little is at stake.

The nineteenth-century novel develops a kind of complexity different from that of its predecessors. No longer do we encounter the dazzling multiplicity of Jane Barker or the exuberant plotting of Henry Fielding, with attendant self-congratulation by the narrator, or, for that matter, the intricate and rigorous psychological concentration of Richardson. *Frankenstein* duplicates the ambivalent emotion and the compelled pursuit of *Caleb Williams*, the work of its author's father. It exercises over the reader imaginative power comparable to, perhaps even greater than, that of its predecessor. But, lacking the political impetus of Godwin's thriller, it conveys less immediately a sense of its urgent relevance to the world we inhabit. Not only had the eighteenth century laid the groundwork for the modern novel; it had explored possibilities that would subsequently be long neglected.

Our investigation of eighteenth-century experiment has demonstrated some of the many ways in which the period's novels are linked to one another and some of the patterns by which their plots operate. It has also attempted to reveal some gratifications of reading these novels. Literary history records not only what has been written but also what has been read. Not every work considered here proved a resounding success in its own time, but most of the fiction we have treated found enthusiastic readers in the past. These books still offer rewards to readers. Such classifications as "sentimental novel" or "political novel" (from a period whose politics may seem of remote interest now) perhaps seem to declare antiquated the works that fall under them, but *Memoirs of Miss Sidney Bidulph* provides a gripping plot and a protagonist of great psychological intricacy, and *Caleb Williams* may well, even now, fulfill its writer's intention of creating an epoch in the lives of all who read it.

The fiction of the eighteenth century illuminates not only its time and place but the possibilities of human life, thought, and feeling. Its varying patterns reflect different ways of confronting the personal and social issues that from the beginning created the novel's material. The novel in its early avatars, as in its later forms, speaks from and for its culture and to and for ours.

SUGGESTIONS FOR FURTHER READING

THESE SUGGESTIONS FOR CRITICAL reading are sorted by chapter, but many of the works cited contain interpretations, theories, or organizing ideas that apply usefully to individual novels or groups of novels discussed in other contexts. The works listed for the first chapter, in particular, often supply guides to specific fictions in addition to constructing large historical arguments. On the whole, I have confined myself to listing books rather than articles, but a few exceptionally important or exceptionally pointed essays also appear. In some instances (e.g., Frances Brooke), no useful books on a specific subject exist, so articles necessarily substitute.

CHAPTER ONE: THE EXCITEMENT OF BEGINNINGS

Armstrong, Nancy. *Desire and Domestic Fiction: A Political History of the Novel.* Oxford: Oxford University Press, 1987.

Bartolomeo, Joseph F. *A New Species of Criticism: Eighteenth-Century Discourse on the Novel.* Newark: University of Delaware Press, 1994.

Black, Jeremy. *Eighteenth-Century Britain, 1688–1783.* New York: Palgrave, 2001.

Brown, Homer O. *Institutions of the English Novel: From Defoe to Scott.* Philadelphia: University of Pennsylvania Press, 1997.

Colley, Linda. *Britons: Forging the Nation, 1707–1837.* New Haven: Yale University Press, 1992.

———. *Captives: Britain, Empire and the World, 1600–1850.* London: Jonathan Cape, 2002.

Doody, Margaret. *The True Story of the Novel*. New Brunswick, N.J.: Rutgers University Press, 1996.

Eighteenth-Century Fiction 12:2–3 (2000). This entire double issue of the journal, entitled *Reconsidering "The Rise of the Novel,"* consists of commentary on Ian Watt's study and on new understandings of the novel as genre.

Hunter, J. Paul. *Before Novels: The Cultural Contexts of Eighteenth-Century English Fiction*. New York: Norton, 1990.

Ingrassia, Catherine. *Authorship, Commerce, and Gender in Early Eighteenth-Century England: A Culture of Paper Credit*. Cambridge: Cambridge University Press, 1998.

Kernan, Alvin. *Printing Technology, Letters, and Samuel Johnson*. Princeton: Princeton University Press, 1987.

Lynch, Deidre. *The Economy of Character: Novels, Market Culture, and the Business of Inner Meaning*. Chicago: University of Chicago Press, 1998.

McKeon, Michael. *The Origins of the English Novel, 1600–1740*. Baltimore: Johns Hopkins University Press, 1987.

Nussbaum, Felicity, and Laura Brown, eds. *The New Eighteenth Century: Theory, Politics, English Literature*. New York: Methuen, 1987.

Porter, Roy. *Enlightenment: Britain and the Creation of the Modern World*. London: Allen Lane, 2000.

Richetti, John. *The English Novel in History, 1700–1780*. London: Routledge, 1999.

Richetti, John, et al., eds. *The Columbia History of the British Novel*. New York: Columbia University Press, 1994.

Salzman, Paul. *English Prose Fiction, 1558–1700: A Critical History*. Oxford: Clarendon, 1985.

Spacks, Patricia Meyer. *Desire and Truth: Functions of Plot in Eighteenth-Century English Novels*. Chicago: University of Chicago Press, 1990.

Todd, Janet. *The Sign of Angellica: Women, Writing and Fiction, 1660–1800*. London: Virago, 1989.

Warner, William. *Licensing Entertainment: The Elevation of Novel Reading in Britain, 1684–1750*. Berkeley: University of California Press, 1998.

Watt, Ian. *The Rise of the Novel: Studies in Defoe, Richardson and Fielding*. Berkeley: University of California Press, 1957.

White, Ian, and Kathleen White. *On the Trail of the Jacobites*. London: Routledge, 1990.

CHAPTER TWO: NOVELS OF ADVENTURE

Ballaster, Ros. *Seductive Forms: Women's Amatory Fiction from 1684 to 1740*. Oxford: Clarendon, 1992.

Gallagher, Catherine. *Nobody's Story: The Vanishing Acts of Women Writers in the Marketplace, 1670–1820*. Berkeley: University of California Press, 1994.

Herman, Ruth. *The Business of a Woman: The Political Writings of Delarivier Manley*. Newark: University of Delaware Press, 2003.

Lund, Roger D., ed. *Critical Essays on Daniel Defoe*. New York: G. K. Hall, 1997.

Novak, Maximillian E. *Daniel Defoe: Master of Fictions, His Life and Ideas.* Oxford: Oxford University Press, 2001.

Richetti, John. *Popular Fiction Before Richardson: Narrative Patterns, 1700–1739.* Oxford: Clarendon, 1992.

Saxon, Kirsten T., and Rebecca P. Bocchicchio, eds. *The Passionate Fictions of Eliza Haywood: Essays on Her Life and Work.* Lexington: University Press of Kentucky, 2000.

Schofield, Mary Anne, and Cecilia Macheski, eds. *Fetter'd or Free? British Women Novelists, 1670–1815.* Athens: Ohio University Press, 1986.

Seidel, Michael. *"Robinson Crusoe": Island Myths and the Novel.* Boston: Twayne, 1991.

CHAPTER THREE: THE NOVEL OF DEVELOPMENT

Brack, O M, Jr. "Smollett's *Peregrine Pickle* Revisited." *Studies in the Novel* 27: 3 (1995): 260–72.

Douglas, Aileen. *Uneasy Sensations: Smollett and the Body.* Chicago: University of Chicago Press, 1995.

Fowler, Patsy S., Alan Jackson, and Peter Sabor, eds. *Launching "Fanny Hill": Essays on the Novel and Its Influences.* New York: AMS, 2003.

Parker, Jo Alyson. *The Author's Inheritance: Henry Fielding, Jane Austen, and the Establishment of the Novel.* DeKalb: Northern Illinois University Press, 1998.

Paulson, Ronald. *The Life of Henry Fielding: A Critical Biography.* Oxford: Blackwell, 2000.

Rivero, Albert J., ed. *Critical Essays on Henry Fielding.* New York: G. K. Hall, 1998.

Rosengarten, Richard A. *Henry Fielding and the Narration of Providence: Divine Design and the Incursions of Evil.* New York: Palgrave, 2000.

Skinner, John. *Constructions of Smollett: A Study of Genre and Gender.* Newark: University of Delaware Press, 1996.

Stuart, Shea. "Subversive Didacticism in Eliza Haywood's *Betsy Thoughtless*." *SEL: Studies in English Literature, 1500–1900* 42:3 (2002): 559–75.

Thompson, Helen. "Charlotte Lennox and the Agency of Romance." *Eighteenth Century: Theory and Interpretation* 43:2 (2002): 91–114.

CHAPTER FOUR: NOVELS OF CONSCIOUSNESS

Alliston, April. *Virtue's Faults: Correspondences in Eighteenth-Century British and French Women's Fiction.* Stanford: Stanford University Press, 1996.

Altman, Janet Gurkin. *Epistolarity: Approaches to a Form.* Columbus: Ohio State University Press, 1982.

Benedict, Barbara M. "The Margins of Sentiment: Nature, Letter, and Law in Frances Brooke's Epistolary Novels." *ARIEL: A Review of International English Literature* 23:3 (1992): 7–25.

Blewett, David, ed. *Passion and Virtue: Essays on the Novels of Samuel Richardson.* Toronto: University of Toronto Press, 2001.

Bree, Linda. *Sarah Fielding.* New York: Twayne, 1996.

Castle, Terry. *Clarissa's Ciphers: Meaning and Disruption in Richardson's "Clarissa."* Ithaca: Cornell University Press, 1982.

Cook, Elizabeth Heckendorn. *Epistolary Bodies: Gender and Genre in the Eighteenth-Century Republic of Letters.* Stanford: Stanford University Press, 1996.

Keymer, Tom. *Richardson's "Clarissa" and the Eighteenth-Century Reader.* Cambridge: Cambridge University Press, 1992.

Krishman, R. S. "'The Vortex of the Tumult': Order and Disorder in *Humphry Clinker.*" *Studies in Scottish Literature* 23 (1988): 239–53.

Lamb, Jonathan. *Sterne's Fiction and the Double Principle.* Cambridge: Cambridge University Press, 1989.

Rogers, Katharine M. "Sensibility and Feminism: The Novels of Frances Brooke." *Genre* 11 (1978): 159–71.

Rosenblum, Michael. "Smollett's *Humphry Clinker.*" *The Cambridge Companion to the Eighteenth-Century Novel,* 175–97. Ed. John Richetti. Cambridge: Cambridge University Press, 1996.

Walsh, Marcus, ed. *Laurence Sterne.* London: Longman, 2002.

Warner, William Beatty. *Reading "Clarissa": The Struggles of Interpretation.* New Haven: Yale University Press, 1979.

Zomchick, John P. "Social Class, Character, and Narrative Strategy in *Humphry Clinker.*" *Eighteenth-Century Life* 10: 3 (1986): 172–85.

CHAPTER FIVE: THE NOVEL OF SENTIMENT

Barker, Gerard A. "*David Simple:* The Novel of Sensibility in Embryo." *Modern Language Studies* 12: 2 (1982): 69–80.

———. *Henry Mackenzie.* Boston: Twayne, 1975.

Barker-Benfield, G. J. *The Culture of Sensibility: Sex and Society in Eighteenth-Century Britain.* Chicago: University of Chicago Press, 1992.

Bredvold, Louis Ignatius. *The Natural History of Sensibility.* Detroit: Wayne State University Press, 1962.

Brissenden, R. F. *Virtue in Distress: Studies in the Novel of Sentiment.* New York: Barnes and Noble, 1974.

Dixon, Peter. *Oliver Goldsmith Revisited.* Boston: Twayne, 1991.

Erickson, Robert. *The Language of the Heart, 1600–1750.* Philadelphia: University of Pennsylvania Press, 1997.

Hopkins, Robert Hazen. *The True Genius of Oliver Goldsmith.* Baltimore: Johns Hopkins University Press, 1969.

Mullan, John. *Sentiment and Sociability: The Language of Feeling in the Eighteenth Century.* Oxford: Clarendon, 1990.

Nussbaum, Felicity. "Effeminacy and Femininity: Domestic Prose Satire and David Simple." *Eighteenth-Century Fiction* 11:4 (1999): 421–44.

Oliver, Kathleen M. "Frances Sheridan's Faulkland, the Silenced, Emasculated, Ideal Male." *SEL: Studies in English Literature, 1500–1900* 43:3 (2003): 683–700.

Rawson, Claude Julien. *Satire and Sentiment, 1660–1830.* Cambridge: Cambridge University Press, 1994.

Van Sant, Ann Jessie. *Eighteenth-Century Sensibility and the Novel: The Senses in Social Context*. Cambridge: Cambridge University Press, 1993.

CHAPTER SIX: THE NOVEL OF MANNERS

Boardman, Michael. "Inchbald's *A Simple Story:* An Anti-Ideological Reading." *Ideology and Form in Eighteenth-Century Literature*, 207–22. Ed. David H. Richter. Lubbock: Texas Tech University Press, 1999.

Cutting-Gray, Joanne. *Woman as "Nobody" and the Novels of Fanny Burney*. Gainesville: University Press of Florida, 1992.

Doody, Margaret Anne. *Frances Burney: The Life in the Works*. New Brunswick, N.J.: Rutgers University Press, 1988.

Epstein, Julia. *The Iron Pen: Frances Burney and the Politics of Women's Writing*. Madison: University of Wisconsin Press, 1989.

Johnson, Claudia L. *Equivocal Beings: Politics, Gender, and Sentimentality in the 1790s: Wollstonecraft, Radcliffe, Burney, Austen*. Chicago: University of Chicago Press, 1995.

Nachumi, Nora. "'Those Simple Signs': The Performance of Emotion in Elizabeth Inchbald's *A Simple Story*." *Eighteenth-Century Fiction* 11:3 (1999): 317–38.

Rogers, Katharine M. *Frances Burney: The World of "Female Difficulties."* New York: Harvester Wheatsheaf, 1990.

Ward, Candace. "Inordinate Desire: Schooling the Senses in Elizabeth Inchbald's *A Simple Story*." *Studies in the Novel* 31:1 (1999): 1–18.

CHAPTER SEVEN: GOTHIC FICTION

Clery, E. J. *Women's Gothic: From Clara Reeve to Mary Shelley*. Tavistock: Northcote House in association with the British Council, 2000.

Emsley, Sarah. "Radical Marriage." *Eighteenth-Century Fiction* 11:4 (1999): 477–98.

Gray, Jennie. *Horace Walpole and William Beckford: Pioneers of the Gothic Revival*. Chislehurst: Gothic Society, 1994.

Haggerty, George E. *Unnatural Affections: Women and Fiction in the Later Eighteenth Century*. Bloomington: Indiana University Press, 1998.

Heiland, Donna. *Gothic and Gender: An Introduction*. Malden, Mass.: Blackwell, 2004.

Kilgour, Maggie. *The Rise of the Gothic Novel*. New York: Routledge, 1995.

Lewis, Jayne Elizabeth. "'Ev'ry Lost Relation': Historical Fictions and Sentimental Incidents in Sophia Lee's *The Recess*." *Eighteenth-Century Fiction* 7:2 (1995): 165–84.

Punter, David, and Glennis Byron. *The Gothic*. Malden, Mass.: Blackwell, 2004.

Reno, Robert Princeton. *The Gothic Visions of Ann Radcliffe and Matthew G. Lewis*. New York: Arno, 1980.

Smith, Nelson C. *The Art of Gothic: Ann Radcliffe's Major Novels*. New York: Arno, 1980.

Stevens, Anne H. "Sophia Lee's Illegitimate History." *Eighteenth-Century Novel* 3 (2003): 263–91.

Wright, Angela. "Early Women's Gothic Writing: Historicity and Canonicity in Clara Reeve's *The Old English Baron* and Sophia Lee's *The Recess.*" *Approaches to Teaching Gothic Fiction: The British and American Traditions,* 99–104. Ed. Diane Long Hoeveler and Tamar Heller. New York: Modern Language Association of America, 2003.

CHAPTER EIGHT: THE POLITICAL NOVEL

Baine, Rodney M. *Thomas Holcroft and the Revolutionary Novel.* Athens: University of Georgia Press, 1965.

Clemit, Pamela. *The Godwinian Novel: The Rational Fictions of Godwin, Brockden Brown, Mary Shelley.* Oxford: Clarendon, 1993.

Faulkner, Peter. *Robert Bage.* Boston: Twayne, 1979.

Grenby, M. O. *The Anti-Jacobin Novel: British Conservatism and the French Revolution.* New York: Cambridge University Press, 2001.

Gunther-Canada, Wendy. *Rebel Writer: Mary Wollstonecraft and Enlightenment Politics.* DeKalb: Northern Illinois University Press, 2001.

Johnson, Claudia L., ed. *The Cambridge Companion to Mary Wollstonecraft.* Cambridge: Cambridge University Press, 2002.

Johnson, Nancy E. *The English Jacobin Novel on Rights, Property and the Law: Critiquing the Contract.* New York: Palgrave Macmillan, 2004.

Keen, Paul. "A 'Memorable Grave': The Abject Subtext of Charles Lloyd's *Edmund Oliver.*" *Authorship, Commerce and the Public: Scenes of Writing, 1750–1850,* 203–17. Ed. E. J. Clery, Caroline Franklin, and Peter Garside. Basingstoke, England: Palgrave Macmillan, 2002.

Kelly, Gary. *The English Jacobin Novel, 1780–1805.* Oxford: Clarendon, 1976.

Watson, Nicola J. *Revolution and the Form of the British Novel, 1790–1825: Intercepted Letters, Interrupted Seductions.* Oxford: Clarendon, 1994.

CHAPTER NINE: *TRISTRAM SHANDY* AND THE DEVELOPMENT OF THE NOVEL

Byrd, Max. *Tristram Shandy.* London: Allen and Unwin, 1985.

Conrad, Peter. *Shandyism: The Character of Romantic Irony.* Oxford: Blackwell, 1978.

Erickson, Robert A. *Mother Midnight: Birth, Sex, and Fate in Eighteenth-Century Fiction (Defoe, Richardson, and Sterne).* New York: AMS, 1986.

Iser, Wolfgang. *Laurence Sterne: "Tristram Shandy."* Trans. David Henry Wilson. Cambridge: Cambridge University Press, 1988.

Keymer, Tom. *Sterne, the Moderns, and the Novel.* Oxford: Oxford University Press, 2002.

Lanham, Richard A. *"Tristram Shandy": The Games of Pleasure.* Berkeley: University of California Press, 1973.

WORKS CITED

Adventures of Lindamira, a Lady of Quality, The. 1702. *Foundations of the Novel,*
    ed. Michael F. Shugrue. New York: Garland, 1972.

Aubin, Penelope. *The Life and Adventures of the Lady Lucy.* 1726. *Foundations of*
    the Novel, ed. Michael F. Shugrue. New York: Garland, 1973.

———. *The Life of Madam de Beaumount.* 1721. *Foundations of the Novel,* ed.
    Michael F. Shugrue. New York: Garland, 1973.

———. *The Strange Adventures of the Count de Vinevil and his Family.* 1721.
    Foundations of the Novel, ed. Michael F. Shugrue. New York: Garland, 1973.

Austen, Jane. *Emma.* 1816. Ed. R. W. Chapman. Vol. 4 of *The Novels of Jane*
    Austen. 3rd ed. Oxford: Oxford University Press, 1933.

———. *"Northanger Abbey" and "Persuasion."* 1818. Ed. R. W. Chapman. Vol. 5 of
    The Novels of Jane Austen. 3rd ed. Oxford: Oxford University Press, 1933.

———. *Pride and Prejudice.* 1813. Ed. R. W. Chapman. Vol. 2 of *The Novels of Jane*
    Austen. 3rd ed. Oxford: Oxford University Press, 1932.

Bage, Robert. *Hermsprong, or, Man As He Is Not.* 1796. Ed. Peter Faulkner. Oxford:
    Oxford University Press, 1985.

Barker, Jane. *The Galesia Trilogy and Selected Manuscript Poems.* Ed. Carol Shiner
    Wilson. New York: Oxford University Press, 1997.

Beckford, William. *"Modern Novel Writing" (1796) and "Azemia" (1797).* Gaines-
    ville, Fla.: Scholars' Facsimiles and Reprints, 1970.

———. *Vathek.* 1786. Ed. Roger Lonsdale. London: Oxford University Press,
    1970.

Behn, Aphra. *Oroonoko.* 1698. *Shorter Novels: Seventeenth Century,* 147–224.
    Ed. Philip Henderson. London: Dent, 1960.

Boswell, James. *The Life of Samuel Johnson.* 1791. Ed. R. W. Chapman. Corrected by J. D. Fleeman. London: Oxford University Press, 1970.

Brooke, Frances. *The History of Emily Montague.* 1769. Ed. Laura Moss. Ottawa: Tecumseh Press, 2001.

———. *The History of Lady Julia Mandeville.* 1763. Ed. E. Phillips Poole. London: E. Partridge, 1930.

Brooke, Henry. *The Fool of Quality, or the History of Henry Earl of Moreland.* 1765–70. London: Routledge, 1906.

Bunyan, John. *The Pilgrim's Progress From This World to That Which Is to Come.* 1678–84. Ed. John F. Thornton and Susan B. Varenne. New York: Vintage, 2004.

Burke, Edmund. *A Philosophical Enquiry into the Origin of our Ideas of the Sublime and Beautiful.* 1757. Ed. Adam Phillips. Oxford: Oxford University Press, 1990.

Burney, Frances. *Camilla or A Picture of Youth.* 1796. Ed. Edward A. Bloom and Lillian D. Bloom. London: Oxford University Press, 1972.

———. *Cecilia, or, Memoirs of an Heiress.* 1782. Ed. Peter Sabor and Margaret Anne Doody. Oxford: Oxford University Press, 1988.

———. *Evelina or The History of a Young Lady's Entrance into the World.* 1778. Ed. Edward A. Bloom. Oxford: Oxford University Press, 1970.

———. *The Wanderer, or, Female Difficulties.* 1814. Ed. Margaret Anne Doody, Robert L. Mack, and Peter Sabor. Oxford: Oxford University Press, 2001.

Cleland, John. *Memoirs of a Woman of Pleasure.* 1748–49. Ed. Peter Sabor. Oxford: Oxford University Press, 1999.

Davys, Mary. *Familiar Letters, Betwixt a Gentleman and a Lady.* 1725. *Foundations of the Novel,* ed. Michael F. Shugrue. New York: Garland, 1973.

———. *The Reform'd Coquet; A NOVEL.* 1724. *Foundations of the Novel,* ed. Michael F. Shugrue. New York: Garland, 1973.

Defoe, Daniel. *The Fortunes and Misfortunes of the Famous Moll Flanders.* 1722. Ed. Juliet Mitchell. New York: Penguin, 1978.

———. *Robinson Crusoe.* 1719. Ed. Michael Shinagel. 2nd ed. New York: Norton, 1994.

———. *Roxana, The Fortunate Mistress.* 1724. Ed. Jane Jack. New York: Oxford University Press, 1964.

Edgeworth, Maria. *Belinda.* 1801. London: Pandora, 1986.

Fenwick, Eliza. *Secresy: or, The Ruin on the Rock.* 1795. Ed. Isobel Grundy. 2nd ed. Peterborough, Ont.: Broadview, 1998.

Fielding, Henry. *Amelia.* 1751. Ed. Martin C. Battestin. Middletown, Conn.: Wesleyan University Press, 1983.

———. *"The History of the Adventures of Joseph Andrews And of his friend Mr. Abraham Adams" and "An Apology for the Life of Mrs. Shamela Andrews."* 1742, 1741. Ed. Douglas Brooks-Davies. Oxford: Oxford University Press, 1980.

———. *Tom Jones.* 1749. Ed. John Bender and Simon Stern. Oxford: Oxford University Press, 1998.

Fielding, Sarah. *The Adventures of David Simple. Containing an Account of His*

Travels Through the Cities of London and Westminster in the Search of a Real Friend. 1744. Ed. Malcolm Kelsall. Oxford: Oxford University Press, 1994.

———. *The Cry*. 1754. Delmar, N.Y.: Scholars' Facsimiles and Reprints, 1986.

Godwin, William. *An Enquiry Concerning Political Justice*. 1793. 2 vols. Ed. Raymond Abner Preston. New York: Knopf, 1926.

———. *Caleb Williams*. 1794. Ed. Gary Handwerk and A. A. Markley. Peterborough, Ont.: Broadview, 2000.

Goldsmith, Oliver. *The Vicar of Wakefield*. 1766. Ed. Stephen Coote. Harmondsworth, England: Penguin, 1984.

Hays, Mary. *Memoirs of Emma Courtney*. 1796. London: Pandora, 1987.

———. *The Victim of Prejudice*. 1799. Ed. Eleanor Ty. Peterborough, Ont.: Broadview, 1999.

Haywood, Eliza. *The City Jilt*. 1726. *Selected Fiction and Drama of Eliza Haywood*. Ed. Paula R. Backscheider. New York: Oxford University Press, 1999.

———. *"Fantomina" and Other Works*. 1725 et al. Ed. Margaret Case Croskery, Anna C. Patchias, and Alexander Pettit. Peterborough, Ont.: Broadview, 2004.

———. *The History of Miss Betsy Thoughtless*. 1751. Ed. Christine Blough. Peterboro, Ont.: Broadview, 1998.

———. *Love in Excess, or, The Fatal Enquiry*. 1719. Ed. David Oakleaf. Peterborough, Ont.: Broadview, 1994.

Haywood, Eliza, and Henry Fielding. *"Anti-Pamela" and "Shamela."* 1742, 1741. Ed. Catherine Ingrassia. Peterborough, Ont.: Broadview, 2004.

Holcroft, Thomas. *Anna St. Ives*. 1792. Ed. Peter Faulkner. London: Oxford University Press, 1970.

Inchbald, Elizabeth. *A Simple Story*. 1791. Ed. Pamela Clemit. New York: Penguin, 1986.

Johnson, Samuel. *The Life of Pope*. Introduction and notes F. Ryland. London: Bell, 1920.

———. "Preface to Shakespeare." *Johnson on Shakespeare*. 1765. Vol. 7 of *The Yale Edition of the Works of Samuel Johnson*, 59–113. Ed. Arthur Sherbo. New Haven: Yale University Press, 1968.

Johnstone, Charles. *Chrysal: or, The Adventures of a Guinea*. 1760–65. *The Novel: 1720–1805*. 4 vols. New York: Garland, 1979.

Lee, Sophia. *The Recess; or, A Tale of Other Times*. 1783. Ed. April Alliston. Lexington: University Press of Kentucky, 2000.

Lennox, Charlotte. *The Female Quixote or The Adventures of Arabella*. 1752. Ed. Margaret Dalziel. Oxford: Oxford University Press, 1998.

Lewis, M. G. *The Monk*. 1795. Ed. Howard Anderson. Oxford: Oxford University Press, 1973.

Lloyd, Charles. *Edmund Oliver*. 1798. Oxford: Woodstock, 1990.

Locke, John. *An Essay Concerning Human Understanding*. 1690. Ed. Peter H. Nidditch. Oxford: Clarendon, 1979.

Mackenzie, Henry. *The Man of Feeling*. 1769. New York: Norton, 1958.

Manley, Delarivier. *The New Atalantis*. 1709. Ed. Ros Ballaster. London: Pickering and Chatto, 1991.

Pratt, Samuel Jackson [Courtney Melmoth]. *The Tutor of Truth.* 1779. 2 vols. London, 1779.

Radcliffe, Ann. *The Italian, or, The Confessional of the Black Penitents.* 1796. Ed. Frederick Garber. London: Oxford University Press, 1968.

———. *The Mysteries of Udolpho.* 1794. Ed. Bonamy Dobrée. Oxford: Oxford University Press, 1980.

Reeve, Clara. *The Old English Baron.* 1778. Ed. James Trainer. Oxford: Oxford University Press, 2003.

Richardson, Samuel. *Clarissa or The History of a Young Lady.* 1747–48. Ed. Angus Ross. Harmondsworth, England: Penguin, 1985.

———. *Pamela; or, Virtue Rewarded.* 1740. Ed. Thomas Keymer and Alice Wakely. Oxford: Oxford University Press, 2001.

———. *Sir Charles Grandison.* 1753–54. 3 vols. Ed. Jocelyn Harris. London: Oxford University Press, 1972.

Robinson, Mary. *Walsingham, or the Pupil of Nature.* 1797. 4 vols. London: Routledge/Thoemmes, 1992.

Rousseau, Jean-Jacques. *Confessions.* 1781. Ed. P. N. Furbank. New York: Knopf, 1992.

Scott, Sarah. *Millenium Hall.* 1762. Ed. Gary Kelly. Peterborough, Ont.: Broadview, 1995.

Scott, Sir Walter. *Waverley; or, 'Tis Sixty Years Since.* 1814. Ed. Claire Lamont. Oxford: Clarendon, 1981.

Shaftesbury, Anthony Ashley Cooper, third earl of. *Characteristicks of Men, Manners, Opinions, Times.* 1711. 2 vols. Ed. Philip Ayres. Oxford: Clarendon, 1999.

Sheridan, Frances. *Memoirs of Miss Sidney Bidulph.* 1761. Ed. Patricia Koster and Jean Coates Cleary. Oxford: Oxford University Press, 1995.

Shklovsky, Victor. *Theory of Prose.* Trans. Benjamin Sher. Elmwood Park, Ill.: Dalkey Archive Press, 1990.

Smith, Adam. *The Theory of Moral Sentiments.* 1759. Ed. Knud Haakonssen. New York: Cambridge University Press, 2002.

Smith, Charlotte. *Emmeline.* 1788. Ed. Lorraine Fletcher. Peterborough, Ont.: Broadview, 2003.

———. *The Old Manor House.* 1793. Ed. Jacqueline M. Labbe. Peterborough, Ont.: Broadview, 2002.

Smollett, Tobias. *The Adventures of Peregrine Pickle, in which are included Memoirs of a Lady of Quality.* 1751. Ed. James Clifford, rev. Paul-Gabriel Boucé. Oxford: Oxford University Press, 1983.

———. *The Expedition of Humphry Clinker.* 1771. Ed. Lewis M. Knapp, rev. Paul-Gabriel Boucé. Oxford: Oxford University Press, 1998.

Sterne, Laurence. *The Life and Opinions of Tristram Shandy, Gentleman.* 1759–67. Ed. Melvyn New and Joan New. London: Penguin, 1997.

———. *A Sentimental Journey through France and Italy.* 1768. Ed. Ian Jack. Oxford: Oxford University Press, 1998.

Walpole, Horace. *The Castle of Otranto.* 1764. Ed. W. S. Lewis. London: Oxford University Press, 1964.

Wollstonecraft, Mary. *"Mary" and "Maria."* 1788, 1798. Ed. Janet Todd. Harmondsworth, England: Penguin, 1992.

———. *A Vindication of the Rights of Woman.* 1792. Vol. 5 of *The Works of Mary
Wollstonecraft.* Ed. Marilyn Butler and Janet Todd. London: Pickering, 1989.

Wordsworth, William, and Samuel Taylor Coleridge. *Lyrical Ballads.* 1798, 1800.
Ed. R. L. Brett and A. R. Jones. London: Methuen, 1963.

INDEX

adventure novel, 26, 28–58, 273; conventions of, 94, 260, 265; enlarged definition of, 28–29, 33–34, 40–42, 45, 203, 224–27, 260, 273; Gothic and, 221; about inanimate object, 53–54; political novel and, 222, 223, 224–27; Sterne and, 260, 261, 262, 263, 265, 267; structuring of, 259, 261

Adventures of Lindamira, a Lady of Quality (anon.), 32–33, 34, 41; multiple stories in, 88–89

allegory, 12, 13–16, 123, 125, 132, 259

American Indians, 234, 239

American Revolution, 11, 12, 217

anxiety, 192, 211

Apuleius, 2

aristocracy, 10, 200

Aristotelian unity, 20

Armstrong, Nancy, 4

associationism, 261, 280

Aubin, Penelope, 13, 29, 48–51; factuality claims of, 50–51; works of: *The Life of Madam de Beaumont*, 48–49, 50; *The Strange Adventures of the Count de Vinevil and his Family*, 50

Austen, Jane, 60, 133, 277–81; forerunners of, 8, 277, 278, 279, 281, 282, 283; innovations of, 281–82; novel of manners and, 175, 176, 190, 277–80; works of: *Emma*, 60, 176, 277, 278–82; *Mansfield Park*, 194; *Northanger Abbey*, 277, 279, 280–81; *Pride and Prejudice*, 277, 279, 280

authority, male. *See under* women

Bage, Robert: novelistic skill of, 240, 241, 244; political intent of, 12, 239, 240, 247; works of: *Hermsprong*, 222, 234, 238–41, 247; *Man As He Is*, 238

Barker, Jane, 13, 34–42, 51, 57; Defoe compared with, 42, 48; multiple stories and, 39, 40, 42, 284; pacing and, 18–19, 35, 41; physical detail and, 19, 36, 57; plotting and, 12, 34–36, 63; subgenres and, 33, 35; works of: *The Lining of the Patch Work Screen*, 18, 34–38; *Love Intrigues*, 34, 35–38; *A Patch-Work Screen for the Ladies*, 19, 34, 35–38

beautiful, the sublime and, 212–14, 216–17

Gramley Library
Salem College
Winston-Salem, NC 27108